# DEFINING DOCUMENTS
# IN WORLD HISTORY

# Women's Rights
# (1429–2017)

"The right of citizens of the United States to vote shall not be denied or abridged by the United States or by any State on account of sex.

"Congress shall have power to enforce this article by appropriate legislation."

*Speaker of the House of Representatives.*

*Vice President of the United States and*
*President of the Senate.*

DEFINING DOCUMENTS
IN WORLD HISTORY

# Women's Rights
# (1429–2017)

Editor

**Michael Shally-Jensen, PhD**

Volume 2

SALEM PRESS
A Division of EBSCO Information Services
Ipswich, Massachusetts

**GREY HOUSE PUBLISHING**

**Publisher's Cataloging-In-Publication Data**
**(Prepared by The Donohue Group, Inc.)**

Names: Shally-Jensen, Michael, editor.
Title: Women's rights (1429-2017) / editor, Michael Shally-Jensen, PhD.
Other Titles: Defining documents in world history.
Description: [First edition]. | Ipswich, Massachusetts : Salem Press, a division of EBSCO Information Services ; [Amenia, New York] : Grey House Publishing, [2018] | Includes bibliographical references and index.
Identifiers: ISBN 9781682175835 (set) | ISBN 9781682178904 (v. 1) | ISBN 9781682178911 (v. 2)
Subjects: LCSH: Women's rights--History--Sources.
Classification: LCC HQ1236 .W664 2018 | DDC 305.42--dc23

# Table of Contents

## Volume 1

### PRECURSORS     1

### SUFFRAGE AND SENSIBILITY     67

# Volume 2

## EQUALITY NOW!          249

## APPENDIXES                                                                503

# EQUALITY NOW!

## THE UNIVERSAL DECLARATION OF Human Rights

**WHEREAS** recognition of the inherent dignity and of the equal and inalienable rights of all members of the human family is the foundation of freedom, justice and peace in the world,

**WHEREAS** disregard and contempt for human rights have resulted in barbarous acts which have outraged the conscience of mankind, and the advent of a world in which human beings shall enjoy freedom of speech and belief and freedom from fear and want has been proclaimed as the highest aspiration of the common people,

**WHEREAS** it is essential, if man is not to be compelled to have recourse, as a last resort, to rebellion against tyranny and oppression, that human rights should be protected by the rule of law,

**WHEREAS** it is essential to promote the development of friendly relations among nations,

**WHEREAS** the peoples of the United Nations have in the Charter reaffirmed their faith in fundamental human rights, in the dignity and worth of the human person and in the equal rights of men and women and have

determined to promote social progress and better standards of life in larger freedom,

**WHEREAS** Member States have pledged themselves to achieve, in co-operation with the United Nations, the promotion of universal respect for and observance of human rights and fundamental freedoms,

**WHEREAS** a common understanding of these rights and freedoms is of the greatest importance for the full realisation of this pledge,

**NOW THEREFORE** THE GENERAL ASSEMBLY PROCLAIMS this Universal Declaration of Human Rights as a common standard of achievement for all peoples and all nations, to the end that every individual and every organ of society, keeping this Declaration constantly in mind, shall strive by teaching and education to promote respect for these rights and freedoms and by progressive measures, national and international, to secure their universal and effective recognition and observance, both among the peoples of Member States themselves and among the peoples of territories under their jurisdiction.

## UNITED NATIONS

The universal declaration of human rights 10 December 1948

# Universal Declaration of Human Rights

**Date:** 1948
**Authors:** Eleanor Roosevelt; John Humphrey; René Cassin
**Genre:** Charter; law

## Summary Overview

The Universal Declaration of Human Rights (UDHR) was adopted unanimously by the General Assembly of the United Nations on December 10, 1948. Eight countries abstained: Saudi Arabia, South Africa, Byelorussia, Czechoslovakia, Poland, Ukraine, the Soviet Union, and Yugoslavia. The Universal Declaration of Human Rights had been drafted by the Commission on Human Rights, chaired by Eleanor Roosevelt, the widow of U.S. president Franklin D. Roosevelt. In a speech before the General Assembly she described the declaration as the "international Magna Carta of all men everywhere." The former secretary general of the United Nations, Kofi Annan, is not alone in his belief that "the principles enshrined in the Declaration are the yardstick by which we measure progress. They lie at the heart of all that the United Nations aspires to achieve in its global mission of peace and development."

The Universal Declaration of Human Rights is the founding document of the International Bill of Human Rights, which was completed by the addition of the International Covenant on Civil and Political Rights and the International Covenant on Economic, Social and Cultural Rights in 1966. The declaration has been translated into more than 350 languages and was written so that ordinary people could understand it. It reflects the complex state of international relations at a particular historical moment—immediately after World War II and at the beginning of the cold war (the state of tension between the United States and its allies and the Soviet bloc). The document has formed the basis of many conventions and treaties and has influenced more than two dozen national constitutions. The Universal Declaration of Human Rights continues to be upheld as a universal standard of morality and is widely recognized as international common law.

## Defining Moment

The declaration was the product of nearly two years of intense and often conflicted discussion among members of the newly formed UN Commission on Human Rights. The United Nations had faced enormous pressure from individuals, nongovernmental organizations (NGOs), and international conferences calling for the United Nations to prioritize human rights in its charter. Instead of including a bill of human rights in its charter, the United Nations established the eighteen-member Commission on Human Rights.

The declaration was written soon after World War II. In 1941, U.S. president Franklin Roosevelt had met with Winston Churchill, the prime minister of England, to discuss the international postwar balance of power. Their major concern was international peace and security. Later, various meetings took place as the circle was enlarged to include the third Allied leader, Josef Stalin of the Soviet Union. Finally, in 1945, fifty nations met in San Francisco. Dominated by the Big Three, who had invited France and China to join them, the assembled nations drafted the United Nations Charter. The charter was intended to provide a mechanism to prevent future aggression, resolve disputes, and ensure that national borders would be kept intact. The principle of national sovereignty was built into the charter, and from the beginning this principle was in tension with the potential for the United Nations to intervene or "interfere" in a nation's internal affairs.

As the horrors of the Nazi genocide against Jews and other "undesirables" became known across the world, global voices demanding attention to human rights grew louder. A shared determination to prevent the rise again of Nazism or Fascism was critical to the drafting of the UDHR. Other effects of the war were also influential, including the plight of refugees and national security concerns. The horrors of the war provided the catalyst that enabled people from so many diverse cultural, political, social, and economic backgrounds to develop a shared moral code.

The declaration was also influenced by the League of Nations, formed after World War I, which had failed to prevent World War II. The league had not mentioned human rights, but the authors of the UDHR wanted to ensure that international security would include the protection of human rights. Many wanted the document to include the means for implementing its proposals, but the document became a statement of shared beliefs in human rights on which more action-based treaties or conventions could be built. (A treaty is a specific agreement between or among nations; a convention is a more general agreement on principles that does not necessarily require specific action.)

Few Asian and African countries were represented in the United Nations and on the commission because so many (other than Japan, which was excluded) were European colonies. A few had gained independence after the war, and these countries played an important role in the process. The delegate from France, René Cassin, sat face to face with the delegate from a former French colony, Charles Malik of Lebanon. (This was also the case with the United States and the Philippines and with Great Britain and its colonies, India and Pakistan.) The question of the human rights of colonized people would be a source of tension, and the word *colony* or its derivations would not appear in the document.

Another contentious issue was the treatment of minorities and the eradication of racism. Although the war had destroyed the moral basis of scientific racism, for example, a number of countries had not yet internalized this lesson. The Soviet Union, for example, was subjected to sharp criticism of its human rights record.

Women's human rights would also present a challenge. Many UN member nations had not granted women full political rights, let alone cultural, social, or economic equality. Two women served on the commission: Eleanor Roosevelt and Hansa Mehta of India. Roosevelt argued that the word "men" included "women," but Mehta insisted on specifically including women in the declaration. The UN Commission on the Status of Women played an important role. No mandate was given for these two commissions to work together, but representatives of the Commission on the Status of Women regularly attended committee meetings and provided crucial input, helping to ensure the removal of sexist language and the full inclusion of women in the category of "men." In several regards, then, the commission had to develop a moral agenda that challenged many of the delegates' own countries' human rights records at that very moment.

NGOs also played a critical role in pushing human rights onto the international agenda. Many people and organizations developed international bills of human rights; even the pope called for such a document.

When the commission began its work, it invited and welcomed comments and suggestions, and NGOs maintained pressure throughout.

International events that help to contextualize the committee's work include the beginnings of decolonization in such countries as the Philippines, Lebanon, India, and Pakistan; the continuation of colonial rule in both Asia and Africa; apartheid laws passed in South Africa the same year as the declaration; Britain's relinquishment of its mandate over Palestine and the formation of Israel; Jewish and Palestinian refugees; and the transition to a Communist government in China. These were the early years of the cold war between the Soviet bloc and the West. It is remarkable that delegates from both sides of the Iron Curtain and across many religious, political, and ideological divides could work together so intensely to develop a shared commitment to a global moral blueprint for human rights. There were seven distinct stages in the drafting process. Small subcommittees worked on the document and then brought it to the entire eighteen-member commission for a vote. This continued for nearly two years. In the process of drafting this document, every word and sentence attracted scrutiny and revision, and the entire committee voted on every article until it was finally adopted in December of 1948.

## Author Biography

The UDHR has no single author. The UN's Economic and Social Council was responsible for the formation of a permanent Commission on Human Rights, established in June 1946. Eleanor Roosevelt, who had worked tirelessly as a social and political activist during her years as first lady and who had been appointed as a delegate to the United Nations by her husband's successor, Harry Truman, chaired the commission as it worked on its first, critical, task: to draft an international bill of human rights.

The Human Rights Commission comprised eighteen members. The United States, the Soviet Union, the United Kingdom, France, and China would be permanent members. The other thirteen seats would rotate among the other UN member nations at three-year intervals; at the time, the additional thirteen countries were Australia, Belgium, Byelorussia, Chile, Egypt, India, Iran, Lebanon, Panama, Philippines, Ukraine, Uruguay, and Yugoslavia. The first director of the Human Rights Division of the UN Secretariat (the UN organ headed by the secretary-general) was a Canadian, John Humphrey, a legal scholar and human rights activist who would play a critical role.

The entire commission may be considered the author of this document, but certain delegates played particularly important roles. Following intensive research, Humphrey drafted the original text on which the declaration was based. The commission then had to revise this document. A subcommittee of four quickly realized that this task would be best conducted by one individual. René Cassin, a French legal expert, revised the document and provided a valuable structure. In addition to Roosevelt, Humphrey, and Cassin, key authors included Charles

Malik of Lebanon, a prominent philosopher, diplomat, and later Lebanon's minister of foreign affairs and member of that nation's National Assembly, and Peng-chun Chang, a well-known Chinese diplomat and playwright who was likely selected as vice-chair of the commission because of his Western education at Princeton University, his English fluency, and his recognized ability to bridge Asian and Western culture. However, everyone had the opportunity to speak and be heard as the document went through many revisions. NGOs, other UN members, and individuals attended the meetings and lobbied for their positions on human rights.

## HISTORICAL DOCUMENT

### Preamble

Whereas recognition of the inherent dignity and of the equal and inalienable rights of all members of the human family is the foundation of freedom, justice and peace in the world,

Whereas disregard and contempt for human rights have resulted in barbarous acts which have outraged the conscience of mankind, and the advent of a world in which human beings shall enjoy freedom of speech and belief and freedom from fear and want has been proclaimed as the highest aspiration of the common people,

Whereas it is essential, if man is not to be compelled to have recourse, as a last resort, to rebellion against tyranny and oppression, that human rights should be protected by the rule of law,

Whereas it is essential to promote the development of friendly relations between nations,

Whereas the peoples of the United Nations have in the Charter reaffirmed their faith in fundamental human rights, in the dignity and worth of the human person and in the equal rights of men and women and have determined to promote social progress and better standards of life in larger freedom,

Whereas Member States have pledged themselves to achieve, in co-operation with the United Nations, the promotion of universal respect for and

observance of human rights and fundamental freedoms, Whereas a common understanding of these rights and freedoms is of the greatest importance for the full realization of this pledge,

Now, therefore the General Assembly proclaims this universal declaration of human rights as a common standard of achievement for all peoples and all nations, to the end that every individual and every organ of society, keeping this Declaration constantly in mind, shall strive by teaching and education to promote respect for these rights and freedoms and by progressive measures, national and international, to secure their universal and effective recognition and observance, both among the peoples of Member States themselves and among the peoples of territories under their jurisdiction.

### Article 1.

All human beings are born free and equal in dignity and rights. They are endowed with reason and conscience and should act towards one another in a spirit of brotherhood.

### Article 2.

Everyone is entitled to all the rights and freedoms set forth in this Declaration, without distinction of any kind, such as race, colour, sex, language, religion, political or other opinion, national or social origin, property, birth or other status. Furthermore, no distinction shall be made on the basis of the political, jurisdictional or international status of the country or territory to which a person belongs, whether it be independent, trust, non-self-governing or under any other limitation of sovereignty.

### Article 3.

Everyone has the right to life, liberty and security of person.

### Article 4.

No one shall be held in slavery or servitude; slavery and the slave trade shall be prohibited in all their forms.

### Article 5.

No one shall be subjected to torture or to cruel, inhuman or degrading treatment or punishment.

### Article 6.

Everyone has the right to recognition everywhere as a person before the law.

### Article 7.

All are equal before the law and are entitled without any discrimination to equal protection of the law. All are entitled to equal protection against any discrimination in violation of this Declaration and against any incitement to such discrimination.

### Article 8.

Everyone has the right to an effective remedy by the competent national tribunals for acts violating the fundamental rights granted him by the constitution or by law.

### Article 9.

No one shall be subjected to arbitrary arrest, detention or exile.

### Article 10.

Everyone is entitled in full equality to a fair and public hearing by an independent and impartial tribunal, in the determination of his rights and obligations and of any criminal charge against him.

### Article 11.

(1) Everyone charged with a penal offence has the right to be presumed innocent until proved guilty according to law in a public trial at which he has had all the guarantees necessary for his defence.
(2) No one shall be held guilty of any penal offence on account of any act or omission which did not constitute a penal offence, under national or international law, at the time when it was committed. Nor shall a heavier penalty be imposed than the one that was applicable at the time the penal offence was committed.

### Article 12.

No one shall be subjected to arbitrary interference with his privacy, family, home or correspondence, nor to attacks upon his honour and reputation. Everyone has the right to the protection of the law against such interference or attacks.

### Article 13.

(1) Everyone has the right to freedom of movement and residence within the borders of each state.
(2) Everyone has the right to leave any country, including his own, and to return to his country.

### Article 14.

(1) Everyone has the right to seek and to enjoy in other countries asylum from persecution.
(2) This right may not be invoked in the case of prosecutions genuinely arising from non-political crimes or from acts contrary to the purposes and principles of the United Nations.

### Article 15.

(1) Everyone has the right to a nationality. (2) No one shall be arbitrarily deprived of his nationality nor denied the right to change his nationality.

### Article 16.

(1) Men and women of full age, without any limitation due to race, nationality or religion, have the

right to marry and to found a family. They are entitled to equal rights as to marriage, during marriage and at its dissolution.

(2) Marriage shall be entered into only with the free and full consent of the intending spouses.

(3) The family is the natural and fundamental group unit of society and is entitled to protection by society and the State.

## Article 17.

(1) Everyone has the right to own property alone as well as in association with others.

(2) No one shall be arbitrarily deprived of his property.

## Article 18.

Everyone has the right to freedom of thought, conscience and religion; this right includes freedom to change his religion or belief, and freedom, either alone or in community with others and in public or private, to manifest his religion or belief in teaching, practice, worship and observance.

## Article 19.

Everyone has the right to freedom of opinion and expression; this right includes freedom to hold opinions without interference and to seek, receive and impart information and ideas through any media and regardless of frontiers.

## Article 20.

(1) Everyone has the right to freedom of peaceful assembly and association.

(2) No one may be compelled to belong to an association.

## Article 21.

(1) Everyone has the right to take part in the government of his country, directly or through freely chosen representatives.

(2) Everyone has the right of equal access to public service in his country.

(3) The will of the people shall be the basis of the authority of government; this will shall be expressed in periodic and genuine elections which shall be by universal and equal suffrage and shall be held by secret vote or by equivalent free voting procedures.

## Article 22.

Everyone, as a member of society, has the right to social security and is entitled to realization, through national effort and international cooperation and in accordance with the organization and resources of each State, of the economic, social and cultural rights indispensable for his dignity and the free development of his personality.

## Article 23.

(1) Everyone has the right to work, to free choice of employment, to just and favourable conditions of work and to protection against unemployment.

(2) Everyone, without any discrimination, has the right to equal pay for equal work.

(3) Everyone who works has the right to just and favourable remuneration ensuring for himself and his family an existence worthy of human dignity, and supplemented, if necessary, by other means of social protection.

(4) Everyone has the right to form and to join trade unions for the protection of his interests.

## Article 24.

Everyone has the right to rest and leisure, including reasonable limitation of working hours and periodic holidays with pay.

## Article 25.

(1) Everyone has the right to a standard of living adequate for the health and well-being of himself and of his family, including food, clothing, housing and medical care and necessary social services, and the right to security in the event of unemployment, sickness, disability, widowhood, old age or other lack of livelihood in circumstances beyond his control.

(2) Motherhood and childhood are entitled to special care and assistance. All children, whether born in or out of wedlock, shall enjoy the same social protection.

### Article 26.

(1) Everyone has the right to education. Education shall be free, at least in the elementary and fundamental stages. Elementary education shall be compulsory. Technical and professional education shall be made generally available and higher education shall be equally accessible to all on the basis of merit.

(2) Education shall be directed to the full development of the human personality and to the strengthening of respect for human rights and fundamental freedoms. It shall promote understanding, tolerance and friendship among all nations, racial or religious groups, and shall further the activities of the United Nations for the maintenance of peace.

(3) Parents have a prior right to choose the kind of education that shall be given to their children.

### Article 27.

(1) Everyone has the right freely to participate in the cultural life of the community, to enjoy the arts and to share in scientific advancement and its benefits.

(2) Everyone has the right to the protection of the moral and material interests resulting from any scientific, literary or artistic production of which he is the author.

### Article 28.

Everyone is entitled to a social and international order in which the rights and freedoms set forth in this Declaration can be fully realized.

### Article 29.

(1) Everyone has duties to the community in which alone the free and full development of his personality is possible.

(2) In the exercise of his rights and freedoms, everyone shall be subject only to such limitations as are determined by law solely for the purpose of securing due recognition and respect for the rights and freedoms of others and of meeting the just requirements of morality, public order and the general welfare in a democratic society.

(3) These rights and freedoms may in no case be exercised contrary to the purposes and principles of the United Nations.

### Article 30.

Nothing in this Declaration may be interpreted as implying for any State, group or person any right to engage in any activity or to perform any act aimed at the destruction of any of the rights and freedoms set forth herein.

*Source: United Nations Web site*

## Document Analysis

The declaration is a product of a specific time and place, yet it has often also been described as a living document. The authors chose not to define several concepts, from "the family" to "torture," so ambiguity is built into the UDHR. The authors believed that human rights are universal. In other words, nations cannot pick and choose certain rights and ignore others. Countries that voted to adopt the declaration were accepting the whole package. The division of the document into thirty separate articles may make it difficult to remember that they are all interconnected and interdependent.

The declaration was given a particular structure by Cassin, and the basic structure still stands. The foundation, or core values, consists of dignity, liberty, equality, and brotherhood. The preamble leads to the four pillars of the declaration: life, liberty, and personal security (Articles 3–11); rights in civil society (Articles 12–17); rights in the polity (political rights; Articles 18–21); and economic, social, and cultural rights (Articles 22–27). The final three articles (28–30) deal with duties, limits, and order. The UDHR does not specifically discuss the human rights of soldiers or civilians during wartime; it focuses on the rights that must be upheld in order to preserve peace.

### Preamble

The preamble introduces the declaration and summarizes its core values. First, international peace and security are not just a matter of diplomacy. They are a function of human rights. Then, dignity is "inherent," a vital part of being human. All people have the right to respect and share certain rights that cannot be taken away. Finally, these rights are shared equally: All people have the same rights, and no one has more of one right than anyone else.

In the preamble's reference to "barbarous acts," the authors clearly had in mind World War II, but they do not mention the war, for they wanted the document to focus on the future. The second paragraph alludes to the "four freedoms" that were articulated by President Roosevelt in a 1941 speech. Although Roosevelt was speaking as an American, the delegates agreed that these are the "highest aspiration of the common people": freedom from fear and want (or poverty) and freedom of speech and belief. This list includes social, economic, political, and cultural rights. In a sense, the UDHR is an expansion of the four freedoms.

Recalling the American Declaration of Independence, the preamble warns governments to protect human rights so as to avoid "rebellion against tyranny and oppression." Such rebellion might be inevitable if human rights are not inscribed in the rule of law. There is a clear, if subtle, warning that national peace can be ensured only through the protection of human rights. The preamble then shifts to a reminder that protecting human rights is a vital aspect of the international peace process and essential for "social progress" or development. The preamble ends with a pledge by member states to ensure the implementation of the UDHR by means of education that will promote respect for human rights and to introduce various measures to "secure their universal and effective recognition and observance." The final sentence includes colonies, people without political, social, or economic rights, though the word *colony* does not appear. Instead, reference is made to "territories" under the "jurisdiction" of the member states.

### Articles 1 and 2

The first two articles spell out the core values of the UDHR. The preamble tells us that we are all members of the "human family," and the first article declares that we should act "in brotherhood." The implication is that a shared humanity is more important than being members of different countries, religions, or other belief systems. The preamble suggests that if we can understand that we are all part of one family, world peace may be possible.

Article 2 states that no one can be discriminated against on any basis. The list begins with physiological

markers. Race and color are listed separately to ensure the greatest protection for minorities and others previously denied their rights on the basis of skin color. Sex is the other genetic marker. The article goes on to cover freedom of belief and opinion and ends with social and economic factors, including national and social status (class or caste). Finally, UN members are reminded that colonized people share these rights. The question arises as to whether a country that colonized other countries *could* adhere to the UDHR. It is a challenge to find an article in this document that does not raise this question.

### Articles 3–11

The individual rights included in Article 3 are absolute. No conditions are attached to the right to life, liberty, and personal security. The right to life is not limited by national or international interests. There is no differentiation or hierarchy of rights: The right to life has the same value as the right to personal security. This implies that both capital punishment and wartime killing may be defined as violations of human rights. These rights might conflict, as in the case of self-defense or national security. The French Declaration of the Rights of Man and of the Citizen included a contradiction between individual rights to liberty and national security concerns. This contradiction remains pertinent today and is recognized in the final set of articles in the UDHR.

Article 4 prohibits slavery and states that no one can be held in "servitude." Forced labor is outlawed. This connects with Article 9 (against arbitrary arrest) and to Article 23, which protects the right to choose one's work.

Article 5 continues the theme of personal security. It deals with the right to protection of the body from torture, or "cruel, inhuman or degrading treatment or punishment." Read with the third article, one might again argue that capital punishment is a violation of human rights. A similar argument has been made about interrogation. Note the inclusion of the word "punishment": Even convicted criminals have the right to humane punishment. "Torture" is an excellent example of how the failure to define a term allows governments to redefine their policies or actions as "not torture" when others claim they are indeed torturous acts. At the same time, it underscores the moral power of the declaration, because governments do not claim the right to torture. This article demonstrates both the weakness and the strength of the declaration. Because it did not define its terms clearly, there is room for maneuvering, which may be used either to demand protection of human rights (normally by NGOs or individuals) or withhold human rights (normally by governments). Later conventions seek to address these kinds of shortcomings.

Articles 6–11 relate the individual to national legal systems. The UDHR states the moral obligation to create laws that protect human rights. These articles assume that such laws and constitutions are in place (see particularly Article 8). Article 6 ensures that every person has a right to fair treatment under the law, whereas Article 7 details the right to equality before the law. Not only is discrimination prohibited, but so too is the *incitement* to discriminate. Articles 8, 9, and 10 focus on the kind of treatment one should expect under a national legal system so as to ensure a fair, effective hearing. People have the right to be "presumed innocent" and to be treated accordingly, with dignity. Article 11 also states that no one can be held guilty of a crime that had not been codified at the time of the action, and if the crime did exist, "no heavier penalty [may] be imposed than the one that was applicable at the time."

### Articles 12–17

Rights related to the family and home in the context of the right to privacy are introduced in Article 12. Note the word *arbitrary* (see Articles 9 and 15). This means that the rights named here are not absolute. Rights to privacy, family, home, and correspondence are protected from "arbitrary interference." If the interference can be justified legally, these rights can be limited.

Articles 13 through 15 discuss the rights to a nationality (including the right to chose a new one) as well as to freedom of movement within and between countries. The word *citizen* does not appear. Whereas the previous articles had assumed that a country would choose to uphold human rights within its constitution and laws, here we discover the rights of citizens whose governments persecute them. The word *enjoy* in Article 14 introduces ambiguity: "Everyone has the right to seek and to enjoy in other countries asylum from persecution." If everyone has the right to "enjoy" asylum, the question arises as to which country has the obligation to grant it.

The family is the focus of Article 16. Marriage, in particular, was the cause of much discussion on the committee, and the delegates worked hard to ensure that different cultural views of this central institution were accommodated. Consent of both spouses is re-

quired, they have to be of "full age" (a specific age is not given, however), and the family is entitled to protection by both "society" and "the State." However, this article contains a provision given by Saudi Arabia as a reason for its decision to abstain from the vote, for the Saudis believed it would not be acceptable for a Muslim to marry a person of another religion. Article 16 also raised other concerns among the members of the commission. Many delegates and lobbyists argued that the word *divorce* should not be included in the declaration; here Muslims and Roman Catholics were in perfect agreement. Note that the family is also protected in Articles 12 and 23, which refer to the right to earn a living wage to ensure the "an existence worthy of human dignity." Article 25 protects the rights of children born out of marriage.

Finally, Article 17 states the absolute right to private property, a Western concept. However, the right to hold on to one's property is not absolute: "No one shall be *arbitrarily* deprived of his property."

### Articles 18–21

These articles focus on two of Franklin Roosevelt's four freedoms: the rights to belief and speech—including the right to change one's belief and even one's religion. This was the second point Saudi Arabia could not accept. Whereas Article 18 focuses on religion, Article 19 is broader in scope, speaking of the right to "freedom of opinion and expression." The next article moves beyond the right to the individual freedom of thought and expression to include the right (but not the obligation) to meet and associate with others, as long as it is done peacefully.

Article 21 shifts to formal political rights: the right to participate in government and to have equal access to public service. This article is important because it permits only one concept of government: "The will of the people shall be the basis of the authority of government." The article goes on to state that regular, public elections incorporating "free voting procedures" should be held and that there should be "universal and equal suffrage"—there shall be no discrimination on the bases outlined in Article 2. The only ambiguity is in the word *equivalent* in reference to methods of voting.

### Articles 22–27

Article 22 sets out the right to "social security," although this is not specifically defined. Nevertheless, cooperation between nations and the international community is specifically invoked in this article, given limitations on countries' resources. Thus every nation individually and within the international community is obliged to ensure a humane standard of living for all people.

Work issues are the focus of Article 23. These rights have particular challenges, as the burden is placed on the state to protect rights; this assumes that nations have the resources to do so. Freedom to work is spelled out, including the right to choose one's employment. Fair labor conditions and the right to "protection against unemployment" are also noted as human rights. Section 2 states the right to equal pay for equal work for everyone, "without discrimination." Fair pay is another right. The concept of a family wage is implied, with the assumption that each family has one male breadwinner. If the wage is insufficient, there has to be a backup, provided presumably by the state. Finally, the right (but not obligation) to unionize is included.

Article 24 includes what might be considered a surprising right: "the right to rest and leisure"; paid holidays are considered a human right. Leisure could be considered part of a dignified standard of living, the topic of Article 25. In this article, basic needs are spelled out, including food, housing, and medical care, that is, to social security because of "lack of livelihood in circumstances beyond [a person's] control." It then specifies the importance of the needs of mothers and children and calls for the protection of children irrespective of the marital status of their parents.

The right to an education is the core of Article 26. The article says that elementary education should be compulsory and free, but it speaks of the right to other levels of education too. The purpose of education is to support the core values of the UDHR. Finally, parents have a right to choose how their children are educated. It should be clear that many of the rights in the UDHR provide a list of objectives toward which countries should strive. Not every country had, or has, the resources to provide free education, but in the spirit of this declaration, they should work toward this goal.

Article 27 refers to cultural rights specifically: All have the right to participate in the "cultural life of the community" and to "enjoy," "share," and benefit from scientific advances. This article also introduces the right to copyright, to "protection of the moral and material interests" that result from any kind of cultural production in the arts or sciences.

## Articles 28–30

The final three articles speak of the duties of the international community. Everyone has the right to peace, but duties accompany rights. This was a point made very clearly by many influential thinkers (including the Indian nationalist leader Mohandas Gandhi and the English critic and novelist Aldous Huxley) who were surveyed as the committee began its work. Article 29 specifies this obligation. This article connects individuals to the community, not as bearers of rights but as bearers of duties to others. In order to claim our own human rights, we need to protect the rights of others. This section states that "the free and full development" of human beings is impossible without "the community." The article goes on to acknowledge that rights may be limited, as for example by the need to protect the rights of others, but it also speaks of the "just requirements" of "public order." Section 3 declares that rights and freedoms may be exercised only in line with the goals of the UN. The UDHR closes (Article 30) with a statement that recognizes that interpretations of the various rights and freedoms may vary, but no person, group, or government has the right to interpret the articles in such a way that human rights are violated.

## Essential Themes

The declaration provides a yardstick or guidepost for setting goals and measuring progress toward those goals. NGOs and grassroots movements have played a critical role in transforming the words of the UDHR into action and in making governments accountable. Governments have often been quick to pay lip service but slow to protect human rights. The greatest impact globally seems to have been in the inspiration, hope, and empowerment that this document has given to "common people" who do not experience human rights but know that they have a right to seek justice.

However, the declaration has also had significant impact on the constitutions of more than two dozen nations that either became independent from colonial rule after 1948 or that have reviewed and rewritten their constitutions. No government is willing to stand in the face of the declaration and deny outright the existence of human rights. Acknowledging the UDHR is an important step toward developing a culture of human rights, but governments must have the political will to implement them within their own national borders as well as internationally, and this has been less forthcoming.

The declaration has been of great importance within the UN system itself. Its moral power has provided the foundation for numerous conventions, treaties, and covenants promoting and protecting human rights. Yet the second half of the twentieth century saw genocide, ethnic cleansing, and continued violence against women and children. However, as former U.S. president Jimmy Carter noted, when countries sign and ratify human rights conventions, at least *some* accountability is required. Political will is also required of the United Nations itself. The Commission on Human Rights presented two human rights covenants to the General Assembly in 1966, but it took a full ten years for them to be ratified.

Scholars and activists continue to debate whether the UDHR recognizes women's rights. Another key concern is the issue of universality. Many have noted the absence of many African and Asian countries, as well as the dominance of three Western nations, on the core committee. There also appears to be an imbalance within the document itself, with considerable weight given to Western Enlightenment views of individuals' rights. Despite the obstacles and challenges that every person faces in the enjoyment of their basic human rights, the Universal Declaration of Human Rights has no doubt played a critical role in the development of awareness of human rights and the need to promote and protect them.

—*Patricia van der Spuy, PhD*

## Bibliography and Additional Reading

Amnesty International. *Human Rights Are Women's Rights*. New York: Amnesty International, 1995.

Ashworth, Georgina. *Of Violence and Violation: Women and Human Rights*. London: CHANGE, 1986.

Bunch, Charlotte, Noeleen Heyzer, Sushma Kapoor, and Joanne Sandler. "Women's Human Rights and Development: A Global Agenda for the 21st Century." In *A Commitment to the World's Women: Perspectives on Development for Beijing and Beyond*, ed. Noeleen Heyzer. New York: UNIFEM, 1995.

Danieli, Yael, Elsa Stamatopoulou, and Clarence J. Dias, eds. *The Universal Declaration of Human Rights: Fifty Years and Beyond*. New York: Baywood, 1998.

Glendon, Mary Ann. A World Made New: Eleanor Roosevelt and the Universal Declaration of Human Rights. New York: Random House, 2001.

Hunt, Lynn. *Inventing Human Rights: A History*. New York: W. W. Norton, 2007.

Korey, William. NGOs and the Universal Declaration of Human Rights: "A Curious Grapevine." New York: St. Martin's Press, 1998.

Morsink, Johannes. *The Universal Declaration of Human Rights: Origins, Drafting, and Intent*. Philadelphia: University of Pennsylvania Press, 1999.

Mutua, Makau. "The Ideology of Human Rights." *Virginia Journal of International Law* 36 (1996): 589–657.

"Ongoing Struggle for Human Rights." Universal Declaration of Human Rights Web site. http://www.udhr.org/history/timeline.htm.

Pollis, Adamantia, and Peter Schwab, eds. *Human Rights: Cultural and Ideological Perspectives*. New York: Praeger, 1979.

Roosevelt, Eleanor. "On the Adoption of the Universal Declaration of Human Rights." American Rhetoric Web site. http://www.americanrhetoric.com/speeches/eleanorrooseveltdeclarationhumanrights.htm.

United Nations. "Human Rights." http://www.un.org/en/rights.

# ■ Simone de Beauvoir: Introduction to *The Second Sex*

**Date:** 1949 (English translation 1953)
**Author:** Simone de Beauvoir
**Genre:** Book chapter

## Summary Overview

Simone de Beauvoir was a French intellectual, political activist, and philosopher active from the 1930s until 1986. Her life and work as a teacher and writer were foundational to the feminist movements of the second half of the 20th century. In addition to her philosophical works, she was a prolific writer of letters and novels. She was in a long-term open relationship with the French existentialist philosopher Jean-Paul Sartre for much of her life and their social circle included many of the most famous thinkers of their time. Her 1949 treatise *The Second Sex* is a meticulously researched two-volume study of the position of women in human society. In it, de Beauvoir covers the role that religious and scientific institutions, marriage, and cultural and sexual mores have contributed to the subjection and domination of women. The book was critically acclaimed at its publication and is considered one of the major influences on second-wave feminism.

## Defining Moment

De Beauvoir was writing in a post-war Europe that idealized domesticity. Abortion and birth control were still illegal in France and French women had only gained the right to vote in 1944. De Beauvoir herself was one of the first women to achieve higher education; opportunities for women outside the home were few and far between. Her direct challenge to women's traditional roles of wife and mother was therefore shocking to many, as was her frankness in addressing sexuality and biology.

*The Second Sex* was one of the first texts to explicitly draw a contrast between sex and gender. Though the distinction is now widely accepted, it was nearly unheard of at the time to think about the idea of femininity without linking it to reproduction and the female body. Moreover, de Beauvoir's concept of the feminine as "the Other" laid the groundwork for a radical shift in thinking about the way social constructs affect individuals. Twenty years before second-wave feminists popularized the idea that "the personal is political", de Beauvoir 's work demonstrates that cultural oppression impacts women in every sphere of life. The notion that women themselves are complicit in this oppression was an innovation, and the publication of *The Second Sex* inspired a new way of thinking about systemic injustice.

*The Second Sex* is a two-volume work of literature aimed at elucidating and dismantling the cultural system that leads to the subjection of women in every sphere of life. De Beauvoir argues throughout the work that society divides people into men and not-men (the Second Sex of the title) and uses this distinction to subjugate women and keep them in a subordinate position in order to ensure the continuation of a patriarchal society. She speaks directly to women, but also to all people interested in advancing the human race as a whole without distinction between gender. The treatise is a call to abandon the old way of thinking that places men at the center of the world and conceives of masculinity in opposition femininity. De Beauvoir asks what it means to be a woman in a male-centered world: she argues that men consider themselves the default race and women are compelled to position themselves as non-men, or Others.

De Beauvoir's work is wide-ranging and demands the reader's engagement; she draws on historical examples from ancient times to the modern era. She also uses zoological and physiological examples and discusses in detail the role that biology has played in the relationship between men and women. At the beginning of volume two, she discusses the contrast between upbringing and education that male and female children receive, arguing that gender differences are taught, not innate. She also explicitly describes the difference between heterosexual and homosexual relationships and the negative impact that marriage has on the inner life of both women and men.

Like many other pioneering but controversial feminist thinkers (such as Elizabeth Cady Stanton and Emma Goldman), De Beauvoir took aim at the hierarchy and misogyny inherent in religious systems. She was also among the first feminist writers to critique the psychoanalytical approach championed by male thinkers of the late-nineteenth century such as Sigmund Freud. She objected to his approach as being overly

Simone de Beauvoir and Jean-Paul Sartre in Beijing, 1955. By 刘东鳌 (Liu Dong'ao) (Xinhua News Agency).

focused on idea of masculinity as an inherently superior state. To de Beauvoir, if women are in fact jealous of masculinity and virility, this envy is not because of their innate inferiority but a result of the power and privilege that social constructs have granted men.

The work was published in French in 1949. The initial English translation differed vastly from de Beauvoir's original, but her message still reached the American women's liberation movement and exerted a huge influence on the feminists of the 1970s.

## Author Biography

Simone de Beauvoir was born in Paris in 1908 to upper-middle-class parents. The family lost most of its money after World War I and struggled to keep up appearances. Her mother was deeply invested in Catholicism and the young Simone was also devoutly religious. De Beauvoir initially attended a convent school and considered becoming a nun, but she lost her faith as a teenager and remained a lifelong atheist.

Encouraged by her father in her untraditional pursuits, de Beauvoir excelled in school and entered the Sorbonne for university studies. Her curiosity and analytical skills drew the attention of teachers and other students, including Jean-Paul Sartre. The two met when de Beauvoir was 21 and Sartre was 24, and they began a relationship that would last for the rest of their lives. They never married, had children, or lived together, but they edited and critiqued each other's work and their complex relationship was central to both of their lives for decades. They took the final exam for their postgraduate philosophy course together, where the jury narrowly awarded Sartre first place and de Beauvoir second; she was the youngest person ever to pass.

Upon graduation, de Beauvoir taught at classes in various lyceums, the equivalent of high school, while writing. She published her first work of fiction at age 29 and continued to write while teaching until she was able to support herself financially with her literary output. In 1943, she left her teaching position and embarked on a distinguished career of research, travel, and writing.

Like Sartre, De Beauvoir became famous for her existentialist works that contrasted the freedom of the individual with the constraints imposed by society. She is famous for her works on the "Otherness" of women and the way that cultural institutions compel women to be thought of, and to think of themselves as, outsiders.

De Beauvoir was an early proponent of the theory that biological sex and cultural gender are not synonymous: there is a distinction between the social/historical construction of gender and the experience of the individual, and people (especially women) are often forced to act in ways that conform with gender stereotypes in order to be accepted in society.

De Beauvoir's personal life has been the subject of such intense interest and controversy. She never married and had no children. Though Sartre did propose to her early in life (at the insistence of de Beauvoir's father), she rejected his proposal and they continued their relationship without the sanction of society. She and Sartre shared an extremely close bond through their entire lives, though both had many other lovers. De Beauvoir carried on several long-term affairs with writers and intellectuals other than Sartre and both led independent lives, but the two maintained an intense and essential connection that informed all of their literary activities. On multiple occasions, both Sartre and de Beauvoir befriended a young or vulnerable woman, introduced her to their intellectual circle, and seduced her, independently or together. The two would discuss their sexual exploits in detail in letters to each other and De Beauvoir included fictionalized versions of these liaisons in many of her novels.

De Beauvoir and Sartre became famous after the end of World War II with his publication of *Being and Nothingness* in 1943 and her publication of *The Second Sex* in 1949. Her novel *The Mandarins*, about the personal lives of people in her circle, was published in 1954 to critical acclaim, but its unvarnished portrayal of personal details angered some of her friends and ex-lovers. She traveled extensively in her later life and her travel journals of time in China were especially popular. Late in life she became active in the women's liberation movement of the 1970s and was one of the signers of the "Manifesto of the 343", a controversial list of famous women who declared publicly that they had had abortions (which were illegal in France until 1974).

Sartre died in 1980. After his death, de Beauvoir published their letters with significant edits to remove personal details. She also published *A Farewell to Sartre*, an account of the end of his life and their relationship. She died in 1986 in Paris and is buried next to Sartre. Her literary heir Sylvie le Bon, her former student and adoptive daughter, later published her unedited letters.

## HISTORICAL DOCUMENT

### Introduction: "Woman as Other"

FOR a long time I have hesitated to write a book on woman. The subject is irritating, especially to women; and it is not new. Enough ink has been spilled in quarrelling over feminism, and perhaps we should say no more about it. It is still talked about, however, for the voluminous nonsense uttered during the last century seems to have done little to illuminate the problem. After all, is there a problem? And if so, what is it? Are there women, really? Most assuredly the theory of the eternal feminine still has its adherents who will whisper in your ear: 'Even in Russia women still are women'; and other erudite persons—sometimes the very same—say with a sigh: 'Woman is losing her way, woman is lost.' One wonders if women still exist, if they will always exist, whether or not it is desirable that they should, what place they occupy in this world, what their place should be. 'What has become of women?' was asked recently in an ephemeral magazine.

But first we must ask: what is a woman? 'Tota mulier in utero', says one, 'woman is a womb'. But in speaking of certain women, connoisseurs declare that they are not women, although they are equipped with a uterus like the rest. All agree in recognising the fact that females exist in the human species; today as always they make up about one half of humanity. And yet we are told that femininity is in danger; we are exhorted to be women, remain women, become women. It would appear, then, that every female human being is not necessarily a woman; to be so considered she must share in that mysterious and threatened reality known as femininity. Is this attribute something secreted by the ovaries? Or is it a Platonic essence, a product of the philosophic imagination? Is a rustling petticoat enough to bring it down to earth? Although some women try zealously to incarnate this essence, it is hardly patentable. It is frequently described in vague and dazzling terms that seem to have been borrowed from the vocabulary of the seers, and indeed in the times of St Thomas it was considered an essence as certainly defined as the somniferous virtue of the poppy

But conceptualism has lost ground. The biological and social sciences no longer admit the existence of unchangeably fixed entities that determine given characteristics, such as those ascribed to woman, the Jew, or the Negro. Science regards any characteristic as a reaction dependent in part upon a *situation*. If today femininity no longer exists, then it never existed. But does the word *woman*, then, have no specific content? This is stoutly affirmed by those who hold to the philosophy of the enlightenment, of rationalism, of nominalism; women, to them, are merely the human beings arbitrarily designated by the word *woman*. Many American women particularly are prepared to think that there is no longer any place for woman as such; if a backward individual still takes herself for a woman, her friends advise her to be psychoanalysed and thus get rid of this obsession. In regard to a work, *Modern Woman: The Lost Sex*, which in other respects has its irritating features, Dorothy Parker has written: 'I cannot be just to books which treat of woman as woman ... My idea is that all of us, men as well as women, should be regarded as human beings.' But nominalism is a rather inadequate doctrine, and the antifeminists have had no trouble in showing that women simply *are* not men. Surely woman is, like man, a human being; but such a declaration is abstract. The fact is that every concrete human being is always a singular, separate individual. To decline to accept such notions as the eternal feminine, the black soul, the Jewish character, is not to deny that Jews, Negroes, women exist today—this denial does not represent a liberation for those concerned, but rather a flight from reality. Some years ago a well-known woman writer refused to permit her portrait to appear in a series of photographs especially devoted to women writers; she wished to be counted among the men. But in order to gain this privilege she made use of her husband's influence! Women who assert that they are men lay claim none the less to masculine consideration and respect. I recall also a young Trotskyite standing on a platform at a boisterous meeting and getting ready to use her fists, in spite of her evident fragility. She was denying her feminine weakness; but it was for love of a militant male whose equal she wished to be. The attitude of defiance of many American women proves that they are haunted by a sense of their femininity. In truth, to go for a walk with one's eyes open is enough to demonstrate that humanity is divided into two classes of individuals whose clothes, faces, bodies, smiles, gaits, interests, and occupations are manifestly different. Perhaps these differences are superficial, perhaps they are destined to disappear. What is certain is that they do most obviously exist.

If her functioning as a female is not enough to define woman, if we decline also to explain her through 'the eternal feminine', and if nevertheless we admit, provisionally, that women do exist, then we must face the question "what is a woman"?

To state the question is, to me, to suggest, at once, a preliminary answer. The fact that I ask it is in itself significant. A man would never set out to write a book on the peculiar situation of the human male. But if I wish to define myself, I must first of all say: 'I am a woman'; on this truth must be based all further discussion. A man never begins by presenting himself as an individual of a certain sex; it goes without saying that he is a man. The terms *masculine* and *feminine* are used symmetrically only as a matter of form, as on legal papers. In actuality the relation of the two sexes is not quite like that of two electrical poles, for man represents both the positive and the neutral, as is indicated by the common use of *man* to designate human beings in general; whereas woman represents only the negative, defined by limiting criteria, without reciprocity. In the midst of an abstract discussion it is vexing to hear a man say: 'You think thus and so because you are a woman'; but I know that my only defence is to reply: 'I think thus and so because it is true,' thereby removing my subjective self from the argument. It would be out of the question to reply: 'And you think the contrary because you are a man', for it is understood that the fact of being a man is no peculiarity. A man is in the right in being a man; it is the woman who is in the wrong. It amounts to this: just as for the ancients there was an absolute vertical with reference to which the oblique was defined, so there is an absolute human type, the masculine. Woman

has ovaries, a uterus: these peculiarities imprison her in her subjectivity, circumscribe her within the limits of her own nature. It is often said that she thinks with her glands. Man superbly ignores the fact that his anatomy also includes glands, such as the testicles, and that they secrete hormones. He thinks of his body as a direct and normal connection with the world, which he believes he apprehends objectively, whereas he regards the body of woman as a hindrance, a prison, weighed down by everything peculiar to it. 'The female is a female by virtue of a certain lack of qualities,' said Aristotle; 'we should regard the female nature as afflicted with a natural defectiveness.' And St Thomas for his part pronounced woman to be an 'imperfect man', an 'incidental' being. This is symbolised in Genesis where Eve is depicted as made from what Bossuet called 'a supernumerary bone' of Adam.

Thus humanity is male and man defines woman not in herself but as relative to him; she is not regarded as an autonomous being. Michelet writes: 'Woman, the relative being ...' And Benda is most positive in his *Rapport d'Uriel*: 'The body of man makes sense in itself quite apart from that of woman, whereas the latter seems wanting in significance by itself ... Man can think of himself without woman. She cannot think of herself without man.' And she is simply what man decrees; thus she is called 'the sex', by which is meant that she appears essentially to the male as a sexual being. For him she is sex—absolute sex, no less. She is defined and differentiated with reference to man and not he with reference to her; she is the incidental, the inessential as opposed to the essential. He is the Subject, he is the Absolute—she is the Other.'

The category of the *Other* is as primordial as consciousness itself. In the most primitive societies, in the most ancient mythologies, one finds the expression of a duality—that of the Self and the Other. This duality was not originally attached to the division of the sexes; it was not dependent upon any empirical facts. It is revealed in such works as that of Granet on Chinese thought and those of Dumézil on the East Indies and Rome. The feminine element was at first no more involved in such pairs as Varuna-Mitra, Uranus-Zeus, Sun-Moon, and Day-Night than it was in the contrasts between Good and Evil, lucky and unlucky auspices, right and left, God and Lucifer. Otherness is a fundamental category of human thought.

Thus it is that no group ever sets itself up as the One without at once setting up the Other over against itself. If three travellers chance to occupy the same compartment, that is enough to make vaguely hostile 'others' out of all the rest of the passengers on the train. In small-town eyes all persons not belonging to the village are 'strangers' and suspect; to the native of a country all who inhabit other countries are 'foreigners'; Jews are 'different' for the anti-Semite, Negroes are 'inferior' for American racists, aborigines are 'natives' for colonists, proletarians are the 'lower class' for the privileged.

Lévi-Strauss, at the end of a profound work on the various forms of primitive societies, reaches the following conclusion: 'Passage from the state of Nature to the state of Culture is marked by man's ability to view biological relations as a series of contrasts; duality, alternation, opposition, and symmetry, whether under definite or vague forms, constitute not so much phenomena to be explained as fundamental and immediately given data of social reality.' These phenomena would be incomprehensible if in fact human society were simply a *Mitsein* or fellowship based on solidarity and friendliness. Things become clear, on the contrary, if, following Hegel, we find in consciousness itself a fundamental hostility towards every other consciousness; the subject can be posed only in being opposed—he sets himself up as the essential, as opposed to the other, the inessential, the object.

But the other consciousness, the other ego, sets up a reciprocal claim. The native travelling abroad is shocked to find himself in turn regarded as a 'stranger' by the natives of neighbouring countries. As a matter of fact, wars, festivals, trading, treaties, and contests among tribes, nations, and classes tend to deprive the concept *Other* of its absolute sense and to make manifest its relativity; willy-nilly, individuals and groups are forced to realize the reciprocity of their relations. How is it, then, that this reciprocity has not been recognised between the sexes, that one of the contrasting terms is set up as the sole essential, denying any relativity in regard to its correlative and defining the latter as pure otherness? Why is it that women do not dispute male sovereignty? No subject will readily volunteer to become the object, the inessential; it is not the Other who, in defining himself as the Other, establishes the One. The Other is posed as such by the One in defining himself as the One. But if the Other is not to regain the status of being the One, he must be submissive enough to accept this alien point of view. Whence comes this submission in the case of woman?

There are, to be sure, other cases in which a certain category has been able to dominate another completely for a time. Very often this privilege depends upon inequality of numbers—the majority imposes its rule upon the minority or persecutes it. But women are not a minority, like the American Negroes or the Jews; there are as many women as men on earth. Again, the two groups concerned have often been originally independent; they may have been formerly unaware of each other's existence, or perhaps they recognised each other's autonomy. But a historical event has resulted in the subjugation of the weaker by the stronger. The scattering of the Jews, the introduction of slavery into America, the conquests of imperialism are examples in point. In these cases the oppressed retained at least the memory of former days; they possessed in common a past, a tradition, sometimes a religion or a culture.

The parallel drawn by Bebel between women and the proletariat is valid in that neither ever formed a minority or a separate collective unit of mankind. And instead of a single historical event it is in both cases a historical development that explains their status as a class and accounts for the membership of *particular individuals* in that class. But proletarians have not always existed, whereas there have always been women. They are women in virtue of their anatomy and physiology. Throughout history they have always been subordinated to men, and hence their dependency is not the result of a historical event or a social change—it was not something that *occurred*. The reason why otherness in this case seems to be an absolute is in part that it lacks the contingent or incidental nature of historical facts. A condition brought about at a certain time can be abolished at some other time, as the Negroes of Haiti and others have proved: but it might seem that natural condition is beyond the possibility of change. In truth, however, the nature of things is no more immutably given, once for all, than is historical reality. If woman seems to be the inessential which never becomes the essential, it is because she herself fails to bring about this change. Proletarians say 'We'; Negroes also. Regarding themselves as subjects, they transform the bourgeois, the whites, into 'others'. But women do not say 'We', except at some congress of feminists or similar formal demonstration; men say 'women', and women use the same word in referring to themselves. They do not authentically assume a subjective attitude. The proletarians have accomplished the revolution in Russia, the Negroes in Haiti, the Indo-Chinese are battling for it in Indo-China; but the women's effort has never been anything more than a symbolic agitation. They have gained only what men have been willing to grant; they have taken nothing, they have only received.

The reason for this is that women lack concrete means for organising themselves into a unit which can stand face to face with the correlative unit. They have no past, no history, no religion of their own; and they have no such solidarity of work and interest as that of the proletariat. They are not even promiscuously herded together in the way that creates community feeling among the American Negroes, the ghetto Jews, the workers of Saint-Denis, or the factory hands of Renault. They live dispersed among the males, attached through residence, housework, economic condition, and social standing to certain men—fathers or husbands—more firmly than they are to other women. If they belong to the bourgeoisie, they feel solidarity with men of that class, not with proletarian women; if they are white, their allegiance is to white men, not to Negro women. The proletariat can propose to massacre the ruling class, and a sufficiently fanatical Jew or Negro might dream of getting sole possession of the atomic bomb and making humanity wholly Jewish or black; but woman cannot even dream of exterminating the males. The bond that unites her to her oppressors is not comparable to any other. The division of the sexes is a biological fact, not an event in human history. Male and female stand opposed within a primordial *Mitsein*, and woman has not broken it. The couple is a fundamental unity with its two halves riveted together, and the cleavage of society along the line of sex is impossible. Here is to be found the basic trait of woman: she is the Other in a totality of which the two components are necessary to one another.

One could suppose that this reciprocity might have facilitated the liberation of woman. When Hercules sat at the feet of Omphale and helped with her spinning, his desire for her held him captive; but why did she fail to gain a lasting power? To revenge herself on Jason, Medea killed their children; and this grim legend would seem to suggest that she might have obtained a formidable influence over him through his love for his offspring. In *Lysistrata* Aristophanes gaily depicts a band of women who joined forces to gain social ends through the sexual needs of their men; but this is only a play. In the legend of the Sabine women, the latter soon abandoned their plan of remaining sterile to punish their ravishers. In truth woman has not been socially emancipated through man's need—sexual desire and the desire for offspring—which makes the male dependent for satisfaction upon the female.

Master and slave, also, are united by a reciprocal need, in this case economic, which does not liberate the slave. In the relation of master to slave the master does not make a point of the need that he has for the other; he has in his grasp the power of satisfying this need through his own action; whereas the slave, in his dependent condition, his hope and fear, is quite conscious of the need he has for his master. Even if the need is at bottom equally urgent for both, it always works in favour of the oppressor and against the oppressed. That is why the liberation of the working class, for example, has been slow.

Now, woman has always been man's dependant, if not his slave; the two sexes have never shared the world in equality. And even today woman is heavily handicapped, though her situation is beginning to change. Almost nowhere is her legal status the same as man's, and frequently it is much to her disadvantage. Even when her rights are legally recognised in the abstract, long-standing custom prevents their full expression in the mores. In the economic sphere men and women can almost be said to make up two castes; other things being equal, the former hold the better jobs, get higher wages, and have more opportunity for success than their new competitors. In industry and politics men have a great many more positions and they monopolise the most important posts. In addition to all this, they enjoy a traditional prestige that the education of children tends in every way to support, for the present enshrines the past—and in the past all history has been made by men. At the present time, when women are beginning to take part in the affairs of the world, it is still a world that belongs to men—they have no doubt of it at all and women have scarcely any. To decline to be the Other, to refuse to be a party to the deal—this would be for women to renounce all the advantages conferred upon them by their alliance with the superior caste. Man-the-sovereign will provide woman-the-liege with material protection and will undertake the moral justification of her existence; thus she can evade at once both economic risk and the metaphysical risk of a liberty in which ends and aims must be contrived without assistance. Indeed, along with the ethical urge of each individual to affirm his subjective existence, there is also the temptation to forgo liberty and become a thing. This is an inauspicious road, for he who takes it—passive, lost, ruined—becomes henceforth the creature of another's will, frustrated in his transcendence and deprived of every value. But it is an easy road; on it one avoids the strain involved in undertaking an authentic existence. When man makes of woman the Other, he may, then, expect to manifest deep-seated tendencies towards complicity. Thus, woman may fail to lay claim to the status of subject because she lacks definite resources, because she feels the necessary bond that ties her to man regardless of reciprocity, and because she is often very well pleased with her role as the Other.

But it will be asked at once: how did all this begin? It is easy to see that the duality of the sexes, like any duality, gives rise to conflict. And doubtless the winner will assume the status of absolute. But why should man have won from the start? It seems possible that women could have won the victory; or that the outcome of the conflict might never have been decided. How is it that this world has always belonged to the men and that things have begun to change only recently? Is this change a good thing? Will it bring about an equal sharing of the world between men and women?

These questions are not new, and they have often been answered. But the very fact that woman *is the Other* tends to cast suspicion upon all the justifications that men have ever been able to provide for it. These have all too evidently been dictated by men's interest. A little-known feminist of the seventeenth century, Poulain de la Barre, put it this way: 'All that has been written about women by men should be suspect, for the men are at once judge and party to the lawsuit.' Everywhere, at all times, the males have displayed their satisfaction in feeling that they are the lords of creation. 'Blessed be God ... that He did not make me a woman,' say the Jews in their morning prayers, while their wives pray on a note of resignation: 'Blessed be the Lord, who created me according to His will.' The first among the blessings for which Plato thanked the gods was that he had been created free, not enslaved; the second, a man, not a woman. But the males could not enjoy this privilege fully unless they believed it to be founded on the absolute and the eternal; they sought to make the fact of their supremacy into a right. 'Being men, those who have made and compiled the laws have favoured their own sex, and jurists have elevated these laws into principles', to quote Poulain de la Barre once more.

Legislators, priests, philosophers, writers, and scientists have striven to show that the subordinate position of woman is willed in heaven and advantageous on earth. The religions invented by men reflect this wish for domination. In the legends of Eve and Pandora men have taken up arms against women. They have made use of philosophy and theology, as the quotations from Aristotle and St Thomas have shown. Since ancient times satirists and moralists have delighted in showing up the weaknesses of women. We are familiar with the savage indictments hurled against women throughout French literature. Montherlant, for example, follows the tradition of Jean de Meung, though with less gusto. This hostility may at times be well founded, often it is gratuitous; but in truth it more or less successfully conceals a desire for self-justification. As Montaigne says, 'It is easier to accuse one sex than to excuse the other'. Sometimes what is going on is clear enough. For instance, the Roman law limiting the rights of woman cited 'the imbecility, the instability of the sex' just when the weakening of family ties seemed to threaten the interests of male heirs. And in the effort to keep the married woman under guardianship, appeal was made in the sixteenth century to the authority of St Augustine, who declared that 'woman is a creature neither decisive nor constant', at a time when the single woman was thought capable of managing her property. Montaigne understood clearly how arbitrary and unjust was woman's appointed lot: 'Women are not in the wrong when they decline to accept the rules laid down for them, since the men make these rules without consulting them. No wonder intrigue and strife abound.' But he did not go so far as to champion their cause.

It was only later, in the eighteenth century, that genuinely democratic men began to view the matter objectively. Diderot, among others, strove to show that woman is, like man, a human being. Later John Stuart Mill came fervently to her defence. But these philosophers displayed unusual impartiality. In the nineteenth century the feminist quarrel became again a quarrel of partisans. One of the consequences of the industrial revolution was the entrance of women into productive labour, and it was just here that the claims of the feminists emerged from the realm of theory and acquired an economic basis, while their opponents became the more aggressive. Although landed property lost power to some extent, the bourgeoisie clung to the old morality that found the guarantee of private property in the solidity of the family. Woman was ordered back into the home the more harshly as her emancipation became a real menace. Even within the working class the men endeavoured to restrain woman's liberation, because they began to see the women as dangerous competitors—the more so because they were accustomed to work for lower wages.

In proving woman's inferiority, the anti-feminists then began to draw not only upon religion, philosophy, and theology, as before, but also upon science—biology, experimental psychology, etc. At most they were willing to grant 'equality in difference' to the other sex. That profitable formula is most significant; it is precisely like the 'equal but separate' formula of the Jim Crow laws aimed at the North American Negroes. As is well known, this so-called equalitarian segregation has resulted only in the most extreme discrimination. The similarity just noted is in no way due to chance, for whether it is a race, a caste, a class, or a sex that is reduced to a position of inferiority, the methods of justification are the same. 'The eternal feminine' corresponds to 'the black soul' and to 'the Jewish character'. True, the Jewish problem is on the whole very different from the other two—to the anti-Semite the Jew is not so much an inferior as he is an enemy for whom there is to be granted no place on earth, for whom annihilation is the fate desired. But there are deep similarities between the situation of woman and that of the Negro. Both are being emancipated today from a like paternalism, and the former master class wishes to 'keep them in their place'—that is, the place chosen for them. In both cases the former masters lavish more or less sincere eulogies, either on the virtues of 'the good Negro' with his dormant, childish, merry soul—the submissive Negro—or on the merits of the woman who is 'truly feminine'—that is, frivolous, infantile, irresponsible the submissive woman. In both cases the dominant class bases its argument on a state of affairs that it has itself created. As George Bernard Shaw puts it, in substance, 'The American white relegates the black to the rank of shoeshine boy; and he concludes from this that the black is good for nothing but shining shoes.' This vicious circle is met with in all analogous circumstances; when an individual (or a group of individuals) is kept in a situation of inferiority, the fact is that he is inferior. But the significance of the verb *to be* must be rightly understood here; it is in bad faith to give it a static value when it really has the dynamic Hegelian sense of 'to have become'. Yes, women on the whole *are* today inferior to men; that is, their situation affords them fewer possibilities. The question is: should that state of affairs continue?

Many men hope that it will continue; not all have given up the battle. The conservative bourgeoisie still see in the emancipation of women a menace to their morality and their interests. Some men dread feminine competition. Recently a male student wrote in the *Hebdo-Latin*: 'Every woman student who goes into medicine or law robs us of a job.' He never questioned his rights in this world. And economic interests are not the only ones concerned. One of the benefits that oppression confers upon the oppressors is that the most humble among them is made to feel superior; thus, a 'poor white' in the South can console himself with the thought that he is not a 'dirty nigger'—and the more prosperous whites cleverly exploit this pride.

Similarly, the most mediocre of males feels himself a demigod as compared with women. It was much easier for M. de Montherlant to think himself a hero when he faced women (and women chosen for his purpose) than when he was obliged to act the man among men—something many women have done better than he, for that matter. And in September 1948, in one of his articles in the *Figaro littéraire*, Claude Mauriac—whose great originality is admired by all—could write regarding woman: 'We listen on a tone [*sic!*] of polite indifference ... to the most brilliant among them, well knowing that her wit reflects more or less luminously ideas that come from *us*.' Evidently the speaker referred to is not reflecting the ideas of Mauriac himself, for no one knows of his having any. It may be that she reflects ideas originating with men, but then, even among men there are those who have been known to appropriate ideas not their own; and one can well ask whether Claude Mauriac might not find more interesting a conversation reflecting Descartes, Marx, or Gide rather than himself. What is really remarkable is that by using the questionable *we* he identifies himself with St Paul, Hegel, Lenin, and Nietzsche, and from the lofty eminence of their grandeur looks down disdainfully upon the bevy of women who make bold to converse with him on a footing of equality. In truth, I know of more than one woman who would refuse to suffer with patience Mauriac's 'tone of polite indifference'.

I have lingered on this example because the masculine attitude is here displayed with disarming in-genuousness. But men profit in many more subtle ways from the otherness, the alterity of woman. Here is a miraculous balm for those afflicted with an inferiority complex, and indeed no one is more arrogant towards women, more aggressive or scornful, than the man who is anxious about his virility. Those who are not fear-ridden in the presence of their fellow men are much more disposed to recognise a fellow creature in woman; but even to these the myth of Woman, the Other, is precious for many reasons. They cannot be blamed for not cheerfully relinquishing all the benefits they derive from the myth, for they realize what they would lose in relinquishing woman as they fancy her to be, while they fail to realize what they have to gain from the woman of tomorrow. Refusal to pose oneself as the Subject, unique and absolute, requires great self-denial. Furthermore, the vast majority of men make no such claim explicitly. They do not *postulate* woman as inferior, for today they are too thoroughly imbued with the ideal of democracy not to recognise all human beings as equals.

In the bosom of the family, woman seems in the eyes of childhood and youth to be clothed in the same social dignity as the adult males. Later on, the young man, desiring and loving, experiences the resistance, the independence of the woman desired and loved; in marriage, he respects woman as wife and mother, and in the concrete events of conjugal life she stands there before him as a free being. He can therefore feel that social subordination as between the sexes no longer exists and that on the whole, in spite of differences, woman is an equal. As, however, he observes some points of inferiority—the most important being unfitness for the professions—he attributes these to natural causes. When he is in a co-operative and benevolent relation with woman, his theme is the principle of abstract equality, and he does not base his attitude upon such inequality as may exist. But when he is in conflict with her, the situation is reversed: his theme will be the existing inequality, and he will even take it as justification for denying abstract equality.

So it is that many men will affirm as if in good faith that women are the equals of man and that they have nothing to clamour for, while *at the same time* they will say that women can never be the equals of man and that their demands are in vain. It is, in point of fact, a difficult matter for man to realize the extreme importance of social discriminations which seem outwardly insignificant but which produce in woman moral and intellectual effects so profound that they appear to spring from her original nature. The most sympathetic of men never fully comprehend woman's concrete situation. And there is no reason to put much trust in the men when they rush to the defence of privileges whose full extent they can hardly measure. We shall not, then, permit ourselves to be intimidated by the number and violence of the attacks launched against women, nor to be entrapped by the self-seeking eulogies bestowed on the 'true woman', nor to profit by the enthusiasm for woman's destiny manifested by men who would not for the world have any part of it.

We should consider the arguments of the feminists with no less suspicion, however, for very often their controversial aim deprives them of all real value. If the 'woman question' seems trivial, it is because masculine arrogance has made of it a 'quarrel'; and when quarrelling one no longer reasons well. People have tirelessly sought to prove that woman is superior, inferior, or equal to man. Some say that, having been created after Adam, she is evidently a secondary being: others say on the contrary that Adam was only a rough draft and that God succeeded in producing the human being in perfection when He created Eve. Woman's brain is smaller; yes, but it is relatively larger. Christ was made a man; yes, but perhaps for his greater humility. Each argument at once suggests its opposite, and both are often fallacious. If we are to gain understanding, we must get out of these ruts; we must discard the vague notions of superiority, inferiority, equality which have hitherto corrupted every discussion of the subject and start afresh.

Very well, but just how shall we pose the question? And, to begin with, who are we to propound it at all? Man is at once judge and party to the case; but so is woman. What we need is an angel—neither man nor woman—but where shall we find one? Still, the angel would be poorly qualified to speak, for an angel is ignorant of all the basic facts involved in the problem. With a hermaphrodite we should be no better off, for here the situation is most peculiar; the hermaphrodite is not really the combination of a whole man and a whole woman, but consists of parts of each and thus is neither. It looks to me as if there are, after all, certain women who are best qualified to elucidate the situation of woman. Let us not be misled by the sophism that because Epimenides was a Cretan he was necessarily a liar; it is not a mysterious essence that compels men and women to act in good or in bad faith, it is their situation that inclines them more or less towards the search for truth. Many of today's women, fortunate in the restoration of all the privileges pertaining to the estate of the human being, can afford the luxury of impartiality—we even recognise its necessity. We are no longer like our partisan elders; by and large we have won the game. In recent debates on the status of women the United Nations has persistently maintained that the equality of the sexes is now becoming a reality, and already some of us have never had to sense in our femininity an inconvenience or an obstacle. Many problems appear to us to be more pressing than those which concern us in particular, and this detachment even allows us to hope that our attitude will be objective. Still, we know the feminine world more intimately than do the men because we have our roots in it, we grasp more immediately than do men what it means to a human being to be feminine; and we are more concerned with such knowledge. I have said that there are more pressing problems, but this does not prevent us from seeing some importance in asking how the fact of being women will affect our lives. What opportunities precisely have been given us and what withheld? What fate awaits our younger sisters, and what directions should they take? It is significant that books by women on women are in general animated in our day less by a wish to demand our rights than by an effort towards clarity and understanding. As we emerge from an era of excessive controversy, this book is offered as one attempt among others to confirm that statement.

But it is doubtless impossible to approach any human problem with a mind free from bias. The way in which questions are put, the points of view assumed, presuppose a relativity of interest; all characteristics imply values, and every objective description, so called, implies an ethical background. Rather than attempt to conceal principles more or less definitely implied, it is better to state them openly, at the beginning. This will make it unnecessary to specify on every page in just what sense one uses such words as *superior, inferior, better, worse, progress, reaction,* and the like. If we survey some of the works on woman, we note that one of the points of view most frequently adopted is that of the public good, the general interest; and one always means by this the benefit of society as one wishes it to be maintained or established. For our part, we hold that the only public good is that which assures the private good of the citizens; we shall pass judgement on institutions according to their effectiveness in giving concrete opportunities to individuals. But we do not confuse the idea of private interest with that of happiness, although that is another common point of view. Are not women of the harem more happy than women voters? Is not the housekeeper happier than the working-woman? It is not too clear just what the word *happy* really means and still less what true values it may mask. There is no possibility of measuring the happiness of others, and it is always easy to describe as happy the situation in which one wishes to place them.

In particular those who are condemned to stagnation are often pronounced happy on the pretext that happiness consists in being at rest. This notion we reject, for our perspective is that of existentialist ethics. Every subject plays his part as such specifically through exploits or projects that serve as a mode of transcendence; he achieves liberty only through a continual reaching out towards other liberties. There is no justification for present existence other than its expansion into an indefinitely open future. Every time transcendence falls back into immanence, stagnation, there is a degradation of existence into the '*en-sois*'—the brutish life of subjection to given conditions—and of liberty into constraint and contingence. This downfall represents a moral fault if the subject consents

to it; if it is inflicted upon him, it spells frustration and oppression. In both cases it is an absolute evil. Every individual concerned to justify his existence feels that his existence involves an undefined need to transcend himself, to engage in freely chosen projects.

Now, what peculiarly signalises the situation of woman is that she—a free and autonomous being like all human creatures—nevertheless finds herself living in a world where men compel her to assume the status of the Other. They propose to stabilise her as object and to doom her to immanence since her transcendence is to be overshadowed and for ever transcended by another ego (*conscience*) which is essential and sovereign. The drama of woman lies in this conflict between the fundamental aspirations of every subject (ego)—who always regards the self as the essential and the compulsions of a situation in which she is the inessential. How can a human being in woman's situation attain fulfilment? What roads are open to her? Which are blocked? How can independence be recovered in a state of dependency? What circumstances limit woman's liberty and how can they be overcome? These are the fundamental questions on which I would fain throw some light. This means that I am interested in the fortunes of the individual as defined not in terms of happiness but in terms of liberty.

Quite evidently this problem would be without significance if we were to believe that woman's destiny is inevitably determined by physiological, psychological, or economic forces. Hence I shall discuss first of all the light in which woman is viewed by biology, psychoanalysis, and historical materialism. Next I shall try to show exactly how the concept of the 'truly feminine' has been fashioned—why woman has been defined as the Other—and what have been the consequences from man's point of view. Then from woman's point of view I shall describe the world in which women must live; and thus we shall be able to envisage the difficulties in their way as, endeavouring to make their escape from the sphere hitherto assigned them, they aspire to full membership in the human race.

## GLOSSARY

**Levi-Strauss:** the French anthropologist Claude Lévi-Strauss (1908-2009), a contemporary of de Beauvoir who studied the impact of patterns and civilization on human development

**proletariat:** a member of the working class in a capitalist society

**somniferous:** sleep-bringing, sleep-inducing

**Trotskyite:** a follower of the Soviet Marxist philosopher Leon Trotsky (1879-1940)

## Document Analysis

Simone de Beauvoir begins the introduction to her two-volume treatise by posing a question that challenges the entire premise of patriarchal society: "what is a woman?" She proposes several traditional definitions of the feminine before moving on to point out that the very act of questioning is significant: a man does not ask himself what it means to be a man.

This is a bold and controversial claim for its time, but de Beauvoir is prepared to substantiate it by quoting the words of writers from all areas of history, from the ancient Greek authority Aristotle to Claude Lévi-Strauss, a contemporary anthropologist. She discusses literature, history, biological differences, and religious constructs from the same point of view: all of these writers have collaborated in reducing women to a state of "Otherness".

De Beauvoir's roots in existentialist and socialist theory can be seen in her comparison of the positions of women and the proletariat. Like many first-wave American feminists, she also draws parallels between women and Black Americans. The systems of capitalism, racism, and patriarchy act in the same way to provide one in-group with dominance over the group that they have made the Other. In a patriarchal system, men compel women to provide sexual satisfaction and offspring for men. To keep women complicit in the system, men provide them with economic and psychological comfort--men allow women to avoid "the strain involved in undertaking an authentic existence."

De Beauvoir's book calls women to have the courage to resist the system and undertake authenticity. She understands, however, that her characterization of these systems of oppression will be difficult for many women to accept. To back up her assertion, then, she provides evidence gathered from every area of life. She begins with religion and moving on to politics, showing how these systems have conspired over the ages "[i]n proving woman's inferiority." With the rise of science, the anti-feminist movement has employed studies and pseudo-scientific reasoning (particularly psychoanalysis, as de Beauvoir discusses in a later chapter) to extend their domination.

She next moves past institutionalized oppression to discuss the systemic oppression that takes place within the family, even by unsuspecting and well-intentioned men. This is one of her most significant contributions: she argues that men benefit, even unconsciously, from the system of oppression. Men, she says, "cannot be blamed for not cheerfully relinquishing all the benefits they derive from the myth" of female inferiority. This inferiority, however, is more destructive to the female psyche than anyone realizes. The very fact that every area of life positions women as the Other makes it appear that any deficiencies a woman might have "spring from her original nature."

De Beauvoir opposes anyone, male or female, participating in this system of oppression. She therefore cannot simply accept the arguments of feminists who are seeking to replace one system of oppression with another. To her, anyone who argues that they are innately superior to another is committing the same harmful fallacy that anti-feminists do. She calls upon men and women alike to "discard the vague notions of superiority, inferiority, equality" that have poisoned rational discussion. Only after the entire system has been overthrown can all humans truly be free to achieve their full potential.

Since this is the introduction to a monumental and wide-ranging work, de Beauvoir takes care throughout the essay to outline the arguments she will use for the entire book. After stating her central question--what does it mean to be a woman?--she offers a wide range of evidence to demonstrate the importance of this question and the failure of previous works to address it thoroughly. She touches on political, societal, and personal oppression, showing that women are treated as Others in every area of life. She finishes her introduction by offering an outline of what she will try to do in the two volumes of *The Second Sex*: she will reveal the oppressive thought inherent in our systems, show the development of this thought, and attempt to explain its consequences from a personal perspective. She knows that a simple call to action will have no power without in-depth research and explanation of the problem. Her introduction lays the groundwork for a thorough investigation of anti-feminist thought.

## Essential Themes

*The Second Sex* was immensely popular upon its publication and it shot de Beauvoir to international fame. Sartre was simultaneously experiencing a surge of interest in his own work, and the two became fixtures of French intellectual life. The book was quickly translated into many languages. An English version appeared in 1953, but it has been criticized since its publication: the publisher knew that the book featured references to biology and ended up finding a zoologist translator with rudimentary French skills who cut or abridged large sections of the work. De Beauvoir herself was unhappy with the final product and felt that important parts of her message had been omitted. A fuller and more faithful English translation was published in 2009.

De Beauvoir's work was, and remains, immensely important to the development of second-wave feminism. Betty Friedan's 1963 book *The Feminine Mystique* was inspired in large part by *The Second Sex*. Her distinction between biological sex and society-created gender remains crucial to our modern understanding of the sex/gender dichotomy.

Modern feminists have expanded upon de Beauvoir's assertions and she has come under fire for what some see as an anti-woman or anti-feminist attitude. Where de Beauvoir hopes for a new world free of oppressive gender distinctions, many modern feminists argue that feminists should use their perspectives to change patriarchal systems rather than dismantling them altogether. Some have also argued that De Beauvoir's opposition to family structures and reproductive customs removes agency from women.

Though perspectives have changed in some ways, it is inarguable that de Beauvoir was a foundational thinker for the feminist movement. Her work argues for the full development and achievement of all humans, and she spurred an entire generation of feminists to action. Second-wave feminism, inspired by her life and work, attempted to confront systemic injustice and oppression head-on. De Beauvoir calls everyone to live a life of full engagement while avoiding complicity. Her words about men are relevant to all humanity: under a patriarchal system, "they realize what they would lose in relinquishing woman as they fancy her to be, while they fail to realize what they have to gain from the woman of tomorrow." Her work and the movement it inspired has helped society realize these gains and move toward equality for all.

—*Hannah Rich, MA*

## Bibliography and Additional Reading

Bair, Deirdre. 1990. *Simone de Beauvoir: A Biography*. New York: Summit Books.

Menand, Louis. 2005. "Stand By Your Man: The strange liaison of Sartre and Beauvoir". *The New Yorker*, September 26, 2005.

Thurman, Judith. 2009. "Introduction to Simone de Beauvoir's *The Second Sex*." Random House: Alfred A. Knopf.

# ■ Women's Political Council Documents

**Date:** May 21, 1954; 1955
**Author:** Jo Ann Robinson
**Genre:** Letter; report

## Summary Overview

The Women's Political Council (WPC) had been active in Alabama since 1946. The professionals and educators involved in the organization initially focused on increasing the number of African Americans who were registered to vote. Starting in 1950, however, the Montgomery chapter of the organization began to focus on bus segregation and civil rights. A majority of the passengers on the Montgomery bus system were black, and yet city ordinances and company practices subjected these passengers to daily indignities. Jo Ann Robinson and the WPC appealed to Montgomery city commissioners in 1953 and the mayor in 1954. The organization asked for more bus stops in black neighborhoods and compromised on seating arrangements: they were repeatedly rebuffed or their requests were met hesitantly. Robinson recognized that the black community needed to assert their civil rights through economic means: they needed to boycott the buses. After the arrest of Rosa Parks for refusing to give up her seat, Robinson finally had a "suitable" figure for the movement to rally behind.

## Defining Moment

The passage of the Fourteenth Amendment in 1868 nominally granted African Americans full citizenship and equal protection under the law. Equal protection, however, was not the reality for the black community for decades afterwards. During the Reconstruction period and later, the rights of newly enfranchised African Americans were continually reduced by the introduction of local and state laws called "Jim Crow laws," likely named after a racist theatrical performance. These laws made unequal service and segregation in public schools, restaurants, transportation, and restrooms legally protected practices. In 1896, the Supreme Court ruling in *Plessy v. Ferguson* upheld the constitutionality of these laws. "Separate but equal" service became the pretext through which white politicians and businesses could offer humiliation and poorer service to keep African Americans disadvantaged. The principle of "separate but equal" affected African Americans in the South to a large extent, but racial discrimination was not exclusive to the South.

It was not until after World War II that dissatisfaction turned into a nationwide protest. Local chapters of activists, like the Women's Political Council, combated racial discrimination piecemeal. Prior to Jo Ann Robinson's leadership, the WPC focused on increasing African American voter registration; the group only made transportation discrimination a priority after 1950. Other groups focused on segregated schooling, unfair housing practices, and unequal treatment from businesses. Ultimately, all these organizations were targeting the same systematic oppression based on skin color.

Jo Ann Robinson had tried appealing to the mayor of Montgomery to improve transportation for African Americans. After the mayor and other Montgomery officials refused to take the polite requests of the WPC seriously, Robinson waited for the right moment to rally the larger black community to action. Several women were arrested for refusing to move seats in the intervening time, including Claudette Colvin, but it was Rosa Parks whom Robinson and other activists deemed "respectable" enough to merit action.

## Author Biography

Jo Ann Richardson was born in Culloden, Georgia, in 1912; she later became the first person in her family to graduate from college. She taught in Atlanta and New York City before eventually moving to teach English at Alabama State College in 1949. In this same year, Robinson experienced treatment similar to the sort that Rosa Parks would later famously defy: a bus driver ordered Robinson off his bus for daring to sit in the front rows. When Robinson became president of the Women's Political Council in 1950, she made it a priority of the organization to challenge bus segregation. She was instrumental in organizing the Montgomery bus boycott that would propel Reverend Martin Luther King, Jr. to prominence. Robinson stayed up late into the night mimeographing leaflets to announce the boycott after news of Rosa Parks' arrest in 1955. Like other civil rights activists at the time, she was subject to repercussions by those who resisted equal rights. Robinson eventually resigned her post at Alabama State College to teach in Los Angeles.

## HISTORICAL DOCUMENT

Harriet St.
Montgomery, Ala.
May 21, 1954

Honorable Mayor W. A. Gayle
City Hall
Montgomery, Alabama

Dear Sir:

The Women's Political Council is very grateful to you and the City Commissioners for the hearing you allowed our representatives during the month of March, 1954, when the "city-bus-fare-increase case" was being reviewed. There were several things that the Council asked for:

1.  A city law that would make it possible for Negroes to sit from back toward front, and whites from front toward back until all the seats are taken.

2.  That Negroes not be asked or forced to pay fare at front and go the rear of the bus to enter.

3.  That busses stop at every corner in residential sections occupied by Negroes as they do in communities where whites reside.

We are happy to report that busses have been stopping at more corners now in some sections where Negroes live than previously. However, the same practices in seating and boarding the bus continue.

Mayor Gayle, three-fourths of the riders of these public conveyances are Negroes. If Negroes did not patronize them, they could not possibly operate.

More and more of our people are already arranging with neighbors and friends to ride to keep from being insulted and humiliated by bus drivers.

There has been talk from twenty-five or more local organizations of planning a city-wide boycott of busses. We, sir, do not feel that forceful measures are necessary in bargaining for a convenience which is right for all bus passengers. We, the Council, believe that when this matter has been put before you and the Commissioners, that agreeable terms can be met in a quiet and unostensible manner to the satisfaction of all concerned.

Many of our Southern cities in neighboring states have practiced the policies we seek without incident whatsoever. Atlanta, Macon and Savannah in Georgia have done this for years. Even Mobile, in our own state, does this and all the passengers are satisfied.

Please consider this plea, and if possible, act favorably upon it, for even now plans are being made to ride less, or not at all, on our busses. We do not want that.

Respectfully yours,
*The Women's Political Council*
*Jo Ann Robinson, President*

\* \* \*

The 1955 leaflet from the Women's Political Council, Montgomery, Alabama:

Another Negro woman has been arrested and thrown in jail because she refused to get up out of her seat on the bus for a white person to sit down. It is the second time since the Claudette Colvin case that a Negro woman has been arrested for the same thing. This has to be stopped. Negroes have rights, too, for if Negroes did not ride the buses, they could not operate. Three-fourths of the riders are Negroes, yet we are arrested, or have to stand over empty seats. If we do not do something to stop these arrests, they will continue. The next time it may be you, or your daughter, or mother. This woman's case will come up on Monday. We are, therefore, asking every Negro to stay off the buses Monday in protest of the arrest and trial. Don't ride the buses to work, to town, to school, or anywhere on Monday. You can afford to stay out of school for one day if you have no other way to go except by bus. You can also afford to stay out of town for one day. If you work, take a cab, or walk. But please, children and grown-ups, don't ride the bus at all on Monday. Please stay off all buses Monday.

## Document Analysis

These two documents from the Women's Political Council in Montgomery, Alabama, show a radical change in approach towards fighting segregation that occurred between 1954 and 1955. The WPC (and other similar organizations) initially attempted to work within existing power structures; after 1955, the tone had changed. No longer were African Americans content to accept unfair treatment as part of the status quo. Rosa Parks' arrest acted as the catalyst for escalated action by civil rights activists.

First, Jo Ann Robinson's letter to the mayor of Montgomery, W. A. Gayle, in 1954 uses a conciliatory tone. She begins the letter by speaking graciously: "The Women's Political Council is very grateful to you and the City Commissioners for the hearing you allowed." Instead of addressing the mayor with anger for the indignities suffered, Robinson tries to appease him. She reports that, although the WPC's four requests have not been met, her organization is "happy to report that busses have been stopping at more corners." There is no open dissatisfaction or hurt from her organization that unfair seating practices still continue. Robinson stresses that her organization (in opposition to the "twenty-five or more local organizations") does not believe in openly protesting. Robinson shows in this letter that she wants to appeal to the city authority first to change local practices to everyone's best interests: "We, sir, do not feel that forceful measures are necessary in bargaining for a convenience which is right for all bus passengers," she writes. She further stresses that the WPC does not want to make a national incident out of the current situation. It would be best if the "terms" were met "in a quiet and unostensible manner to the satisfaction of all concerned."

However, the mayor of Montgomery did not accept the terms of Robinson and the WPC. Over a year after Robinson sent that letter to the mayor, the goals of the WPC changed. Robinson changes her tone dramatically in the leaflet she stayed up late to mimeograph for African American families following Rosa Parks' arrest on December 1, 1955. Robinson appeals to other African Americans in Montgomery to engage in the very boycott she initially said the WPC did not wish to start. She uses much of the same reasoning for fairer practices in this leaflet as in the letter, but the tone of this leaflet is outraged. "This has to be stopped," says the leaflet simply. This leaflet does not appeal to the economic repercussions as the main purpose of the boycott as the letter to the mayor does, but rather puts the rights of African Americans first: "Negroes have rights, too, for if Negroes did not ride the buses, they could not operate." A series of imperative phrases follow and are repeated: "don't ride the busses," stresses the leaflet. There are no more polite requests, but urgent commands.

To conclude, the shift in tone between these two documents shows a new phase in the civil rights movement. The WPC's decision to abandon appealing to authority is reflected in the divergence in language between the letter to the mayor and the leaflet to the African American community. It is easy to see from the difference in tone before Rosa Parks' arrest and after how her simple act of resistance soon gained her the name of "mother of the Civil Rights Movement." Her arrest started the mass boycott of the Montgomery transportation system, which in turn encouraged more people across the nation to participate in fighting segregation in the South.

## Essential Themes

Jo Ann Robinson turned her own humiliating experience on a Montgomery bus in 1950 into a movement that affected the entire nation. She correctly pinpointed that the right to be respected equally by the law was connected to as mundane an experience as riding the bus. By boycotting the bus in Montgomery, African Americans could show the government that discrimination had economic repercussions: it was more profitable to the state to treat citizens equally. Additionally, by as simple an act as refusing to ride the bus, average people could participate in making a powerful statement that they refused to be oppressed anymore by racist statutes. The grassroots movement that Robinson started in 1955 was part of a chain of protests that focused on daily indignities suffered by the black community, such as unfair housing practices, voter discrimination, and separate schooling, to name a few issues.

Although Martin Luther King, Jr. has become the face of the civil rights movement of the 1950s and 60s, the tireless work of female activists, such as Jo Ann Robinson and her colleagues in the Women's Political Council, propelled the machinery of these grassroots campaigns. Later activists, particularly in the Black Lives Matter movement, have copied the work of these female activists in networking between groups. Formed by three women, Black Lives Matter utilizes social media to disseminate ideas for protest and connect people across the country. Hailed as the "new civil rights movement," Black Lives Matter shows the lasting influence of the ideas of Jo Ann Robinson and the female educators who made up the Women's Political Council.

—*Ashleigh Fata, MA*

## Bibliography and Additional Reading

Brooks, Pamela E. Boycotts, Buses, and Passes: Black Women's Resistance in the U.S. South and South Africa. Amherst, MA: University of Massachusetts Press, 2008. Print.

Burns, Stewart. Daybreak of Freedom: The Montgomery Bus Boycott. Chapel Hill, NC: UNC Press, 1997. Print.

Day, Elizabeth. "#BlackLivesMatter: the birth of a new civil rights movement." The Guardian. The Guardian Media Limited, 19 Jul. 2015. Web.

Robinson, Jo Ann. The Montgomery Bus Boycott and the Women Who Started It: The Memoir of Jo Ann Gibson Robinson. Knoxville, TN: UT Press, 1987. Print.

Theocharis, Jeanne. The Rebellious Life of Mrs. Rosa Parks. Boston: Beacon, 2014. Print.

# ■ Equal Pay Act

**Date:** 1963
**Author:** 88th Congress of the United States and Esther Peterson
**Genre:** Law

## Summary Overview

As women came into the American workforce in larger numbers, many sought, and obtained, employment in areas outside those traditionally filled by women. As a result, in some businesses, men and women worked in the same, or comparable, positions, with the women often being paid less than the men. The Equal Pay Act, passed as an amendment to the Fair Labor Standards Act of 1938, was an attempt to force businesses to pay women and men the same amount when undertaking "equal work." Esther Peterson, a former labor organizer appointed as an Assistant Secretary in the Department of Labor, overseeing the Women's Bureau, wrote the first draft of the bill for President Kennedy who submitted it to Congress early in 1963. Having been transformed into an amendment of the Fair Labor Standards Act, the bill moved through the legislative process relatively quickly. Implementation of the Act's provisions has been far from perfect, and in 2007 the Supreme Court ruling in *Ledbetter v. Goodyear Tire and Rubber Co.* raised questions regarding its future usefulness. However, new legislation has given new life to the Act. Thus, while during the first fifty-five years the goal has not been reached, the Act has been a major factor in the move toward equal salaries for men and women.

## Defining Moment

At the end of the nineteenth century, the twin societal changes of industrialization and urbanization created a situation in which women could more readily obtain paid employment. Although most jobs were unofficially classified as men's or women's, there were many women ready to challenge the male dominated society. While women won the right to vote, the push for full civil rights faltered in the 1920s. Thus the proposed Equal Rights Amendment and many other pieces of legislation guaranteeing greater equality sat in the various legislative bodies. With the Great Depression of the 1930s, gender equality took a backseat to regaining a vital economy for the nation. World War II not only created a revitalized economy, the demand for women in the labor force was great. With so many men in the military, but women filled a wide variety of positions from which they had previously been excluded. A law mandating equal pay for women was introduced

in 1945, as some feared that if industry could pay women less, at the end of the war there would be no jobs for the men being demobilized. However, nothing passed and when the war ended, most of the women were pushed out of the workforce. Many who remained were paid less than men who were hired for the same, or similar, positions.

By the end of the 1950s, more than a third of the workforce was female. President Kennedy campaigned for change, offering a plan called the New Frontier. The New Frontier included greater civil rights for all people, including women in the work-place. Kennedy created the Presidential Commission on the Status of Women (PCSW) with Esther Peterson becoming its chair upon the death of Eleanor Roosevelt, its first chair. In line with one of the PCCSW goals, Peterson wrote the original draft of the bill which became the Equal Pay Act. (The full report of the PCSW was not submitted until October, 1963.) Although an equal pay bill had passed the House in 1962, Peterson submitted a new bill to Congress in February, 1963, seeking to overcome problems identified in the earlier bill, including putting the implementation of the new law within the framework of the Fair Labor Standards Act of 1938. In May, 1963, the bill passed by voice vote in the Senate and then the House, with the Senate then accepting the minor changes made by the House.

As part of the New Frontier legislative initiative of President Kennedy, the law assisted in acknowledging women's civil rights. In line with the full report of the PCSW, the Equal Pay Act was a positive step in Kennedy's desire to end gender-based discrimination throughout society. Although much progress has been made in all eight areas identified by the PCSW, the Equal Pay Act was the first to be passed by Congress. While other areas of the report, totally under government control, have been fully implemented, the push for equal pay has made some progress with women moving from 59 percent of men's pay in 1962 to 87 percent in 2016.

## Author Biography

The 88th Congress of the United States was controlled by the Democratic Party as a result of the 1962 elections. As it opened, in the House of Representatives there were 258

Democrats, 178 Republicans, and 1 Independent Democrat. The Senate was comprised of 66 Democrats, 33 Republicans, with one vacancy. As with the previous Congress, the 88th was an active body, generally supporting the major legislative initiatives put forward by Presidents Kennedy and Johnson. The Equal Pay Act was the first major piece of civil rights legislation, although overshadowed by the more comprehensive 1964 Civil Rights Act.

Esther Peterson, born Esther Eggertsen, in 1906, started her career as a physical education teacher following graduation from Brigham Young University. While attending Columbia University, she began her activities in social reform as well as marrying Oliver Peterson. She taught in workers' schools and assisted in labor union activities, as well as pushing for equal rights for women. She held numerous positions in the United States and Europe before organizing the Committee of Labor Women for Kennedy. In early 1961, she was the highest ranking woman in Kennedy's administration, as Assistant Secretary for the Bureau of Labor Standards and the Director of the Women's Bureau, serving in the Department of Labor until 1969. Following that period, she worked as a consumer advocate, both domestically and at the United Nations. Peterson died in 1997, having received the Presidential Medal of Freedom, and having been a leading force for social change for seven decades.

## HISTORICAL DOCUMENT

Sec. 206. Minimum Wage . . .

(d) Prohibition of sex discrimination

(1)  No employer having employees subject to any provisions of this section shall discriminate, within any establishment in which such employees are employed, between employees on the basis of sex by paying wages to employees in such establishment at a rate less than the rate at which he pays wages to employees of the opposite sex in such establishment for equal work on jobs the performance of which requires equal skill, effort, and responsibility, and which are performed under similar working conditions, except where such payment is made pursuant to
  (i) a seniority system;
  (ii) a merit system;
  (iii) a system which measures earnings by quantity or quality of production; or
  (iv) a differential based on any other factor other than sex:

Provided, That an employer who is paying a wage rate differential in violation of this subsection shall not, in order to comply with the provisions of this subsection, reduce the wage rate of any employee.

(2)  No labor organization, or its agents, representing employees of an employer having employees subject to any provisions of this section shall cause or attempt to cause such an employer to discriminate against an employee in violation of paragraph (1) of this subsection.

(3)  For purposes of administration and enforcement, any amounts owing to any employee which have been withheld in violation of this subsection shall be deemed to be unpaid minimum wages or unpaid overtime compensation under this chapter.

(4)  As used in this subsection, the term "labor organization" means any organization of any kind, or any agency or employee representation committee or plan, in which employees participate and which exists for the purpose, in whole or in part, of dealing with employers concerning grievances, labor disputes, wages, rates of pay, hours of employment, or conditions of work.

## GLOSSARY

**equal work:** a crucial term in the law, designating employee positions with the same or comparable responsibilities or tasks

**sex discrimination:** gender discrimination is currently the more usual term

## Document Analysis

On June 10, 1963, President John F. Kennedy signed into law the Equal Pay Act, a law passed to amend the Fair Labor Standards Act of 1938. The goal of the law was simple: to ensure that in the matter of pay, employers did not discriminate on the basis of gender, generally meaning that they could not pay women less than men for the same work. The Equal Pay Act was intended to provide a broad remedial framework for ending gender discrimination. Within this framework, the U.S. Supreme Court has had to adjudicate claims of gender discrimination. In doing so, the Supreme Court has applied a three-part test: Are higher wages paid to employees of the opposite sex? Do the employees perform substantially equal work on jobs requiring equal effort, skill, and responsibility? Are the jobs performed under similar conditions? If the answers to these questions were yes, the employer was strictly liable, regardless of the employer's intent.

The Equal Pay Act arose in the context of "second-wave feminism" in the 1960s. While first-wave feminism dealt with such issues as the right to vote, second-wave feminism took on more subtle forms of discrimination and prejudice, including gender discrimination with regard to pay. While estimates varied, the gender disparity in pay for full-time year-round employees at the time meant that women were paid less than 60 percent of what men were paid. Since that time, the situation has improved considerably, so that by 2016 the figure had risen to 87 percent—and researchers have noted that in many areas (primarily urban) and job categories, women, particularly younger women, actually earned more than their male counterparts. (Part of the increase in the average wages paid to women has been due to the fact that by the beginning of this century, more women graduated from college than men.) According to Bureau of Labor Statistics data, in the 106 job categories in which female participation has increased since 1990, women earn 101 percent of what their male counterparts earn.

The issue of what constituted wage disparity has been hotly debated. When two people have exactly the same job/position, seniority, and so forth, gender based differences are easy to document. The Equal Pay Act gave solid ground for seeking remediation of the situation. However, there have been many cases in which jobs seem to require similar skills, or comparable education, and yet the jobs are not exactly the same. This is where the courts have expended great effort to understand the situation in order to enforce the provisions of this Act.

Comparing the average wages of all women versus all men has been criticized by some economists. These economists, and others, have pointed to a wide range of other factors that might contribute to any disparities that still exist between the averages wages for women and men. These have included educational level, age, number of hours worked, occupational choices (for example, teaching and social work versus medicine and engineering), decisions about family responsibilities (particularly child care), the "danger premium" paid for certain jobs (mining, firefighting), the prevalence of men in blue-collar jobs that pay overtime (in contrast to the salaried white-collar jobs more likely to be held by women), and the like. This means that some of the difference has been from men and women having been guided into different career paths. While gender bias in pay, sometimes motivated by the antiquated belief that "men have families to support," undoubtedly still exists, the Equal Pay Act was a significant step in remedying the matter.

Part (d)(1) of Section 206 ("Minimum Wage") of the Equal Pay Act made the intent of the law clear: "No employer . . . shall discriminate . . . between employees on the basis of sex by paying wages . . . at a rate less than the rate at which he pays wages to employees of the opposite sex." This section limited the scope of the Equal Pay Act, by the inclusion of several exceptions. Also, the law at that time did not cover white-collar and professional employees; it also did not include outside sales representatives. In this regard, the Equal Pay Act was consistent with the Fair Labor Standards Act. That provision was changed nine years later to exempt professionals from the 1938 act and thus included them in the provisions of the Equal Pay Act.

Within the act itself, four exceptions were allowed, as regarded equal pay. Payment disparities were allowed if they were part of a seniority system, if they were part of a merit system, if they were part of a system that awards pay based on production (for example, commissions or piecework in manufacturing), and any other factor than gender. Further, this section anticipated the possibility that to comply with the law an employer might lower wages paid to the favored group. The act forbade this practice. Additionally, the act extended its provisions to the activities of labor organizations—that was, unions—so unions could not discriminate in matters pertaining to grievances, disputes, hours, or conditions of work.

In the introduction to this section of the law, not printed in this volume, it was stated that the Equal Pay Act was an amendment to the Fair Labor Standards Act of 1938. This was an important change from the previous equal pay proposal, because there was great dissatisfaction with the possible creation of a new agency to oversee economic activity. Having a twenty-five year track record of working with industry and labor under the 1938 law, expectations were that both would be comfortable working with the Department of Labor via an expansion of responsibilities. Thus, this provision was added. However, this also limited the application of the Equal Pay Act to businesses which were covered under the Fair Labor Standards Act. For some this was an unintended consequence, but for most members of Congress, it was intentional. However, Kennedy and Peterson were willing to accept this limitation, since they envisioned it as only a first step toward their goal of full gender equality.

## Essential Themes

In his inaugural speech, President Kennedy stated that the transformations he envisioned for American society would not be "finished in the first one hundred days . . . (nor) in our lifetime," however, he was determined to begin the process. This included equity in economic opportunity for all people. The Equal Pay Act was the first step in this process, by guaranteeing gender equity in wages. In the same month in which he signed the Equal Pay Act, Kennedy pushed economic opportunity further by presenting to Congress what eventually became the Civil Rights Act of 1964. Following Kennedy's lead, during the next three decades, additional laws were enacted to outlaw gender discrimination in hiring and education. Although true equality in economic opportunity for all people has not yet been attained, failure to overcome all problems immediately, has not been considered an acceptable reason to do nothing.

In addition to the desire for equal economic opportunity, Kennedy and Peterson did not want the new law to be used as an excuse to reduce wages for anyone. They wanted to increase the standard of living for all, by mandating equal wages. They also did not want some companies gaining an advantage by hiring women at a lower wage, thereby hurting men's economic opportunities. Thus, they included provisions which mandated all be paid at the higher wage.

With the passage of the Civil Rights Act of 1964, some of the guarantees of the Equal Pay Act were blended with Title VII of the Civil Rights Act. Among these was the provision that any complaint regarding gender wage discrimination be filed within 180 days, as mandated by the 1964 law. This became the focal point in a landmark case, *Ledbetter v. Goodyear Tire and Rubber Co.* Nineteen years after being hired, Lilly Ledbetter learned that men in similar positions were paid more than she was. Although winning at the district court level, her victory was overturned by the Supreme Court, which threw out her case based on the 180-day limitation of the 1964 law. As a result, the Equal Pay Act became a law with limited effect. However, the Lilly Ledbetter Fair Pay Act was passed in 2009 which transformed the 180 day period from the time a salary was established to 180 days since the last time either a wage decision was made or a paycheck was issued based upon a discriminatory wage decision. This once again made the Equal Pay Act a viable tool in enforcing equal opportunity for all genders.

—*Donald A. Watt, PhD and Michael J. O'Neal, PhD*

## Bibliography and Additional Reading

Castro, Ida L. and Alexis M. Herman. *Equal Pay: A Thirty-Five Year Perspective*. Washington: US Dept. of Labor, Women's Bureau, 1998. Print and Online. 14 November 2017.

Cobble, Dorothy Sue and Julia Bowes. ""Esther Peterson." *American National Biography Online*. New York: Oxford University Press/The American Council of Learned Societies, 2005. Web. 15 November 2017.

Kennedy, John F. "Remarks upon Signing the Equal Pay Act." White House, Washington, DC. 10 June 1963. *American Presidency Project*. Santa Barbara CA: University of California Santa Barbara: American Presidency Project, 2017. Web. 14 November 2017.

National Equal Pay Task Force. *Fifty Years after the Equal Pay Act: Assessing the Past, Taking Stock of the Future*. Washington: White House, 2013. Print and Web. 14 November 2017.

National Park Service. "Equal Pact of 1963." *Civil Rights*. Washington: National Park Service, 2016. Web. 14 November 2017.

# ■ Betty Friedan: *The Feminine Mystique*

**Date:** 1963
**Author:** Betty Friedan
**Genre:** Book excerpt; political tract

## Summary Overview

*The Feminine Mystique*, by Betty Friedan (1921–2006), is one of a relative handful of modern books that can truly be said to have altered dramatically the course of thinking—in this case, about the role of women. After the book was published in 1963, it touched off a national debate about women's roles and quickly became a central text in modern feminism. Indeed, that debate sometimes became fierce, for Friedan and her family were forced to move out of their New York City neighborhood because of threats from angry neighbors.

Friedan wrote *The Feminine Mystique* after surveying other graduates of her alma mater, Smith College. She believed that her own less than positive feelings about her traditional, and limited, role as a house-wife was likely shared with other women of her time. In Chapter 1, excerpted below, Friedan tackles her feelings and her findings, asking and trying to answer the question: "Is this all?"

## Defining Moment

This text both is a defining moment, as it shows a tension within the traditional woman's role in the household, and it leads to a defining moment, as it sets off a radical shift in how people view women and how women view themselves. After defining the problem in chapter 1, Friedan provides a detailed analysis of the root causes of the problem. In her view, the problem stems from an idealized image of what it means to be a woman. Women, she says, have been encouraged, if not forced, to adopt the roles of mother and "house-wife," in the process abandoning their education and any career goals they might have had. These roles prevented women from developing their unique identities. She sees the problem as an outgrowth of World War II and the Cold War that followed, which produced the baby boom and the sprawling suburbs that limited and defined womanhood. The overwhelming response to *The Feminine Mystique* turned Betty Friedan into a household name and launched her career as a leading feminist speaker, writer, and cofounder and president of the National Organization for Women.

The arguments within *The Feminine Mystique* sparked a change in the United States. Not only did Friedan show that women wanted more from their lives, her book is often credited with starting second-wave feminism in the United States. Second-wave feminism essentially came about because of this work and the continuation of these ideas after its publication. Not satisfied with this text alone, however, Friedan pursued political change for women. For example, the Equal Pay Act of 1963, grew out of these tensions and attempted to end pay equality, demanding that men and women be paid equally for equal work. But political changes did not end there. New and, occasionally, radical groups were founded in order to pursue goals outside of strict gender equality. Friedan's ideas were also applicable to racism, anti-Semitism, and working-class issues for men and women alike. Possibly, it was in her accessibility that Friedan's ideas, fairly radical at the time, had such a wide impact on the country. But this text was not simply a flash in the pan either. In 2013, fifty years after its original publication, the U.S. Department of Labor placed *The Feminine Mystique* in the top ten on a list of 100 books that shaped work in America.

## Author Biography

Friedan was born in 1921 in Illinois and lived a fairly ordinary early life, eventually earning a bachelor's degree in 1942 in psychology from Smith College and continued her studies in psychology at the University of California at Berkeley. She then moved to New York City, where, in addition to writing freelance magazine articles, she married, had children, and adopted the traditional role of homemaker. The genesis of *The Feminine Mystique* was her fifteen-year class reunion at Smith. She later distributed a questionnaire to two hundred of her classmates (all women, since Smith is a women's college). The results of the questionnaire led her to the conclusion that many of her classmates—and by implication many American women—were unhappy and did not know why, causing her to title the first chapter of her book "The Problem That Has No Name." Initially she had difficulty finding a publisher for a magazine article she wrote based on her findings, but after several years of further research and writing, she published her results in *The Feminine Mystique*. Friedan continued her work in activism throughout her life. After her divorce in 1967, she founded the National Women's Political Caucus, about which she famously stated "made policy, not coffee." Friedan passed away in 2006 in Washington, D.C.

## HISTORICAL DOCUMENT

### Chapter 1: "The Problem That Has No Name"

The problem lay buried, unspoken, for many years in the minds of American women. It was a strange stirring, a sense of dissatisfaction, a yearning that women suffered in the middle of the twentieth century in the United States. Each suburban wife struggled with it alone. As she made the beds, shopped for groceries, matched slipcover material, ate peanut butter sandwiches with her children, chauffeured Cub Scouts and Brownies, lay beside her husband at night—she was afraid to ask even of herself the silent question—"Is this all?"

For over fifteen years there was no word of this yearning in the millions of words written about women, for women, in all the columns, books and articles by experts telling women their role was to seek fulfillment as wives and mothers. Over and over women heard in voices of tradition and of Freudian sophistication that they could desire—no greater destiny than to glory in their own femininity. Experts told them how to catch a man and keep him, how to breastfeed children and handle their toilet training, how to cope with sibling rivalry and adolescent rebellion; how to buy a dishwasher, bake bread, cook gourmet snails, and build a swimming pool with their own hands; how to dress, look, and act more feminine and make marriage more exciting; how to keep their husbands from dying young and their sons from growing into delinquents. They were taught to pity the neurotic, unfeminine, unhappy women who wanted to be poets or physicists or presidents. They learned that truly feminine women do not want careers, higher education, political rights—the independence and the opportunities that the old-fashioned feminists fought for. Some women, in their forties and fifties, still remembered painfully giving up those dreams, but most of the younger women no longer even thought about them. A thousand expert voices applauded their femininity, their adjustment, their new maturity. All they had to do was devote their lives from earliest girlhood to finding a husband and bearing children.

By the end of the nineteen-fifties, the average marriage age of women in America dropped to 20, and was still dropping, into the teens. Fourteen million girls were engaged by 17. The proportion of women attending college in comparison with men dropped from 47 per cent in 1920 to 35 per cent in 1958. A century earlier, women had fought for higher education; now girls went to college to get a husband. By the mid-fifties, 60 per cent dropped out of college to marry, or because they were afraid too much education would be a marriage bar. Colleges built dormitories for "married students," but the students were almost always the husbands. A new degree was instituted for the wives—"Ph.T" (Putting Husband Through).

Then American girls began getting married in high school. And the women's magazines, deploring the unhappy statistics about these young marriages, urged that courses on marriage, and marriage counselors, be installed in the high schools. Girls started going steady at twelve and thirteen, in junior high. Manufacturers put out brassieres with false bosoms of foam rubber for little girls of ten. And on advertisement for a child's dress, sizes 3–6x, in the *New York Times* in the fall of 1960, said: "She Too Can Join the Man-Trap Set."

By the end of the fifties, the United States birth-rate was overtaking India's. The birth-control movement, renamed Planned Parenthood, was asked to find a method whereby women who had been advised that a third or fourth baby would be born dead or defective might have it anyhow. Statisticians were especially astounded at the fantastic increase in the number of babies among college women. Where once they had two children, now they had four, five, six. Women who had once wanted careers were now making careers out of having babies. So rejoiced *Life* magazine in a 1956 paean to the movement of American women back to the home.

In a New York hospital, a woman had a nervous breakdown when she found she could not breast-feed her baby. In other hospitals, women dying of cancer refused a drug which research had proved might save their lives: its side effects were said to be unfeminine. "If I have only one life, let me live it as a blonde," a larger-than-life- sized picture of a pretty, vacuous woman proclaimed from newspaper, magazine, and drugstore ads. And across America, three out of every ten women dyed their hair blonde. They ate a chalk called Metrecal, instead of food, to shrink to the size of the thin young models. Department-store buyers reported that American women, since 1939, had become three and four sizes smaller. "Women are out to fit the clothes, instead of vice-versa," one buyer said.

Interior decorators were designing kitchens with mosaic murals and original paintings, for kitchens were once again the center of women's lives. Home sewing became a million-dollar industry. Many women no longer left their homes, except to shop, chauffeur their children, or attend a social engagement with their husbands. Girls were growing up in America without ever having jobs outside the home. In the late fifties, a sociological phenomenon was suddenly remarked: a third of American women now worked, but most were no longer young and very few were pursuing careers. They were married women who held part-time jobs, selling or secretarial, to put their husbands through school, their sons through college, or to help pay the mortgage. Or they were widows supporting families. Fewer and fewer women were entering professional work. The shortages in the nursing, social work, and teaching professions caused crises in almost every American city. Concerned over the Soviet Union's lead in the space race, scientists noted that America's greatest source of unused brain-power was women. But girls would not study physics: it was "unfeminine." A girl refused a science fellowship at Johns Hopkins to take a job in a real-estate office. All she wanted, she said, was what every other American girl wanted—

to get married, have four children and live in a nice house in a nice suburb.

The suburban housewife—she was the dream image of the young American women and the envy, it was said, of women all over the world. The American housewife—freed by science and labor-saving appliances from the drudgery, the dangers of child-birth and the illnesses of her grandmother. She was healthy, beautiful, educated, concerned only about her husband, her children, her home. She had found true feminine fulfillment. As a housewife and mother, she was respected as a full and equal partner to man in his world. She was free to choose automobiles, clothes, appliances, supermarkets, she had everything that women ever dreamed of.

In the fifteen years after World War II, this mystique of feminine fulfillment became the cherished and self-perpetuating core of contemporary American culture. Millions of women lived their lives in the image of those pretty pictures of the American suburban housewife, kissing their husbands goodbye in front of the picture window, depositing their station wagons full of children at school, and smiling as they ran the new electric waxer over the spotless kitchen floor. They baked their own bread, sewed their own and their children's clothes, kept their new washing machines and dryers running all day. They changed the sheets on the beds twice a week instead of once, took the rug-hooking class in adult education, and pitied their poor frustrated mothers, who had dreamed of having a career. Their only dream was to be perfect wives and mothers; their highest ambition to have five children and a beautiful house, their only fight to get and keep their husbands. They had no thought for the unfeminine problems of the world outside the home; they wanted the men to make the major decisions. They gloried in their role as women, and wrote proudly on the census blank: "Occupation: housewife."

For over fifteen years, the words written for women, and the words women used when they talked to each other, while their husbands sat on the other side of the room and talked shop or politics or septic tanks, were about problems with their children, or how to keep their husbands happy, or improve their children's school, or cook chicken or make slipcovers.

Nobody argued whether women were inferior or superior to men; they were simply different. Words like "emancipation" and "career" sounded strange and embarrassing; no one had used them for years. When a Frenchwoman named Simone de Beauvoir wrote a book called *The Second Sex*, an American critic commented that she obviously "didn't know what life was all about," and besides, she was talking about French women. The "woman problem" in America no longer existed.

If a woman had a problem in the 1950's and 1960's, she knew that something must be wrong with her marriage, or with herself. Other women were satisfied with their lives, she thought. What kind of a woman was she if she did not feel this mysterious fulfillment waxing the kitchen floor? She was so ashamed to admit her dissatisfaction that she never knew how many other women shared it. If she tried to tell her husband, he didn't understand what she was talking about. She did not really understand it herself.

For over fifteen years women in America found it harder to talk about the problem than about sex. Even the psychoanalysts had no name for it. When a woman went to a psychiatrist for help, as many women did, she would say, "I'm so ashamed," or "I must be hopelessly neurotic." "I don't know what's wrong with women today," a suburban psychiatrist said uneasily. "I only know something is wrong because most of my patients happen to be women. And their problem isn't sexual." Most women with this problem did not go to see a psychoanalyst, however. "There's nothing wrong really," they kept telling themselves, "There isn't any problem."

But on an April morning in 1959, I heard a mother of four, having coffee with four other mothers in a suburban development fifteen miles from New York, say in a tone of quiet desperation, "the problem." And the others knew, without words, that she was not talking about a problem with her husband, or her children, or her home. Suddenly they realized they all shared the same problem, the problem that has no name. They began, hesitantly, to talk about it. Later, after they had picked up their children at nursery school and taken them home to nap, two of the women cried, in sheer relief, just to know they were not alone.

Gradually I came to realize that the problem that has no name was shared by countless women in America. As a magazine writer I often interviewed women about problems with their children, or their marriages, or their houses, or their communities. But after a while I began to recognize the telltale signs of this other problem. I saw the same signs in suburban ranch houses and split-levels on Long Island and in New Jersey and Westchester County; in colonial houses in a small Massachusetts town; on patios in Memphis; in suburban and city apartments; in living rooms in the Midwest. Sometimes I sensed the problem, not as a reporter, but as a suburban housewife, for during this time I was also bringing up my own three children in Rockland County, New York. I heard echoes of the problem in college dormitories and semiprivate maternity wards, at PTA meetings and luncheons of the League of Women Voters, at suburban cocktail parties, in station wagons waiting for trains, and in snatches of conversation overheard at Schrafft's. The groping words I heard from other women, on quiet afternoons when children were at school or on quiet evenings when husbands worked late, I think I understood first as a woman long before I understood their larger social and psychological implications.

Just what was this problem that has no name? What were the words women used when they tried to express it? Sometimes a woman would say "I feel empty somehow…incomplete." Or she would say, "I feel as if I don't exist." Sometimes she blotted out the feeling with a tranquilizer. Sometimes she thought the problem was with her husband or her children, or that what she really needed was to redecorate her house, or move to a better neighborhood, or have an affair, or another baby. Sometimes, she went to a doctor with symptoms she could hardly describe: "A tired feeling… I get so angry with the children it scares me… I feel like crying without any reason." (A Cleveland doctor called it "the housewife's syndrome.") A number of women told me about great bleeding blisters that break out on their hands and arms. "I call it the house wife's blight" said a family doctor in Pennsylvania. "I see it so often lately in these young women with four, five and six children who bury themselves in their dishpans. But it isn't caused by detergent and it isn't cured by cortisone."

Sometimes a woman would tell me that the feeling gets so strong she runs out of the house and walks through the streets. Or she stays inside her house and cries. Or her children tell her a joke, and she doesn't laugh because she doesn't hear it. I talked to women who had spent years on the analyst's couch, working out their "adjustment to the feminine role," their blocks to "fulfillment as a wife and mother." But the desperate tone in these women's voices, and the look in their eyes, was the same as the tone and the look of other women, who were sure they had no problem, even though they did have a strange feeling of desperation.

A mother of four who left college at nineteen to get married told me:

"I've tried everything women are supposed to do—hobbies, gardening, pickling, canning, being very social with my neighbors, joining committees, running PTA teas. I can do it all, and I like it, but it doesn't leave you anything to think about—any feeling of who you are. I never had any career ambitions. All I wanted was to get married and have four children. I love the kids and Bob and my home. There's no problem you can even put a name to. But I'm desperate. I begin to feel I have no personality. I'm a server of food and putter-on of pants and a bed maker, somebody who can be called on when you want something. But who am I?"

A twenty-three-year-old mother in blue jeans said:

"I ask myself why I'm so dissatisfied. I've got my health, fine children, a lovely new home, enough money. My husband has a real future as an electronics engineer. He doesn't have any of these feelings. He says maybe I need a vacation, let's go to New York for a weekend. But that isn't it. I always had this idea we should do everything together. I can't sit down and read a book alone. If the children are napping and I have one hour to myself I just walk through the house waiting for them to wake up. I don't make a move until I know where the rest of the crowd is going. It's as if ever since you were a little girl, there's always been

somebody or something that will take care of your life: your parents, or college, or falling in love, or having a child, or moving to a new house. Then you wake up one morning and there's nothing to look forward to."

A young wife in a Long Island development said:

"I seem to sleep so much. I don't know why I should be so tired. This house isn't nearly so hard to clean as the cold-water flat we had when I was working. The children are at school all day. It's not the work. I just don't feel alive."

In 1960, the problem that has no name burst like a boil through the image of the happy American housewife. In the television commercials the pretty housewives still beamed over their foaming dishpans and *Time*'s cover story on "The Suburban Wife, an American Phenomenon" protested: "Having too good a time... to believe that they should be unhappy." But the actual unhappiness of the American housewife was suddenly being reported—from the *New York Times* and *Newsweek* to *Good Housekeeping* and CBS Television ("The Trapped Housewife"), although almost everybody who talked about it found some superficial reason to dismiss it. It was attributed to incompetent appliance repairmen (*New York Times*), or the distances children must be chauffeured in the suburbs (*Time*), or too much PTA (*Redbook*). Some said it was the old problem—education: more and more women had education, which naturally made them unhappy in their role as housewives. "The road from Freud to Frigidaire, from Sophocles to Spock, has turned out to be a bumpy one," reported the *New York Times* (June 28, 1960). "Many young women—certainly not all—whose education plunged them into a world of ideas feel stifled in their homes. They find their routine lives out of joint with their training. Like shut-ins, they feel left out. In the last year, the problem of the educated housewife has provided the meat of dozens of speeches made by troubled presidents of women's colleges who maintain, in the face of complaints, that sixteen years of academic training is realistic preparation for wifehood and motherhood."

There was much sympathy for the educated housewife. ("Like a two-headed schizophrenic… once she wrote a paper on the Graveyard poets; now she writes notes to the milkman. Once she determined the boiling point of sulphuric acid; now she determines her boiling point with the overdue repairman…. The housewife often is reduced to screams and tears…. No one, it seems, is appreciative, least of all herself, of the kind of person she becomes in the process of turning from poetess into shrew.")

Home economists suggested more realistic preparation for housewives, such as high-school workshops in home appliances. College educators suggested more discussion groups on home management and the family, to prepare women for the adjustment to domestic life. A spate of articles appeared in the mass magazines offering "Fifty-eight Ways to Make Your Marriage More Exciting." No month went by without a new book by a psychiatrist or sexologist offering technical advice on finding greater fulfillment through sex.

A male humorist joked in *Harper's Bazaar* (July, 1960) that the problem could be solved by taking away woman's right to vote. ("In the pre-19th Amendment era, the American woman was placid, sheltered and sure of her role in American society. She left all the political decisions to her husband and he, in turn, left all the family decisions to her. Today a woman has to make both the family and the political decisions, and it's too much for her.")

A number of educators suggested seriously that women no longer be admitted to the four-year colleges and universities: in the growing college crisis, the education which girls could not use as housewives was more urgently needed than ever by boys to do the work of the atomic age.

The problem was also dismissed with drastic solutions no one could take seriously. (A woman writer proposed in *Harper's* that women be drafted for compulsory service as nurses' aides and baby-sitters.) And it was smoothed over with the age-old panaceas: "love is their answer," "the only answer is inner help," "the secret of completeness—children," "a private means of intellectual fulfillment," "to cure this toothache of the spirit—the simple formula of handling one's self and one's will over to God."

The problem was dismissed by telling the housewife she doesn't realize how lucky she is—her own boss, no time clock, no junior executive gunning for her job. What if she isn't happy—does she think men are happy in this world? Does she really, secretly, still want to be a man? Doesn't she know yet how lucky she is to be a woman?

The problem was also, and finally, dismissed by shrugging that there are NO solutions: this is what being a woman means, and what is wrong with American women that they can't accept their role gracefully? As *Newsweek* put it (March 7, 1960):

"She is dissatisfied with a lot that women of other lands can only dream of. Her discontent is deep, pervasive, and impervious to the superficial remedies which are offered at every hand…. An army of professional explorers have already charted the major sources of trouble…. From the beginning of time, the female cycle has defined and confined woman's role. As Freud was credited with saying: 'Anatomy is destiny.' Though no group of women has ever pushed these natural restrictions as far as the American wife, it seems that she still cannot accept them with good grace…. A young mother with a beautiful family, charm, talent and brains is apt to dismiss her role apologetically. 'What do I do?' you hear her say. 'Why nothing. I'm just a housewife.' A good education, it seems, has given this paragon among women an understanding of the value of everything except her own worth."…

And so she must accept the fact that "American women's unhappiness is merely the most recently won of women's rights," and adjust and say with the happy housewife found by *Newsweek*: "We ought to salute the wonderful freedom we all have and be proud of our lives today. I have had college and I've worked, but being a housewife is the most rewarding and satisfying role…. My mother was never included in my father's business affairs… she couldn't get out of the house and away from us children. But I am an equal to my husband; I can go along with him on business trips and to social business affairs."

The alternative offered was a choice that few women would contemplate. In the sympathetic words of the *New York Times*: "All admit to being deeply frustrated at times by the lack of privacy, the physical burden, the routine of family life, the confinement of it. However, none would give up her home and family if she had the choice to make again." *Redbook* commented: "Few women would want to thumb their noses at husbands, children and community and go off on their own. Those who do may be talented individuals, but they rarely are successful women."

The year American women's discontent boiled over, it was also reported (*Look*) that the more than 21,000,000 American women who are single, widowed, or divorced do not cease even after fifty their frenzied, desperate search for a man. And the search begins early—for seventy per cent of all American women now marry before they are twenty-four. A pretty twenty-five-year-old secretary took thirty-five different jobs in six months in the futile hope of finding a husband. Women were moving from one political club to another, taking evening courses in accounting or sailing, learning to play golf or ski, joining a number of churches in succession, going to bars alone, in their ceaseless search for a man.

Of the growing thousands of women currently getting private psychiatric help in the United States, the married ones were reported dissatisfied with their marriages, the unmarried ones suffering from anxiety and, finally, depression. Strangely, a number of psychiatrists stated that, in their experience, unmarried women patients were happier than married ones. So the door of all those pretty suburban houses opened a crack to permit a glimpse of uncounted thousands of American housewives who suffered alone from a problem that suddenly everyone was talking about, and beginning to take for granted, as one of those unreal problems in American life that can never be solved-like the hydrogen bomb. By 1962 the plight of the trapped American housewife had become a national parlor game. Whole issues of magazines, newspaper columns, books learned and frivolous, educational conferences and television panels were devoted to the problem.

Even so, most men, and some women, still did not know that this problem was real. But those who had faced it honestly knew that all the superficial remedies, the sympathetic advice, the scolding words and the cheering words were somehow drowning the problem in unreality. A bitter laugh was beginning to be heard from American women. They were admired, envied, pitied, theorized over until they were sick of it, offered drastic solutions or silly choices that no one could take seriously. They got all kinds of advice from the growing armies of marriage and child guidance counselors, psychotherapists, and armchair psychologists, on how to adjust to their role as housewives. No other road to fulfillment was offered to American women in the middle of the twentieth century. Most adjusted to their role and suffered or ignored the problem that has no name. It can be less painful for a woman, not to hear the strange, dissatisfied voice stirring within her.

It is NO longer possible to ignore that voice, to dismiss the desperation of so many American women. This is not what being a woman means, no matter what the experts say. For human suffering there is a reason; perhaps the reason has not been found because the right questions have not been asked, or pressed far enough. I do not accept the answer that there is no problem because American women have luxuries that women in other times and lands never dreamed of; part of the strange newness of the problem is that it cannot be understood in terms of the age-old material problems of man: poverty, sickness, hunger, cold. The women who suffer this problem have a hunger that food cannot fill. It persists in women whose husbands are struggling intern and law clerks, or prosperous doctors and lawyers; in wives of workers and executives who make $5,000 a year or $50,000. It is not caused by lack of material advantages; it may not even be felt by women preoccupied with desperate problems of hunger, poverty or illness. And women who think it will be solved by more money, a bigger house, a second car, moving to a better suburb, often discover it gets worse.

It is no longer possible today to blame the problem on loss of femininity: to say that education and independence and equality with men have made American women unfeminine. I have heard so many women try to deny this dissatisfied voice within themselves because it does not fit the pretty picture of femininity the experts have given them. I think, in fact, that this is the first clue to the mystery; the problem cannot be understood in the generally accepted terms by which scientists have studied women, doctors have treated them, counselors have advised them, and writers have written about them. Women who suffer this problem, in whom this voice is stirring, have lived their whole lives in the pursuit of feminine fulfillment. They are not career women (although career women may have other problems); they are women whose greatest ambition has been marriage and children. For the oldest of these women, these daughters of the American middle class, no other dream was possible. The ones in their forties and fifties who once had other dreams gave them up and threw themselves joyously into life as housewives. For the youngest, the new wives and mothers, this was the only dream. They are the ones who quit high school and college to marry, or marked time in some job in which they had no real interest until they married. These women are very "feminine" in the usual sense, and yet they still suffer the problem.

Are the women who finished college, the women who once had dreams beyond housewifery, the ones who suffer the most? According to the experts they are, but listen to these four women:

"My days are all busy, and dull, too. All I ever do is mess around. I get up at eight—I make breakfast, so I do the dishes, have lunch, do some more dishes, and some laundry and cleaning in the afternoon. Then it's supper dishes and I get to sit down a few minutes, before the children have to be sent to bed.... That's all there is to my day. It's just like any other wife's day. Humdrum. The biggest time, I am chasing kids."

"Ye Gods, what do I do with my time? Well, I get up at six. I get my son dressed and then give him breakfast. After that I wash dishes and bathe and feed the baby. Then I get lunch and while the children nap, I sew or mend or iron and do all the other things I can't get done before noon. Then I cook supper for the family and my husband watches TV while I do the dishes. After I get the children to bed, I set my hair and then I go to bed."

"The problem is always being the children's mommy, or the minister's wife and never being myself."

"A film made of any typical morning in my house would look like an old Marx Brothers' comedy. I wash the dishes, rush the older children off to school, dash out in the yard to cultivate the chrysanthemums, run back in to make a phone call about a committee meeting, help the youngest child build a blockhouse, spend fifteen minutes skimming the newspapers so I can be well-informed, then scamper down to the washing machines where my thrice-weekly laundry includes enough clothes to keep a primitive village going for an entire year. By noon I'm ready for a padded cell. Very little of what I've done has been really necessary or important. Outside pressures lash me through the day. Yet I look upon myself as one of the more relaxed housewives in the neighborhood. Many of my friends are even more frantic."

In the past sixty years we have come full circle and the American housewife is once again trapped in a squirrel cage. If the cage is now a modern plate-glass-and-broadloom ranch house or a convenient modern apartment, the situation is no less painful than when her grandmother sat over an embroidery hoop in her gilt-end-plush parlor and muttered angrily about women's rights.

The first two women never went to college. They live in developments in Levittown, New Jersey, and Tacoma, Washington, and were interviewed by a team of sociologists studying workingmen's wives. The third, a minister's wife, wrote on the fifteenth reunion questionnaire of her college that she never had any career ambitions, but wishes now she had. The fourth, who has a PhD in anthropology, is today a Nebraska housewife with three children. Their words seem to indicate that housewives of all educational levels suffer the same feeling of desperation.

The fact is that NO one today is muttering angrily about "women's rights," even though more and more women have gone to college. In a recent study of all the classes that have graduated from Barnard College, a significant minority of earlier graduates blamed their education for making them want "rights," later classes blamed their education for giving them career dreams, but recent graduates blamed the college for making them feel it was not enough simply to be a housewife and mother; they did not want to feel guilty if they did not read books or take part in community activities. But if education is not the cause of the problem, the fact that education somehow festers in these women may be a clue.

If the secret of feminine fulfillment is having children, never have many women, with the freedom to choose, had so many children in so few years, so willingly. If the answer is love, never have women marched for love with such determination. And yet there is a growing suspicion that the problem may not be sexual, though it must somehow relate to sex. I have heard from many doctors evidence of new sexual problems between man and wife—sexual hunger in wives so that their husbands cannot satisfy it. "We have made women a sex creature," said a psychiatrist at the Margaret Sanger marriage counseling clinic. "She has no identity except as a wife and mother. She does know who she is herself. She waits all day for her husband to come home at night to make her feel alive. And now it is the husband who is interested. It is terrible for the women, to lie there, night after night, waiting for her husband to make her feel alive." Why is there such a market for books and articles offering sexual advice? The kind of sexual orgasm which Kinsey found in statistical plenitude in the recent generations of American women does not seem to make this problem go away.

On the contrary, new neuroses are being seen among women—and problems as yet unnamed as neuroses—which Freud and his followers did not predict, with physical symptoms, anxieties, and defense mechanisms equal to those caused by sexual repression. And strange new problems are being reported in the growing generations of children whose mothers were always there, driving them around, helping them with their homework—an inability to endure pain or discipline or pursue any self-sustained goal of any sort, a devastating boredom with life. Educators are increasingly uneasy about the dependence, the lack of self-reliance, of the boys and girls who are entering college today. "We fight a continual battle to make our students assume manhood," said a Columbia dean.

A White House conference was held on the physical and muscular deterioration of American children: were they being over-nurtured? Sociologists noted the astounding organization of suburban children's lives: the lessons, parties, entertainments, play and study groups organized for them. A suburban housewife in Portland, Oregon, wondered why the children "need" Brownies and Boy Scouts out here. "This is not the slums. The kids out here have the great outdoors. I think people are so bored. They organize the children, and then try to hook ever'one else on it. And the poor kids have no time left just to lie on their beds and daydream."

Can the problem that has no name be somehow related to the domestic routine of the housewife? When a woman tries to put the problem into words, she often merely describes the daily life she leads. What is there in this recital of comfortable domestic detail that could possibly cause such a feeling of desperation? Is she trapped simply by the enormous demands of her role as modern housewife: wife, mistress, mother, nurse, consumer, cook, chauffeur, expert on interior decoration child care, appliance repair, furniture refinishing, nutrition, and education? Her day is fragmented as she rushes from dishwasher to washing machine to telephone to dryer to station wagon to supermarket, and delivers Johnny to the Little League field, takes Janey to dancing class, gets the lawn mower fixed and meets the 6:45. She can never spend more than 15 minutes on any one thing; she has no time to read books, only magazines; even if she had time, she has lost the power to concentrate. At the end of the day, she is so terribly tired that sometimes her husband has to take over and put the children to bed.

This terrible tiredness took so many women to doctors in the 1950's that one decided to investigate it. He found, surprisingly, that his patients suffering from "housewife's fatigue" slept more than an adult needed to sleep—as much as ten hours a day—and that the actual energy they expended on housework did not tax their capacity. The real problem must be something else, he decided—perhaps boredom. Some doctors told their women patients they must get out of the house for a day, treat themselves to a movie in town. Others prescribed tranquilizers. Many suburban housewives were taking tranquilizers like cough drops. "You wake up in the morning, and you feel as if there's no point in going on another day like this. So you take a tranquilizer because it makes you not care so much that it's pointless."

It is easy to see the concrete details that trap the suburban housewife, the continual demands on her time. But the chains that bind her in her trap are chains in her own mind and spirit. They are chains made up of mistaken ideas and misinterpreted facts, of incomplete truths and unreal choices. They are not easily seen and not easily shaken off.

How can any woman see the whole truth within the bounds of her own life? How can she believe that voice inside herself, when it denies the conventional, accepted truths by which she has been living? And yet the women I have talked to, who are finally listening to that inner voice, seem in some incredible way to be groping through to a truth that has defied the experts.

I think the experts in a great many fields have been holding pieces of that truth under their microscopes for a long time without realizing it. I found pieces of it in certain new research and theoretical developments in psychological, social and biological science whose implications for women seem never to have been examined. I found many clues by talking to suburban doctors, gynecologists, obstetricians, child-guidance clinicians, pediatricians, high-school guidance counselors, college professors, marriage counselors, psychiatrists and ministers—questioning them not on their theories, but on their actual experience in treating American women. I became aware of a growing body of evidence, much of which has not been reported publicly because it does not fit current modes of thought about women—evidence which throws into question the standards of feminine normality, feminine adjustment, feminine fulfillment, and feminine maturity by which most women are still trying to live.

I began to see in a strange new light the American return to early marriage and the large families that are causing the population explosion; the recent movement to natural childbirth and breastfeeding; suburban conformity, and the new neuroses, character pathologies and sexual problems being reported by the doctors. I began to see new dimensions to old problems that have long been taken for granted among women: menstrual difficulties, sexual frigidity, promiscuity, pregnancy fears, childbirth depression, the high incidence of emotional breakdown and suicide among women in their twenties and thirties, the menopause crises, the so-called passivity and immaturity of American men, the discrepancy between women's tested intellectual abilities in childhood and their adult achievement, the changing incidence of adult sexual orgasm in American women, and persistent problems in psychotherapy and in women's education.

If I am right, the problem that has no name stirring in the minds of so many American women today is not a matter of loss of femininity or too much education, or the demands of domesticity. It is far more important than anyone recognizes. It is the key to these other new and old problems which have been torturing women and their husbands and children, and puzzling their doctors and educators for years. It may well be the key to our future as a nation and a culture. We can no longer ignore that voice within women that says: "I want something more than my husband and my children and my home."

## GLOSSARY

**paean:** a victory song or shout; originally a song sung in Ancient Greece after a victory in war

**groping:** showing or reflecting a desire to understand or explain, especially something that is puzzling; stumbling

**Frigidaire:** a home appliance company that was founded in 1916

**panacea:** a answer or solution for all problems; a so-called cure-all

**plate glass:** a type of glass made in large, thick sheets; very common in mid-nineteenth-century homes

**broadloom:** a type of carpet woven in wide widths; often used in wall-to-wall carpeting in homes

**gilt:** gilded; colored or covered with a thin gold plate, fairly common in higher-end furniture during the Victorian and Progressive periods

## Document Analysis

The essence of *The Feminine Mystique* can be found in its first paragraph. Friedan begins by saying that "the problem lay buried, unspoken, for many years in the minds of American women." She calls it "a strange stirring, a sense of dissatisfaction, a yearning that women suffered in the middle of the twentieth century in the United States." She notes that "each suburban wife struggled with it alone" and itemizes the activities of a typical suburban housewife: "As she made the beds, shopped for groceries, matched slipcover material, ate peanut butter sandwiches with her children, chauffeured Cub Scouts and Brownies, lay beside her husband at night—she was afraid to ask even of herself the silent question—'Is this all?'"

Friedan locates the source of this dissatisfaction in "columns, books and articles by experts telling women their role was to seek fulfillment as wives and mothers." She cites statistics showing that the average marriage age of women was falling, a high percentage of women were dropping out of college, and the American birthrate was rising. Fewer women, she says, were entering professional work. Meanwhile, the American woman was the envy of the world: "She was healthy, beautiful, educated, concerned only about her husband, her children, her home."

Friedan then turns to her own experience, including the routine in her own home and how she became aware of the feminine mystique and the "problem that has no name." She began seeing symptoms of the problem in her own community and among the women with whom she associated, and she cites conversations she had with dissatisfied women, such as a mother of four who left college at nineteen. Women with educations were relegated to domestic tasks, and schools and colleges recommended courses designed to prepare women for their roles as mothers and homemakers. She discusses the efforts women went through to snare a husband and the therapy women underwent to cope with their unhappiness. She states that "it is NO longer possible to ignore that voice, to dismiss the desperation of so many American women" and that "it is no longer possible today to blame the problem on loss of femininity: to say that education and independence and equality with men have made American women unfeminine." She concludes that "the chains that bind her in her trap are chains in her own mind and spirit," and the remainder of the book is an effort to unbind the chains.

## Essential Themes

The most impressive outcome of Betty Friedan's work was the outbreak of Second-Wave Feminism. Unlike First-Wave Feminism, which focused mostly on voting rights, basic equality, and citizens' rights, Second-Wave began to branch out into different issues, including reproductive rights, sexuality, familial roles, custody issues, and even divorce law. Essentially spanning from the 1960s to the 1990s, Second-Wave feminism shaped the United States in ways that are very recognizable today. Although it is often remembered for facing issues commonly faced by middle-income, white women and their families, women (and men) of color, lower-income families, and LGBT women played a significant role in shaping gender relations and interactions (though these changes often took place much slower for minority groups).

Because of these pushes for more equal standards, there were several distinct political and educational changes that swept the country. Many male-only colleges, for example, began to merge with women-only colleges, such as Radcliff College merging with Harvard University, creating the University that is well-known in the US today. Moreover, Title IX laws, as part of the Education Amendments of 1972, were put into effect which were intended to prohibit discrimination based on sex or gender and, now, deal with issues of sexual harassment on college campuses. Furthermore, purely political acts were passed in order to protect women and ensure greater rights. One of the most famous was the Supreme Court case, Roe v. Wade, which gave women the inalienable right to make decisions about her own body, specifically whether or not she wished to carry a pregnancy to term.

Finally, in a mix of the social and political, Second-Wave feminism opened up opportunities for women's groups to emerge and make their own marks on the U.S. and on the international community. Groups, such as the National Women's Political Caucus and the Women's Aid Federation, were formed around the world in an attempt to offer protection and aid to women from all walks of life. These progressive pushes are perhaps best exemplified in International Women's Day, first formally recognized in 1977 by the United Nations General Assembly in order to honor women's rights and peace around the world.

*—Anna Accettola, MA, and Michael J. O'Neal, PhD*

## Bibliography and Additional Resources

"Betty Friedan." History.com, A&E Television Networks, 2009, www.history.com/topics/womens-history/betty-friedan.

Bradley, Patricia. *Mass Media and the Shaping of American Feminism, 1963-1975*. University Press of Mississippi, 2004.Friedan, Betty. *The Second Stage: with a New Introduction*. Harvard University Press, 1998.

Horowitz, Daniel. *Betty Friedan and the Making of the Feminine Mystique: the American Left, the Cold War, and Modern Feminism*. University of Massachusetts Press, 2000.

Tong, Rosemarie, and Tina Fernandes Botts. *Feminist Thought: a More Comprehensive Introduction*. Westview Press, 2018.

# ■ Testimony of Fannie Lou Hamer before the Credentials Committee of the Democratic National Convention

**Date:** August 22, 1964
**Authors:** Fannie Lou Hamer
**Genre:** Testimony; speech

## Summary Overview

On June 9, 1963, Fannie Lou Hamer, an African American woman who had recently attended a voter registration training, was arrested and beaten in prison, along with several other black women. A year later, she participated in the formation of a new wing of the Democratic Party in order to challenge the entrenched Democratic Party in Mississippi. She testified about her violent experience at the Democratic presidential nominating convention in August 1964, as the delegates from her new group sought to be seated in place of those from the mainstream Democratic Party in Mississippi. Her speech was moving, as she described the horrible details of her arrest, imprisonment, and beating. She also simultaneously embraced the fundamental civil rights due her as an American citizen, while also questioning the true nature of an America that continued to allow its citizens to be beaten and murdered as they pursued their basic rights. Hamer's beating and testimony occurred during one of the most disturbing periods of racial violence in American history, the two years between President John F. Kennedy's June 1963 public embrace of civil rights and the final passage of the 1965 Voting Rights Act in August of that year. Her experience was one part, but an important one, of the larger, violent transition to full civil and voting rights for African Americans.

## Defining Moment

Hamer's testimony occurred within the context of what amounted to a revolutionary political challenge to the established Democratic Party in Mississippi. In 1964, Hamer and other activists formed the Mississippi Freedom Democratic Party (MFDP) in order to send their own delegates to the party's national presidential nominating convention that year. Altogether, this new branch of the party gained 80,000 supporters and tried to get sixty-four of its members seated at the national convention as representatives of the Democratic Party of Mississippi. As part of the controversy they stimulated when they arrived at the convention, Hamer provided some of her own personal testimony as evidence that the members of the MFDP

should be seated either in place of or alongside the regular Democratic delegates. Despite increasing attention to civil rights by the national leaders of the Democratic Party and despite offers of a negotiated arrangement, the MFDP refused any accommodation and ended up failing in this specific endeavor in August 1964.

Beyond the immediate context of the MFDP's efforts to supplant the main Democratic Party's Mississippi delegation in August 1964, the beating that Hamer suffered and the attempts to form a rival branch of the party took place in the larger context of the troubling period between President John F. Kennedy's long overdue public embrace of civil rights in his famous June 1963 speech and the passing of the Voting Rights Act in August 1965. Of course, this period directly included the arrest and beating of Harmer, and overall, it was marked by a sharp uptick in violence against African American and white civil rights activists who sought to register black voters in the South. Even after the 1964 Civil Rights Act became law, voting protections for black Americans still remained weak, and therefore, voter registration efforts—of the kind that lead to Harmer's arrest and beating—continued. Of course, as she notes, her ordeal occurred because she had been at a "voter registration workshop" and was on the return journey. As historian Taylor Branch notes, in the ten weeks after the end of violence in Birmingham, Alabama, in May 1963, a period that included both Hamer's beating and the murder of activist Medgar Evers, "statisticians counted 758 racial demonstrations and 14,733 arrests in 186 American cities" (85). Support for, and opposition against, black civil rights was at a fevered pitch across the nation in 1963 and 1964. Hamer's experience was a small, although important and impactful, part of this larger moment in American history before the Voting Rights Act finally passed into law.

## Author Biography

Fannie Lou Hamer was born in 1917 and was a politically inactive plantation worker until she tried to register to vote in 1962. She subsequently lost her

Fannie Lou Hamer, American civil rights leader, at the Democratic National Convention, Atlantic City, New Jersey, August 1964. By Warren K. Leffler, U.S. News & World Report Magazine; Restored by Adam Cuerden.

job and home and then joined the Student Nonviolent Coordinating Committee (SNCC), despite being in her mid-forties and not being a student, to advocate for civil rights and to help other African Americans register to vote. As Hine, Hine, and Harrold note, af-

ter her experiences in jail and at the 1964 Democratic convention and until her death in 1977, she pursued various efforts designed to help impoverished rural African Americans working in agriculture, where she had spent most of her life.

## HISTORICAL DOCUMENT

...[On] June the 9th, 1963, I had attended a voter registration workshop; was returning back to Mississippi. Ten of us was traveling by the Continental Trailway bus. When we got to Winona, Mississippi, which is Montgomery County, four of the people got off to use the washroom, and two of the people—to use the restaurant—two of the people wanted to use the washroom. The four people that had gone in to use the restaurant was ordered out... I stepped off of the bus to see what was happening and somebody screamed from the car that the five workers was in and said, "Get that one there." When I went to get in the car, when the man told me I was under arrest, he kicked me.

I was carried to the county jail and put in the booking room. They left some of the people in the booking room and began to place us in cells. I was placed in a cell with a young woman called Miss Ivesta Simpson. After I was placed in the cell I began to hear sounds of licks and screams, I could hear the sounds of licks and horrible screams...And it wasn't too long before three white men came to my cell. One of these men was a State Highway Patrolman and he asked me where I was from. I told him Ruleville and he said, "We are going to check this."

They left my cell and it wasn't too long before they came back. He said, "You are from Ruleville all right," and he used a curse word. And he said, "We are going to make you wish you was dead."

I was carried out of that cell into another cell where they had two Negro prisoners. The State

Highway Patrolmen ordered the first Negro to take the blackjack.

The first Negro prisoner ordered me, by orders from the State Highway Patrolman, for me to lay down on a bunk bed on my face.

I laid on my face and the first Negro began to beat. I was beat by the first Negro until he was exhausted. I was holding my hands behind me at that time on my left side, because I suffered from polio when I was six years old.

After the first Negro had beat until he was exhausted, the State Highway Patrolman ordered the second Negro to take the blackjack.

The second Negro began to beat and I began to work my feet, and the State Highway Patrolman ordered the first Negro who had beat me to sit on my feet—to keep me from working my feet. I began to scream and one white man got up and began to beat me in my head and tell me to hush.

One white man—my dress had worked up high—he walked over and pulled my dress—I pulled my dress down and he pulled my dress back up.

I was in jail when Medgar Evers was murdered.

All of this is on account of we want to register, to become first-class citizens. And if the Freedom Democratic Party is not seated now, I question America. Is this America, the land of the free and the home of the brave, where we have to sleep with our telephones off the hooks because our lives be threatened daily, because we want to live as decent human beings, in America?

## Document Analysis

Most of the document is a narrative of the events leading up to her beating, but the details include important windows into the nature and mechanisms of ongoing white control in the South during the early 1960s. Essentially, she faced state-sponsored terrorism in that

government officials imprisoned her without cause, simply for attempting to practice her constitutional rights, and then physically assaulted her in prison.

Her arrest, along with several other black women, occurred at a rural bus stop in Winona, Mississippi, and shows the strict control exercised by whites who disliked the push for black civil rights. According to historian Taylor Branch, even just the black women entering the bus stop "caused the waitress behind the counter to wad up her check pad and fling it at them all in disgust, crying out, 'I can't take no more.'" Law enforcement officials then arrived and forced them outside. When Annell Ponder, a member of the Southern Christian Leadership Conference (SCLC) who was leading the trip, began to protest, they were arrested.

As Hamer describes, upon arrival in jail, they were all beaten, although Hamer was beaten by two fellow black male prisoners. They likely did not want to participate, but were probably under threat of physical violence themselves. Even as it went on, Hamer noted that she tried to keep her dress down in order to maintain even the tiniest bit of dignity, but the white man pulling her dress back up and the fact that the white officers made two black men beat her both revealed the extensive efforts that whites went to in order to degrade and humiliate blacks in the South at this time. She also noted that while in prison, Medgar Evers, the National Association for the Advancement of Colored People's executive secretary in Jackson, Mississippi, and a leading figure of the civil rights movement, was murdered in front of his home. Both the beating of several black women in Winona and the death of Evers in Jackson showed that in the summer of 1963, white resistance to civil rights in Mississippi was extremely violent.

## Essential Themes

In addition to the themes of the violence against African Americans and the humiliation often forced on them, the final section of Hamer's speech was a resounding call for the nation to fulfill its promise to all its citizens. She noted once again the constant threat they felt, describing how African Americans had "to sleep with our telephones off the hooks because our lives be threatened daily." She went on to claim that black Americans wanted "to become first-class citizens" and "to live as decent human beings." Key to this, Hamer and many others thought, was the ability of African Americans to vote without intimidation or violence. Beyond human decency in a country that claimed to be democratic, she implicitly invoked the Fourteenth Amendment to the Constitution, which states that everyone born in the United States is a citizen and has certain rights based

on that status, including the right to vote as guaranteed in the Fifteenth Amendment to the Constitution. While she did not explicitly invoke these protections in her speech before the Credentials Committee, she was certainly voicing their core ideas and claiming those ideas on behalf of all black Americans.

Interestingly, there was a bit of a note of doubt in her final statement as well. While Hamer was not herself a young woman at this time, many younger African American activists, often in SNCC, were by the mid-1960s at odds over strategies with groups that usually had older leaders, such as the Congress of Racial Equality (CORE) or the SCLC. Younger activists pushed for more direct tactics, and some would turn to the Black Power movement and the Black Panther Party by the late 1960s as they embraced more direct confrontations with whites in order to challenge both racism and problems related to urban poverty, especially bad housing and unemployment. While Hamer was not specifically invoking those ideas, her note of doubt about what America truly was pointed in that direction. Even while claiming that she, and others, wanted the protections due an American citizen, she said that if they weren't given, "I question America." In her next sentence, she noted the threats to black Americans and asked, "Is this America?" In one way, she was asking if this was the true nature of America. Therefore, she simultaneously sought to invoke the highest ideals of the United States and claim them for African Americans, while also implicitly wondering whether, in fact, violent racism was closer to the core of the definition of America than she had perhaps realized.

—*Kevin Grimm, PhD*

## Bibliography and Additional Reading

Branch, Taylor. *Parting the Waters: America in the King Years, 1954–63*. New York: Simon and Schuster, 1988. Print.

Hine, Darlene Clark, William C. Hine, & Stanley Harrold. *The African-American Odyssey*. Combined Vol. 2nd ed. Upper Saddle River, NJ: Pearson Education, 2005. Print.

Mills, Kay. *This Little Light of Mine: The Life of Fannie Lou Hamer*. Lexington, KY: U P Kentucky, 2007. Print.

# ■ *Griswold v. Connecticut*

**Date:** June 7, 1965
**Author:** Justice William O. Douglas (majority opinion)
**Genre:** Court opinion

## Summary Overview

A Connecticut law passed in 1879 forbade citizens from accessing birth control for purposes of contraception. Citizens were not allowed to have access to information regarding birth control, were prohibited from receiving counsel about birth control, and were not able to access instruments or medication that would prevent reproduction. Furthermore, medical professionals and their assistants and staff were forbidden to provide birth control services to individuals. Those found in violation of this law could be fined up to $100.00, face imprisonment, or both. In 1961, two workers at a New Haven Planned Parenthood clinic were arrested and charged with violating the Connecticut law. Upon reviewing the case, the Supreme Court struck down the statute on the basis that the law violated a series of constitutional amendments, which guaranteed American citizens the right to privacy.

## Defining Moment

After women gained the right to vote in 1920 through the passage of the Nineteenth Amendment, the movement towards women's rights significantly slowed down in this country. It was not until the mid-1960s that the movement began to see a resurgence. Betty Friedan's publication, *The Feminine Mystique*, helped women across the nation realize they were not alone in their lukewarm feelings towards their position in society. Prior to this revitalization in the fight for women's rights, a struggle regarding the legality and accessibility of birth control was taking place in the country. By 1936, birth control was no longer considered obscene, but advocates for accessible birth control struggled throughout the 40s and 50s to defeat state laws preventing women from gaining access to contraception. In 1960, the Food and Drug Administration approved the birth control pill, but states were still reluctant to allow citizens access to the medication.

In Connecticut, a state law had been in place since 1879 forbidding any person from selling birth control mechanisms, or giving advice on birth control for purposes of preventing pregnancy. Any individual found guilty of violating this law would be subject to a fine of $100.00, imprisonment, or both, including any individual who assisted in providing information or access to birth control. In Connecticut, this law had been challenged repeatedly, but held strong for over eighty years. In 1961, under Planned Parenthood, a birth control clinic was established in New Haven, Connecticut. Estelle Griswold, the executive director of the clinic, and C. Lee Buxton, the attending physician, were providing information and offering advice to patients regarding methods of birth control specifically for the purpose of preventing pregnancy. Authorities raided the clinic, resulting in convictions and fines for both Griswold and Buxton, who willingly admitted to violating the state law. The state of Connecticut upheld the convictions, and Griswold and Buxton petitioned the Supreme Court for a chance at having their case heard.

## Biography

William O. Douglas was born in 1898, and after the death of his father early in his life, Douglas was forced to work from a young age to help support his family and earn his education. Douglas attended Whitman College on scholarship and went on to attend law school at Columbia, where he would later teach. Douglas served as a faculty member at Yale Law and received a political appointment to serve on the United States Securities and Exchange Commission. After Justice Brandeis retired from the Supreme Court in 1939, Douglas was nominated by Roosevelt to serve on the Court. Upon his confirmation at just forty years old, Douglas became one of the youngest ever appointed to the Court. With almost thirty-seven years of service on the Court to his name, Douglas holds the record for serving the longest term on the Supreme Court. William O. Douglas passed away on January 19, 1980.

Estelle Griswold standing outside the Planned Parenthood clinic in April, 1963, which was closed pending a decision of the U.S. Supreme Court regarding a Connecticut state law forbidding the sale or use of contraceptives. By Lee Lockwood (Time & Life pictures) [CC0]

## HISTORICAL DOCUMENT

### MR. JUSTICE DOUGLAS delivered the opinion of the Court.

Appellant Griswold is Executive Director of the Planned Parenthood League of Connecticut. Appellant Buxton is a licensed physician and a professor at the Yale Medical School who served as Medical Director for the League at its Center in New Haven—a center open and operating from November 1 to November 10, 1961, when appellants were arrested. They gave information, instruction, and medical advice to married persons as to the means of preventing conception. They examined the wife and prescribed the best contraceptive device or material for her use. Fees were usually charged, although some couples were serviced free.

The statutes whose constitutionality is involved in this appeal are 53–32 and 54–196 of the General Statutes of Connecticut (1958 rev.). The former provides:

"Any person who uses any drug, medicinal article or instrument for the purpose of preventing conception shall be fined not less than fifty dollars or imprisoned not less than sixty days nor more than one year or be both fined and imprisoned."

Section 54–196 provides:

"Any person who assists, abets, counsels, causes, hires or commands another to commit any offense may be prosecuted and punished as if he were the principal offender."

The appellants were found guilty as accessories and fined $100 each, against the claim that the accessory statute as so applied violated the Fourteenth Amendment....

Coming to the merits, we are met with a wide range of questions that implicate the Due Process Clause of the Fourteenth Amendment. Overtones of some arguments suggest that *Lochner v. New York*, 198 U.S. 45, should be our guide. But we decline that invitation. We do not sit as a super-legislature to determine the wisdom, need, and propriety of laws that touch economic problems, business affairs, or social conditions. This law, however, operates directly on an intimate relation of husband and wife and their physician's role in one aspect of that relation.

The association of people is not mentioned in the Constitution nor in the Bill of Rights. The right to educate a child in a school of the parents' choice—whether public or private or parochial—is also not mentioned. Nor is the right to study any particular subject or any foreign language. Yet the First Amendment has been construed to include certain of those rights.

By *Pierce v. Society of Sisters*, supra, the right to educate one's children as one chooses is made applicable to the States by the force of the First and Fourteenth Amendments. By *Meyer v. Nebraska*, supra, the same dignity is given the right to study the German language in a private school. In other words, the State may not, consistently with the spirit of the First Amendment, contract the spectrum of available knowledge... And so we reaffirm the principle of the *Pierce* and the *Meyer* cases.

In *NAACP v. Alabama* we protected the "freedom to associate and privacy in one's associations," noting that freedom of association was a peripheral First Amendment right. Disclosure of membership lists of a constitutionally valid association, we held, was invalid "as entailing the likelihood of a substantial restraint upon the exercise by petitioner's members of their right to freedom of association." Ibid. In other words, the First Amendment has a penumbra where privacy is protected from governmental intrusion. The right of "association," like the right of belief (*Board of Education v. Barnette*, 319 U.S. 624), is more than the right to attend a meeting; it includes the right to express one's attitudes or philosophies by membership in a group or by affiliation with it or by other lawful means. Association in that context is a form of expression of opinion; and while it is not expressly included in the First Amendment its existence is necessary in making the express guarantees fully meaningful.

The foregoing cases suggest that specific guarantees in the Bill of Rights have penumbras, formed by emanations from those guarantees that help give them life and substance. Various guarantees create zones of privacy. The right of association contained in the penumbra of the First Amendment is one, as we have seen. The Third Amendment in its prohibition against the quartering of soldiers "in any house" in time of peace without the consent of the owner is another facet of that privacy. The Fourth Amendment explicitly affirms the "right of the people to be secure in their persons, houses, papers, and effects, against unreasonable searches and seizures." The Fifth Amendment in its Self-Incrimination Clause enables the citizen to create a zone of privacy which government may not force him to surrender to his detriment. The Ninth Amendment provides: "The enumeration in the Constitution, of certain rights, shall not be construed to deny or disparage others retained by the people."

The Fourth and Fifth Amendments were described... as protection against all governmental invasions "of the sanctity of a man's home and the privacies of life."

We have had many controversies over these penumbral rights of "privacy and repose." These cases bear witness that the right of privacy which presses for recognition here is a legitimate one.

The present case, then, concerns a relationship lying within the zone of privacy created by several fundamental constitutional guarantees. And it concerns a law which, in forbidding the use of contraceptives rather than regulating their manufacture or sale, seeks to achieve its goals by means having a maximum destructive impact upon that relationship. Such a law cannot stand in light of the familiar principle, so often applied by this Court, that a "governmental purpose to control or prevent activities constitutionally subject to state regulation may not be achieved by means which sweep unnecessarily broadly and thereby invade the area of protected freedoms." . Would we allow the police to search the sacred precincts of marital bedrooms for telltale signs of the use of contraceptives? The very idea is repulsive to the notions of privacy surrounding the marriage relationship.

We deal with a right of privacy older than the Bill of Rights—older than our political parties, older than our school system. Marriage is a coming together for better or for worse, hopefully enduring, and intimate to the degree of being sacred. It is an association that promotes a way of life, not causes; a harmony in living, not political faiths; a bilateral loyalty, not commercial or social projects. Yet it is an association for as noble a purpose as any involved in our prior decisions.

*Reversed.*

## MR. JUSTICE GOLDBERG, whom THE CHIEF JUSTICE and MR. JUSTICE BRENNAN join, concurring.

I agree with the Court that Connecticut's birth-control law unconstitutionally intrudes upon the right of marital privacy, and I join in its opinion and judgment. Although I have not accepted the view that "due process" as used in the Fourteenth Amendment incorporates all of the first eight Amendments, I do agree that the concept of liberty protects those personal rights that are fundamental, and is not confined to the specific terms of the Bill of Rights. My conclusion that the concept of liberty is not so restricted and that it embraces the right of marital privacy though that right is not mentioned explicitly in the Constitution is supported both by numerous decisions of this Court, referred to in the Court's opinion, and by the language and history of the Ninth Amendment. In reaching the conclusion that the right of marital privacy is protected, as being within the protected penumbra of specific guarantees of the Bill of Rights, the Court refers to the Ninth Amendment, I add these words to emphasize the relevance of that Amendment to the Court's holding.

The Court stated many years ago that the Due Process Clause protects those liberties that are "so rooted in the traditions and conscience of our people as to be ranked as fundamental."

The Ninth Amendment reads, "The enumeration in the Constitution, of certain rights, shall not be construed to deny or disparage others retained by the people." The Amendment is almost entirely the work of James Madison. It was introduced in Congress by him and passed the House and Senate with little or no debate and virtually no change in language. It was proffered to quiet expressed fears that a bill of specifically enumerated rights could not be sufficiently broad to cover all essential rights and that the specific mention of certain rights would be interpreted as a denial that others were protected.

In presenting the proposed Amendment, Madison said:

"It has been objected also against a bill of rights, that, by enumerating particular exceptions to the grant of power, it would disparage those rights which were not placed in that enumeration; and it might follow by implication, that those rights which were not singled out, were intended to be assigned into the hands of the General Government, and were consequently insecure. This is one of the most plausible arguments I have ever heard urged against the admission of a bill of rights into this system; but, I conceive, that it may be guarded against. I have attempted it, as gentlemen may see by turning to the last clause of the fourth resolution [the Ninth Amendment]."

Mr. Justice Story wrote of this argument against a bill of rights and the meaning of the Ninth Amendment:

"In regard to…[a] suggestion, that the affirmance of certain rights might disparage others, or might lead to argumentative implications in favor of other powers, it might be sufficient to say that such a course of reasoning could never be sustained upon any solid basis…. But a conclusive answer is, that such an attempt may be interdicted (as it has been) by a positive declaration in such a bill of rights that the enumeration of certain rights shall not be construed to deny or disparage others retained by the people."

He further stated, referring to the Ninth Amendment:

"This clause was manifestly introduced to prevent any perverse or ingenious misapplication of the well-known maxim, that an affirmation in particular cases implies a negation in all others; and, *e converso*, that a negation in particular cases implies an affirmation in all others."

These statements of Madison and Story make clear that the Framers did not intend that the first eight amendments be construed to exhaust the basic and fundamental rights which the Constitution guaranteed to the people.

To hold that a right so basic and fundamental and so deep-rooted in our society as the right of privacy in marriage may be infringed because that right is not guaranteed in so many words by the first eight amendments to the Constitution is to ignore the Ninth Amendment and to give it no effect whatsoever. Moreover, a judicial construction that this fundamental right is not protected by the Constitution because it is not mentioned in explicit terms by one of the first eight amendments or elsewhere in the Constitution would violate the Ninth Amendment, which specifically states that "[t]he enumeration in the Constitution, of certain rights, shall not be construed to deny or disparage others retained by the people.…"

In determining which rights are fundamental, judges are not left at large to decide cases in light of their personal and private notions. Rather, they must look to the "traditions and [collective] conscience of our people" to determine whether a principle is "so rooted [there]… as to be ranked as fundamental." The inquiry is whether a right involved "is of such a character that it cannot be denied without violating those 'fundamental principles of liberty and justice which lie at the base of all our civil and political institutions'.… ."

Although the Constitution does not speak in so many words of the right of privacy in marriage, I cannot believe that it offers these fundamental rights no protection. The fact that no particular provision of the Constitution explicitly forbids the State from disrupting the traditional relation of the family—a relation as old and as fundamental as our entire civilization—surely does not show that the Government was meant to have the power to do so. Rather, as the Ninth Amendment expressly recognizes, there are fundamental personal rights such as this one, which are protected from abridgment by the Government though not specifically mentioned in the Constitution.

The logic of the dissents would sanction federal or state legislation that seems to me even more plainly unconstitutional than the statute before us. Surely the Government, absent a showing of a compelling subordinating state interest, could not decree that all husbands and wives must be sterilized after two children have been born to them. Yet by their reasoning such an invasion of marital privacy would not be subject to constitutional challenge because, while it might be "silly," no provision of the Constitution specifically prevents the Government from curtailing the marital right to bear children and raise a family. While it may shock some of my Brethren that the

Court today holds that the Constitution protects the right of marital privacy, in my view it is far more shocking to believe that the personal liberty guaranteed by the Constitution does not include protection against such totalitarian limitation of family size, which is at complete variance with our constitutional concepts. Yet, if upon a showing of a slender basis of rationality, a law outlawing voluntary birth control by married persons is valid, then, by the same reasoning, a law requiring compulsory birth control also would seem to be valid. In my view, however, both types of law would unjustifiably intrude upon rights of marital privacy which are constitutionally protected.

**MR. JUSTICE BLACK, with whom MR. JUSTICE STEWART joins, dissenting.**

I agree with my Brother STEWART'S dissenting opinion. And like him I do not to any extent whatever base my view that this Connecticut law is constitutional on a belief that the law is wise or that its policy is a good one. In order that there may be no room at all to doubt why I vote as I do, I feel constrained to add that the law is every bit as offensive to me as it is to my Brethren of the majority and my Brothers HARLAN, WHITE and GOLDBERG who, reciting reasons why it is offensive to them, hold it unconstitutional. There is no single one of the graphic and eloquent strictures and criticisms fired at the policy of this Connecticut law either by the Court's opinion or by those of my concurring Brethren to which I cannot subscribe— except their conclusion that the evil qualities they see in the law make it unconstitutional.

The Court talks about a constitutional "right of privacy" as though there is some constitutional provision or provisions forbidding any law ever to be passed which might abridge the "privacy" of individuals. But there is not. There are, of course, guarantees in certain specific constitutional provisions which are designed in part to protect privacy at certain times and places with respect to certain activities. Such, for example, is the Fourth Amendment's guarantee against "unreasonable searches and seizures." But I think it belittles that Amendment to talk about it as though it protects nothing but "privacy." To treat it that way is to give it a niggardly interpretation, not the kind of liberal reading I think any Bill of Rights provision should be given. The average man would

very likely not have his feelings soothed any more by having his property seized openly than by having it seized privately and by stealth. He simply wants his property left alone. And a person can be just as much, if not more, irritated, annoyed and injured by an unceremonious public arrest by a policeman as he is by a seizure in the privacy of his office or home.

One of the most effective ways of diluting or expanding a constitutionally guaranteed right is to substitute for the crucial word or words of a constitutional guarantee another word or words, more or less flexible and more or less restricted in meaning. This fact is well illustrated by the use of the term "right of privacy" as a comprehensive substitute for the Fourth Amendment's guarantee against "unreasonable searches and seizures." "Privacy" is a broad, abstract and ambiguous concept which can easily be shrunken in meaning but which can also, on the other hand, easily be interpreted as a constitutional ban against many things other than searches and seizures. I like my privacy as well as the next one, but I am nevertheless compelled to admit that government has a right to invade it unless prohibited by some specific constitutional provision. For these reasons I cannot agree with the Court's judgment and the reasons it gives for holding this Connecticut law unconstitutional.

The due process argument which my Brothers HARLAN and WHITE adopt here is based, as their opinions indicate, on the premise that this Court is vested with power to invalidate all state laws that it considers to be arbitrary, capricious, unreasonable, or oppressive, or on this Court's belief that a particular state law under scrutiny has no "rational or justifying" purpose, or is offensive to a "sense of fairness and justice." If these formulas based on "natural justice," or others which mean the same thing, are to prevail, they require judges to determine what is or is not constitutional on the basis of their own appraisal of what laws are unwise or unnecessary. The power to make such decisions is of course that of a legislative body. Surely it has to be admitted that no provision of the Constitution specifically gives such blanket power to courts to exercise such a supervisory veto over the wisdom and value of legislative policies and to hold unconstitutional those laws which they believe unwise or dangerous.

I repeat so as not to be misunderstood that this Court does have power, which it should exercise, to hold laws unconstitutional where they are forbidden by the Federal Constitution. My point is that there is no provision of the Constitution which either expressly or impliedly vests power in this Court to sit as a supervisory agency over acts of duly constituted legislative bodies and set aside their laws because of the Court's belief that the legislative policies adopted are unreasonable, unwise, arbitrary, capricious or irrational. The adoption of such a loose, flexible, uncontrolled standard for holding laws unconstitutional, if ever it is finally achieved, will amount to a great unconstitutional shift of power to the courts which I believe and am constrained to say will be bad for the courts and worse for the country. Subjecting federal and state laws to such an unrestrained and unrestrainable judicial control as to the wisdom of legislative enactments would, I fear, jeopardize the separation of governmental powers that the Framers set up and at the same time threaten to take away much of the power of States to govern themselves which the Constitution plainly intended them to have.

I realize that many good and able men have eloquently spoken and written, sometimes in rhapsodical strains, about the duty of this Court to keep the Constitution in tune with the times. The idea is that the Constitution must be changed from time to time and that this Court is charged with a duty to make those changes. For myself, I must with all deference reject that philosophy. The Constitution makers knew the need for change and provided for it. Amendments suggested by the people's elected representatives can be submitted to the people or their selected agents for ratification. That method of change was good for our Fathers, and being some-what old-fashioned I must add it is good enough for me. And so, I cannot rely on the Due Process Clause or the Ninth Amendment or any mysterious and uncertain natural law concept as a reason for striking down this state law. The Due Process Clause with an "arbitrary and capricious" or "shocking to the conscience" formula was liberally used by this Court to strike down economic legislation in the early decades of this century, threatening, many people thought, the tranquility and stability of the Nation. See, e.g., *Lochner v. New York*, 198 U.S. 45. That formula, based on subjective considerations of "natural justice," is no less dangerous when used to enforce this Court's views about personal rights than those about economic rights. I had thought that we had laid that formula, as a means for striking down state legislation, to rest once and for all.

## MR. JUSTICE STEWART, whom MR. JUSTICE BLACK joins, dissenting.

Since 1879 Connecticut has had on its books a law which forbids the use of contraceptives by anyone. I think this is an uncommonly silly law. As a practical matter, the law is obviously unenforceable, except in the oblique context of the present case. As a philosophical matter, I believe the use of contraceptives in the relationship of marriage should be left to personal and private choice, based upon each individual's moral, ethical, and religious beliefs. As a matter of social policy, I think professional counsel about methods of birth control should be available to all, so that each individual's choice can be meaningfully made. But we are not asked in this case to say whether we think this law is unwise, or even asinine. We are asked to hold that it violates the United States Constitution. And that I cannot do.

## Document Analysis

The question before the Court was this: do individual citizens have a fundamental right to privacy within a marriage, and if so, does the Connecticut law violate this right? The Court interpreted the Constitution as protecting a fundamental right to privacy, specifically in marriage, as their basis for the ruling. The justices were certain no one specific provision found within the Bill of Rights was applicable to the question they were facing, and nowhere does the Constitution discuss or identify a person's right to privacy. Justice Douglas, writing for the Court, stated there were "penumbras" found within the Constitution that created zones of privacy. In other words, within the shadowy language of the Constitution, there can be found a protection of marital privacy. Justice Douglas wondered, if the marital right to privacy was not honored, would laws such as Connecticut's allow the police to search married couple's homes "for telltale signs of the use of contraceptives"? Concurring justices' opinions supported the general idea of a right to privacy, but there was disagreement on the source for interpreting this right.

In dissenting opinions, Justices Black and Stewart argued that while the Connecticut law may be "uncommonly silly," the right to privacy is nowhere to be found in the Constitution. Both Black and Stewart found the Connecticut law offensive in its purpose, but both justices felt strongly the Court did not have the authority to create rights not reasonably interpreted as being found within the Constitution. Regardless of the dissents and the lack of specific language citing privacy, the right to privacy was interpreted as existing through the First, Third, Fourth, Fifth, and Ninth Amendments to the Constitution. Additionally, the concurring justices believed the notion of privacy could be interpreted through the Due Process Clause found in the Fourteenth Amendment. These amendments, taken together, should be interpreted to mean citizens have a fundamental right to privacy within a marriage. These zones of privacy work together to protect the marital relationship from legal scrutiny. Because the zones of privacy were found to exist, and due to the fact Connecticut was unable to prove the law criminalizing birth control was mandatory and compelling, the Court struck down the law by a vote of 7–2 five years after the FDA approved oral birth control medication and forty-nine years after the first birth control clinic was opened in this country. Moreover, the ruling made it possible for women to access birth control without fear of legal punishment. This case proved to be extraordinarily important not only to women and the women's rights movement as a whole, but to anyone who values their right to privacy as we know it today.

## Essential Themes

The significance of *Griswold v. Connecticut* still holds major importance, not just for women, but for all citizens of America today. The case of *Griswold v. Connecticut* established the notion that our rights, as protected by the Constitution, include a fundamental right to privacy. While privacy in itself is arguably a valued right, the ruling of this case had other major repercussions, particularly when examining women's rights associated with reproduction. This case was the predecessor of important women's rights cases like *Roe v. Wade* and *Planned Parenthood v. Casey*, and without the precedent set in the *Griswold* case, the struggle for women's reproductive rights could have been prolonged even further. Just eight years later, in the

case of *Roe v. Wade*, the zones of privacy cited in the *Griswold* case were used to make a ruling on a woman's right to have an abortion. Without the ruling in *Griswold v. Connecticut*, it is reasonable to wonder whether the *Roe* ruling would have been the same, thereby altering the scope of women's reproductive rights in America.

Women's reproductive rights issues will always be a political point of contention in American whether women have a fundamental right to make certain choices regarding reproduction. Since the Court's decision in the *Griswold* case, women have been able to control whether or not they reproduce, which has had major beneficial impacts on society. For example, there have been positive changes associated with infant health, including a drop in the infant mortality rate. Women have been able pursue educational or professional goals they may have been unable to engage in if their attention had been focused solely on motherhood. Moving forward, the case of *Griswold v. Connecticut* will undoubtedly serve as a fundamental basis for decisions regarding women's rights debates and other issues of privacy as they move to the forefront of political and legislative agendas across the country.

—*Amber R. Dickinson, PhD*

## Bibliography and Further Reading

Chemerinsky, Erwin. "Rediscovering Brandeis's Right to Privacy." *Brandeis LJ* 45 (2006): 643.

Douglas, William O. *The Court Years, 1939–1975: The Autobiography of William O. Douglas.* New York: Vintage Books, 1981.

Fisher, Louis. *American Constitutional Law.* 5th ed. Vol. 2. Durham, NC: Carolina Academic Press, 2003.

Franklin, Cary. "Griswold and the Public Dimension of the Right to Privacy." *The Yale LJ Forum.* The Yale Law Journal, 2 Mar. 2015. Web.

Irons, Peter. *A People's History of the Supreme Court.* New York: Penguin Books, 2000.

Katin, Ernest. "*Griswold v. Connecticut*: The Justices and Connecticut's Uncommonly Silly Law." *Notre Dame LR* 42 (1967) 5.

Kauper, Paul G. "Penumbras, Peripheries, and Emanations, Things Fundamental and Things Forgotten." *Michigan LR* 46 (1965): 2.

McClosky, Robert. *The American Supreme Court.* 4th ed. Chicago: University of Chicago Press, 2005.

Rothman, Sheila M. *Women's Proper Place: A History of Changing Ideals and Practices, 1870 to the Present.* Vol. 5053. Phoenix, AZ: Basic Books, 1980.

# ■ National Organization for Women (NOW) Founding Statement

**Date:** October 29, 1966
**Author:** Betty Friedan
**Genre:** Charter; political tract

## Summary Overview

In 1966, the National Organization for Women, known as NOW, convened its organizing conference in Washington, DC. The event came in the wake of the federal Equal Employment Opportunity Commission's failure to enforce protections provided under Title VII of the Civil Rights Act of 1964 that banned sex discrimination in employment. The time had come; women activists understood they needed to organize and advocate on behalf of their own civil rights. One of NOW's founders, Betty Friedan, had written the book *The Feminine Mystique* (1963), which ignited a rise in feminism. Friedan also authored the Statement of Purpose reprinted here, using a logic, as she later wrote that "was inexorable. Once we broke through that feminine mystique and called ourselves human—no more, no less—surely we were entitled to enjoyment of the values which were our American, democratic human right" (105). Today, NOW defines itself on its website as the grassroots arm of the women's movement, with more than 500 chapters in the fifty states and Washington, DC.

## Defining Moment

The late nineteenth and early twentieth centuries saw progress for women's rights in the United States, perhaps most definitively with the arrival of women's right to vote in 1920 after the passage of the Nineteenth Amendment. This era is generally considered feminism's "first wave." Following World War II, however, came renewed pressure on women to stay home, take care of their children, and embrace the role of homemaker and wife.

During this time, efforts on behalf of women came slowly. President John F. Kennedy established the President's Commission on the Status of Women, which released a final report in October 1963 that advocated workplace equality. However, it ignored the Equal Rights Amendment that had been proposed, repeatedly, since 1923. Although advisory in nature, the commission's report did spawn similar commissions in many states, a national advisory council, and the Equal Pay Act of 1963.

The Civil Rights Act of 1964 banned discrimination based on race, color, religion, sex or national origin—

and, perhaps inadvertently, created the defining moment of feminism's "second wave." From that act came the Equal Employment Opportunity Commission (EEOC), created to implement Title VII. And from the EEOC, frankly, came mostly only lip service, rather than action to protect women's employment rights. In 1965, the commission voted to continue to allow gender-specific job advertising. Thus, job announcements advertising "men only" or "women only" remained in place—and, in the process, reinforced the norm of men in professional jobs and women limited to helper positions.

At a conference in spring 1966, activists were brought to the boiling point after delegates were denied the opportunity to pass a resolution to demand the EEOC do its job and enforce the ban on sex discrimination. Friedan and others realized that they needed to take action. Friedan wrote the basic tenets of NOW at that conference, writing that the organization would "take the actions needed to bring women into the mainstream of American society, now, full equality for women, in fully equal partnership with men." As she wrote some years later in *It Changed My Life,* "I was forced to spell out in my own mind the implications of 'equality' for women" (4).

The group agreed to convene an organizing conference that fall. Of approximately 300 inaugural NOW members, thirty attended the conference and adopted the Statement of Purpose. NOW moved quickly to take action on the matter of EEOC employment discrimination enforcement and, a year later, turned its attention to a campaign to pass the Equal Rights Amendment.

## Author Biography

Born Bettye Naomi Goldstein in Peoria, Illinois, on February 4, 1921, Friedan graduated from Smith College in 1942 and is best known as the author of *The Feminine Mystique.* Considered groundbreaking upon its publication in 1963, the book—which focused on the unfulfilling and confined role of post-World War II housewives—is widely credited with launching the so-called "second wave" of feminism. Friedan studied psychology on a graduate fellowship at the University of California, Berkeley, where she studied with famed psychologist

NOW founder and president Betty Friedan with, lobbyist Barbara Ireton (1932-1998) and feminist attorney Marguerite Rawalt.

Erik Erikson. She married theater director Carl Friedan in 1947 and went on to write for union-oriented publications. She wrote *The Feminine Mystique* as a suburban mother of three. She and her husband divorced in 1969. She served as founding president of the National Organization for Women and went on to help found the National Association for the Repeal of Abortion Laws, now known as NARAL Pro-Choice America. Friedan authored numerous books and died on her eighty-fifth birthday, February 4, 2006.

## HISTORICAL DOCUMENT

### Statement of Purpose

We, men and women who hereby constitute ourselves as the National Organization for Women, believe that the time has come for a new movement toward true equality for all women in America, and toward a fully equal partnership of the sexes, as part of the world-wide revolution of human rights now taking place within and beyond our national borders.

The purpose of NOW is to take action to bring women into full participation in the mainstream of American society now, exercising all the privileges and responsibilities thereof in truly equal partnership with men.

We believe the time has come to move beyond the abstract argument, discussion and symposia over the status and special nature of women which has raged in America in recent years; the time has come to confront, with concrete action, the conditions that now prevent women from enjoying the equality of opportunity and freedom of choice which is their right, as individual Americans, and as human beings.

NOW is dedicated to the proposition that women, first and foremost, are human beings, who, like all other people in our society, must have the chance to develop their fullest human potential. We believe that women can achieve such equality only by accepting to the full the challenges and responsibilities they share with all other people in our society, as part of the decision-making mainstream of American political, economic and social life.

We organize to initiate or support action, nationally, or in any part of this nation, by individuals or organizations, to break through the silken curtain of prejudice and discrimination against women in government, industry, the professions, the churches, the political parties, the judiciary, the labor unions, in education, science, medicine, law, religion and every other field of importance in American society.

Enormous changes taking place in our society make it both possible and urgently necessary to advance the unfinished revolution of women toward true equality, now. With a life span lengthened to nearly 75 years it is no longer either necessary or possible for women to devote the greater part of their lives to child-rearing; yet childbearing and rearing which continues to be a most important part of most women's lives—still is used to justify barring women from equal professional and economic participation and advance.

Today's technology has reduced most of the productive chores which women once performed in the home and in mass-production industries based upon routine unskilled labor. This same technology has virtually eliminated the quality of muscular strength as a criterion for filling most jobs, while intensifying American industry's need for creative intelligence. In view of this new industrial revolution created by automation in the mid-twentieth century, women can and must participate in old and new fields of society in full equality—or become permanent outsiders.

Despite all the talk about the status of American women in recent years, the actual position of women in the United States has declined, and is declining, to an alarming degree throughout the 1950's and 60's. Although 46.4% of all American women between the ages of 18 and 65 now work outside the home, the overwhelming majority—75%—are in routine clerical, sales, or factory jobs, or they are household workers, cleaning women, hospital attendants. About two-thirds of Negro women workers are in the lowest paid service occupations. Working women are becoming increasingly—not less—concentrated on the bottom of the job ladder. As a consequence full-time women workers today earn on the average only 60% of what men earn, and that wage gap has been increasing over the past twenty-five years in every major industry group. In 1964, of all women with a yearly income, 89% earned under $5,000 a year; half of all full-time year round women workers earned less than $3,690; only 1.4% of full-time year round women workers had an annual income of $10,000 or more.

Further, with higher education increasingly essential in today's society, too few women are entering and finishing college or going on to graduate or professional school. Today, women earn only one in three of the B.A.'s and M.A.'s granted, and one in ten of the PhD's.

In all the professions considered of importance to society, and in the executive ranks of industry and government, women are losing ground. Where they are present it is only a token handful. Women comprise less than 1% of federal judges; less than 4% of all lawyers; 7% of doctors. Yet women represent 51% of the U.S. population. And, increasingly, men are replacing women in the top positions in secondary and elementary schools, in social work, and in libraries—once thought to be women's fields.

Official pronouncements of the advance in the status of women hide not only the reality of this dangerous decline, but the fact that nothing is being done to stop it. The excellent reports of the President's Commission on the Status of Women and of the State Commissions have not been fully implemented. Such Commissions have power only to advise. They have no power to enforce their recommendation; nor have they the freedom to organize American women and men to press for action on them. The reports of these commissions have, however, created a basis upon which it is now possible to build. Discrimination in employment on the basis of sex is now prohibited by federal law, in Title VII of the Civil Rights Act of 1964. But although nearly one-third of the cases brought before the Equal Employment Opportunity Commission during the first year dealt with sex discrimination and the proportion is increasing dramatically, the Commission has not made clear its intention to enforce the law with the same seriousness on behalf of women as of other victims of discrimination. Many of these cases were Negro women, who are the victims of double discrimination of race and sex. Until now, too few women's organizations and official spokesmen have been willing to speak out against these dangers facing women. Too many women have been restrained by the fear of being called "feminist." There is no civil rights movement to speak for women, as there has been for Negroes and other victims of discrimination. The National Organization for Women must therefore begin to speak.

WE BELIEVE that the power of American law, and the protection guaranteed by the U.S. Constitution to the civil rights of all individuals, must be effectively applied and enforced to isolate and remove patterns of sex discrimination, to ensure equality of opportunity in employment and education, and equality of civil and political rights and responsibilities on behalf of women, as well as for Negroes and other deprived groups.

We realize that women's problems are linked to many broader questions of social justice; their solution will require concerted action by many groups. Therefore, convinced that human rights for all are indivisible, we expect to give active support to the common cause of equal rights for all those who suffer discrimination and deprivation, and we call upon other organizations committed to such goals to support our efforts toward equality for women.

WE DO NOT ACCEPT the token appointment of a few women to high-level positions in government and industry as a substitute for serious continuing effort to recruit and advance women according to their individual abilities. To this end, we urge American government and industry to mobilize the same resources of ingenuity and command with which they have solved problems of far greater difficulty than those now impeding the progress of women.

WE BELIEVE that this nation has a capacity at least as great as other nations, to innovate new social institutions which will enable women to enjoy the true equality of opportunity and responsibility in society, without conflict with their responsibilities as mothers and homemakers. In such innovations, America does not lead the Western world, but lags by decades behind many European countries. We do not accept the traditional assumption that a woman has to choose between marriage and motherhood, on the one hand, and serious participation in industry or the professions on the other. We question the present expectation that all normal women will retire from job or profession for 10 or 15 years, to devote their full time to raising children, only to reenter the job market at a relatively minor level. This, in itself, is a deterrent to the aspirations of women, to their acceptance into management or professional training courses, and to the very possibility of equality of opportunity or real choice, for all but a few women. Above all, we reject the assumption that these problems are the unique responsibility of each individual woman, rather than a basic social dilemma which society must solve. True equality of opportunity and freedom of choice for women requires such practical, and possible innovations as a nationwide network of child-care centers, which will make it unnecessary for women to retire completely from society until their children are grown, and national programs to provide retraining for women who have chosen to care for their children full-time.

WE BELIEVE that it is as essential for every girl to be educated to her full potential of human ability as it is for every boy—with the knowledge that such education is the key to effective participation in today's economy and that, for a girl as for a boy, education can only be serious where there is expectation that it will be used in society. We believe that American educators are capable of devising means of imparting such expectations to girl students. Moreover, we consider the decline in the proportion of women receiving higher and professional education to be evidence of discrimination. This discrimination may take the form of quotas against the admission of women to colleges, and professional schools; lack of encouragement by parents, counselors and educators; denial of loans or fellowships; or the traditional or arbitrary procedures in graduate and professional training geared in terms of men, which inadvertently discriminate against women. We believe that the same serious attention must be given to high school dropouts who are girls as to boys.

WE REJECT the current assumptions that a man must carry the sole burden of supporting himself, his wife, and family, and that a woman is automatically entitled to lifelong support by a man upon her marriage, or that marriage, home and family are primarily woman's world and responsibility—hers, to dominate—his to support. We believe that a true partnership between the sexes demands a different concept of marriage, an equitable sharing of the responsibilities of home and children and of the economic burdens of their support. We believe that proper recognition should be given to the economic and social value of homemaking and child-care. To these ends, we will seek to open a reexamination of laws and mores governing marriage and divorce, for we believe that the current state of "half-equity" between the sexes discriminates against both men and women, and is the cause of much unnecessary hostility between the sexes.

WE BELIEVE that women must now exercise their political rights and responsibilities as American citizens. They must refuse to be segregated on the basis of sex into separate-and-not-equal ladies' auxiliaries in the political parties, and they must demand representation according to their numbers in the regularly constituted party committees—at local, state, and national levels—and in the informal power structure, participating fully in the selection of candidates and political decision-making, and running for office themselves.

IN THE INTERESTS OF THE HUMAN DIGNITY OF WOMEN, we will protest, and endeavor to change, the false image of women now prevalent in the mass media, and in the texts, ceremonies, laws, and practices of our major social institutions. Such images perpetuate contempt for women by society and by women for themselves. We are similarly opposed to all policies and practices—in church, state, college, factory, or office—which, in the guise of protectiveness, not only deny opportunities but also foster in women self-denigration, dependence, and evasion of responsibility, undermine their confidence in their own abilities and foster contempt for women.

NOW WILL HOLD ITSELF INDEPENDENT OF ANY POLITICAL PARTY in order to mobilize the political power of all women and men intent on our goals. We will strive to ensure that no party, candidate, president, senator, governor, congressman, or any public official who betrays or ignores the principle of full equality between the sexes is elected or appointed to office. If it is necessary to mobilize the votes of men and women who believe in our cause, in order to win for women the final right to be fully free and equal human beings, we so commit ourselves.

WE BELIEVE THAT women will do most to create a new image of women by acting now, and by speaking out in behalf of their own equality, freedom, and human dignity—not in pleas for special privilege, nor in enmity toward men, who are also victims of the current, half-equality between the sexes—but in an active, self-respecting partnership with men. By so doing, women will develop confidence in their own ability to determine actively, in partnership with men, the conditions of their life, their choices, their future and their society.

## Document Analysis

At a time when the civil rights movement was making strides for African Americans, the group that came together to form NOW drew a line in the sand on behalf of women. No more dodging equal employment by installing token women in the occasional position of influence. Women deserve equal partnership with men, and Friedan's statement reflects clear, forceful positions backed by the intent of action to gain those goals.

The statement opens by putting women's rights in the context of "the world-wide revolution of human rights now taking place within and beyond our national borders" and soon calls for moving "beyond the abstract argument, discussion, and symposia" to "confront, with concrete action, the conditions that now prevent women from enjoying the equality of opportunity and freedom of choice which is their right." A prevailing attitude at the time believed that women belonged at home because, as mothers, their primary job was to bear and raise children and take care of the home. The statement pushes back against that notion, pointing out that, given a seventy-five-year lifespan, child-rearing consumes only a portion of a woman's life. The language used reflects how recently that lifespan was seen to have lengthened; "it is no longer either necessary or possible for women to devote the greater part of their lives to child-rearing."

Similarly, technology had "virtually eliminated the quality of muscular strength as a criterion" for filling the types of unskilled labor jobs often held by women, not to mention household chores. This freed them to contribute economically, intellectually, and creatively to their country, the statement goes on to argue. And yet a list of statistics showed the decline of American women during the 1950s and 60s: only a token few held significant professional positions, such as lawyers or doctors, and, with 75 percent in routine lower-level jobs, women brought home an average of only 60 percent of men's earnings.

The plight of African American women is addressed as "double discrimination," and highlights a major contributor to the formation of NOW. Sex discrimination was banned under Title VII of the Civil Rights Act of 1964, yet nearly one-third of the cases brought before the Equal Employment Opportunity Commission in its first year "dealt with sex discrimination and the proportion is increasing dramatically." Still, the commission,

proffers the statement, "has not made clear its intention to enforce the law with the same seriousness on behalf of women as of other victims of discrimination." Many of the cases were those of African American women.

Women did not have to choose between motherhood and marriage on the one hand, or a career on the other. Rather, their full participation as equal partners to men, and in the US economy, both benefits society and recognizes the human rights of women. Such were the views that led to the founding of NOW.

## Essential Themes

Bringing women out of the home and into "full participation in the mainstream of American society" recognizes a fundamental right held by women and also benefits the society. This is one point stressed in the document. Women, it says, deserve equal access to employment opportunities, education, and the responsibilities of marriage, including homemaking and child-rearing. Thus is the need for women to be financially dependent on men rejected by the NOW organizers. Instead, action to attain the organization's goals is promised by the Statement of Purpose. NOW was formed as an action group, but it also needed to articulate, as here, its purpose, goals, and methods.

—Allison Blake

## Bibliography and Additional Reading

Friedan, Betty. *It Changed My Life: Writings on the Women's Movement.* Cambridge, MA: Harvard UP, 1998. Print.

_____. *The Feminine Mystique.* 1963. Cambridge, MA: Harvard UP, 1998. Print.

Keetley, Dawn & John Pettegrew. *Public Women, Public Words: A Documentary History of American Feminism.* Vol. 2. Lanham, MD: Rowman & Littlefield, 2005. Print.

Lewis, Jone Johnson. "President's Commission on the Status of Women." *About Education.* About.com, 2015. Web.

Murray, Pauli & Mary O. Eastwood. *Jane Crow and the Law: Sex discrimination and Title VII.* Durham, NC: Sallie Bingham Center for Women's History and Culture, 1965. Print.

*National Organization for Women Official Website.* National Organization for Women, 2015. Web.now.org.

# ■ An Act Ending Sex Discrimination in Government Employment

**Date:** October 13, 1967
**Author:** Lyndon Baines Johnson
**Genre:** Executive order

## Summary Overview

Looking back on the presidency of Lyndon Baines Johnson, it is easy to focus entirely on the failures inherent to the Vietnam War and ignore the administration's many achievements in the field of civil rights. It was under Johnson that the United States saw the dismantling of Jim Crow, the completion of racial integration, and the first large steps toward gender equality. What Johnson could not negotiate through Congress, he pushed through by the power of the executive branch, often through the use of executive orders. In fact, few other presidential decrees had as much impact on women's rights as executive order 11375, signed on October 13, 1967. An attempt to strengthen the gender provisions of the Civil Rights Act of 1964, the executive order had wide-ranging and long-lasting societal consequences and reshaped both public and private employment practices. While the push for governmental action helped launch the National Organization for Women (NOW), the order itself ultimately led to millions more American women entering the workplace.

## Defining Moment

Immediately following the ratification of the Nineteenth Amendment in 1920, women's rights groups began vigorously campaigning for greater equality in American society, arguing that the right to vote alone would not be enough to level the playing field. Citing employment discrimination and lower wages based on gender, along with expectations for women to remain in traditional roles inside the home, they pushed for legally guaranteed protection and opportunity. In 1923, Alice Paul, the suffragist leader of the National Women's Party introduced the Equal Rights Amendment (ERA) to Congress, where—despite wide support—it languished, often failing to move past committee. In the 1950s, President Dwight Eisenhower urged Congress to pass the ERA; however, as a means to slow the legislation's progress, conservatives added provisions to the amendment, forcing its sponsors to withdraw and resubmit. As a way to appease the women's movement, President John F. Kennedy created the President's Commission on the Status of Women, a group of twenty presidentially appointed legislators and philanthropists led by Eleanor Roosevelt, who was personally opposed to the ERA. In 1963, the commission helped win passage of the Equal Pay Act, a law that banned unequal pay based on gender across numerous professions. Then in 1964, the commission, working with feminist leaders such as Paul, helped win the inclusion of gender in the Civil Rights Act of 1964, which banned workplace discrimination on the basis of race, religion, and national origin.

Despite this victory, the gender provision in the Civil Rights Act was largely ignored, much to the frustration of women's groups across the country. Even the newly created Equal Employment Opportunity Commission (EEOC) led by Franklin Roosevelt, Jr. decreed that job advertisements segregated by gender were permissible. In direct response to repeated failures to enforce the law, twenty-eight feminist leaders, among them such notables as Betty Friedan and Pauli Murray, established the National Organization for Women (NOW) in 1966 and began to put pressure on the president to enforce the gender provisions. Franklin Roosevelt, Jr. and others argued that without the direction of the congressional or executive branches, gender employment equality could not be achieved, as no clear guidance existed on how to enforce the law. It was in this light that President Johnson signed Executive Order 11375, adding gender to earlier anti-discrimination provisions outlined in his Executive Order 11246. With the stroke of a pen, Johnson made it illegal for women to be discriminated against in a wide swath of professions, including administration and teaching.

## Author Biography

Lyndon Baines Johnson was born in Stonewall, Texas, on August 27, 1908. The oldest of five children, Johnson gravitated toward debate and public speaking at an early age. After receiving a degree in education, Johnson first went into teaching and then, in 1930, politics.

After receiving a law degree and having worked as a congressional aide, Johnson was elected to Congress as a Democrat in 1937 to represent Texas' tenth congressional district. A devoted member of Roosevelt's New Deal coalition, Johnson soon made a name for himself as a wheeler and dealer, able to convince even the most obstinate foes of the righteousness of his cause. After a distinguished naval career during World War II, Johnson was elected to the United States Senate and quickly rose through the ranks, first to become majority whip and later the leader of the Senate Democrats. Respected, admired, and feared, Johnson ran for president in the 1960 Democratic primary. Having lost to his chief rival, the junior senator from Massachusetts, John F. Kennedy, Johnson begrudgingly, and much to the chagrin of the Kennedys, accepted the nomination as vice president. Often marginalized by the Kennedy administration, Johnson became president after Kennedy's assassination in November 1963 and was elected in his own right in 1964 by an impressive margin. Despite having done considerable work on social welfare and civil rights, Johnson's presidency was marred by the growing war in Vietnam. Facing ever more hostile public opinion, Johnson chose not to run for reelection in 1968 and withdrew from public life. Lyndon Baines Johnson died on January 22, 1973.

## HISTORICAL DOCUMENT

It is the policy of the United States Government to provide equal opportunity in Federal employment and in employment by Federal contractors on the basis of merit and without discrimination because of race, color, religion, sex or national origin.

The Congress, by enacting Title VII of the Civil Rights Act of 1964, enunciated a national policy of equal employment opportunity in private employment, without discrimination because of race, color, religion, sex or national origin.

Executive Order No. 11246 of September 24, 1965, carried forward a program of equal employment opportunity in Government employment, employment by Federal contractors and subcontractors and employment under Federally assisted construction contracts regardless of race, creed, color or national origin.

It is desirable that the equal employment opportunity programs provided for in Executive Order No. 11246 expressly embrace discrimination on account of sex.

Now, THEREFORE, by virtue of the authority vested in me as President of the United States by the Constitution and statutes of the United States, it is ordered that Executive Order No. 11246 of September 24, 1965, be amended as follows:

(1) Section 101 of Part I, concerning nondiscrimination in Government employment, is revised to read as follows:

"SECTION 101. It is the policy of the Government of the United States to provide equal opportunity in Federal employment for all qualified persons, to prohibit discrimination in employment because of race, color, religion, sex or national origin, and to promote the full realization of equal employment opportunity through a positive, continuing program in each executive department and agency. The policy of equal opportunity applies to every aspect of Federal employment policy and practice."

(2) Section 104 of Part I is revised to read as follows:

"SECTION 104. The Civil Service Commission shall provide for the prompt, fair, and impartial consideration of all complaints of discrimination in Federal employment on the basis of race, color, religion, sex or national origin. Procedures for the consideration of complaints shall include at least one impartial review within the executive department or agency and shall provide for appeal to the Civil Service Commission."

(3) Paragraphs (1) and (2) of the quoted required contract provisions in section 202 of Part II, concerning nondiscrimination in employment by Government contractors and subcontractors, are revised to read as follows:

"(1) The contractor will not discriminate against any employee or applicant for employment because of race, color, religion, sex, or national origin. The contractor will take affirmative action to ensure that applicants are employed, and that employees are treated during employment, without regard to their race, color, religion, sex or national origin. Such action shall include, but not be limited to the following: employment, upgrading, demotion, or transfer; recruitment or recruitment advertising; layoff or termination; rates of pay or other forms of compensation; and selection for training, including apprenticeship. The contractor agrees to post in conspicuous places, available to employees and applicants for employment, notices to be provided by the contracting officer setting forth the provisions of this nondiscrimination clause.

"(2) The contractor will, in all solicitations or advertisements for employees placed by or on behalf of the contractor, state that all qualified applicants will receive consideration for employment without regard to race, color, religion, sex or national origin."

(4) Section 203 (d) of Part II is revised to read as follows:

"(d) The contracting agency or the Secretary of Labor may direct that any bidder or prospective contractor or subcontractor shall submit, as part of his Compliance Report, a statement in writing, signed by an authorized officer or agent on behalf of any labor union or any agency referring workers or providing or supervising apprenticeship or other training, with which the bidder or prospective contractor deals, with supporting information, to the effect that the signer's practices and policies do not discriminate on the grounds of race, color, religion, sex or national origin, and that the signer either will affirmatively cooperate in the implementation of the policy and provisions of this order or that it consents and agrees that recruitment, employment, and the terms and conditions of employment under the proposed contract shall be in accordance with the purposes and provisions of the order. In the event that the union, or the agency shall refuse to execute such a statement, the Compliance Report shall so certify and set forth what efforts have been made to secure such a statement and such additional factual material as the contracting agency or the Secretary of Labor may require."

The amendments to Part I shall be effective 30 days after the date of this order. The amendments to Part II shall be effective one year after the date of this order.

LYNDON B. JOHNSON
The White House
October 13, 1967

## GLOSSARY

**apprenticeship:** the process by which someone learns a trade by working under someone skilled in that trade

**contractors:** a person, working under contract, who performs a job

**enunciated:** said clearly

## Document Analysis

Johnson's Executive Order 11375 begins by laying out the reasons for the decree. The United States must ensure equal protection against discrimination, as spelled out in the Civil Rights Act of 1964. A previous executive order, 11246, pushed forward a program of equal government workplace protection, but it did not go far enough. Executive Order 11375 is an amendment of 11246 to include gender. Section 101 expressly stipulates that the government has to give equal opportunity for federal employment to all persons no matter their "race, color, religion, sex or national origin." Section 104 empowers the Civil Service Commission to promptly investigate "all complaints of discrimination in Federal employment." The process for such investigation is to include impartial review. Johnson's executive order further extends beyond federal employees to include contractors and subcontractors and anyone who accepts federal funds. More importantly, equality must extend to: "employment, upgrading, demotion, or transfer; recruitment or recruitment advertising; layoff or termination; rates of pay or other forms of compensation; and selection for training, including apprenticeship." Equal treatment must extend to all hiring practices and regulations. Finally, Section 203 directs the secretary of labor to only accept bid for federal money from contractors who have similarly agreed to equal treatment of all employees. In other words, not only government workers are ensured equal treatment, but anyone who might also do business with the government or accept federal funds. All of the various provisions would be enacted within the next year. Overall, the executive order is a clear legal stipulation, outlining the need to promote universal equality, while outlining how it's to be achieved.

## Essential Themes

Lyndon Johnson's signing of Executive Order 11375 represents both the many small victories of the women's movement and simultaneously its biggest failure. On the one hand, the signing of Executive Order 11375 was another small step toward greater equality between the sexes. Building on the incremental success of the Equal Pay Act and the larger success of the inclusion of gender in the Civil Rights Act of 1964, the executive order focused gender equality enforcement, giving federal agencies the recourse needed to better investigate and police instances of discrimination. Over the next several decades, the presidential order would be strengthened even more and used to bring greater equality to professions across the public and private sector. By the 1970s, the Carter administration used Johnson's order to promote equality in corporations and across colleges and universities. As the rate of women entering the workforce steadily increased, the Department of Labor and the equality agencies created in the 1960s helped promote fairer pay and fairer treatment for all Americans, regardless of gender.

Yet, in many ways, Executive Order 11375 represents the limit of what the government was willing to do on the question of gender equality. By including gender in the Civil Rights Act of 1964 and later passing smaller pieces of legislation strengthened by executive order, the Equal Rights Amendment first introduced to Congress in 1923 lost even more momentum. Anti-ERA conservatives and feminist leaders such as Eleanor Roosevelt similarly argued that the ERA was no longer relevant, given the protections included in civil rights legislation. In 1980, the Republican Party officially dropped its support for the ERA and Ronald Reagan became the first president to come out openly in opposition against its ratification. Without the protection afforded by a constitutional amendment, gender equality took a step back as a feminist backlash, led by conservative activist Phyllis Schlafly, called for a return to traditional gender roles. Although the majority of women work, often right alongside men, women's wages continue to lag behind. The United States is still one of the few developed countries that does not offer paid family leave or require of companies mandatory maternity leave. The United States is also one of the few major industrialized nations that has never had a woman serve in the highest office of the government.

—*KP Dawes, MA*

## Bibliography and Additional Reading

Berry, Mary Frances. *Why the ERA Failed: Politics, Women's Rights, and the Amending Process of the Constitution.* New York: Indiana UP, 1988. Print.

Collins, Gail. *When Everything Changed: The Amazing Journey of American Women from 1960 to the Present.* New York: Little Brown, 2009. Print.

Flexner, Eleanor & Ellen Fitzpatrick. *Century of Struggle: The Woman's Rights Movement in the United States.* Boston: Belknap Press, 1996. Print.

# ■ Position Paper Regarding the Equal Rights Amendment (ERA)

**Date:** 1967
**Author:** National Organization for Women (NOW)
**Genre:** Political tract

## Summary Overview

The year after the National Organization for Women (NOW) was founded in 1966, the feminist organization issued this informational paper backing the Equal Rights Amendment (ERA). Already devoted to the idea that women should share equally with men in social and economic responsibilities, NOW subsequently took on the ERA as a priority plank in its platform, calling it the "Bill of Rights for Women."

The ERA was nothing new; it had been introduced in every Congress since 1923. The National Women's Party, originally formed to lobby for women's suffrage, turned its attention to the ERA after women finally gained the right to vote in 1920. Alice Paul, founder of the party, drafted the amendment, which was adopted by her party as a resolution seeking "[t]he security of an amendment to the United States Constitution stating men and women shall have equal rights throughout the United States and every place subject to its jurisdiction." But it was perennially bottled up in committee and had come to a vote only once, in 1946, when it failed to command even a simple majority in the Senate.

Finally, in 1972, the required two-thirds of both the US House of Representatives and the US Senate proposed the Equal Rights Amendment for ratification by the state legislatures. Under Article V of the Constitution, it needed approval of three-quarters, or thirty-eight states, in order for it to become part of the US Constitution. Thirty states approved it within a year. Then came opposition leader Phyllis Schlafly and her Stop ERA, arguing that financially dependent housewives and women in the workforce needed special protections that would be prohibited by the amendment and that young women would be made subject to the draft if it were revived. Many labor unions had worked hard for such protections, and although the AFL-CIO, for example, abandoned its opposition in 1973, some unions remained strongly allied with the socially conservative Schlafly forces.

By 1978, a year before its stated deadline, thirty-five states had ratified the amendment. The time limit was extended by three years, but no additional state ratified it. It had been ratified by thirty-five states—although five later voted to rescind their ratifications, a procedure of uncertain validity. The amendment died in 1982.

## Defining Moment

NOW's position paper—and the organization itself—arrived during the first years of the so-called "second wave" of feminism that emerged as the civil rights movement gathered steam, decades after the first wave that achieved a woman's right to vote. The ERA's passage was an early priority after the organization tackled its galvanizing goal of holding the federal Equal Employment Opportunity Commission (EEOC) accountable for equal employment opportunities. In addition to backing the ERA, NOW became the first organization to back legalized abortion. At a time when the equal rights of women were front and center, passage of the ERA gained momentum.

NOW's commitment to the Equal Rights Amendment came in 1967, only three years after passage of the Civil Rights Act. Title VII of the act, which bans employment discrimination against women and minorities, was seen by NOW as not being enforced by the EEOC, which had determined, for example, that men-only and women-only job listings and hiring criteria did not represent illegal discrimination.

U.S. Representative Martha Griffiths championed the ERA. By Leffler, Warren K.

## HISTORICAL DOCUMENT

### ERA POSITION PAPER— CONSTITUTIONAL PROTECTION AGAINST SEX DISCRIMINATION

An informational memorandum prepared for the National Organization for Women (NOW) regarding the Equal Rights Amendment and similar proposals.

NOW's Statement of Purpose endorses the principle that women should exercise all the privileges and responsibilities of American society in equal partnership with men and states that:

"the power of American law, and the protection guaranteed b the U. S. Constitution to the civil rights of all individuals, must be effectively applied and enforced to isolate and remove patterns of sex discrimination, to ensure equality of opportunity in employment and education, and equality of civil and political rights and responsibilities on behalf of women, as well as for Negroes and other deprived groups."

The Fourteenth Amendment to the United States Constitution provides that no State shall "deprive any person of life, liberty or property, without due process of law; nor deny to any person with its jurisdiction the equal protection of the laws." The Fourteenth Amendment restricts the States and the "due process" clause of the Fifth Amendment similarly restricts the Federal Government from interfering with these individual rights. These are the constitutional provisions under which much of the civil rights for Negroes litigation has been brought and it is now clear that any radical distinction in law or official practice is unconstitutional.

The President's commission on the Status of Women recommendation.

The issue of constitutionality of sex distinctions in the law has been raised in a number of cases under the 5th and 14th Amendments. However, the Civil and Political Rights Committee of the President's Commission found in 1963:

"The courts have consistently upheld laws providing different treatment for women than for men, usually on the basis of the State's special interest in protecting the health and welfare of women. In no 14th Amendment case alleging discrimination on account of sex has the United States Supreme Court held that a law classifying persons on the basis of sex is unreasonable and therefore unconstitutional. Until such time as the Supreme Court reexamines the doctrine of 'sex as a basis for legislative classification' and promulgates the standards determining which types of laws and official practices treating men and women differently are reasonable and which are not, it will remain unclear whether women can enforce their rights under the 14th amendment or whether there is a constitutional gap which can only be filled by a Federal constitutional amendment."

The President's Commission on the Status of Women in its report to President Kennedy in October, 1963, declared:

"Equality of rights under the law for all persons, male or female, is so basic to democracy and its commitment to the ultimate value of the individual that it must be reflected in the fundamental law of the land."

The Commission went on to say that it believed that the principle of equal rights for men and women was embodied in the 5th and 14th amendments, and accordingly, "a constitutional amendment need not now be sought in order to establish this principle." The Commission stated further:

"Early and definitive court pronouncement, particularly by the U.S. Supreme Court, is urgently needed with regard to the validity under the 5th and 14th amendments of laws and official practices discriminating against women, to the end that the principle of equality become firmly established in constitutional doctrine."

The Commission report optimistically does not include any recognition of the possibility that the Court might rule against women seeking to invoke the protection of the Constitution.

## History of the Equal Rights Amendment
The constitutional amendment which the Commission stated it did not deem necessary to endorse in 1963 was the proposed Equal Rights Amendment. That amendment, which has been introduced in every Congress since 1923, in its present form would provide (see S.J. Res. 54, 90th Congress. 1st Sess.):

"Equality of Rights under the law shall not be denied or abridged by the United States or by any State on account of sex."

Congress has in the past held hearings on the Equal Rights Amendment, most recently in 1948 and in 1956, and the amendment has twice passed the Senate, but with a provision added that the amendment "shall not be construed to impair any rights, benefits, or exemptions now or hereafter conferred by law, upon persons of the female sex." The effect of the added provision, known as the "Hayden rider," has been to kill the Equal Rights Amendment, since proponents of the amendment obviously would not wish to support the addition. The Senate Judiciary Committee has frequently reported favorably on the amendment and the recent reports specifically oppose the "Hayden rider" pointing out that the qualification "is not acceptable to women who want equal rights under the law. It is under the guise of so-called 'rights' or 'benefits' that women have been treated unequally and denied opportunities which are available to men".

## Effect of the Equal Rights Amendment

Constitutional amendments, like statutes, are interpreted by the courts in light of intent of Congress. Committee reports on a proposal are regarded by the courts as the most persuasive evidence of the intended meaning of a provision. Therefore, the probable meaning and effect of the Equal Rights Amendment can be ascertained from the Senate Judiciary Committee reports (which have been the same in recent years):

1.  The amendment would restrict only governmental action, and would not apply to purely private action. What constitutes "State action" would be the same as under the 14th amendment and as developed in the 14th amendment litigation on other subjects.

2.  Special restrictions on property rights of married women would be unconstitutional; married women could engage in business as freely as a member of the male sex; inheritance rights of widows would be the same as for widowers.

3.  Women would be equally subject to jury service and to military service, but women would not be required to serve (in the Armed Forces) where they are not fitted any more than men are required to so serve.

4.  Restrictive work laws for women only would be unconstitutional.

5.  Alimony laws would not favor women solely because of their sex, but a divorce decree could award support to a mother if she was granted custody of the children. Matters concerning custody and support of children would be determined in accordance with the welfare of the children and without favoring either parent because of sex.

6.  Laws granting maternity benefits to mothers would not be affected by the amendment, nor would criminal laws governing sexual offenses become unconstitutional.

## Support of and opposition to the Equal Rights Amendment

The National Woman's Party, which continued to carry on the feminist movement following the adoption of the Nineteenth Amendment, has led the fight for an Equal Rights Amendment. Other organizations which have supported the amendment include the National Federation of Business and Professional Women's Clubs, the General Federation of Women's Clubs, National Association of Women Lawyers, National Association of Colored Business and Professional Women, St. Joan's Alliance, American Federation of Soroptimist Clubs, and various women's professional and civic organizations. Strong opposition to the amendment has come from the labor unions. Other organizations opposing the amendment have included the Americans for Democratic Action, National Council of Jewish Women, National Council of Catholic Women, National Council of Negro Women.

The most recent Congressional hearings on the amendment were held in 1956. There does not appear to be any record which would indicate that any of the opponents of the amendment who objected to the amendment's effect of eliminating special labor laws for women, have re-examined their position since the enactment of Title VII of the Civil Rights Act of 1964. Some of the organizations opposed to the amendment have urged the

Equal Employment Opportunity Commission not to enforce Title VII in a manner which would affect State laws restricting the employment of women. On the other hand, some labor unions, notably the U.A.W., Chemical Workers and Typographical Workers, have urged the EEOC to rule that the equal employment opportunity provisions of the Federal law supersede special hours and weight lifting restrictions on women workers.

## Current sex discrimination cases

In a 1966 case, *White v. Crook,* a three judge federal court in Alabama held the Alabama law excluding women from serving on juries violate the 14th amendment. The court said that "the plain effect (of the equal protection clause of the 14th amendment) is to prohibit prejudicial disparities before the law. This means prejudicial disparities for all citizens—including women." The State did not appeal to the U.S. Supreme Court and the Alabama legislature amended its law to permit women to serve on juries on the same basis as men. A similar case challenging the constitutionality of a Mississippi jury law excluding women is currently pending before a three judge federal court in Mississippi. (*Willis v. Carson*) The Mississippi jury law is also at issue in *Bass v. Mississippi*, pending before the Fifth Circuit U.S. Court of Appeals. The Mississippi Supreme Court, in the case of *Hall v. Mississippi*, declined to apply the doctrine of *White v. Crook* and held that the Mississippi law did not violate the 14th amendment. The U.S. Supreme Court dismissed the appeal in that case on jurisdictional grounds and did not hear the case.

The exclusion of women from draft boards under selective service regulations (which have recently been amended to permit women to serve) is at issue in a conscientious objector case in Georgia.

In *Mengelkoch v. Industrial Welfare Commission* the constitutionality of the California hours restriction law for women workers is being challenged. This case is pending before a three judge federal court in Los Angeles. NOW attorneys Marguerite Rawalt and Evelyn Whitlow are representing the plaintiff women workers. A Federal court in Indiana recently ruled in *Bowe v. Col-*

*gate-Palmolive Co.* that Title VII does not prohibit an employer from excluding women from jobs which require the lifting of more than 35 pounds. Although Indiana does not have a weight lifting restriction law for women, the court reasoned that some States do and this justifies employers in other States in adopting the same "protective" practices. A California weight lifting limitation on women workers is alleged as violating their right to equal employment opportunity under Title VII in *Regguinti v. Rocketdyne and North American Aviation*, pending in a Federal court in that State. However, plaintiff's attorney did not raise the issue of a violation of the 14th amendment. There may be other Title VII cases as well which could involve testing the validity under the 14th amendment of State restrictive laws, but in which the attorneys have failed to raise the issue.

A Pennsylvania State court held that a statute providing longer prison sentences for women than for men does not deny to women the equal protection of the laws under the 14th amendment. (*Commonwealth v. Daniels*). This case is currently being appealed to the Pennsylvania Supreme Court. A county court in Oregon held, in January, 1967, that a city ordinance providing for punishment of female prostitutes is unconstitutional because it does not apply equally to males.

This listing of pending litigation does not, of course, purport to be exhaustive.

## Suggested new interpretations of the 5th and 14th amendment

In "Jane Crow and the Law" (34 G.W. Law Rev. 232 (1965) authors Murray and Eastwood suggest that the doctrine that sex is a reasonable basis for classifying persons under the law, which has been used to justify upholding the constitutionality of laws which treat women differently from men, should be discarded by the courts. They point out that it could be argued that any sex differentiation in law or official practice today is inherently unreasonable and discriminatory and therefore violates the Constitution. The prospective effect of such an interpretation of the Constitution by the courts is outlined on pages 240 and 241 of that article.

NOW's brief in the Mengelkoch case asserts that the doctrine that sex is a valid basis for classifying persons does not even apply where there is involved the right to pursue lawful employment, since this is an individual right and a liberty and property which the State cannot restrict.

If these suggested constitutional interpretations are adopted by the courts in all areas of sex discrimination, the principle of equality set forth in the Equal Rights Amendment might in effect be "read into" the 5th and 14th amendments.

## Analysis of Arguments Against the Equal Rights Amendment

Reasons which have been given for opposing the Equal Rights Amendment are as follows:

1. The amendment would be difficult to interpret and would result in a great deal of litigation.

2. The amendment is not necessary because women can achieve constitutional equality through litigation under the 5th and 14th amendments.

3. Any constitutional requirement of equal treatment of the sexes is undesirable because it would require equal treatment of men and women in (a) state labor laws, (b) family law, (c) criminal laws, (d) social benefits law, and (e) obligations to the State and to the Nation.

\* \* \*

(1) "The amendment would be difficult to interpret and would result in a great deal of litigation."

The meaning of "equality of rights under the law" would be a question for interpretation by the courts. The language of the Equal Rights Amendment is patterned after the 19th Amendment:

ERA: "Equality of rights under the law shall not be denied.
19th: "The right of citizens of the United States to vote shall not be denied or abridged by the United States or by any State on account of sex."

However, the 19th amendment is specific and applies only to the right to vote. Its meaning is therefore more clear than the Equal Rights Amendment, which applies to all "rights." Excessive litigation (and possible undesirable decisions) under the Equal Rights Amendment might be avoided if "equality of rights" were more clearly defined in the legislative history of the amendment as meaning the right to equal treatment without differentiation based on sex.

As noted in the cases mentioned above, women are now seeking to invoke the protection of the 14th amendment in the courts. In part because of the enactment of Title VII of the Civil Rights Act of 1964, it is likely that litigation under the 14th amendment will increase. It is possible that the adoption of the Equal Rights Amendment would actually have the effect of reducing the amount of litigation necessary to secure equal treatment of the sexes under the law. Of course, litigation is not necessarily bad. Indeed under our legal system litigation is a proper means for correcting discriminatory treatment.

(2) The amendment is not necessary because women can achieve constitutional equality through litigation under the 5th and 14th amendments.

Women have been seeking equal rights under these amendments since 1872. (For a summary of the cases see the Report of the Committee on Civil and Political Rights, Appendix B, President's Commission on the Status of Women.) Women can and should continue to do so until discrimination in laws and official practices is eliminated. In "Jane Crow and the Law" (op. cit. supra) Murray and Eastwood state (page 237):

"Although the Supreme Court has in no case found a law distinguishing on the basis of sex to be a violation of the fourteenth amendment, the amendment may nevertheless be applicable to sex discrimination. The genius of the American Constitution is its capacity, through judicial interpretation, for growth and adaptation to changing conditions and human values. Recent Supreme Court decisions in cases involving school desegregation, reapportionment, the right to counsel, and the extension of the concept of state action illustrate the modern trend towards insuring equality of status and recognizing individual rights. Courts have not yet fully realized that women's rights are a part of human rights; but the climate appears favorable to renewed judicial attacks on sex discrimination..."

Supporters of the Equal Rights Amendment believe that the potential of the 14th amendment is too unclear and that women's constitutional rights to equality are too insecure to rely exclusively on the possibility of getting more enlightened court decisions under that amendment.

In a 1963 case, the Supreme Court stated: "The Fifteenth Amendment prohibits a State from denying or abridging a Negro's right to vote. The Nineteenth Amendment does the same for women.... Once a geographical unit for which a representative is to be chosen is designated, all who participate in the election are to have an equal vote—whatever their race, whatever their sex.... This is required by the Equal Protection Clause of the Fourteenth Amendment." *Gray v. Sanders,* 372 U.S. 368, 379.

This interpretation of the 14th amendment reinforced and made doubly secure the right to vote. There are numerous cases in which the Supreme Court has interpreted the 14th amendment to reinforce or to extend rights guaranteed by earlier or, as in the above case, later amendments to the Constitution. For example, the more general due process and equal protection concepts of the Fifth and Fourteenth Amendments have been used to strengthen more specific rights of individuals to freedom of speech, assembly and religion guaranteed by the First Amendment; and the right to a speedy trial and right to counsel guaranteed by the Sixth. If the Equal Rights Amendment is adopted, the courts might well subsequently interpret the Fourteenth Amendment as reinforcing constitutional equality for women.

A question might be asked as to why there should be a special equality guarantee for women and not for Negroes or for the aged. As a result of successful litigation under the Fifth and Fourteenth Amend-

ments, Negroes today have the constitutional right to equal treatment and both the Federal Government and the States are absolutely prohibited from treating persons differently because of race. The same is true as to national origin and religion. With respect to age, absolute equality of rights and responsibilities is not desirable. If age were added to the Equal Rights Amendment, child labor laws would be rendered void, as would social security and government retirement systems. Selective service laws could not place the responsibility to serve in military service on a certain age group, and state requirements that children attend school could not be based on age.

If the Fourteenth Amendment had been drafted so as to absolutely and unequivocally require equal treatment without differentiation based on race, Negroes would not have had to painstakingly, step by step, achieve equality of rights under the law through litigation and legislation. The general language of the 14th amendment guarantees of due process and equal protection of the law for all persons has enabled the courts to give recognition to important human rights concepts of freedom of speech and religion and protection of the rights of persons accused of crimes. These are unrelated to race and it is not suggested that the 14th amendment should have been limited to requiring racial equality. Nevertheless, one might ask those who oppose the Equal Rights Amendment on the ground that equality of rights for women might ultimately be achieved under the present constitutional framework whether, at this day in history, women should be asked to repeat the painful, costly and uncertain course of litigation which Negro Americans had to endure.

(3.) Any constitutional requirement of equal treatment of the sexes is undesirable because it would require equal treatment of men and women in (a) state labor laws, (b) family law, (c) criminal laws, (d) social benefits law, and (e) obligations to the State and to the Nation.

At the time of the last Congressional hearings on the amendment (1956) it was assumed by both proponents and opponents of the amendment that there is no existing constitutional requirement that women be accorded equal rights and responsibilities under the law. The debate centered on whether the constitution should require equal treatment of the sexes. Those who opposed the amendment simply opposed equal treatment of men and women.

It is assumed that all members of NOW favor equal rights and responsibilities for women. Nevertheless, before endorsing or rejecting the Equal Rights Amendment one would want to know the consequences and effects of the amendment.

The precise effect in a particular case alleging denial of equal rights under the amendment would be a question for the courts. As noted above, the courts, in making their determinations, would be guided by the intended meaning or the "legislative history" of the amendment. Organizations such as NOW could help in shaping the legislative history and in clarifying the effect the amendment is intended to have.

The President's Commission on the Status of Women and the various State Commissions have outlined the areas of law and official practice which treat men and women differently. All of these studies have been made since the last hearings on the amendment.

The Equal Rights Amendment would require equal treatment without differentiation based on sex. Purely private discrimination, whether based on race, religion, sex or national origin, is not reached and is not prohibited by the U.S. Constitution. Laws and actions of agents of the Government are clearly reached. The question in each instance would be whether the right to equal treatment is denied or abridged the State or Federal Government.

The precise effect of the amendment in a given situation cannot be predicted with absolute certainty since this would be determined by the courts. The following discussion indicates how the amendment might affect various laws and practices which treat men and women differently.

(a) State labor laws

(1) Minimum wage laws and other laws giving rights to women workers. If the State guarantees to women workers a minimum wage, men workers would be entitled to equal treatment by virtue of the Equal Rights Amendment. The same reasoning applies as to any state protected guarantees of seating facilities, lunch periods, or similar benefits provided for women workers. These laws or regulations would be automatically extended to persons of both sexes in the same way the State voting laws which applied only to men were automatically extended to women by virtue of the 19th amendment.

(2) State laws limiting and restricting the hiring and employment of female workers-hours restrictions, night work restrictions and weight lifting limitations. These laws are all limitations on the freedom of women workers because of their sex. They limit the right to pursue lawful employment and to work when and how long they choose. They confer no rights on women. Both men and women are, of course, free to not work longer than they so choose or at such times as they choose, by virtue of the 13th amendment's prohibition against slavery and forced labor. State restrictive laws would not be extended to men; they would be nullified by the Equal Rights Amendment because they place restrictions on women not placed on men.

(3) Laws totally prohibiting the employment of women in certain occupations, such as bar tending and mining, likewise would be void, because they clearly deprive women, because of their sex, of the right to employment in these occupations. State laws providing a higher minimum age for employment for girls would be affected by the amendment by reducing the age to that provided for boys.

(4) Maternity laws would not be affected by the amendment because such laws are not based on sex; they do not apply women as a class. (See "Jane Crow and the Law," pages 239–240.)

(b) Family law.

(1) Both mothers and fathers are now generally responsible for the support of children under state laws. This would not be changed by the Equal

Rights Amendment. In case of divorce or separation, where the mother (or father, as the case may be) has custody and care of the children, courts could continue to require the other parent, be it mother or father, to contribute to the financial support of the children .Present laws do not give recognition to the financial worth of homemaking and child care. The Equal Rights Amendment would probably not require that such worth be recognized in determining the relative responsibilities of parents in case of divorce. However, recognizing the value of child care and homemaking would be consistent with the principle of equality of rights under the amendment.

(2) Alimony for wives solely because they are female would be prohibited by the Equal Rights Amendment. However, continued support by one spouse for the other after divorce or separation based on actual necessary economic dependency, relative ability to provide family support or past relationships and obligations of the particular parties would not be prohibited by the amendment because the alimony or support would not be based on sex but upon some other criteria. The states would continue to be free to establish these values and criteria; they would simply be prohibited from discriminating against either men or women because of sex.

(3) Minimum age for marriage. Some states provide a lower minimum age for marriage for women that for men. The amendment would prohibit treating men and women differently in regard to age for marriage. If under state law women have the right to marry at age 18 and men at age 21, the amendment would give men the right to marry at 18. The state could, of course, amend its law to provide that the age be 21 for both sexes.

(4) Age of right to parental support. Some states give girls a right to be supported to age 18 and boys to age 21. Since the girls would have the right to be treated equally under the amendment, their right in these states would be automatically extended to age 21. The states would be free, of course, to provide a different age, so long as it is the same for boys and girls.

(5) State laws placing special limitations and restrictions on married women but not on married men would be nullified by the amendment.
(c) Criminal law.

States would be prohibited from providing greater penalties for female law violators than for males. There are certain sex crimes, such as rape, which apply only to males. These would not be affected by the Equal Rights Amendment since the state in enacting these laws has not made any classification of persons by sex; if these laws were drafted so as to refer to persons instead of males, their meaning would be the same. (see "Jane Crow and the Law," page 240.)

(d) Social benefits laws.

There are certain differences in benefits which men and women receive under the social security and government retirement laws. There may be similar state retirement systems which give greater or lesser benefits to women. Legislation is currently pending in Congress to correct some of the inequities in the Federal law (see, e.g., H.R.643, 90th Congress, to eliminate differences in government employees' fringe benefits.). It could reasonably be expected that by the time an Equal Rights Amendment became effective, differences between the sexes in these laws would have been corrected. However, insofar as differences remained, the State or Federal Government, as the case may be, would be obligated by the Equal Rights Amendment to give the same benefits to both sexes.

(e) Service to the State and to the Nation. (Government employment, jury service and military service.)

The Equal Rights Amendment would prohibit discrimination against women in public employment at all levels of government. The Administration's Civil Rights Bill would prohibit any sex discrimination in juror qualification or in selection of jurors. This would eliminate laws excluding or discouraging women from serving on juries. It is generally agreed that a state law relieving women from jury service responsibilities relegated them to second class citizenship and should be forbidden. The Equal Rights Amendment would make women eligible to serve on all juries on the same basis as men. With regard to military service the same reasoning might apply. It could be argued that failure of a nation to give its women the same responsibilities as it requires of its men makes women second class citizens. The Military Selective Service Act of 1967 requires men but not women to register for military service. The Equal Rights Amendment would have the effect of extending this requirement to women and make women eligible for selection just as women would be eligible for jury selection on the same basis as men. The present selective service law will automatically expire on July 1, 1971.

\*\*\*

Some lawyers might disagree that the Equal Rights Amendment would have the effects outlined above. However, to the extent that supporters of the amendment can agree on the desired effects of the amendment on existing laws, such effects could be made more certain if they are carefully set forth and made a part of the amendment's legislative history.

## Document Analysis

The position paper begins with the obvious: NOW's stated reason for existing, which aligns with the ERA's essential goal. The organization then goes on to show the amendment's history, as well as the long list of backing organizations, including noted women's professional groups. The document not only lays out the arguments on behalf of the Equal Rights Amendment, but the reasons to oppose it—which the paper then refutes, point by point. Indeed, the opposition is clearly on the mind of the document's creator.

The president's Commission on the Status of Women, created by President John F. Kennedy, reported back to him in the fall of 1963. While the report declared that equality is "basic to democracy," it also rejected the idea of a constitutional amendment because the equal rights in question were already covered by the Fifth and Fourteenth Amendments. That said, the Commission felt a "definitive" court decision—preferably from the US Supreme Court—was needed in regard to the two amendments to ensure that women's equality was "firmly established in Constitutional doctrine." The Fifth Amendment, part of the original "Bill of Rights" ratified promptly after the Constitution itself, protects any "person" from being "deprived of life, liberty, or property without due process of law" by the federal government. The Fourteenth Amendment, added after the Civil War (along with the Thirteenth, abolishing slavery, and the Fifteenth, outlawing race-based restrictions on voting rights), extends that restriction to state governments, and also guarantees to "any person" the "equal protection of the laws."

The NOW paper addressed the commission's view that the amendment was unnecessary because already encompassed in those existing amendments, as well as other arguments that had been advanced against it. Outlining what the amendment would and would not affect, it points out that the provision would restrict only government action and not purely private action; the sometimes hazy boundary between them would be defined as it was for purposes of the application of the equal-protection clause to racial classifications. Married women would not find their property rights under special restrictions, giving control to their husbands; both genders would share the same inheritance rights as well as engage in business equally. Women would be subject to jury and military duty, but, like men, they would not be required to serve if they were found not to be fit. Restrictive work laws—already under scrutiny at the time—would be unconstitutional. Women would not receive either alimony or custody of children solely due to their gender; custody, child support, and alimony decisions would be based on the spouses' individual circumstances, with no presumptions in favor of one sex or the other. And laws granting mothers maternity benefits would not be affected, nor would criminal laws governing sexual offenses become unconstitutional.

The paper's rebuttal of the argument that women's equality is assured by the Fifth and Fourteenth Amendments started with the observation: "Women have been seeking equal rights under these amendments since 1872." Ninety-five years later, NOW encouraged women to continue to demand full legal equality "until discrimination in laws and official practices is eliminated." The Fourteenth Amendment was too unclear to accomplish that goal, they argued. Examining the existing judicial precedents, the paper shows that the two amendments had been used to strengthen rights under other amendments—including individuals' rights to freedom of speech, assembly, and religion guaranteed by the First Amendment—but had taken nearly a century of interpretation by the courts even to approach their original purpose of equal treatment of *races* because the Fourteenth Amendment was so general in its terms; women, it suggests, should not have to repeat that long process because of the absence of express reference to gender discrimination in the text of the post-Civil-War amendments.

The opposition argument that the ERA would be difficult to interpret and result in a great deal of litigation was refuted by the simple fact that abundant litigation was already underway and likely to increase, in part due to the new Title VII of the Civil Rights Act of 1964. Perhaps the ERA would reduce litigation by avoiding the need to determine how the equal-protection and due-process clauses applied to distinctions based on sex. Opposition arguments focused on the impact that requiring equal treatment of the sexes would have on existing law in a series of categories that treated men and women differently. The paper addresses each category in turn—protective labor laws and restrictive licensing laws; family law; criminal law; social benefit law; and citizens' obligations to the State and Nation. NOW's central points are that the amendment would: properly extend to men the benefits that protective laws reserved for women; require that women be allowed to do whatever men were allowed to do; and confirm that equality for both genders should be the defining goal notwithstanding the need for women to give up the special protections and exemptions they were afforded in existing laws in order to escape second-class citizenship.

The paper concludes by urging as a political strategy that "...to the extent that supporters of the amendment can agree on the desired effects of the amendment on existing laws, such effects could be made more certain if they are carefully set forth and made a part of the amendment's legislative history." Indeed, the paper can be seen as an attempt to model the "legislative history" that would guide the courts' implementation of the amendment once adopted.

## Essential Themes

NOW's 1967 ERA Position Paper is essentially a legal analysis designed to show the long history of the slow march to equal rights between women and men and to refute the arguments against the amendment. These arguments include the following: that the amendment would be difficult to interpret and result in additional litigation; that the Fifth and Fourteenth Amendments already protect women's rights; and that a number of areas of existing law would be disrupted by a constitutional requirement that men and women and men be treated equally. The key underlying point was that women could avoid second-class citizenship only by a guarantee of completely equal legal treatment—no restrictions specifically applicable to them as well as no special protections. Although women in general were divided on the desirability of the ERA, NOW's position was unequivocal, and the organization referred to its own founding statement of purpose: that men and women should equally share in the responsibilities and privileges of American society.

Today, hope that the amendment might be revived remains. On May 8, 2015, US Senator Ben Cardin (D–MD) reintroduced a joint resolution to ratify the ERA, while US Representative Jackie Speier (D–CA) did the same in the House of Representatives. Their measures would remove a deadline for ratification.

*—Allison Blake*

## Bibliography and Additional Reading

Friedan, Betty. *The Feminine Mystique*. 1963. Cambridge, MA: Harvard UP, 1998. Print.

Keetley, Dawn & John Pettegrew. *Public Women, Public Words: A Documentary History of American Feminism*. vol. 2. Lanham, MD: Rowman & Littlefield, 2005. Print.

Murray, Pauli & Mary O. Eastwood. *Jane Crow and the Law: Sex discrimination and Title VII*. Durham, NC: Sallie Bingham Center for Women's History and Culture, 1965. Print.

*National Organization for Women Official Website*. National Organization for Women, 2015. Web. now.org.

# ■ Kate Millett: "Sexual Politics"

**Date:** 1968
**Author:** Kate Millett
**Genre:** Essay

## Summary Overview

Kate Millett's essay, which would later be incorporated into her classic book *Sexual Politics*, establishes the theoretical basis that she would use in the longer work to critique the discussion and presentation of sex by male authors. This essay also introduced the term "patriarchy" to second-wave feminist theory, and it would provide an academic system of thought for the larger radical feminist movement. Patriarchy, which originally signifies an anthropological category of kinship structures dominated by a male elder, became in Millett's analysis a distinct social system across cultures designed specifically to reinforce male supremacy and maintain female oppression. This system of power preceded both racial and class oppression, and contributed to a history of male political and economic privilege. The subordination based on sex was pervasive, affecting everything from interpersonal relations all the way to governmental institutions. Second-wave feminists would use the ideas and questions stimulated by Millett's text to argue for widespread change in cultural attitudes and policies.

## Defining Moment

The United States experienced a culture shift at the end of World War II: security and prosperity contributed to a renewed emphasis on the "cult of domesticity" for women. Returning soldiers were eager to marry and return to normal life: they returned to their prewar occupations, and drove many women who had taken on these jobs traditionally held by men out and into the occupation of fulltime homemakers. This domestic ideal emphasized the role of caretaker, too, since increased economic prosperity made it feasible for couples to have more children. This resulting "baby boom" was a sharp increase in live births and lasted until the 1960s. Advertising and popular media also reinforced domestic roles as ideal for women. Popular television shows like *Leave It to Beaver* and the marketing of many consumer goods contributed to increased pressure on young women to lead the idealized American life by marrying early, starting a family, and concentrating on the home.

More people began to question the prevalence of these cultural ideals in the 1960s. The availability of the oral contraceptive pill at the beginning of the decade meant that women could take control of their reproductive lives and pursue careers without the fear of pregnancy. Betty Friedan's 1963 book *The Feminine Mystique* was a reaction to the postwar domestic ideal and incited the start of the second-wave feminist movement. Friedan's book revealed the widespread phenomenon of unhappiness that many women faced as they felt compelled to confine themselves to marriage, children, and a life of domesticity at the cost of their professional development and personal goals. As a result of the great support for her book and the struggle to implement political measures for gender equality, Friedan helped found the National Organization for Women in 1966. This organization often led the way in many political fights during the Kennedy and Johnson administrations for protections against sex-based discrimination and violence.

This was the era of landmark legislation like the Civil Rights Act of 1964 and Title IX, but also, as the decade went on, a time of increased social divisions. The Vietnam War, the student protest movement, and other pushes for racial and sexual orientation equality interacted with the women's rights movement. In Kate Millett's case, this interaction could be occasionally contentious. Although she participated in the student antiwar protests, Millett would soon find herself struggling to negotiate her identity with the growing gay rights movement and the internal quarrels among other contemporary feminists.

## Author Biography

The success of Kate Millett was only possible, as she herself says, because she was fired from her job teaching English at Barnard College in 1968. Born in 1934, Millett was a diligent feminist and anti-war protestor: her part in the student demonstrations cost her a teaching job; however, this dismissal gave her more time to work on her sculpture and a PhD thesis at Columbia on power structures, sex, and literature. This thesis would

Sexual Politics book cover.

become the book *Sexual Politics*, which would make her one of the giants of second-wave feminism. *Time* magazine even featured her on its cover and called her the "Mao Tse-tung of Women's Liberation." Although her first book often defines her career, Millett continued her involvement in the arts by creating a women's art colony in New York; she also continued to publish writing on issues she was interested in as a political activist, including the use of state-sanctioned torture in prisons and prostitution. Millett documented her struggles in and with the feminist movement in several memoirs: after the publication of *Sexual Politics*, she found herself criticized for not identifying publically as a lesbian sooner, was eventually left behind by the evolution of the feminist movement, and her book went out of print. However, her work remained a touchstone for many feminist thinkers, and a new edition of Millett's first and most famous book had recently been published when she died suddenly of cardiac arrest in Paris with her wife in 2017.

## HISTORICAL DOCUMENT

Is it possible to regard the relation of the sexes in a political light at all? It depends on how one defines politics. I do not define the political area here as that narrow and exclusive sector known as institutional or official politics of the Democrat or Republican—we have all reason to be tired and suspicious of them. By politics I mean powerstructured relationships, the entire arrangement whereby one group of people is governed by another, one group is dominant and the other subordinate.

It is time we developed a more cogent and relevant psychology and philosophy of power relationships not yet considered in out institutional politics. It is time we gave attention to defining a theory of politics which treats of power relationships on the less formal than establishmentarian grounds of personal intercourse between members of well defined and coherent groups—races, castes, classes and sexes. It is precisely because such groups have no representation in formal political structures that their oppression is so entire and so continuous.

In the recent past, we have been forced to acknowledge that the relationship between the races in the United States is indeed a political one—and one of the control of collectivity defined by birth, or another collectivity also defined by birth. Groups who rule by birth are fast disappearing in the West and white supremacists are fated to go the way of aristocrats and other extinct upper castes. We have yet one ancient and universal arrangement for the political exploitation of one birth group by another—in the area of sex.

Just as the study of racism has convinced us that there exists a truly political relationship between races, and an oppressive situation from which the subordinated group had no redress through formal political structures whereby they might organize into conventional political struggle and opposition—just so any intelligent and objective examination of our system of sexual politics or sex role structure will prove that the relationship between the sexes now—and throughout history—is one of what Max Weber once termed "Herrschaft"—or dominance and subordination—the birthright control of one group by another-the male to rule and the female to be ruled. Women have been placed in the position of minority status throughout history and even after the grudging extension of certain minimal rights of citizenship and suffrage at the beginning of this century. It is fatuous to suppose that women—white or black—have any greater representation now that they vote—than that they ever did. Previous history has made it clear that the possession of the vote for 100 years has done the black man precious little good at all.

Why, when this arrangement of male rule and control of our society is so obvious—why is it never acknowledged or discussed? Partly, I suspect because such discussion is regarded as dangerous in the extreme and because a culture does not discuss its most basic assumptions and most cherished bigotries. Why does no one ever remark that the military, industry, the universities, the sciences, political office and finance (despite absurd declarations to the contrary on the evidence that some little old lady owns stock over which she has no control). Why does no one ever remark that every avenue of power in our culture including the repressive forces of the police—entirely in male hands? Money, guns, authority itself, are male provinces. Even God is male—and a white male at that.

The reasons for this gigantic evasion of the very facts of our situation are many and obvious. They are also rather amusing. Let's look at a few of the thousand defenses the masculine culture has built against any infringement or even exposure of its control: is to react with ridicule and the primitive mechanism of laughter and denial. Sex is funny—it's dirty—and it is something women have. Men are not sexual beings—they are people—they are humanity. Therefore, any rational discussion of the realities of sexual life degenerate as quickly as men can make them into sniggering sessions, where through cliché so ancient as to have almost ritual value, women who might be anxious to carry on an adult dialogue are bullied back into "their place".

At the level of common attitude—sex and particularly that very explosive subject of the relationship of the sexes—is a subject closed to intelligent investigation and accessible only to persiflage and levity.

The second evasion our culture has evolved is via folk myth. From Dagwood to the college professor, sex is folklore and the official version of both is that the male is the "victim" of a widespread conspiracy. From the folk figure of Jiggs or Punch to the very latest study of the damage which mothers wreak upon their sons, we are assailed by the bogey of the overbearing woman—woman as some terrible and primitive natural evil—our twentieth-century remnant of the primitive fear of the unknown, unknown at least to the male, and remember, it is the male in our culture who defines reality. Man is innocent, he is put upon, everywhere he is in danger of being dethroned. Dagwood—the archetypal henpecked husband—is a figure of folk fun only because the culture assumes that a man will rule his wife or cease to be very much of a man. Like a dimwitted plantation owner who is virtually controlled by his far-cleverer steward or valet, Dagwood is a member of the ruling class held up both to scorn and to sympathy-scorn for being too human or too incompetent to rule, yet sympathetic because every other member of the privileged group knows in his heart how burdensome it is to maintain the illusory facade of superiority over those who are your natural equals.

The phantasy of the male victim is not only a myth, it is politically expedient myth, myth either invented or disseminated to serve the political end of a rationalization or a softening and partial denial of power. The actual relation of the sexes in our culture from the dawn of history has been diametrically opposite to official cult of the downtrodden. Yet our culture seeks on every level of discussion to deny logical charge of oppression which any objective view of the sex structure would bring up; masculine society has a fascinating tactic of appropriating all sympathy for itself. It has lately taken up the practice of screaming out that it is the victim of unnatural surgery ... it has been "castrated". Even Albert Shanker has discovered of late that black community control, the Mayor, and the Board of Education have performed this abomination upon his person. To those in fear of castration word one word of comfort. The last instance of its practice on a white man in western culture was the late 18th century when the last castrati lost a vital section of his anatomy in the cause of the art of music—at the hands of another male, I must add. For castration is an ancient cruelty which males practice on each other. In the American South it was as a way to humiliate black victims of the Klan. In the Ancient East it was a barbarous form of punishment for crime. In the courts of the Italian Renaissance castration was a perverse method of providing soprano voices for the Papal Choir. It was felt that women were too profane to sing the holy offices so to supply the demand for the higher musical register, eunuchs were created through putting young men to the knife

As the practice of physical castration has been abolished clear that the word in current usage must be accepted in a metaphoric rather than literal connotation, if we are to any sense of the fantastic anxiety contemporary male egos, for on every hand, in the media and in the culture both high and low, men today have come to see the terrible specter of the "castrating female" all about them, their paranoiac delusions are taken for social fact. Having in a confused way, associated his genitals with his power, the male now bellows in physical pain and true hysteria every time his social and political prerogatives are threatened. If by castration is meant a loss through being forced to share power with oppressed groups deprived of power- or even of human status, then there are many white men in America who will suffer this psychic operation, but it will be the removal of a cancer in the brain and heart not of any. pleasurable or creative organ. To, argue that any woman who insists on full human, status is a "castrating bitch" or guilty of the obscure evil: of "penis envy" (only the consummate male chauvinist could have imagined this term) is as patently silly as to argue that dispossessed blacks want to become white men issue is not to be Whitey, but to have a fair share of what Whitey has the whole world of human possibility

While I am fully aware that equal rights entail equal responsibility there are some things Whitey has which I am very sure I don't want, for example, a Green Beret, a Zippo for burning down villages the ear of a dead of peasant, the burden of the charred flesh a Vietnamese child. Nor do I have an any interest in acquiring the habits of violence, warfare (unless in the just cause of self-defense—a cause I cannot foresee ever happening in American foreign policy), or the white man's imperialist racism, or rape or the capitalist exploitation of poverty and ignorance.

Because of the smoke-screen of masculine propaganda one hears endless cant about castration—whereas real and actual crimes men commit against women are never mentioned. It is considered bad taste, unsportsmanlike to refer to the fact that the are thousands of rapes or crimes against the female personality in New-York City every year—I speak only of those instances which are reported—probably one tenth of those which occur. It is also generally accepted that to regard Richard Speck and so many others like him in anything, but the light, of exceptional and irrelevant instances of individual pathology, is another instance of not playing that Speck merely enacted the presupposition of the majority male supremacists of the sterner sort—and they are legion. That his murders echo in the surrealist chambers of masculine phantasy and wish fulfillment is testified to by every sleazy essay into sadism and white slave traffic on the dirty movie belt of 42nd St, and anti-social character of hard core pornography. The Story of O tells it like it is about masculine phantasy better than does Romeo and Juliet. So does the Playboy, chortling over the con-game he has played on that Rabbit, he dreams of screwing the Bunny, or woman reduced to a meek and docile animal toy.

For the extent and depth of the male's hatred and hostility toward his subject colony of women is a source of continual astonishment.' Just as behind the glowing' mirage of "darkeys" crooning in the twilight—is reality the block, the whip and the manacle, the history of women is full of colorful artifact....the bound feet of all of old China's women—women deliberately deformed—that they might be the better controlled—(you can work with those useless feet, but you cannot run away)—the veil of Islam (or an attenuated existence as a human soul condemned to wear a cloth sack over her head all the days of her half-life);—the lash, the rod, domestic imprisonment through most of the world's history—rape, concubinage, prostitution. Yes, we have our own impressive catalogue of open tyrannies. Women are still sold in Saudi Arabia and elsewhere. In Switzerland, they are even today disenfranchised. And in nearly every rod of ground on this earth they live only via the barter system of sex in return for food of the latter. Like every system of oppression male supremacy rests finally on force, physical power, rape, assault and the threat of assault. A final resource when all else has failed the male resorts to attack. But the fear of force is there before every woman always as a deterrent—dismissal, divorce, violence—personal sexual or economic.

As in any society in a state of war, the enforcement of male rule which euphemism calls "the battle of the sexes", is possible only through the usual lies convenient to countries at war—The Enemy is Evil—the Enemy is not Human. And men have always been able to believe in the innate evil of women. Studies of primitive societies just as studies of our own religious texts—illustrate over and over—the innumerable instances of taboos practiced against women. A group of aborigines agree with Judaism in the faith that a menstruating, woman is "unclean," taboo, untouchable. Should she have access to weapons or other sacred and ritual articles the male, she will place a hex or spell upon them that their "masculine" owners will not survive. Everything that pertains to her physical make-up or function is despicable or subversive. Let side the village and inhabit a hut alone and without food during her period—let her be forbidden the temple—even those outer precincts assigned to her for a-specified number of-days after, as the Gospels-coolly inform us she has given birth to the very savior of the world for she is still, dirty. Dirty and mysterious. Have you ever thought it curious that 'nocturnal' emissions were not regarded as either dirty or mysterious, that the penis was (until Industrialism decided to veil it again for greater effect) never considered as dirty—but so regal and imperious that its shape is the one assigned to scepters, bombs, guns, and airplanes?

In history vast numbers of peoples have worshipped the phallus openly. It may also be true that ever larger numbers of peoples once worshipped the womb or the fertility powers of the earth. It may also be true that one of the many causes for the commencement of that now-universal oppression and contempt for women lay in the male's very fear of the female powers of giving life and perhaps inspired that enormous change in world affairs we call the patriarchal take-over. Living so close to the earth, without having yet developed toys of his own in warfare and the rise of princely city-states full of toiling slaves building him empty monuments, and unaware of his own vital role in conception the male may well have past glances of envy on the woman and what was—in those conditions—her miraculous capacity to bring another human life out of her very belly—and seen in it a connection with the phases of the moon, and the seasons of the earth's vegetation—and stood both in awe and terror—and finally in hatred—and decided to cast this function down from what he rather naturally I assumed was its collusion with the supernatural, the terrible, the uncontrollable forces of nature—and denigrate it to the level of the bestial, the pernicious and the obscene. And thus the filthy totem was appropriated by the male and taboo assigned in a thousand ways to operate against the female.

Having vitiated all effects of the female power the male set about aggrandizing his own. Having finally appropriated all access to the supernatural for himself he established an alliance with the new male god (both his brother his father, depending on auspicious or inauspicious circumstance), he then proceeded to announce his kinship with the divine through a long and impressive list of patriarchs and prophets, high priests and emperors. Now that he had gone into partnership with God, the male set himself up as God to the female. Milton puts it this way: "He for God only, she for God in him".

In some cultures females were allowed to participate on an inferior level as figures of identification for human females—useful in encouraging them to an enforced cooperation in their own control. So they can see themselves as honored through the rapes of Jove on Europa and Leda, favored in divine seduction scenarios as an endless series of wood nymphs, possibly debased versions of other tribal goddesses at loose ends now their matriarchal reign had ended—or incarnate in that first troublesome woman, Juno—the insubordinate wife.

But in sterner patriarchal societies such as the Judaic and Christian, there was never any kidding around about goddesses. Christianity did not elevate the Virgin to goddess status until the 12th Century and the Protestants dethroned her a mere 4 hundred years later. The device of making her both virgin and mother not only excites admiration for its ingenuity but astonishment as its perfection of effect—here is divine or nearly divine woman completely relieved of that insidious sexuality by which woman herself has always been defined.

Mere mortal women in the Christian ages were continuously assured of their inherent evil and inferiority by a whole procession of fanatic male supremacists—from Paul who found even the exhibition of their hair in church a powerful provocation and an indelicate enticement to hellish practices more apparent in his mind than in others—(such it is to represent the sexuality of the whole race in only one half of it)—to Jerome, Augustine, Aquinas and a whole parade of ascetics, hermits, and other nonparticipating types who have projected their own teeming sexuality onto the female. For so strong is the hold of the Christian assumption through Eve and other notable exempla that the "evil" of sex was introduced via the female alone—that today even Women think of Women when they think of sex, sexiness, sex objects, sexuality and sex symbols—a state of rather surprising paradox in a society which rigidly enforces heterosexuality for women.

Judaism is even more punctilious than Christianity in the matter of male supremacy. First thing in the morning every male Jew is enjoined to thank God for creating him a male and therefore a superior order of being. I have never been informed as to what Jewish women are instructed to say on such occasions of coming to consciousness—perhaps it is some little bit of advice to themselves not to fall into the much-satirized posture of the overbearing Jewish mother.

Of course it is not surprising that religion as we know it takes the enforcement of male supremacy by divine fiat as part of its function in a patriarchy—so too does literature, all traditional and contemporary notions of government, those platitudes which currently pass for social science—and even—despite the influence of the Enlightenment—science itself cooperates in a number of transparently expedient rationalizations in maintaining the traditional sexual politics on grounds so specious as to have a certain comic charm.

A further way in which contemporary masculine culture refuses to face the issue of sexual politics is through the reduction of the two sexual collectivities of male and female into an endless variety of purely individual situations, whereby all cases are unique—each a delicate matter of adjustment of one diverse character to another—all of them merely the very private matter of one-to-one relationships. That this is so largely our favorite method of portraying sexual relationships today—since Freud and the development of that very private science of psychoanalysis—is probably due in good part to the convenience it offers in shielding us from the unpleasant reality of sexual relations should we begin to view them on general or class/caste terms as we have learned to see race. For we know very well now that race is not a matter between one employer and his "boy" or one family and its "maid", but it is to be perceived in the far more pertinent light of one race's control over the other

The Individual Case translates our older myth of the dangerous Female into a newer but by now rather shop-worn cliché of the bitch stereotype—the most stock figure of the contemporary media. It is interesting to note how this bitch leads one to fancy—without ever coming right out and saying it—that all women are bitches. It is puzzling too how, as woman—with woman's minority status and therefore a creature completely out of the male power structure—she is arbitrarily and unjustly blamed for nearly every fault in American life today—and turned into a veritable symbol of the Hateful Establishment. As beauty queen, the male establishment is willing to allow woman a place as mascot or cheerleader—but it is a long way from admitting her to any personal stake in the establishment's show. As a girlfriend or a wife, she may participate vicariously for a time,—but she is easy to replace and the trade-in on old models of wife and mistress is pretty brisk. She may sleep with so many thousands a year or such and such an office, but she is dreaming if she ever fancies such glory is her own.

For the purpose of male propaganda, one of the most felicitous effects of the Individual Case myth is that it immediately translates any resistance to the present political situation in sex relations into a damning conviction of the sin of neurosis. As Psychology has replaced religion as the conformist in social behavior, it has branded any activity at odds with the force quo (which, by the way, it has taken to be "normality") as deranged, pitiable or dangerous behavior. By this criteria, current "normality" in the United States is racism, police brutality and ruthless economic exploitation.

This is what happens, if, like the Shrinks, you take 19th Century social life as both the State of Nature and the State of a Healthy Society. Any woman who fails to conform to the sterile stereotype of wife and motherhood as all and only, or who fails to bow in elaborate deference to male authority and opinion on any and all questions—is clearly off her nut. Men have said it.

One other device to maintain the current and traditional sexual politics is to claim that the whole thing has already been settled a long time ago "we gave you the vote" as the male authoritarian puts it with such stunning arrogance—we went to the polls and elected you into the human race because one day you mentioned the oversight of your exclusion and, obliging fellow that we are, we immediately rectifies this very trivial detail.

The foregoing is both a distortion of history and a denial of reality. Women fought hard and almost without hope, driven to massive and forceful protest which has served as a model both for the labor movement and the black movement. They struggled on against overwhelming odds of power and repression for over one hundred and fifty years to get this worthless rag known as the ballot. We got it last of all,—black and white—women are the last citizens of the United States'—and we had to work hardest of all to get it.

And now we have it we realize how badly we were cheated—we had fought so long, worked so hard, pushed back despair so many times that we were exhausted—we just said then give us that and we will do the rest ourselves. But we didn't realize, as perhaps blacks never realized until the Civil Rights Movement, that the ballot is no real admission to civil life in America; it means nothing at all if you are not represented in a representative democracy. And we are not represented now any more than black people... both groups have only one senator one Tom apiece. The United States has fewer women in public office than hardly any nation in the world— we are more effectively ostracized from political life—in this country than any other constituency in America—and we are 53% of its population. Political nominees announced their intention of helping asthmatic children and the mentally retarded of every age, if elected—but not a word about women half the population- but not a word—the largest minority status group in history. But not one word.

It is time the official fallacy of the West and of the United States particularly—that the sexes are now equal socially and politically—be exploded for the hoax it really is. For at present any gainsaying of this piety is countered with the threat that "women have got too much power, they're running the world", and other tidbits of frivolity which the speaker, strange as it may seem, might often enough believe. For the more petty male ego (like that of the cracker or the Union man in the North who voted for Wallace)—

in his paranoia is likely to believe that because one woman or one black man in millions can make nearly or even a bit more than he does—the whole bunch are taking over that sordid little corner of the world he regarded as his birthright because the was white and male—and on which he had staked his very identity-just because it prevented him from seeing himself as exploited by the very caste he had imagined he was part of and with whom, despite all evidence to the contrary, he fancied he shared the gifts of the earth and the American dream—. Nightmare that it is.

The actual facts of the situation of woman in America today are sufficient evidence that, white or black, women are at the bottom unless they sleep with the top. On their own they are Nobody and taught every day they are Nobody and taught so well they have come to internalize that destructive notion and even believe it. The Department of Labor statistics can't hide the fact that this is a man's world—a white man's world: the average year-round income of the white male is $6,704, of a black male $4,277, of a white female $3,991, and of the black woman $2,816. As students you live in a Utopia—enjoy it, for it is the only moment in your lives when you will be treated nearly as equals. When you get married or get a job you will be made to see where power is, but then it will be too late. That is why you should organize now: look at your curriculum and look at your housing rules,—that's a start at realizing how you are treated unfairly.

But the oppression of women is not only economic; that's just a part of it. The oppression of women is Total and therefore it exists in the mind, it is psychological oppression. Let's have a look at how it works, for it works like a charm. From earliest childhood every female child is carefully taught that she is to be a life-long incompetent at every sphere of significant human activity therefore she must convert herself into a sex object—a Thing. She must be pretty and assessed by the world: weighed, judged and measured by her looks alone. If she's pretty, she can marry; then she can concentrate her energies on pregnancy and diapers. That's life—that's female life. That's what it is to reduce and limit the expectations and potentialities of one half of the human race to the level animal behavior.

It is time we realized that the whole structure of male and female personality is arbitrarily imposed by social conditioning, a social conditioning which has taken all the possible traits of human personality—which Margaret Mead once, by way of analogy, compared to the many colors of the rainbow's spectrum—and arbitrarily assigned traits into two categories; thus aggression is masculine, passivity-feminine violence- masculine, tenderness feminine, intelligence masculine and emotion feminine, etc., etc... arbitrarily departmentalizing human qualities into two neat little piles which are drilled into children by toys, games, the social propaganda of television and the board of education's deranged whim as to what is proper male—female Role-Building. What we must now set about doing is to reexamine this whole foolish and segregated house of cards, and pick from it what we can use: Dante, Shakespeare, Lady Murasaki and Mozart, Einstein and the care for life which we have bred into women—and accept these as human traits. Then we must get busy to eliminate what are not properly humane or even human ideas—the warrior, the killer, the hero as homicide, the passive, dumb cow victim.

We must now begin to realize and to retrain ourselves to see that both intelligence and a reverence for life are HUMAN qualities. It is high time we began to be reasonable about the relationship of sexuality to personality and admit the facts—the present assignment of temperamental traits to sex is moronic, limiting and hazardous. Virility—the murderer's complex- or self definition in terms of how many or how often or how efficiently he can oppress his fellow—This has got to go. There is a whole generation coming of age in America who have already thoroughly sickened of the military male ideal, who know they were born men and don't have to prove it by killing someone or wearing crew cuts. There is also a vast number of women who are beginning to wake out of the long sleep known as cooperating in one's own oppression and self-denigration, and they are banding together, in nationwide chapters of the National Organization for Women—in the myriad groups of Radical Women springing up in cities all over the country and the world, in the women's liberation groups of SDS and in other groups or, on campus,

and they are joining together to make the beginnings of a new and massive women's movement in America and in the world—to establish true equality between the sexes, to break the old machine of sexual politics and replace it with a more human and civilized world for both sexes, and to end the present system's oppression of men as well as women.

There are other forces at work to change the whole face of American society: the black movement to end racism, the student movement with its numbers and powers for spreading the idea of a new society founded on democratic principles, free of the war reflex, free of the economic and racial exploitation reflex. Black people, students and women—that's a lot of people with our combined numbers it is probably 70% of the population or more. It is more than enough to change the course and character of our society—surely enough to cause a radical social revolution. And maybe it will also be the first Revolution to avoid the pitfall of bloodshed, a mere change of dictators and the inevitable counter-revolution which follows upon such betrayal and loss of purpose.

We are numbers sufficient to alter the course of human history—by changing fundamental values by affecting an entire change of consciousness. We cannot have such a change of consciousness unless we rebuild values—-we cannot rebuild values unless we 'restructure personality.' But we cannot do this or solve racial and economic crimes unless we end the oppression of all people—unless we end the idea of violence, of dominance, of power, unless we end the idea of oppression itself—unless we realize-that a revolution in sexual policy is not only part of but basic to any real change in the quality life. Social and cultural revolution in America and the world depend on a change of consciousness of which a new relationship between the sexes and a new definition of humanity and human personality are an integral part.

As we awake and begin to take action, there will be enough of us and we will have both a purpose and a goal—the first truly human condition, the first really human society. Let us begin the revolution and let us begin it with love: All of us, black, white, and gold, male and, female, have it, within our power to create a world we could bear out of the desert we inhabit for we hold our very fate in our hands.

## Document Analysis

*Sexual Politics* radically transformed the women's rights movement in the 1960s and provided an academic theoretical background to explain why systemic inequalities existed between the sexes. Learned as Millett's analysis is, the vision of patriarchy presented in this essay shows the influence of structuralist thought. Structuralism is a school of thought, often used in sociology and anthropology, that proposes that human culture can be understood in relation to overarching systems or structures. Structuralist scholars use these systems or structures, often identified as different binaries, to analyze the concerns and prevailing beliefs in universal human thought. The prevailing binary that Millett uses as her heuristic is obviously the male/female dichotomy.

The influence of structuralist thought allows Millett to use Chinese foot binding, the hijab of Muslim women, and sexual practices in the West to make the same point about the patriarchy: it systematically frames women as an aberration or Other compared to men, and uses violence to maintain the dichotomy between powerful and powerless. Her focus on the male/female binary also allows her to use broad characterizations of Judeo-Christian religions as if the comparison between ethnic identities and religions was valid; this analysis does not consider that even within Judaism and Christianity there are multiple sects, and that different peoples practice these sects in different ways with different histories. As her essay continues, it becomes clear that Millett is actually focused on a narrative of sexual politics in the modern United States, but even then this reduction to binaries has the unintended consequence of eliding the different experiences of oppression experienced by white women and women of color into the same story.

Millett occasionally recognizes that experiences of oppression are not universal, but it is not the defining feature of her essay. She says that "white or black, women are at the bottom unless they sleep with the top," but then writes two sentences later the much lower average salaries of black women compared to white men, black men, and white women. She also notices that the number of other people fighting for equal rights includes black people and students, and that these people would outnumber their oppressors. Although this is a tempting vision, Millett does not stop to examine whether other women might follow her same egalitarian ideas or perhaps carry implicit biases as a result of their upbringing; Millett also does not consider whether she

has made any assumptions about the totality of experience because of her upbringing as a middle class white woman. Even in her closing remarks, she subtly reveals her tendency toward structuralist binaries. She says: "All of us, black, white, and gold, male and, female, have it, within our power to create a world we could bear out of the desert we inhabit for we hold our very fate in our hands." Notwithstanding the artistic flourish of "gold," Millett's thinking revolves around the dichotomy between male and female, black and white and subsequently erases the experiences of numerous other discriminated individuals in the United States.

Millet's identification of the patriarchy and her description of the ubiquitous ways it has affected interrelations between the sexes was groundbreaking: she effectively created a new discipline of study, feminist theory, in this essay and later book chapter. Although there are certainly commonalities between cultures, the broad characterizations in this study cannot explain completely or accurately certain behaviors, rituals, or histories of diverse peoples. Millett probably did not intend to be considered the supreme authority on a theory of sexual politics, but her work became a valuable resource for reconsiderations, especially by post-structuralist scholars, who resist the overarching narratives favoured by structuralists, and intersectional feminists, who question how race and sexual orientation affect discrimination.

## Essential Themes

Although second-wave feminism was concomitant with and often interacted with other civil rights movements at the time, the women's rights movement was largely represented by middle and upper class white women and focused on their interests to the exclusion of people of color and individuals with nonbinary gender and sexual orientation. Third-wave feminists began to define their goals in the early 1990s as a reaction to the limited scope of their predecessors' initiatives and their restricted ideas of what was "feminine." Although it is not a cohesive movement, followers of third-wave feminism have repudiated the anti-pornography stance of many second-wave feminists, focused on maintaining reproductive rights, fought against sexual harassment, worked for marriage equality, and continued to define and institute measures to eradicate rape culture.

Third-wave feminism still struggles with some of the class, sex, and race identity issues of the second-wave movement. In 1989, Kimberlé Crenshaw coined the term intersectionality, which means that there are multiple elements to a person's identity and those elements combine to create a compound that is different from any of the individual elements. For example, a woman who is black faces both gender and racial discrimination in a matrix of oppression; a black woman who also identifies as homosexual would face additional discrimination based on sexual orientation. In 2017, intersectionality continues to be a legitimate concern, as women of color often face significant resistance from white feminists in recognizing and prioritizing the issues of other marginalized identities.

—*Ashleigh Fata, MA*

## Bibliography and Additional Reading

Millett, Kate. *Flying*. Chicago: University of Illinois Press, 2000 [1974].

_____. *Sexual Politics*. New York: Columbia UP, 2016 [1970].

Ryan, Barbara. *Feminism and the Women's Movement: Dynamics of Change in Social Movement, Ideology, and Activism*. New York: Routledge, 1992.

Whelehan, Imelda. *Modern Feminist Thought: From the Second Wave to 'Post-Feminism.'* New York: NYU Press, 1995.

# ■ Ella Baker: "The Black Woman in the Civil Rights Struggle"

**Date:** 1969
**Author:** Ella Baker
**Genre:** Speech

## Summary Overview

In 1969 civil rights activist Ella Baker delivered a speech, "The Black Woman in the Civil Rights Struggle" to a conference of supporters. Although she was a forty-year veteran of the civil rights movement, the speech is one of the few verbatim accounts of her appeals. Baker highlighted the important role played by black women in resisting both slavery and segregation. In the speech she argued that while women were unquestionably the "backbone" of the civil rights movement, their contributions often went unappreciated by male civil rights leaders and the public. She also criticized unnamed civil rights leaders for creating and continuing a disconnect between the "leaders" of the movement and the communities they served. She maintained that the only way to achieve truly radical change was to engage the masses in the struggle for their freedom. Only when the people learned to lead themselves would real change be possible.

## Defining Moment

Ella Baker's speech "The Black Woman in the Civil Rights Struggle" is an important speech in many respects. When she delivered this speech, she had been an active and outspoken participant in the fight for black equality for more than four decades; yet, much of what she said and wrote during those years has been lost. She did not commit her words to paper, and the speeches that survived have been reconstructed from notes or tapes made while she spoke. This is one of the few verbatim accounts of her many speeches. Given her importance in the civil rights movement, the fact that only a few of her speeches survived is significant.

The tape recording reveals that her voice was deep. Her speech pattern and accent sounded educated, and she made no attempt to imitate the speech of her audiences, preferring to speak as she normally did. She often said that if she spoke "like the person" she was—educated and raised in a middle-class family—her audiences would have no trouble understanding her; she, in turn, had no trouble understanding them because she listened carefully.

Not surprisingly, this speech reveals her remarkable ability to galvanize audiences with her words. Eyewitness accounts indicate that Baker was an inspirational speaker who appealed to her audiences by initially recounting unfamiliar history. She then would move to a statement of objectives and outline what she thought could be done.

When Ella Baker delivered this speech in 1969, she had already done much for the cause of civil rights. The speech was delivered by someone who had more than forty years of experience fighting for African American political and social equality. Baker's speech was also delivered only a few years after the successful passing of the Civil Rights Act of 1964 and the Voting Rights Act of 1965. Given her impact on the movement that achieved these momentous legislative victories, it is hardly surprising that she would discuss her own involvement.

However, Baker was not only looking back on her own contributions, she was also looking forward and examining possible future challenges. This largely explains why Baker did not spend her time glorifying the civil rights movement and its participants. Instead, she examined the movement from a critical perspective. Considering that she had never refrained from criticizing civil rights leaders, this would not have surprised anyone who knew her. In her speech, she challenged the idea that the civil rights movement needed any sort of centralized or controlling leadership. Throughout her life, Baker argued that "strong people don't need strong leaders," and her comments were a further reflection of this belief.

As well, she portrayed critically the treatment of women in the civil rights movement. She believed that women were not given sufficient credit for their work and the risks they took. Civil rights activists fought for black equality, but they often fell short in their treatment of black women.

## Author Biography

Ella Baker, born in Norfolk, Virginia, in 1903, was an enigmatic figure. She spent most of her career working behind the scenes, helping to organize the National Association for the Advancement of Colored People (NAACP), the Southern Christian Leadership Conference (SCLC), the Student Nonviolent Coordinating Committee (SNCC), and other civil rights groups, yet she was a charismatic public speaker. She had an ordinary childhood in a middle-class family, but when she went to live in the Harlem neighborhood of New York City, she was exposed to much of the leftist thought that was then popular among many African American intellectuals. She studied the works of Karl Marx, the nineteenth-century socialist and economic theorist, and adapted the rhetoric of Marxism to her speeches.

It is likely that her numerous conversations with other leftists helped her form the notion that society should be changed to suit people, instead of insisting that people adapt to society. As her career in the civil rights movement developed, she dropped much of her commitment to Socialism, even though she continued occasionally to use Marxist terminology in her speeches. Indeed, her belief that power should build from the bottom up instead of the top down put her in a long tradition of American political thought dating back to before the Revolutionary War. Much of her work helped bring closer to realization the ideals held by many of those who fought that war and who eventually wrote the Constitution.

When Baker graduated from college in April, 1927, she wanted to become a missionary or social worker, but she could not afford the additional education she needed to get a job as one or the other, so she moved to New York City to look for opportunities. By 1930 she was involved in the management of the Young Negroes' Cooperative League and served as its national director for about four years. The league was part of an international movement in which people pooled their resources to provide food and other necessities for themselves; since poor African Americans made up significant members of the league, Baker developed skills in organizing people who had little money and often had never voted.

The Great Depression of the 1930s was difficult for Baker, and during that decade she learned how to organize people with few funds and how to motivate them with her speeches. She worked as a publicist for the National Negro Congress and as a teacher and project supervisor for the federal government's Works Progress Administration. Her work from 1938 to 1946 for the NAACP—and with the New York Urban League beginning in 1946—contributed greatly to its growth and success, and during that period she honed her motivational speaking skills into the style displayed in "The Black Woman in the Civil Rights Struggle." During the 1950s and 1960s, Baker tried to work quietly behind the scenes to organize civil rights workers; she did so because she wanted people themselves, and not outsiders, to make important choices about their lives. By the 1970s she was a respected figure among civil rights leaders but not well known outside the civil rights movement. This changed when historians began recognizing her achievements, and Baker was sought out by interviewers who wished to record her views of the civil rights movement.

## HISTORICAL DOCUMENT

I think that perhaps because I have existed much longer than you and have to some extent maintained some degree of commitment to a goal of freedom that this is the reason Vincent Harding invited me to come down as an exhibit of what might possibly be the goal of some of us to strive toward—that is, to continue to identify with the struggle as long as the struggle is with us.

I was a little bit amazed as to why the selection of a discussion on the role of black women in the world. I just said to Bernice Reagon that I have never been one to feel great needs in the direction of setting myself apart as a woman. I've always thought first and foremost of people as individuals ... [but] wherever there has been struggle, black women have been identified with that struggle. During slavery there was a tremendous amount of resistance in various forms. Some were rather subtle and some were rather shocking. One of the subtle forms was that of feigning illness.... One of the other forms of resistance which was perhaps much more tragic and has not been told to a great extent is the large number of black women who gave birth to children and killed them rather than have them grow up as slaves. There is a story of a woman in Kentucky who had borne thirteen children and strangled each of them with her own hands rather than have them grow up as slaves. Now this calls for a certain kind of deep *commitment* and *resentment*. *Commitment* to freedom and deep *resentment* against slavery.

I would like to divide my remaining comments into two parts. First, the aspect that deals with the struggle to get into the society, the struggle to be a part of the American scene. Second, the struggle for a different kind of society. The latter is the more radical struggle. In the previous period, the period of struggling to be accepted, there were certain goals, concepts, and values such as the drive for the "Talented Tenth." That, of course, was the concept that proposed that through the process of education black people would be accepted in the American culture and they would be accorded their rights in proportion to the degree to which they qualified as being persons of learning and culture....

[There was] an assumption that those who were trained were not trained to be *part* of the community, but to be *leaders* of the community. This carried with it another false assumption that being a leader meant that you were separate and apart from the masses, and to a large extent people were to look up to you, and that your responsibility to the people was to *represent* them. This means that the people were never given a sense of their own values.... Later, in the 1960s, a different concept emerged: the concept of the right of the people to participate in the decisions that affected their lives. So part of the struggle was the struggle toward intellectualism [which] so often separated us so far from the masses of people that the gulf was almost too great to be bridged.

The struggle for being a part of the society also led to another major phase of the civil rights struggle. That was the period in which legalism or the approach to battling down the barriers of racial segregation through the courts [which] was spearheaded by the National Association for the Advancement of Colored People.... We moved from the question of equal educational opportunity in terms of teachers' salaries into another phase: equality in travel accommodations.... One of the young persons who was part of the first efforts to test [segregated travel] was Pauli Murray. Pauli Murray and I were part of a committee that was organized to try to go into the South to test Jim Crow in bus travel. But the decision was made that only the men could go.... I had just finished a tour of duty with the NAACP and had ridden a lot of Jim Crow buses and wanted very much to go, but I guess it was decided that I was too frail to make such a journey.

I think the period that is most important to most of us now is the period when we began to question whether we really wanted in. Even though the sit-in movement started off primarily as a method of getting in, it led to the concept of questioning whether it was worth trying to get in. The first effort was to be able to sit down at the lunch counters. When you look back and think of all the tragedy and suffering that the first sit-iners went through you begin to wonder, Why pay a price like that for the privilege of eating at lunch counters? There were those who saw from the beginning that it was part of the struggle for full dignity as a human being. So out of that came two things that to me are very significant. First, there was the concept of the trained finding their identity with the masses. Another thing that came out of it at a later period was that of leadership training. As the young people moved out into the community and finally were able to be accepted, they began to discover indigenous leaders....

Around 1965 there began to develop a great deal of questioning about what is the role of women in the struggle. Out of it came a concept that black women had to bolster the ego of the male. This implied that the black male had been treated in such a manner as to have been emasculated both by the white society and black women because the female was the head of the household. We began to deal with the question of the need of black women to play the subordinate role. I personally have never thought of this as being valid because it raises the question as to whether the black man is going to try to be a man on the basis of his capacity to deal with issues and situations rather than be a man because he has some people around him who claim him to be a man by taking subordinate roles.

I don't think you could go through the Freedom Movement without finding that the backbone of the support of the Movement were women. When demonstrations took place and when the community acted, usually it was some woman who came to the fore....

I think at this stage the big question is, What is the American society? Is it the kind of society that ... permits people to grow and develop according to their capacity, that gives them a sense of value, not only for themselves, but a sense of value for other human beings? Is this the kind of society that is going to permit that? I think there is a great question as to whether it can become that kind of society....

In order for us as poor and oppressed people to become a part of a society that is meaningful, the system under which we now exist has to be radically changed. This means that we are going to have to learn to think in *radical* terms. I use the term radical in its original meaning—getting down to and understanding the root cause. It means facing a system that does not lend itself to your needs and devising means by which you change the system. That is easier said than done. But one of the things that has to be faced is, in the process of wanting to change the system, how much have we got to do to find out who we are, where we have come from and where we are going? About twenty-eight years ago I used to go around making speeches, and I would open up my talk by saying that there was a man who had a health problem and he was finally told by the doctor that they could save his sight or save his memory, but they couldn't save both. They asked him which did he want and he said, "Save my sight because I would rather see where I am going than remember where I have been." I am saying as you must say, too, that in order to see where we are going, we not only must remember where we've been, but *we must understand where we have been*. This calls for a great deal of analytical thinking and evaluation of methods that have been used. We have to begin to think in terms of where do we really want to go and how we want to get there.

Finally, I think it is also to be said that it is not a job that is going to be done by all the people simultaneously. Some will have to be in cadres, the advanced cadres, and some will have to come later. But one of the guiding principles has to be that we cannot lead a struggle that involves masses of people without getting the people to understand what their potentials are, what their strengths are.

SOURCE: Reprinted from Joanne Grant, *Ella Baker: Freedom Bound*. Copyright © 1998 Joanne Grant. Reproduced with permission of John Wiley & Sons, Inc.

## GLOSSARY

**cadres:** groups of trained leaders

**feigning:** pretending

**Jim Crow:** a term, based on an African American character in a stage show, for the system of legalized segregation that prevailed in the southern United States from 1876 to 1965

## Document Analysis

Baker begins by reminding the audience, "I have existed much longer than you," evoking both her long-term involvement in the civil rights movements and her status as an elder. Baker became an active participant in the fight for black civil and political rights in the late 1920's. Few had the level of experience or the perspective that she possessed. Her remarks suggest that she was speaking to an audience of young people whose experiences with and knowledge of the civil rights movement may have been fairly limited. In the first few sentences, she mentions such notable figures as Vincent Harding and Bernice Reagon. Harding worked with Baker in the 1960s and in the 1980s and became a noted historian; Reagon was Baker's longtime friend. She noted that Harding played a role in facilitating her speech that day and that Reagon accompanied her to the talk to provide support

Baker highlighted the important role played by African American women in resisting slavery, racial discrimination, and Jim Crow segregation. She noted, "Wherever there was a struggle, black women have been identified with that struggle." Baker touches on the forms of resistance that were open to women. One was to pretend to be too sick to work; another was to commit infanticide to prevent their children from growing up as slaves. She recalled, "There is a story of a woman in Kentucky," she says, "who had borne thirteen children and strangled each of them with her own hands rather than have them grow up as slaves." As a rhetorical device, this has shock value: It tends to rivet one's attention on the speaker while one wonders what other horrors may be in the offing. It also serves to emphasize the point that Baker wanted to make—that the lives of slaves were severely circumscribed, leaving them little opportunity to express their frustration and anger. However, as she notes, even in the most restricted situations, these women held a degree of agency. Further, Baker points out that commitment to freedom and resentment of unjust treatment were part of the lives of African American women even among those who were slaves and, in fact, stood explained such dire acts as infanticide.

Baker and her own generation knew of many contemporary African American women who were also committed to freedom and who resented how their lives were restricted the laws and customs of segregation. Baker saw herself as born into an era where a limited number of African Americans had the opportunity to be educated. In turn the educated were to become leaders of the uneducated. This relationship between the educated leadership and the uneducated masses was born out of the "struggle to get into the society, the struggle to be a part of the American scene" and the belief that "through the process of education black people would be accepted in the American culture." However, Baker believed that this program for advancement embodied a wrongheaded approach to civil rights. To her, educating some blacks to become leaders would make African Americans conform to standards of behavior favored by their oppressors rather than to actually benefit those who most needed help in obtaining their rights. It accepted, if not embraced, the idea that it was acceptable to grant African Americans "their rights in proportion to the degree to which they qualified as being

persons of learning and culture." This viewpoint was problematic as it suggested that uneducated African Americans might be undeserving of full political and civil equality. It also suggested that African Americans needed to earn the rights that were guaranteed to white Americans.

Baker also pointed out that the idea that African Americans needed a "talented tenth" to lead them in the struggle for greater equality placed too much power in the hands of a few figures and created a disconnect or barrier between the well-educated leaders of the civil rights movement and the very people these leaders were supposed to be representing.

Although she cites the 1960s as the era for the emergence of a new idea, actually she had been advocating that very idea at least since the time she joined the NAACP: that liberation would come when the people being helped were helping themselves. To her, the civil rights movement's organizations should listen to what average African Americans wanted and then help them realize their hopes. Much of her life was spent listening to even the poorest of the poor because she believed a lack of formal education did not prevent people from thinking about their lives and understanding what they most needed.

In her account of the history of the shift from conforming to society to reshaping society, Baker perhaps gives too short shrift to what she calls "legalism"—the effort to eliminate segregation through legal action and the courts. For instance, the outlawing by the Supreme Court of racial segregation in education was a momentous event in the civil rights movement, changing how money was spent on education and who benefited from public education. Her misgivings about legalism stemmed from her belief that legal fighting was a top-down affair, with an African American social elite guiding the process on the assumption that they knew better than other African Americans what would be best for them. She hoped that the 1960s marked a shift to what she called "indigenous leaders," meaning people who were members of the communities they represented rather than external elites telling the communities what was best for them.

Baker was critical of the way female participants in the civil rights movement were sometimes treated. She recalled when she and civil rights activist Pauli Murray worked to coordinate a trip to the South to test legally required segregation on bus travel. However, despite the fact that she had "just finished a tour of duty with the NAACP and had ridden a lot of Jim Crow buses and very much wanted to go" it was decided that only men would be able to go on the trip. Baker argued that black women were unquestionably the "backbone" of the civil rights movement, but that their ideas and opinions weren't always taken seriously. She explained that the continued mistreatment and degrading of black men by white society led some members of the civil rights movement to conclude that the primary responsibility of black women in the movement was to "bolster the ego" of black men. She flatly rejected this argument, maintaining that this would only place black women in a subordinate position and would do little to improve the lives of black men.

Baker's advocacy of feminist ideas is noteworthy. She had been asked to speak about African American women, so her espousal of a feminist perspective is no surprise, but it is unclear whether Baker thought of herself as a feminist. She had long chafed under restrictions she believed had been placed on her only because she was a woman, and she had sometimes expressed her resentment of such restrictions.

Baker concluded her speech by outlining the importance of pushing for radical change. She noted, "In order for us as poor and oppressed to become part of a society that is meaningful, the system under which we now exist has to be radically changed." While she does not state explicitly what needs to change or how it needs to be changed, she does provide a definition of what she means by radical. She stated, "I use the term radical in its original meaning—getting down to and understanding the root cause. It means facing a system that does not lend itself to your needs and devising means by which you change the system." As suggested by the preceding statement, Baker believed that the first step to accomplishing radical change was to become knowledgeable about the subject at hand. Not surprisingly, considering her views about hierarchies, Baker asserted that the only way for radical change to occur would be with the participation of the masses and this could only occur once they "understand what their potentials are, what their strengths are."

## Essential Themes

When Ella Baker delivered "The Black Woman in the Civil Rights Struggle," she had already been involved in the fight for black equality for more than four decades.

She had worked as an organizer with the National Association for the Advancement of Colored People (NAACP), Southern Christian Leadership Conference (SCLC), and the Student Non-Violent Coordinating Committee (SNCC), among others. She had given many speeches over the years. However, because her speeches were rarely recorded and she didn't keep written copies, this particular speech is likely the most accurate version of a Baker speech that we have. Most of what we know about Baker and her contributions comes from other civil rights activists who knew her, but the speech provides us with some insight as to how she viewed both the civil rights movement and the role of women in the movement.

The speech was delivered in 1969, five years after the passage of the Civil Rights Act of 1964 and four years after the Voting Rights Act of 1965, the civil rights movement's two greatest legislative victories. Her speech was far different from what it would have been had she given it in 1960, when segregation was the law of the land and the vast majority of African Americans were unable to vote in the South.

Baker provided a critique of the leadership structure of the civil rights movement. She believed that a few leaders possessed too much power at the expense of the larger community who, she believed, needed to be encouraged to lead themselves. Throughout her career she had felt free to criticize the civil rights movement; thus this speech was consistent with her lifelong perspective. In particular she argued that the contributions of African American women to the movement had been unrecognized and undervalued. She was committed to gender equality. She would continue to be an activist for both causes until her death in 1986.

—*Gerald F. Goodwin, PhD and Kirk H. Beetz, PhD*

## Bibliography and Additional Reading

Moye, J. Todd. *Ella Baker: Community Organizer of the Civil Rights Movement*. Lanham, MD: Rowman & Littlefield Publishers, 2015. Print.

Payne, Charles. *I've Got the Light of Freedom: The Organizing Tradition and the Mississippi Freedom Struggle*. Oakland: University of California Press, 2007. Print.

Ransby, Barbara. *Ella Baker and the Black Freedom Movement: A Radical Democratic Vision*. Chapel Hill: The University of North Carolina Press, 2005. Print.

# Gloria Steinem: "Living the Revolution"

**Date:** May 31, 1970
**Author:** Gloria Steinem
**Genre:** Speech

## Summary Overview

Gloria Steinem, already a prolific journalist and renowned activist, gave this speech to Vassar College's graduating class of 1970. The transcript was later published by the *Vassar Quarterly*, making her words available to a wider audience. The 1960's had just ended, but the Women's and the Civil Rights Movements were still going strong, both of which Steinem elaborates upon in her speech. Although Steinem claims to be a reluctant speaker, she presents the case for gender and racial equality with grace and eloquence. She encourages the graduating students to lean into these movements and live these revolutions. The speech presents a number of myths present in American culture that act to perpetuate the American patriarchy and the oppression of women. She exhorts her audience to "un-learn" these myths and offers alternative ways of thinking. Despite the lucidity and vehemence of the speech, one might recognize many of the myths still prevalent nearly five decades later.

## Defining Moment

The audience members at any commencement speech, as college graduates, are at a turning point in their respective lives. Given in the year 1970, this particular commencement speech to and about the Women's Movement marks a symbolic coming of age for this ongoing movement.

Although Gloria Steinem is not a woman of color, she ties the Women's Movement to the Civil Rights Movement in important ways in this speech, both of which have long roots in the United States. Many observers point to the women's convention at Seneca Falls, New York in 1848 as the inception of the Women's Movement. Another hard-fought milestone came in the form of the Nineteenth Amendment, which finally gave women the right to vote, though not until 1920. The Civil Rights movement also has nineteenth century antecedents, such as the Emancipation Proclamation which freed the slaves in 1863. Nevertheless, through the first half of the twentieth century, open racism and sexism remained pervasive in American society and culture.

The 1960's questioned this status quo. The Civil Rights Acts of 1964 prohibited discrimination based on race, color, religion, sex, or national origin. The Voting Rights Act of 1965 reinforced the right of African Americans to vote established under the Fifteenth Amendment. Betty Friedan penned her influential book *The Feminine Mystique* in 1963, which galvanized a new generation of feminist thinkers and activists, sometimes dubbed Second Wave Feminism. The Sexual Revolution disputed women's subservient role in the household and bedroom and worked to normalize female sexuality. The 1970's saw more progress. In 1972, Title IX prohibited discrimination based on sex in educational programs that receive federal funds. In the same year, the landmark *Roe v. Wade* affirmed the legality of abortion.

Gender and racial discrimination remain pervasive in America. The same battles the Steinem discusses are being fought today. Local and State governments pass laws with the sole intent of lowering minority voter turnout. As of 2017, women make up less than twenty percent of congress. The wage gap persists along lines of both gender and race. Nevertheless, if today's activists for equality can take solace in one thing, it is the manifest progress won by the hard work of the women and men of previous generations.

## Author Biography

Following her paternal grandmother's lead, who had been a part of the women's suffrage movement in the early 1900's, Gloria Steinem became a leading voice in the women's movement of the 1960s, 70s and beyond. She was born on March 25, 1934 to working class parents. She graduated from Smith College in 1956 and lived for two years in India as a Chester Bowles Asian Fellow. In the early 1960s, Steinem cut her teeth in journalism, and by the end of the decade, she had become a renowned journalist and writer. For a 1963 article in *Show* magazine exposing the exploitation of women, Steinem famously worked as a playboy bunny at New York Playboy Club. By 1968, she was helping to found *New York* magazine. Four years later, she co-founded

The first issue of Ms., released in 1972. *Ms.* magazine [CC BY-SA 4.0 (https://creativecommons.org/licenses/by-sa/4.0)]

the feminist *Ms.* magazine; she served as editor for the magazine for a decade and a half and remains a consulting editor till this day. As Steinem was becoming a journalistic heavyweight throughout the 1960s and 70s, the Women's Movement raged, due in no small part to her activism. She has been an outspoken activist for progressive causes such as abortion rights and gay marriage (long before they became politically popular). She has worked as an advocate for presidential candidates from George McGovern in 1968 to Hillary Clinton in 2016. Today she continues to be a prolific writer and passionate champion for the causes that she believes in.

## HISTORICAL DOCUMENT

President Simpson, members of the faculty, families and friends, first brave and courageous male graduates of Vassar—and Sisters.

You may be surprised that I am a commencement speaker. You can possibly be as surprised as I am. In my experience, commencement speakers are gray-haired, respected creatures, heavy with the experience of power in the world and with Establishment honors. Which means, of course, that they are almost always men.

But this is the year of Women's Liberation. Or at least, it the year the press has discovered a movement that has been strong for several years now, and reported it as a small, privileged, rather lunatic event instead of the major revolution in consciousness—in everyone's consciousness—male or female that I believe it truly is.

It may have been part of that revolution that caused the senior class to invite me here—and I am grateful. It is certainly a part of that revolution that I, a devout non-speaker, am managing to stand before you at all: I don't know whether you will be grateful or not. The important thing is that we are spending this time together, considering the larger implications of a movement that some call "feminist" but should more accurately be called humanist; a movement that is an integral part of rescuing this country from its old, expensive patterns of elitism, racism, and violence.

The first problem for all of us, men and women, is not to learn, but to un-learn. We are filled with the Popular Wisdom of several centuries just past, and we are terrified to give it up. Patriotism means obedience, age means wisdom, woman means submission, black means inferior—these are preconceptions imbedded so deeply in our thinking that we honestly may not know that they are there.

Unfortunately, authorities who write textbooks are sometimes subject to the same Popular Wisdom as the rest of us. They gather their proof around it, and end by becoming the theoreticians of the status quo. Using the most respectable of scholarly methods, for instance, English scientists proved definitively that the English were descended from the angels, while the Irish were descended from the apes. It was beautifully done, complete with comparative skull-measurements, and it was a rationale for the English domination of the Irish for more than 100 years. I try to remember that when I'm reading Arthur Jensen's current and very impressive work on the limitations of black intelligence. Or when I'm reading Lionel Tiger on the inability of women to act in groups.

The apes-and-angels example is an extreme one, but so may some of our recent assumptions be. There are a few psychologists who believe that anti-Communism may eventually be looked upon as a mental disease.

It wasn't easy for the English to give up their mythic superiority. Indeed, there are quite a few Irish who doubt that they have done it yet. Clearing our minds and government policies of outdated myths is proving to be at least difficult. But it is also inevitable. Whether it's woman's secondary role in society or the paternalistic role of the United States in the world, the old assumptions just don't work anymore.

Rollo May has a theory that I find comforting. There are three periods in history, he says—one in which myths are built up, one in which they obtain, and one in which they are torn down. Clearly, we are living in a time of myths being torn down. We look at the more stable period just past, and we think that such basic and terrifying change has never happened before. But, relatively, it has. Clinging to the comfortable beliefs of the past serves no purpose, and only slows down the growth of new forms to suit a new reality.

Part of living this revolution is having the scales fall from our eyes. Every day we see small obvious truths that we had missed before. Our histories, for instance, have generally been written for and about white men. Inhabited countries were "discovered" when the first white male set foot there, and most of us learned more about any one European country than we did about Africa and Asia combined.

I confess that, before some consciousness-changing of my own, I would have thought the Women History courses springing up around the country belonged in the same cultural ghetto as home economics. The truth is that we need Women's Studies almost as much as we need Black Studies, and for exactly the same reason: too many of us have been allowed from a "good" education believing that everything from political power to scientific discovery was the province of white males. I don't know about Vassar, but at Smith we learned almost nothing about women.

We believed, for instance, that the vote had been "given" to women in some whimsical, benevolent fashion. We never learned about the long desperation of women's struggle, or about the strength and wisdom of the women who led it. We heard about the men who risked their lives in the Abolitionist Movement, but seldom about the women; even though women, as in many movements of social reform, had played the major role. We knew a great deal more about the outdated, male-supremacist theories of Sigmund Freud than we did about societies in which women had equal responsibility, or even ruled.

"Anonymous," Virginia Woolf once said sadly, "was a woman." I don't mean to equate our problems of identity with those that flowed from slavery. But, as Gunnar Myrdal pointed out in his classic study, An American Dilemma, "In drawing a parallel between the position of, and the feeling toward, women and Negroes, we are uncovering a fundamental basis of our culture." Blacks and women suffer from the same myths of childlike natures; smaller brains; in-

ability to govern themselves, much less white men; limited job skills; identity as sex objects—and so on. Ever since slaves arrived on these shores and were given the legal status of wives—that is, chattel—our legal reforms have followed on each other's heels. (With women, I might add, still lagging considerably behind. Nixon's Commission on Women concluded that the Supreme Court was sanctioning discrimination against women—discrimination that it had long ago ruled unconstitutional in the case of blacks—but the Commission report remains mysteriously unreleased by the White House. An Equal Rights Amendment, now up again before the Senate, has been delayed by a male-chauvinist Congress for 47 years.) Neither blacks nor women have role-models in history: models of individuals who have been honored in authority outside the home.

I remember when I was interviewing Mrs. Nixon just before the 1968 election, I asked her what woman in history she most admired and would want to be like. She said, "Mrs. Eisenhower." When I asked her why, she thought for a moment, and said, "Because she meant so much to young people."

It was the last and most quizzical straw in a long, difficult interview, so I ventured a reply. I was in college during the Eisenhower years, I told her, and I didn't notice any special influence that Mrs. Eisenhower had on youth. Mrs. Nixon just looked at me warily, and said, "You didn't?" But afterwards, I decided I had been unfair. After all, neither one of us had that many people to choose from. As Margaret Mead has noted, the only women allowed to be dominant and respectable at the same time are widows. You have to do what society wants you to do, have a husband who dies, and then have power thrust upon you through no fault of your own. The whole thing seems very hard on the men.

Before we go on to other reasons why Women's Liberation is Man's Liberation, too—and why this incarnation of the women's movement is inseparable from the larger revolution–perhaps we should clear the air of a few more myths.

The myth that women are biologically inferior, for instance. In fact, an equally good case could be made for the reverse. Women live longer than men. That's always being cited as proof that we work them to death, but the truth is: women live longer than men even when groups being studied are monks and nuns. We survived Nazi concentration camps better, are protected against heart attacks by our female hormones, are less subject to many diseases, withstand sugar better, and are so much more durable at every stage of life that nature conceives 20 to 50 percent more males just to keep the balance going. The Auto Safety Committee of the American Medical Association has come to the conclusion that women are better drivers because they are less emotional than men. I never thought I would hear myself quoting the AMA, but that one was too good to resist.

Men's hunting activities are forever being pointed to as proof of Tribal Superiority. But while they were out hunting, women built houses, tilled the fields, developed animal husbandry, and perfected language. Men, isolated from each other out there in the bush, often developed into creatures that were fleet of foot, but not very bright.

I don't want to prove the superiority of one sex to another. That would only be repeating a male mistake. The truth is that we're just not sure how many of our differences are biological, and how many are societal. In spite of all the books written on the subject, there is almost no such thing as a culture-free test. What we do know is that the differences between the two sexes, like the differences between races, are much less great than the differences to be found within each group. Therefore, requirements of a job can only be sensibly suited to the job itself. It deprives the country of talent to bundle any group of workers together by condition of birth.

A second myth is that women are already being treated equally in this society. We ourselves have been guilty of perpetuating this myth, especially at upper economic levels where women have grown fond of being lavishly maintained as ornaments and children. The chains may be made of mink and wall-to-wall carpeting, but they are still chains.

The truth is that a woman with a college degree working full-time makes less than a black man with a high school degree working full-time. And black women make least of all. In many parts of the country, New York City, for instance, woman has no legally-guaranteed right to rent an apartment, buy a house, get accommodations in a hotel, or be served in a public restaurant. She can be refused simply because of her sex. In some states, women cannot own property, and get longer jail sentences for the same crime. Women on welfare must routinely answer humiliating personal questions; male welfare recipients do not. A woman is the last to be hired, the first to be fired. Equal pay for equal work is the exception. Equal chance for advancement, especially at upper levels or at any level with authority over men, is rare enough to be displayed in a museum.

As for our much-touted economic power, we make up only 5 percent of all the people in the country receiving $10,000 a year or more. And that includes all the famous rich widows. We are 51 percent of all stockholders, a dubious honor these days, but we hold only 18 percent of the stock—and that is generally controlled by men. The power women have as consumers is comparable to that power all of us currently have as voters: we can choose among items presented to us, but we have little chance to influence the presentation. Women's greatest power to date is her nuisance value. The civil rights, peace, and consumer movements are impressive examples of that.

In fact, the myth of economic matriarchy in this country is less testimony to our power than to the resentment of the little power we do have.

You may wonder why we have submitted to such humiliations all these years; why, indeed, women will sometimes deny that they are second-class citizens at all.

The answer lies in the psychology of second-classness. Like all such groups, we come to accept what society says about us. And that is the most terrible punishment of all. We believe that we can only make it in the world by "uncle Tom-ing," by a real or pretended subservience to white males.

Even when we come to understand that we, as individuals, are not second class, we still accept society's assessment of our group—a phenomenon psychologists refer to as Internalized Aggression. From this stems the desire to be the only woman in an office, an academic department, or any other part of the man's world. From this also stems women who put down their sisters—and my own profession of journalism has some of them. By writing or speaking of their non-conformist sisters in a disapproving, conformist way, they are essentially saying, "See what a real woman I am," and expecting to be rewarded by ruling-class approval and favors. That is only beginning to change.

It shouldn't be surprising that women behave this way, too. After all, Internalized Aggression has for years been evident in black people who criticized each other ("See what a good Nigger I am"), or in Jews who ridiculed Jewishness ("See how I am different from other Jews"). It has been responsible for the phenomenon of wanting to be the only black family in the block, or the only Jew in the club.

With women, the whole system reinforces this feeling of being a mere appendage. It's hard for a man to realize just how full of self-doubt we become as a result. Locked into suburban homes with the intellectual companionship of three-year-olds; locked into bad jobs, watching less-qualified men get promoted above us; trapped into poverty by a system that supposes our only identity is motherhood—no wonder we become pathetically grateful for small favors.

I don't want to give the impression, though, that we want to join society exactly as it is. I don't think most women want to pick up slimline briefcases and march off to meaningless, de-personalized jobs. Nor do we want to be drafted—and women certainly should be drafted: even the readers of Seventeen Magazine were recently polled as being overwhelmingly in favor of women in National Service—to serve in an unconstitutional, racist, body-count war like the one in Indochina.

We want to liberate men from those inhuman roles as well. We want to share the work and responsibility, and to have men share equal responsibility for the children.

Probably the ultimate myth is that children must have full-time mothers, and that liberated women make bad ones. The truth is that most American children seem to be suffering from too much mother and too little father. Women now spend more time with their homes and families than in any past or present society we know about. To get back to the sanity of the agrarian or joint-family system, we need free universal daycare. With that aid, as in Scandinavian countries, and with laws that permit women equal work and equal pay, men will be relieved of their role as sole breadwinner and stranger to his own children.

No more alimony. Fewer boring wives, fewer child-like wives. No more so-called "Jewish mothers," who are simply normal ambitious human beings with all their ambitions confined to the house. No more wives who fall apart with the first wrinkle, because they've been taught their total identity depends on their outsides. No more responsibility for another adult human being who has never been told she is responsible for her own life, and who sooner or later comes up with some version of, "If I hadn't married you, I could have been a star." And let's say it one more time because it such a great organizing tool, no more alimony. Women Liberation really is Men's Liberation, too.

The family system that will emerge is a great subject of anxiety. Probably there will be a variety of choice. Colleague marriages, such as young people have now, with both partners going to law school or the Peace Corps together: that's one alternative. At least they share more than the kitchen and the bedroom. Communes, marriages that are valid for the child-rearing years only … there are many possibilities, but they can't be predicted. The growth of new forms must be organic.

The point is that Women's Liberation is not destroying the American family; it is trying to build a human, compassionate alternative out of its ruins. Engels said that the paternalistic, 19th Century family system was the prototype of capitalism—with man, the capitalist; woman, the means of production; children the labor—and that the family would only change as the economic system did. Well, capitalism and the mythical American family seem to be in about the same shape.

Of course, there are factors other than economic ones. As Margaret Mead says: "No wonder marriage worked so well in the 19th century; people only lived to be fifty years old." And there are factors other than social reform that will influence women's work success. "No wonder women do less well in business," says a woman-executive. "They don't have wives." But the family is the first political unit, and to change it is the most radical act of all.

Women have a special opportunity to live the revolution. By refusing to play their traditional role, they upset and displace the social structure around them. We may be subject to ridicule and suppression, just as men were when they refused to play their traditional role by going to war. But those refusals together are a hope for peace. Anthropologist Geoffrey Gorer discovered that the few peaceful human tribes had a common characteristic: sex roles were not polarized, boys weren't taught that manhood depended on aggression (or short hair or military skills), and girls weren't taught that womanhood depended on submission (or working at home instead of the fields).

For those who still fear that Women Liberation involves some loss of manhood, let me quote from the Black Panther code. Certainly, if the fear with which they are being met is any standard, the Panthers are currently the most potent male symbol of all. In Seize the Time, Bobby Seale writes, "Where there's a Panther house, we try to live socialism. When there's cooking to be done, both brothers and sisters cook. Both wash the dishes. The sisters don't just serve and wait on the brothers. A lot of black nationalist organizations have the idea of regulating women to the role of serving their men, and they relate this to black manhood. But a real manhood is based on humanism, and it not based on any form of oppression."

One final myth: that women are more moral than men. We are not more moral, we are only uncorrupted by power. But until the leaders of our country put into action the philosophy that Bobby Seals has set down until the old generation of male chauvinists is out of office—women in positions of power can increase our chances of peace a great deal. I personally would rather have had Margaret Mead as president during the past six years of Vietnam than either Johnson or Nixon. At least, she wouldn't have had her masculinity to prove.

Much of the trouble this country is in has to do with the Masculine Mystique: the idea that manhood somehow depends on the subjugation of other people. It's a bipartisan problem.

The challenge to all of us, and to you men and women who are graduating today, is to live a revolution, not to die for one. There has been too much killing, and the weapons are now far too terrible. This revolution has to change consciousness, to upset the injustice of our current hierarchy by refusing to honor it, and to live a life that enforces a new social justice.

Because the truth is none of us can be liberated if other groups are not. Women's Liberation is a bridge between black and white women, but also between the construction workers and the suburbanites, between Nixon's Silent Majority and the young people they hate and fear. Indeed, there's much more injustice and rage among working-class women than among the much-publicized white radicals.

Women are sisters, they have many of the same problems, and they can communicate with each other. "You only get radicalized, as black activists always told us, on your own thing." Then we make the connection to other injustices in society. The Women's Movement is an important revolutionary bridge. And we are building it.

I know it's traditional on such an occasion to talk about "entering the world." But this is an untraditional generation: you have made the campus part of the world. I thank you for it.

I don't need to tell you what awaits you in this country. You know that much better than I. I will only say that my heart goes with you, and that I hope we will be working together. Divisions of age, race, class, and sex are old-fashioned and destructive.

One more thing, especially to the sisters, because I wish someone had said it to me; it would have saved me so much time.

You don't have to play one role in this revolutionary age above all others. If you're willing to pay the price for it, you can do anything you want to do. And the price is worth it.

Source: Gloria Steinem. "Living the Revolution." Vassar Quarterly (Fall 1970): 12–15.

## Document Analysis

This document is the transcription of the commencement speech that Gloria Steinem gave to Vassar College's graduating class of 1970. Her immediate audience is, of course, the graduating seniors listening to her that day. Yet Steinem uses the opportunity to sum up the state of the Women's Movement to a larger audience. She speaks to both those within the Movement and those not, to both those present at the speech and those afterward reading the transcript (later published in the *Vassar Quarterly*). Early in the speech she says that the first problem "is not to learn, but to un-learn," and she, in fact, follows this advice throughout the speech. She frames her talk around several myths that must be dispelled.

Steinem begins with an admittedly "extreme" myth. She explains how "English scientists proved definitively that the English were descended from the angels, while the Irish were descended from the apes." She describes how the purveyors of this myth were not fringe elements in society but the very authorities who set the standard of scientific knowledge and wrote the textbooks. Science is not objective but can be manufactured to suit any purpose, even bigoted ones. These eugenic theories had long fallen out of the scientific and cultural mainstream by the time Steinem gave her speech and must have sounded quite ridiculous to the audience, but there lay the whole point. By beginning with an absurd theory that was nonetheless once widely accepted, she paves the way to overturn myths more familiar to her audience.

She moves on to contemporary myths that many of the audience was more likely to have heard themselves. These myths can be embedded in our everyday language. She commences with an example not from the history of gender relations but from the history of colonization: We are apt to say that "Inhabited countries were 'discovered' when the first white male set foot there." Still today, this period is often labelled as the Age of Discovery, even though these colonizers were embarking on previously inhabited lands. Moving back to the American women, she adds another example in which a common verb usage provides an insight into the prejudices of our culture. She explains how "We believed, for instance, that the vote had been 'given' to women in some whimsical, benevolent fashion." As she explains, this passive construction glosses over the hard struggles and large sacrifices of the women and men of the suffrage movement.

Moving from nuances of our language to larger cultural myths, she disproves "The myth that women are biologically inferior." She does so by citing the fact that women on average live longer than men, adding the related facts that women are less susceptible to many diseases and considered to be better drivers by the American Medical Association. The point is not to argue for the superiority of one sex over the other, she asserts, but rather she hopes to show that gender differences are given too much weight. The next myth moves from false inequality in biology to false equality in treatment: "A second myth is that women are already being treated equally in this society." This still prevalent myth then as now can be disproved with straightforward statistics. Among other data, the wage gap clearly exposes discrimination against women (particularly against women of color).

She coves two more myths. First, she asserts, "Probably the ultimate myth is that children must have full-time mothers, and that liberated women make bad ones." In fact, she argues, American children would benefit from more fathering. She calls on free, universal daycare to help ease mothers' transition back into the work force. With this suggestion as with many other points throughout the speech, it is jarring—and depressing—how relevant Steinem's advice remains nearly fifty years on. Some might be surprised at the last myth she overturns: "One final myth: that women are more moral than men." She argues that it is not that women are less immoral but that they have been less corrupted by power. She calls for more women in positions of power, positing that this would bring about a more peaceful world.

This speech is aptly titled "Living the Revolution." Not only does Steinem explicitly encourage her audience to live the revolution, but her speech also does so, by advocating for revolutionary thinking. As the capstone to at least four years of learning, the speech's primary audience is told to start unlearning.

## Essential Themes

Though never mentioned explicitly, a strong thread of intersectionality runs throughout the entire speech, especially the intersectionality between sexism and racism. The term intersectionality holds that forms of oppression are best understood not in a vacuum but when we examine how they intersect with other forms of oppression. In other words, we achieve a more complete comprehension of sexism when we understand how it is effected and amplified by racism, classism, and other forms of oppression. Intersectionality is most often associated with more recent feminist thinking, sometimes dubbed Third Wave Feminism. In fact, one of the main critiques of Second Wave Feminism, the wave that crested in the 1960's and 70's, is that it does not engage in intersectionality enough. Therefore, this speech and its inclusion of intersectionality showcase how Gloria Steinem was well ahead of her time.

Steinem is quick to connect the plight of women to that of people of color. Both groups are used as foils to normative white maleness, and this otherness is employed to keep both groups in subservient positions. She states "The truth is that we need Women's Studies almost as much as we need Black Studies, and for exactly the same reason: too many of us have been allowed from a 'good' education believing that everything from political power to scientific discovery was the province of white males." She is careful to assert that she is not trying to equate American women's plight with that of slavery. After this distinction has been made, she shows how both groups get exploited by white men. She continues from the perspective of the problematic but historically normative point of view: "Blacks and women suffer from the same myths of childlike natures; smaller brains; inability to govern themselves, much less white men; limited job skills; identity as sex objects—and so on." The intersectionality continues when she is dispelling the myth that women are treated as men's equals. Bringing class into the discussion, she faults some women of higher economic levels for perpetuating this myth. She then cites the wage gap to help her refute it. Women make significantly less than men, and "black women make least of all." By including an examination of race within her discussion of sexuality, she not only broadens her scope but she also enhances and refines her look at sexuality itself. Towards the end, she sums up much of her argument with a line the encapsulates the essence of intersectionality: "Divisions of age, race, class, and sex are old-fashioned and destructive." No type of division is given preference; they are all mentioned together and qualified with the same two negative adjectives, old-fashioned and destructive.

—*Anthony Vivian, MA*

## Bibliography and Additional Reading

Friedan, Betty. *The Feminine Mystique*. New York: W. W. Norton & Co., 1963. Print

Heilbrun, Carolyn G. *Education of a Woman: The Life of Gloria Steinem*. New York: Ballantine Books, 1996. Print

Steinem, Gloria. *My Life on the Road*. New York: Random House, 2015. Print.

Steinem, Gloria. *Outrageous Acts and Everyday Rebellions*. New York: Henry Holt & Co., 1987. Print.

# Conversations with Alice Paul: Woman Suffrage and the Equal Rights Amendment

**Date:** November 24-26, 1972
**Author:** Alice Paul
**Genre:** Interview

## Summary Overview

Alice Paul did not produce a large body of written documents. Modern students of the woman's suffrage and early feminist movements can gain insight into Paul's values and beliefs from oral sources, including an interview, "Conversations with Alice Paul," she gave in November of 1972, near the end of her life. In speaking with Amelia Fry, Paul provided personal insight into the push for women's suffrage at the turn of the century and reflections on the controversy over the attempted passage of the Equal Rights Amendment in the 1960s and 1970s.

## Defining Moment

By the 1960s the feminist movement had entered what historians call the "second wave." In essence this modern form of feminism was a delayed reaction to the domesticity of the 1940s and 1950s, driven by the post-war baby boom and increased resettlement in suburbs. Books such as *The Second Sex* by Simone de Beauvoir began to examine the role of women in western society, arguing that male-centered ideology was considered the norm, while women were considered "the other."

Second-wave feminism was a direct reaction to patriarchy and called for increased equality. Fueling this movement was the approval of the first oral contraceptive pill in 1960, which allowed women to delay childbirth and enter into the workforce in increasing numbers, where they uniformly faced discrimination and harassment based solely on their gender. In 1963 Betty Friedan published her wildly influential *The Feminine Mystique,* objecting to the depiction of women in mass media as objects to be possessed rather than individuals to be respected, and arguing that domesticity is a form of captivity. Only by being allowed to have lives and careers of their own could women find satisfaction in life. That same year freelance journalist Gloria Steinem published an undercover expose of the Playboy Club, documenting the systematic mistreatment of women in order to please male customers.

In response to the growing movement, the Kennedy administration established the Presidential Commission on the Status of Women, chaired by Eleanor Roosevelt, and Congress began to enact reforms in the name of gender equality on issues such as pay, participation, and access. In 1966 Friedan joined other influential feminists to form the National Organization for Women (NOW), created to empower women and lobby for legislative action. Across academia new women's studies departments were formed in an attempt to begin to study the role of women in culture, and gender segregated schools were increasingly made coeducational. In order to arm the struggle for equality, it was very quickly recognized that there were a lot of gaps in the scholarship, most notably on the history of suffrage and first-wave feminism. As a result a government, private organizations, and academia came together to document as much of the past of women's movements as possible before it disappeared.

The interview with Alice Paul and other early feminists became critical in not only understanding the history of those past efforts, but also in terms of knowledge sharing about techniques and strategies to affect change. The interviews helped to inform the composition and direction of second-wave feminism at a time when the Equal Rights Amendment was being steered through an attempt at ratification. Although passage of the legislation ultimately failed, the result of the imposition of a time limit, in its wake came other legal victories never achieved in the first wave. As many of the women interviewed left little in terms of writing, the interviews remain crucial to both women's studies and history today.

## Author Biography

Alice Paul, one of the nation's most outspoken suffragists and feminists in the early twentieth century and beyond, was born to a Quaker family at their Paulsdale estate in Mount Laurel, New Jersey, on January 11, 1885. Her religious background is relevant because the Hicksite Quakerism the family practiced placed a great deal of emphasis on gender equality. She came from a prominent family, with ancestors who included William Penn on her mother's side and the Massachusetts Winthrops on her father's. Her maternal grandfather was one of the founders of Swarthmore College, where Paul earned a bachelor's degree in biology in 1905. After attending the New York School of Philanthropy, she earned a master's degree from the University of Pennsylvania in 1907 and then went on to study at England's University of Birmingham and the London School of Economics before returning to the University of Pennsylvania, where she earned a PhD in sociology in 1912.

Her years in England, 1907 to 1910, were eventful. It was there that she served her apprenticeship in the struggle for women's rights. She came under the influence of the militant feminists Emmeline Pankhurst and her daughters, Christabel and Sylvia, and during those years she earned her stripes as an activist through demonstrations, arrests, imprisonment, hunger strikes, and force-feeding. On her return to the United States, she enlisted in the suffrage movement, first with the National American Woman Suffrage Association, though she and the young women she attracted to the movement were impatient with the association's conservative tactics. Accordingly, she broke with the association to found the Congressional Union for Woman Suffrage in 1913. The purpose of the new organization was to seek a federal constitutional amendment granting women the right to vote. In 1915 she appeared before the Judiciary Committee of the U.S. House of Representatives to testify on behalf of the proposed amendment.

In 1916 the Congressional Union evolved into the National Woman's Party. Paul and her followers, dubbed the Silent Sentinels, gained notoriety by launching a two-and-a-half-year picket (with Sundays off) of the White House, urging President Woodrow Wilson to support a suffrage amendment. After the United States entered World War I in 1917, few people believed that the picketers would continue. They did, often writing such incendiary phrases as "Kaiser Wilson" on placards, leading many people to conclude that the women were unpatriotic. (The reference was to Kaiser Wilhelm, ruler of Germany, America's enemy in the war.) Public opinion began to sway in favor of the suffragists when it was learned that more than 150 picketers had been arrested and sentenced to jail, usually on thin charges of obstructing traffic, and that the conditions the jailed women endured were often brutal. Paul, in particular, was subjected to inhuman treatment and launched a hunger strike in protest until she and the other protestors were released after a court of appeals ruled the arrests illegal. Meanwhile, the National Woman's Party continued to campaign against U.S. legislators who opposed the suffrage amendment.

After the passage by Congress (1919) and successful ratification (1920) of the Nineteenth Amendment recognizing the right of women to vote, Paul remained active in the woman's rights movement. In 1921 she wrote an equal rights amendment in the face of opposition from more conservative women's groups, who feared that such an amendment might strip women of protective legislation—in such areas as labor conditions—that had been passed during the Progressive Era. Nevertheless, she campaigned to make an equal rights amendment a plank in the platforms of both major political parties, which she succeeded in doing by 1944. In November 1972 and May 1973 she shared her reflections on the women's movement with an interviewer as part of an oral history project conducted by the University of California, Berkeley. She lived long enough to see Congress approve the Equal Rights Amendment in 1972, though the amendment was not ratified by enough states to allow it to become part of the Constitution. Paul died on July 9, 1977.

## HISTORICAL DOCUMENT

[AMELIA] FRY: … You had another meeting at Seneca Falls like the original one [in July of 1923].

[ALICE] PAUL: No, that Seneca Falls meeting was just to commemorate Seneca Falls. It was the seventy-fifth anniversary.

FRY: But you did submit an equal rights amendment wording.

PAUL: Yes by that time I think I had gotten all my awful bills out of the way and paid…. I always sympathize at the end of these Republican campaigns, Democrat campaigns, because I know that somebody is being left with these awful bills. Because you really would have thought, with wealthy women like Mrs. Belmont and so on that, while certainly one couldn't be too grateful for all she did, after all they all sailed away on their own lives. Suffrage was won and now the thing is over. We certainly had a hard time then.

But I would end up, it seems to me, by saying that when the ratification was over, we celebrated by putting in the Capitol the statues of the great pioneers who in large measure had started the modern campaign at Seneca Falls [in 1848]. It was one of the really big things we did, because it was starting women to have a feeling of respect for women and by putting statues of women in the Capitol when it had always been a Capitol of men. Until Jeannette Rankin no woman was venturing into the … Cosmos Club…. Then when we had a convention on and presented the statue to the Capitol, the last thing that we did in the suffrage campaign was that we voted to go on. Elsie Hill was very gallant and courageous and took the leadership….

By the end of two years …, we sort of, I guess, gathered up some more strength. And this was a really very wonderful meeting up at Seneca Falls. There we proposed not only would we work for equality but we would work for an equal rights amendment to the Constitution. And we started on that campaign. That's enough to finish up with.

FRY: And you did submit a wording of the amendment, which is in that issue of the *Suffragist* (or I guess maybe it was called the *Equal Rights* by that time).

PAUL: … I made the speech, you know, presenting this [amendment]. Of course, by this time I had recovered enough strength I think to feel convinced that we ought to go ahead with the campaign and we ought to do it in the form of another amendment to have *complete* emancipation as our goal…. I said, "This is just a tentative proposal because we have asked a good many lawyers to work on the form and so on, and the wording doesn't make much difference if we agree on what we want." So I presented this:

> "Men and women shall have equal rights throughout the United States and every place subject to its jurisdiction."

That said it all, and I said, "That's what we want, let's say what we want…."

That's when I started in to study law because I thought, "I can't do anything without knowing as much as the people who will be our opponents. I don't know anything whatsoever about law."

So I then went up and lived at the headquarters and early morning about six I went to the American University and enrolled in the law department, and I got my bachelor's degree in law.

And then I thought, "I really don't know much, I must say, still about law, as far as being able to cope with the people who say you can't have any such amendment as that." So you see we went around from person to person who was supposed to be a great authority. I went up myself to see Dean Pound at Harvard, who was supposed to be the greatest authority on constitutional law in the country, and Mrs. Lewis had her son work on it, and Elsie Hill met her husband when she and I went down to see him in the George Washington University law school to ask him to work on some kind of an amendment to the Constitution.

FRY: You mean, a man she later married?

PAUL: Yes, her later husband. That's where she met him. Everybody drew up things, and we knew they wouldn't do. But I thought I wasn't very well-equipped to be making judgments on this subject, so then I went on and took a master's degree in law at the American University. And then I thought, "Still, I really don't know very much about this—it is such a vast subject"—we had to study Roman law and all kinds of laws ..., things like that, quite a lot to do. So I then took the doctor of law. By that time I felt really I could talk to people on this subject, because I knew that they didn't know very much either. My feeling of complete ignorance they seemed pretty much to share.

So then the Judiciary Committee of the Senate paid no attention to us at all. We went to all the national conventions of the Republican party and the Democratic party that intervened ... but 1923 was the first hearing on the subject of the new amendment, and the amendment was "Men and women shall have equal rights throughout the United States and every place subject to its jurisdiction."

Well, at that hearing—and this seems almost impossible to believe—all the women's organizations that came, with the votes in their hands so they counted for something (while before nobody paid much attention to us or to anybody else when we went to hearings because we were all voteless), now became a great power, even more power in the minds of the congressmen and the senators than they really had, because they didn't have back of themselves any united, strong group that would always stand together on this subject. But they got up and spoke and the congressmen certainly felt they had power then. All of them spoke, I think, *against* the Equal Rights Amendment. And if they didn't speak against us they remained silent. They didn't speak for us. So we were the only group that spoke for the Equal Rights Amendment when it was first put in.

Then we saw just what Lucy Burns and all these people thought we would find. Our problem would not be the Senate and Congress and the President, because now we were voters and had this power; but it would be changing the thought of American women, because more than half the country were now new voters. And if the new voters through their own organizations went up and said, "Please don't have a thing to do with this. We don't want women working at night. We don't want women standing up to work, and we don't want women to lose their alimony, and we don't want married women working when their husbands are working," and all these things that they said.... Well, we said, "Now we have a wholly different task, which is to change the thought of American women, really."

So we started then to one convention after another after another and kept it up until this year. We are still keeping it up, the last one being the League of Women Voters and the one before that the AAUW [American Association of University Women]. I have told you all this, I think, before.

FRY: Well, yes, and I remember myself taking long lists of women's organizations to use with congressmen for you. By 1971 huge numbers had gotten behind the Amendment.

PAUL: I know, but you see our task through these years was this monotonous one of getting these women to change their minds to make them see what this principle meant and so on. So that's what has taken, more or less, all these years to do. Well now, we went to convention after convention of the political parties. It was in 1940....

Well, in 1940 for the first time we got in the Republican platform. Then in 1944 we got it in the Democratic one. That was a very hard-fought fight. Then we had it in both. Well, by that time Congress began to—

FRY: When did Republicans—?

PAUL: 1940. 1944—Democrats. And that's when we finally began to work with Mrs. Emma Guffey Miller because she was so prominent in the Democratic party. She came in and joined us then and laid our fight before the Democratic National Convention to put it in the platform, and we got it in.

Well, then Congress began to pay more attention to us. It was in the political party platforms, and the Judiciary Committee of the Senate began seriously to consider the wording....

While I was not national chairman, I went down whenever I could to try to help—I went in to see Senator Burton, I remember, from Ohio, who was on the Supreme Court later. At that time he was on the Senate Judiciary Committee. I went to talk about how it could be worded. I remember him saying, "Well, Senator Austin of Vermont, who is perhaps the most concerned man on the Judiciary Committee, and I have worked and worked and worked and worked and we still cannot find the wording that we think will express what you want."

So this went on. We had asked Dean Pound, and the versions that everybody had given us we knew enough at least about law to know we didn't want it. A great deal of this responsibility fell on me because I was now beginning to know a little bit about law, you see. So I think it was in 1943 that finally we took a draft to—Mrs. Broy went with me; she didn't know very much about it but she was our political chairman so she went with me—to see Senator Austin. We handed him a draft, "Equality of rights under the law shall not be denied or abridged"

The Amendment read, "Equality of rights under the law shall not be denied or abridged by the United States or by any state on account of sex. Congress and the several states shall have the power, within their respective jurisdictions, to enforce this article by appropriate legislation...." It was to take effect five years after ratification.

—what we now have, you see, the one that is now through Congress. So he studied it for a time and then he said, "Well, I really think perhaps this is just exactly right. I don't see anything the matter with it. And I think it will probably give you just what we all have in mind. But I wouldn't want to do it without Senator [Joseph Christopher] O'Mahoney of Wyoming who, on the Democratic side, is the chief person working for this measure."

So Mrs Broy and I then went up to Senator O'Mahoney's office. He was just departing for Wyoming where he lived, but he studied it and he said, "Well, you can go back and tell the senator that you just left that I will be, anyway, the second senator and I will support it, so you will have probably the man who is most concerned on the Republican side and the man who is the most concerned on the Democratic side." So we did.

Then we were asked to make sure that the women of the country who had already (in a few cases, not many, but a few organizations had) endorsed the old amendment, "Men and women shall have equal rights," these two men said, "We don't want to put this in and then find that the women won't stand back of us. So will you get the signature of the responsible person in every woman's organization that has endorsed the old amendment ('Men and women shall have equal rights') saying that they approve of the new amendment." So that's what we started and did.

We drew up a paper with the new proposed amendment addressed to the Senate Judiciary and called up each women's organization or had them come to see us, or in some form or other had them consider it, and we got a page of signatures of all these different women's groups. None of them knew enough to have any objection! Especially when we said we thought we could get the Senate Judiciary to support this. You see, the difference was, the old one said, "Men and women shall have equal rights throughout the United States and every place subject to its jurisdiction." They took the position that while they personally were for equal rights throughout the United States, they didn't think Congress had the right to interfere so much in the lives of *individual* people; they thought it ought to deal with the *government*; the *government* should not deny equal rights. So when we changed it to saying, "Equality of rights under the law shall not be denied or abridged *by the United States or any state* on account of sex," then they all signed, they all signed their approval of the new one.

## GLOSSARY

**Cosmos Club:** a private social club in Washington, D.C., for people distinguished in the arts, literature, and science and which first admitted women in 1988

**Elsie Hill:** a leading feminist and officer of the National Woman's Party and the Congressional Union for Woman Suffrage

**Emma Guffey Miller:** prominent Pennsylvania Democrat, active as a member of the state's Democratic National Committee and delegate to the Democratic National Convention

**Jeannette Rankin:** the first woman to be elected to the U.S. House of Representatives

**Lucy Burns:** one of the founders of the National Woman's Party

**Mrs. Broy:** Cecil Norton Broy, well-known member of the National Woman's Party

**Mrs. Lewis:** Dora Lewis, one of the leaders of the National Woman's Party who served several stints in jail for participating in suffrage demonstrations and pickets

**Senator Austin:** Senator Warren Austin

**Senator Burton:** Harold H. Burton

**Seneca Falls:** a city in New York that was the site of a pivotal women's rights convention in 1848

## Document Analysis

In these interview sessions in late 1972 and the spring of 1973, Alice Paul looks back on her six decades of feminist activism, with particular focus on the Equal Rights Amendment. She begins by laughingly noting that the suffrage campaign had generated heavy expenses and that the bills had to be paid. She mentions "Mrs. Belmont." Alva Belmont, though hardly a familiar name today, was a prominent and wealthy socialite who donated large amounts of money to suffrage organizations. She herself founded one of these organizations, the Political Equality League, in 1909, and she was a member of the National American Woman Suffrage Association. In an effort to broaden support among immigrants, African Americans, and working-class women, she established a "suffrage settlement house" in Harlem, New York. Later she merged her organization with Paul's Congressional Union for Woman Suffrage, and she was instrumental in helping Paul found the National Woman's Party. Using her own money, she purchased the party's headquarters building in Washington, D.C., now the Sewall-Belmont House and Museum.

Paul goes on to discuss her uncertainties about legal matters surrounding an equal rights amendment. Characteristically, in the face of her own perceived lack of knowledge, she went back to school and earned bachelor's, master's, and doctoral degrees in law from the American University. Armed with solid academic credentials, she was able to persuade the Republican and Democratic parties to include support for an equal rights amendment in their platforms. Interestingly, she notes that some of the strongest opposition she encountered came not from men but from women—a pattern that would continue for the next half century. Many women, women's groups, and labor organizations, including the League of Women Voters, the Women's Bureau of the U.S. Department of Labor, the National Consumers' League, and the American Federation of Labor, opposed such an amendment at some point. They feared that it would nullify protective legislation that had been passed to improve working conditions for women in factories and that it could deny women rights to alimony in cases of divorce.

One of the most prominent organizations that opposed Paul's efforts was the National Women's Trade

Union League, which argued that an equal rights amendment would benefit primarily educated women who wanted to enter professions but would not benefit working-class women, who labored for wages and who had fought hard for laws that shortened their working hours and bettered the conditions under which they worked. The league feared that an equal rights amendment could bring into question the constitutionality of labor laws that recognized the distinctive experiences of men and women in the labor force, thereby forcing women to work under the same conditions as men. In later decades some women opposed an equal rights amendment in the belief that it could require women to, among other things, register for the draft, serve in the military, and use unisex restrooms, and that it would preclude the existence of exclusively women's (and men's) organizations.

In her discussion of efforts to gain support for an equal rights amendment as part of the Democratic Party platform, Paul makes reference to Emma Guffey Miller, who played a prominent role in this effort. Miller campaigned for Democrats as early as 1920. In 1924, after seconding the nomination of Al Smith for president at the Democratic National Convention, she earned the distinction of being the first woman in the party's history to receive a vote (though actually it was a half vote) for the presidential nomination. Later she served as chair of the National Woman's Party (1960–1965) and as the party's life president (1965–1970). Throughout her career she was a vigorous supporter of an equal rights amendment.

Paul goes on to discuss the mechanics of the proposed amendment. She and her supporters received advice from a number of people, including members of the Senate Judiciary Committee. In particular, she discusses the change in the wording of the amendment. It was feared that the original wording—"Men and women shall have equal rights throughout the United States and every place subject to its jurisdiction"—allowed too much interference in personal issues, which would endanger support for the amendment. Accordingly, the amendment was reworded to focus more on the action of government: "Equality of rights under the law shall not be denied or abridged by the United States or by any state on account of sex."

## Essential Themes

Compared with such towering figures as Susan B. Anthony, Alice Paul is not as widely remembered as a leader in the movements for women's suffrage and an equal rights amendment, except among students of these movements. She produced little in the way of ringing eloquence that is still quoted today. Yet it is fair to say that without her efforts and those of hundreds of her colleagues, the success of the campaign for a suffrage amendment would have been considerably delayed. Arguably, the pressure she and the "Silent Sentinels" exerted on President Woodrow Wilson induced him to change his position on the suffrage amendment, and the pressure she brought to bear on Congress moved the glacially slow process along. Additionally, her militancy brought the issue to the attention of the American public, so that by the end of the 1910s growing numbers of both women and men were willing to accept woman's suffrage.

Paul's campaign for an equal rights amendment was, in the final analysis, not successful. Thirty-eight states had to ratify the amendment for it to become part of the Constitution. After an initial flurry of ratifications, the pace slowed, and only thirty-five states ratified it—and five of those states rescinded their ratifications. The campaign did, however, succeed in putting equal rights on the national agenda and making it a topic of discussion. The amendment failed, but in the minds of many legal scholars and members of the public, it had its desired effect in a more roundabout way, for numerous pieces of legislation were passed that took into account the status of women. One prominent example is the 1964 Civil Rights Act; Paul led a coalition that succeeded in getting a sexual discrimination clause added to the bill. In 1938 Paul helped found the World Woman's Party, with headquarters in Geneva, Switzerland. The organization later worked to include gender equality as part of the United Nations Charter and to establish the United Nations Commission on the Status of Women.

Although she was certainly a feminist hero, Paul has been the subject of scholarly debate over two issues. One was the attitude of her organizations toward African Americans. The other was her position on abortion. Paul and her colleagues have been accused of a subtle form of racism, given that the movement she spearheaded consisted almost entirely of white middle- and upper-class women, typically to the exclusion of working-class and African American women. It has been argued that the movement excluded African Americans out of fear that including them in any visible way would alienate the southern states, diminishing the ratification prospects of a suffrage amendment. Additionally, Paul appears to have opposed any effort to link the Equal Rights Amendment to abortion rights. Some observers have claimed that this opposition was a political decision based on a desire not to muddy the waters with the volatile and divisive issue of abortion. Others, however, have argued that throughout her life Paul explicitly opposed abortion and is reputed to have said that abortion rights exploited women, given that half the babies aborted were female.

—*Michael J. O'Neal, PhD and KP Dawes, MA*

## Bibliography and Additional Reading

Adams, Katherine H.; Keene, Michael L. *Alice Paul and the American Suffrage Campaign.* University of Illinois Press, 2008.

Baker, Jean H. *Sisters: The Lives of America's Suffragists.* Hill and Wang, 2005.

Bausum, Ann. *With Courage and Cloth: Winning the Fight for a Woman's Right to Vote.* National Geographic, 2004

Bederman, Gail. *Manliness and Civilization: A Cultural History of Gender and Race in the United States, 1880-1917* (Women in Culture and Society). University of Chicago Press, 1995.

Dubois, Ellen Carol. *Feminism and Suffrage: The Emergence of an Independent Women's Movement in America, 1848-1869.* Cornell University Press, 1999.

Friedan, Betty. *The Feminine Mystique* (50th Anniversary Edition). Norton Press, 2001.

Lunardini, Christine. *Alice Paul: Equality for Women.* Boulder: Westview Press, 2013.

Zahniser, J. D.; Fry, Amelia R. *Alice Paul: Claiming Power.* Oxford University Press, 2014.

# ■ Equal Rights Amendment

**Date:** 1972
**Author:** Alice Paul
**Genre:** Constitutional Amendment (voted but not ratified)

## Summary Overview

The Equal Rights Amendment (ERA), originally written by Alice Paul in 1921 and first proposed to Congress in 1923, was intended to guarantee full rights for women under the law. Following the passage of the Nineteenth Amendment, which extended suffrage to women, in August 1920, some believed that the U.S. Constitution should be amended to guarantee full rights for women in all aspects of life, from employment to education to divorce to property ownership. In fact, not all feminists agreed that such a constitutional amendment was necessary. Nevertheless, Paul and other members of the National Woman's Party (NWP) discussed language for the proposed Equal Rights Amendment. In the ensuing years the fight over the amendment waxed and waned, with the proposed legislation being introduced to every session of Congress from 1923 onward but remaining bottled up in committees. Paul rewrote the Equal Rights Amendment into the current language in 1943, aiming to echo the language of the Fifteenth Amendment (which bars governments from preventing a person from voting on the basis of race or previous slave status) and the Nineteenth Amendment.

With the revitalization of the women's movement in the 1960s, the demand for the passage of the Equal Rights Amendment gained new life. Feminists, male and female, recognized that inequities still existed under American law, despite the passage of such landmark legislation as the Equal Pay Act of 1963 and Title VII of the Civil Rights Act of 1964 (protecting people against discrimination in the workplace on the basis of race or national origin or gender). The revised version of the Equal Rights Amendment was finally pushed through Congress and presented to the states for ratification on March 22, 1972. The amendment's proponents saw it as the culmination of the long struggle for women's rights that began with the American Revolution and the adoption of the U.S. Constitution.

By 1977, thirty-five of the needed thirty-eight states had ratified the proposed twenty-seventh amendment. At the time of its introduction, the Equal Rights Amendment was given a seven-year limit for ratification; in 1978, ratification was still needed from three more states, and the limit was extended to 1982. By 1982 the United States had become a more conservative country than it had been ten years earlier, as exemplified by the election of the Republican Ronald Reagan to the presidency in 1980. The anti-ERA forces, playing on fears that the amendment would cause the downfall of society and other such propaganda, were remarkably well organized and successfully pressured politicians to allow the Equal Rights Amendment's defeat.

## Defining Moment

When the NWP proposed the first version of the ERA, the Nineteenth Amendment to the U.S. Constitution had just been passed, giving women the right to vote. This major victory spurred some feminists to seek further legal guarantees for women's equality. The 1920s, however, marked the beginning of an era of conservatism, with business-minded politicians controlling Congress and the White House. Generally, Americans were tired of war, weary of the radicalism of the immediate post–World War I years, and longing for a return to "normalcy," as Warren G. Harding put it in a speech given in Boston in 1920. The popular image of the 1920s is of the Jazz Age, when women bobbed their hair, shortened their skirts, danced the Charleston until dawn, and drank bootleg gin with handsome young men, making out in the backseat of, say, a Stutz Bearcat when appropriate. In the eyes of their late-Victorian-period mothers, the women of this new era were liberated and free.

In reality, however, most people did not live the life of F. Scott Fitzgerald's bon vivant literary character Jay Gatsby and his friends: African Americans were subject to the brutalities of racism; the Ku Klux Klan revitalized and added immigrants, Catholics, and Jews to its hate list; and the typical American woman was hardly a liberated flapper in the model of the actress and sex symbol Clara Bow. Indeed, women were still subject to inequities in employment, divorce law, property rights, and other matters of daily life. Still, the feminists who sought equal rights under the law had a difficult time finding allies in their quest for justice. With the arrival of the Great Depression in the late 1920s, more pressing matters than women's rights occupied the nation. Despite the national presence in the 1930s of First Lady Eleanor Roosevelt, who championed the cause of women, such as by trying to ensure that they were given fair treatment in her husband Franklin's New Deal programs, few were concerned about trying to gain passage for the ERA. With World War II coming on the heels of the Great Depression, other issues again pushed women's rights far into the background.

The post–World War II years gave birth to the complacent "Eisenhower fifties" (under President Dwight D. Eisenhower). While women had made extraordinary contributions to the American war effort, society in general demanded that most now return home and proceed with the business of finding husbands and raising families. While the popular image of the 1950s became one of consumerism-driven Americans living in neat suburban houses, going to malt shops, and dancing to the new "rock and roll," the reality again was quite different; the 1950s were generally prosperous but were still a time when America was more turbulent than the mythology indicates. The decade opened with undeclared war in Korea, where U.S. and United Nations troops fought the Chinese and their allies. The cold war, which had begun at the end of World War II, raged on, as the United States and its allies faced off against Communism. In one of the bitterest episodes in American history, the Wisconsin senator Joseph McCarthy instigated a witch hunt against people over a broad spectrum of American society who he believed to be Communists or Communist sympathizers. The allegations, rumors, and outright lies put forth during the McCarthy hearings ruined many lives. Actors, politicians, labor leaders, academicians, writers, musicians, and many others consequently lost their livelihoods and good names.

The 1950s also saw the rise of the civil rights movement, which in turn sparked a new women's rights movement. While some people had long supported equal rights for African Americans, they amounted to a small minority. Black men did get the right to vote after the Civil War, but few proved able to actually exercise the right, especially in the segregated South. At the beginning of the twentieth century, organizations such as the National Association for the Advancement of Colored People and the National Urban League formed to fight for the rights of African Americans. For many years, these were voices crying out in the wilderness, as African Americans continued to be systematically denied basic rights, such as equal access to employment and to decent schools. Furthermore, African Americans who dared to challenge the system were intimidated and risked their very lives, with lynching becoming widespread.

At the end of World War II, many African Americans came home after bravely serving their deeply segregated nation and realized that the time to systematically fight back had come. After President Harry S. Truman took the courageous step of desegregating the armed forces in 1948, which nearly cost him the subsequent election, African Americans were further encouraged to stand up for themselves. One of the first major episodes in the modern civil rights movement came in 1954, when the U.S. Supreme Court declared segregation unconstitutional in public schools in the landmark decision in *Brown v. Board of Education*. This case paved the way for the desegregation of the nation in other aspects of life. The following year, Rosa Parks, secretary of the Montgomery branch of the National Association for the Advancement of Colored People, further fueled the movement when she refused to relinquish her bus seat to a white person in Montgomery, Alabama. Parks's actions sparked the Montgomery bus boycott, in which African Americans refused to ride city buses until the buses were desegregated in 1956. Dr. Martin Luther King, Jr., first established his name and reputation by leading the Montgomery bus boycott.

Over the next decade, men and women of conscience battled discrimination in numerous ways, on the streets and in the halls of Congress and state legislatures. Young people, such as the African American students who desegregated Central High School in Little Rock, Arkansas, in 1956 and who sometimes feared for their very lives in the classroom, were an important part of the movement. The U.S. Congress finally saw the need to pass legislation guaranteeing equal protection under the law regardless of the color of one's skin. The first piece of landmark legislation in this respect was the Civil Rights Act of 1964, which forbade discrimination on the basis of race, religion, or national origin. Title VII of that act also became important for the nascent women's movement, since it outlawed discrimination on the basis of gender as well. The Twenty-fourth Amendment to the U.S. Constitution, also passed in 1964, finally abolished the poll tax, which had prevented many poor and working-class people from casting ballots. The Voting Rights Act of 1965 made it easier for people to register to vote without having to take literacy tests.

The turmoil over civil rights for African Americans inspired American women to demand equal treatment as well. Impetus for the women's movement came from a number of sources. Generally, middle-class women in the 1950s were better educated than previous generations, with many earning college degrees. Still, society dictated that every woman's goal in life should be to find a husband, settle down, and raise a family as the perfect housewife and mother. The trouble was that not all women were happy in the restrictive role dictated by society. While these women loved their families, being the domestic wife and mother was sometimes not fulfilling enough. In 1963 Betty Freidan published her seminal work *The Feminine Mystique*, which questioned the popular vision that women could find true happiness only in the domestic realm. Freidan referred to the discontent many women felt as the problem without a name. *The Feminine Mystique* became a best seller and is considered one of the major works of the modern feminist canon. Around the time of this book's appearance, the President's Commission on the Status of Women, which President John F. Kennedy had appointed in 1961 and which was originally headed by Eleanor Roosevelt, issued its report on women in American society. The report noted that women still faced enormous discrimination in the workplace, including lower pay, denial of promotions, and other unfair labor practices. The report led to the passage of the Equal Pay Act in 1963, making it illegal for employers to pay women less than they paid men for the same job.

While the federal commission's report retained societal notions regarding women's responsibility for family life, it was revolutionary for the era, calling for an end to discriminatory practices based on gender in realms such as divorce law, eligibility for jury duty, and property rights of married women. The commission also triggered the establishment of a number of state commissions on the status of women. Most of the members of the federal commission, however, saw no need for the ERA, assuming that other legislation would eventually give women equal rights, such as with Title VII of the Civil Rights Act of 1964, which ended discriminatory labor practices based on gender. However, the Equal Employment Opportunity Commission, created to enforce the Civil Rights Act, was lackadaisical in addressing women's complaints about work situations. Betty Freidan and other feminist leaders, such as Pauli Murray, a member of the President's Commission on the Status of Women, were particularly incensed by the commission's obstinacy in refusing to end sex-segregated advertisements for wanted help.

At the third annual conference of the Commission on the Status of Women, held in 1966, Freidan, Murray, and twenty-six other participants set up what they thought at the time was a temporary organization to fight for women's rights. This group became the National Organization for Women (NOW). At the first organizational meeting, the members adopted a lengthy statement of purpose, which was drafted by Freidan. At the core of the statement of purpose is NOW's mission: "to take action to bring women into full participation in the mainstream of American society now, exercising all the rights and responsibilities thereof in truly equal partnership with men." At the second national conference the following year, NOW adopted the passage of the ERA as one of its major goals.

The formation of NOW owed much to the civil rights movement. As inspired by the activism of African Americans and other justice-minded people, the women and men who formed NOW believed that women deserved to be given an equal place in society. The general air of liberalism in the 1960s, coupled with the rise of the anti–Vietnam War movement, also affected the development of the contemporary women's rights movement. In this atmosphere the revised ERA was introduced into Congress and in 1972 passed the Senate by a vote of 84–8. By 1977, thirty-five of the needed thirty-eight states had ratified the proposed twenty-seventh amendment. At the time of its introduction, the ERA was given a seven-year limit for ratification; in 1978, ratification was still needed from three more states, and the limit was extended to 1982. By 1982 the United States had become a more conservative country than it had been ten years earlier, as exemplified by the election of the Republican Ronald Reagan to the presidency in 1980. The anti-ERA forces, playing on fears that the amendment would cause the downfall of society and other such propaganda, were remarkably well organized and successfully pressured politicians to allow the amendment's defeat.

Despite setbacks, progress has been made in the protection of women's hard-won rights, such as the passage of Title IX of the Education Amendments of 1972, which guarantees equal access to education for women, including in athletics. NOW and other feminist organizations are still committed to the passage of the ERA and continue to work for the empowerment of women.

## Author Biography

Alice Paul was born on January 11, 1885, in Mount Laurel, New Jersey, to Tacie Parry and William Mickle Paul. Alice's father was a successful banker and businessman. The Pauls were Quakers, and Alice received her earliest education at the Moorestown Friends School, where she graduated in 1901. The young Alice Paul's Quaker upbringing instilled in her the principle of equality of the sexes. She went on to Swarthmore College, where she received a BA in 1905. She then attended the New York School of Philanthropy to train for social work and later received an MA in sociology from the University of Pennsylvania. After attending the London School of Economics and the University of Birmingham in England, she returned to the United States and earned a doctorate in political science in 1912 from the University of Pennsylvania. She later received a master of laws and a doctorate in civil law from American University's Washington College of Law.

Paul's sojourn in England exposed her to the ideas of the British suffragette Christabel Pankhurst. She joined the radical Women's Social and Political Union, which advocated aggressive action in the fight for women's rights, including hunger strikes, rock throwing, and window breaking. Paul brought these tactics home to the United States, where she joined the National American Woman Suffrage Association (NAWSA), to be appointed head of the group's Congressional Committee and lead the campaign for a federal suffrage amendment. Paul and her friends Crystal Eastman and Lucy Burns traveled to Washington, D.C., to work on their cause, organizing a parade up Pennsylvania Avenue in March 1913 that coincided with President Woodrow Wilson's inauguration. While the march began peacefully, male onlookers quickly turned verbally abusive and physically violent, insulting, jeering at, and assaulting the suffragists. The police did nothing to help the marchers.

Although she was a member of NAWSA, Paul did not agree with all of the organization's tactics. In 1914 Paul and her followers formed the Congressional Union for Woman Suffrage, which was technically an arm of NAWSA but eventually separated, becoming the National Woman's Party (NWP) in 1916. As did their British sisters, the NWP held the party in power responsible for the failure to get the women's suffrage amendment passed. Despite the fact that the United States was engaged in the Great War, the NWP picketed the White House, going so far as to chain themselves to the fence. The NWP members' actions led to their imprisonment and outraged many who felt that they had gone too far while America was at war. While in prison, Paul and others went on hunger strikes but were forcibly fed in an exceedingly cruel manner; the harsh treatment they received in prison did gain the women much sympathy.

The contributions of women to the war effort, in conjunction with the hard work of the various suffrage camps and perhaps even the sympathy generated by the imprisonment of Paul and her allies, finally led to women's gaining the vote when the Nineteenth Amendment to the U.S. Constitution was ratified on August 18, 1920. When the idea of suffrage for women finally became a reality, some American feminists were unsure as to what their next goal would be. NAWSA morphed into the League of Women Voters, a nonpartisan organization dedicated to fostering an informed electorate. Paul, aware of the fact that in spite of having the vote women were still victimized by discrimination in most areas of life, believed that women still needed a federal amendment guaranteeing all of their rights. In 1923, on the seventy-fifth anniversary of the Seneca Falls Convention, Paul and the NWP proposed the ERA. Paul dubbed it the "Lucretia Mott Amendment" in honor of that pioneer feminist, one of the organizers of the Seneca Falls Convention.

Throughout her life, Alice Paul tirelessly sought to secure passage of the ERA, which was rewritten in 1943 and later redubbed the "Alice Paul Amendment" in her honor. She traveled widely and even started the World Woman's Party in Geneva, Switzerland, in 1938, to work for worldwide gender equality. Upon the formation of the United Nations in 1945, Paul worked to ensure that the charter would include a call for equal rights for women and helped establish the United Nations' Commission on the Status of Women. Paul was one of the people who pushed for the inclusion of gender in Title VII of the Civil Rights Act of 1964. She supported the ratification of the ERA as a twenty-seventh amendment to the Constitution but did not live to see it become law. Paul died on July 9, 1977, in Moorestown, New Jersey, having given her long life to the cause of equal rights for women.

## HISTORICAL DOCUMENT

SECTION 1. Equality of rights under the law shall not be denied or abridged by the United States or by any State on account of sex.

SECTION 2. The Congress shall have the power to enforce, by appropriate legislation, the provisions of this article.

SECTION 3. This amendment shall take effect two years after the date of ratification.

### GLOSSARY

**abridged:** lessened, diminished, or curtailed

**ratification:** approval or confirmation; formal sanction

### Document Analysis

The text of both versions of the ERA is relatively short. Alice Paul's original 1921 text is deceptively simple, stating that both genders shall have equal rights under the law. The revised version is subtly different, dropping the word *men* and stating that women's rights shall not be denied by the federal government or by any of its states. The revised version also includes two additional clauses, one stating that Congress shall have the right to enforce the law and one giving the time frame for compliance. Ostensibly, Paul revised the ERA to conform the language to that of the Fifteenth and Nineteenth Amendments to the U.S. Constitution. The Fifteenth Amendment, passed in 1870, states that "the right of citizens of the United States to vote shall not be denied or abridged by the United States or by any State on account of race, color, or previous condition of servitude" and that "Congress shall have power to enforce this article by appropriate legislation." The language of the Nineteenth Amendment is nearly identical, with "sex" replacing the wording on racial considerations; the enforcement clause is the same.

The simplicity of the language in both versions of the ERA actually triggered opposition to the amendment. Indeed, the ERA was a source of controversy and division even among feminists from the outset of its introduction in 1923. Many women feared that such an amendment would negate various pieces of labor legislation, particularly laws designed to "protect" female workers. Organized labor was especially opposed to the ERA, largely because of the protective labor laws, well into the late 1960s. Paul and other supporters felt that some of the labor legislation ostensibly protecting women was actually harmful, in that employers often used the legislation as an excuse to pay women less, not promote them, or not hire them at all. From the 1920s to the 1960s this was one of the biggest arguments against the ERA. Even Eleanor Roosevelt, one of the staunchest supporters of women's rights, felt that the ERA was unnecessary, believing that other legislation would eliminate legal inequities based on gender.

In 1972, after Congress finally approved the ERA, the amendment seemed on the verge of sailing through to ratification by the needed thirty-eight states, with thirty-five ratifying within five years. However, ERA opponents led by Phyllis Schlafly marshaled their forces and launched an attack on the proposed amendment. The simplicity of the language left the amendment open to all sorts of interpretations as to what would happen should it be adopted. Schlafly's group—Stop ERA, which became the Eagle Forum—and other right-wing pundits argued that the ERA would allow for same-sex marriages, the drafting of women into the armed forces, the creation of unisex public restrooms, and the negation of other "privileges" granted to American women. Despite the fact that the pro-ERA forces—

led by NOW, ERAmerica, and more than eighty other mainstream organizations—were also well organized and well funded, the amendment was not ratified by the needed number of states, and it is still not a part of the U.S. Constitution.

After ratification of the Nineteenth Amendment in 1920, many women drifted away from the movement, feeling that its major goal, suffrage for women, had been achieved. Doubtless adding to this flagging interest in feminist issues was the prosperity of the 1920s, a prosperity that, combined with fatigue brought on by the privations of World War I, produced the so-called Roaring Twenties. This was a decade of relief characterized by loosened moral strictures and a belief that new technologies (the automobile, the radio, and the refrigerator, among many others) could solve social and economic problems and create a better life for Americans.

Alice Paul and the members of the National Woman's Party, which numbered about ten thousand members at its apogee, disagreed. Paul believed that while the Nineteenth Amendment was a major step, full equality for women could not be achieved without an equal rights amendment. Accordingly, in 1921 she wrote the first version of the Equal Rights Amendment that nearly a half century later Congress would approve and submit to the states for ratification. The amendment she wrote, which she called the Lucretia Mott Amendment to honor the prominent nineteenth-century abolitionist and feminist, consisted of a single statement: "Men and women shall have equal rights throughout the United States and every place subject to its jurisdiction." She presented the amendment at a convention in Seneca Falls, New York, held to commemorate the 1848 Seneca Falls Convention that essentially launched the suffrage movement.

Paul's Equal Rights Amendment was first submitted to Congress in 1923. It was submitted to every session of Congress until it was passed in 1972. By 1944 both the Democratic and Republican parties included the amendment in their platforms. The amendment was revised in 1943 to read, "Equality of rights under the law shall not be denied or abridged by the United States or by any state on account of sex," and by this time it was referred to as the Alice Paul Amendment.

### Essential Themes

When Alice Paul and the NWP began discussing what is now called the ERA, M. Carey Thomas, the president of Bryn Mawr College, offered her support for the legislation, stating, "How much better by one blow to do away with discriminating against women in work, salaries, promotion and opportunities to compete with men in a fair field with no favor on either side!" (Cott, p. 125). While the need for the ERA may have been self-evident to women like Paul and Thomas, many long-time supporters of women's rights were in the opposite camp. The whole issue of protective labor legislation for women was thorny; feminists who tried to look out for the interests of working-class women in particular believed protective legislation to be necessary, especially for women engaged in industrial labor. In the 1920s, the NWP's insistence on a federal amendment addressing women's equality divided the ranks of American feminists. Many leading women's organizations, such as the League of Women Voters (the successor to the National American Woman Suffrage Association), the National Consumers League (led by the feminist Florence Kelley), and the Women's Trade Union League, believed that the ERA was not necessary and could in fact be detrimental to women workers, especially in the area of protectionist legislation.

By the late 1960s, with the revitalization of the feminist movement, the ERA had become a cornerstone of women's rights issues. With NOW urging its ratification as early as 1967, the ERA came to symbolize the cause of feminism in the United States. Instead of dividing supporters of women's rights at this time, the cause of the ERA proved to have a galvanizing effect. As part of the liberal, reformist spirit of the 1960s and early 1970s, other legislation affecting the lives of women was enacted. Beginning with the Equal Pay Act of 1963 and Title VII of the Civil Rights Act of 1964, much progress was made in the elimination of legal barriers to women in the United States.

Despite the fact that the ERA has not been adopted as part of the U.S. Constitution, the movement that coalesced around it raised consciousness about women's second-class status in American society. The women's movement sparked many women's desires to enter the professions, politics, and other areas of employment not traditionally considered "feminine." Partly because of the women's movement, the Democrats nominated the first woman vice presidential candidate in 1984, the New York representative Geraldine Ferraro. In the run-up to the 2008 presidential election, a woman, Senator Hillary Rodham Clinton, was considered one of the leading contenders for the Democratic nomination. While women like Clinton have been very visible, many more women not in the public eye have also benefited from the feminist movement, even without the ERA. Women throughout the nation have gone to college on athletic scholarships thanks to Title IX; have won sex discrimination lawsuits against employers who broke labor laws regarding equal employment; and have become stay-at-home mothers because they chose to be, not because society dictated that they do so. While gender inequities still exist—and the ERA remains unratified—American women have made gains in most aspects of life.

—*Donna M. DeBlasio and Michael J. O'Neal, PhD*

## Bibliography and Additional Reading

Alice Paul Institute Web site. http://www.alicepaul.org/. Accessed on March 4, 2008.

Barakso, Maryann. *Governing NOW: Grassroots Activism in the National Organization for Women*. Ithaca, N.Y.: Cornell University Press, 2004.

Butler, Amy E. Two Paths to Equality: Alice Paul and Ethel M. Smith in the ERA Debate, 1921–1929. Albany: State University of New York Press, 2002.

Chafe, William H. The American Woman: Her Changing Social, Economic, and Political Roles, 1920–1970. New York: Oxford University Press, 1972.

———. The Paradox of Change: American Women in the Twentieth Century. New York: Oxford University Press, 1991.

Cott, Nancy F. *The Grounding of Modern Feminism*. New Haven, Conn.: Yale University Press, 1987.

Echols, Alice. *Daring to Be Bad: Radical Feminism in America, 1967–1975*. Minneapolis: University of Minnesota Press, 1989.

Evans, Sara M. *Born for Liberty: A History of Women in America*. New York: Free Press, 1989.

———. Tidal Wave: How Women Changed America at Century's End. New York: Free Press, 2003.

Friedan, Betty. *The Feminine Mystique*. New York: W. W. Norton, 1963.

Lunardini, Christine. From Equal Suffrage to Equal Rights: Alice Paul and the National Woman's Party, 1910–1928. New York: New York University Press, 1986.

National Organization for Women Web site. http://www.now.org/. Accessed on March 4, 2008.

National Women's History Project Web site. http://www.nwhp.org/. Accessed on March 4, 2008.

The Equal Rights Amendment Web site. http://www.equalrightsamendment.org/. Accessed on March 4, 2008.

Woloch, Nancy. *Women and the American Experience*. New York: Knopf, 1984.

# ■ Title IX

**Date:** June 23, 1972
**Author:** Birch Bayh, original bill by Patsy Mink and Edith Green
**Genre:** Law

## Summary Overview

Although Title IX is generally referred to in the context of sports, this law goes well beyond this limited, albeit very public, aspect of educational institutions. It outlaws most gender-based discrimination in education. While there are very specific exceptions, any educational entity that receives federal money for any part of its program is subject to this law. Thus, while opportunities to participate in athletics is one area where great changes had to be made at most schools, this law also applies to admission to schools and academic programs.

Equal opportunity in education had been at the center of the civil rights movement since the filing of *Brown v. Board of Education*. As women pushed for equal rights, education was one area which was understood to be of vital importance. In 1970, Representative Edith Green held hearings on the issue and, with Representative Patsy Mink, introduced legislation. In February, 1972, with the assistance of Representatives Mink and Green, Senator Birch Bayh introduced essentially the same bill, which ultimately passed. This transformed educational opportunities for girls and women.

## Defining Moment

While the push for gender equality in American society, as well as racial and ethnic equality, had existed for decades, the 1960s brought new strength to these efforts. What was called the women's liberation movement, or the feminist movement, not only advocated changes in the role women were expected to play within society, but it also advocated equal opportunity and treatment for women in education and employment. In the 1950s, only men were considered for most professional positions, giving rise to the thought that women did not need educational opportunities to be housewives or part of the clerical staff. Even within the professional roles allocated for women, such as nursing, training was generally offered only to unmarried women. Fighting against these expectations, women sought the freedom to choose how to live their lives, including the educational opportunities necessary to succeed in their choices. Although by the 1960s the number of women in higher education had increased since World War II, not all programs were open to them. Title IX was a step toward opening most programs to women and to insuring equal opportunity and treatment within these institutions and fields of study.

President Nixon was willing to work on many issues with the much more liberal Congress, controlled by the Democratic Party. Women's rights were a part of the legislative agenda for this Congress, which passed the Equal Rights Amendment (never ratified by enough states) in March 1972. Previously, in 1970, Representative Green had chaired hearings on discrimination against women in education, but the resulting bill did not get through that session of Congress. In 1972, Senator Bayh added an amendment to a bill on higher education, reflecting Mink's/Green's bill and the Equal Rights Amendment, which, at that time, was stalled in Congress. In many ways, Title IX was slipped through Congress, as supporters were urged by Green to be quiet, keeping opposition to a minimum. The bill (S 659) was also being propelled though Congress because it contained provisions to stop public school busing for desegregation until 1974 and to limit the use of federal money for busing. When President Nixon signed the bill, he said nothing about Title IX, focusing his remarks on the issue of busing for desegregation. Thus, what was a major victory for those seeking educational equality for women became law, virtually unnoticed.

Author Biography

Birch Evans Bayh, Jr. (b. 1928) of Indiana was a Democrat who served three terms in the Senate. His undergraduate degree was from Purdue University, and he had a law degree from Indiana University School of Law. He authored the Twenty-fifth and Twenty-sixth Amendments to the Constitution, as well as the failed Equal Rights Amendment.

Edith Starrett Green (1910–1987), a Democrat from Oregon, was a graduate of the University of Oregon and served ten full terms in the House of Representatives. While she might have moved to the Senate, she stayed in the House because the seniority system, then in place, did not allow House leaders to bypass her in committee assignments. A former teacher, she was an influential member of the Committee on Education.

Patsy Takemoto Mink (1927–2002) from Hawaii was the first woman of color in Congress and the first woman representative from Hawaii. She had a BA from the University of Hawaii and a law degree from the University of Chicago Law School. She had wanted to be a doctor, but was denied admission to twelve medical schools because most allowed only a few women entry each year. A Democrat, she served twelve and a half terms in the House (1965–77, 1990–2003).

## HISTORICAL DOCUMENT

Title IX, Education Amendments of 1972
(Under Title 20 U.S.C. Sections 1681–1688)

### Section 1681. Sex

**(a) Prohibition against discrimination; exceptions.** No person in the United States shall, on the basis of sex, be excluded from participation in, be denied the benefits of, or be subjected to discrimination under any education program or activity receiving Federal financial assistance, except that:

**(1) Classes of educational institutions subject to prohibition**

In regard to admissions to educational institutions, this section shall apply only to institutions of vocational education, professional education, and graduate higher education, and to public institutions of undergraduate higher education;

**(2) Educational institutions commencing planned change in admissions**

In regard to admissions to educational institutions, this section shall not apply (A) for one year from June 23, 1972, nor for six years after June 23, 1972, in the case of an educational institution which has begun the process of changing from being an institution which admits only students of one sex to being an institution which admits students of both sexes, but only if it is carrying out a plan for such a change which is approved by the Secretary of Education or (B) for seven years from the date an educational institution begins the process of changing from being an institution which admits only students of one sex to being an institution which admits students of both sexes, but only if it is carrying out a plan for such a change which is approved by the Secretary of Education, whichever is the later;

**(3) Educational institutions of religious organizations with contrary religious tenets**

This section shall not apply to any educational institution which is controlled by a religious organization if the application of this subsection would not be consistent with the religious tenets of such organization;

**(4) Educational institutions training individuals for military services or merchant marine**

This section shall not apply to an educational institution whose primary purpose is the training of individuals for the military services of the United States, or the merchant marine;

**(5) Public educational institutions with traditional and continuing admissions policy**

In regard to admissions this section shall not apply to any public institution of undergraduate higher education which is an institution that traditionally and continually from its establishment has had a policy of admitting only students of one sex;

4. **(6) Social fraternities or sororities; voluntary youth service organizations**

This section shall not apply to membership practices—

(A) of a social fraternity or social sorority which is exempt from taxation under section 501(a) of Title 26, the active membership of which consists primarily of students in attendance at an institution of higher education, or

(B) of the Young Men's Christian Association, Young Women's Christian Association; Girl Scouts, Boy Scouts, Camp Fire Girls, and voluntary youth service organizations which are so exempt, the membership of which has traditionally been limited to persons of one sex and principally to persons of less than nineteen years of age;

### (7) Boy or Girl conferences

This section shall not apply to—

(A) any program or activity of the American Legion undertaken in connection with the organization or operation of any Boys State conference, Boys Nation conference, Girls State conference, or Girls Nation conference; or

(B) any program or activity of any secondary school or educational institution specifically for—

(i) the promotion of any Boys State conference, Boys Nation conference, Girls State conference, or Girls Nation conference; or

(ii) the selection of students to attend any such conference;

### (8) Father-son or mother-daughter activities at educational institutions

This section shall not preclude father-son or mother-daughter activities at an educational institution, but if such activities are provided for students of one sex, opportunities for reasonably comparable activities shall be provided for students of the other sex; and

### (9) Institutions of higher education scholarship awards in "beauty" pageants

This section shall not apply with respect to any scholarship or other financial assistance awarded by an institution of higher education to any individual because such individual has received such award in any pageant in which the attainment of such award is based upon a combination of factors related to the personal appearance, poise, and talent of such individual and in which participation is limited to individuals of one sex only, so long as such pageant is in compliance with other nondiscrimination provisions of Federal law.

### (b) Preferential or disparate treatment because of imbalance in participation or receipt of Federal benefits; statistical evidence of imbalance.

Nothing contained in subsection (a) of this section shall be interpreted to require any educational institution to grant preferential or disparate treatment to the members of one sex on account of an imbalance which may exist with respect to the total number or percentage of persons of that sex participating in or receiving the benefits of any federally supported program or activity, in comparison with the total number or percentage of persons of that sex in any community, State, section, or other area: *Provided*, that this subsection shall not be construed to prevent the consideration in any hearing or proceeding under this chapter of statistical evidence tending to show that such an imbalance exists with respect to the participation in, or receipt of the benefits of, any such program or activity by the members of one sex.

### (c) Educational institution defined.

For the purposes of this chapter an educational institution means any public or private preschool, elementary, or secondary school, or any institution of vocational, professional, or higher education, except that in the case of an educational institution composed of more than one school, college, or department which are administratively separate units, such term means each such school, college or department.

### Section 1682. Federal administrative enforcement; report to Congressional committees

Each Federal department and agency which is empowered to extend Federal financial assistance to any education program or activity, by way of grant, loan, or contract other than a contract of insurance or guaranty, is authorized and directed to effectuate the provisions of section 1681 of this title with respect to such program or activity by issuing rules, regulations, or orders of general applicability which shall be consistent with achievement of the objectives of the statute authorizing the financial assistance in connection with which the action is taken. No such rule, regulation, or order shall become effective unless and until approved by the President. Compliance with any requirement adopted pursuant to this section may be effected (1) by the termination of or refusal to grant or to continue assistance under such program or activity to any recipient as to whom there has been an express finding on the record, after opportunity for hearing, of a failure to comply with such requirement, but such termination or refusal shall be limited to the particular political entity, or part thereof, or other recipient as to whom such a finding has been made, and shall be limited in its effect to the particular program, or part thereof, in which such noncompliance has been so found, or (2) by any other means authorized by law: *Provided, however*, that no such action shall be taken until the department or agency concerned has advised the appropriate person or persons of the failure to comply with the requirement and has determined that compliance cannot be secured by voluntary means. In the case of any action terminating, or refusing to grant or continue, assistance because of failure to comply with a requirement imposed pursuant to this section, the head of the Federal department or agency shall file with the committees of the House and Senate having legislative jurisdiction over the program or activity involved a full written report of the circumstances and the grounds for such action. No such action shall become effective until thirty days have elapsed after the filing of such report.

## Section 1683. Judicial Review

Any department or agency action taken pursuant to section 1682 of this title shall be subject to such judicial review as may otherwise be provided by law for similar action taken by such department or agency on other grounds. In the case of action, not otherwise subject to judicial review, terminating or refusing to grant or to continue financial assistance upon a finding of failure to comply with any requirement imposed pursuant to section 1682 of this title, any person aggrieved (including any State or political subdivision thereof and any agency of either) may obtain judicial review of such action in accordance with chapter 7 of title 5, United States Code, and such action shall not be deemed committed to unreviewable agency discretion within the meaning of section 701 of that title.

## Section 1684. Blindness or visual impairment; prohibition against discrimination

No person in the United States shall, on the ground of blindness or severely impaired vision, be denied admission in any course of study by a recipient of Federal financial assistance for any education program or activity; but nothing herein shall be construed to require any such institution to provide any special services to such person because of his blindness or visual impairment.

## Section 1685. Authority under other laws unaffected

Nothing in this chapter shall add to or detract from any existing authority with respect to any program or activity under which Federal financial assistance is extended by way of a contract of insurance or guaranty.

## Section 1686. Interpretation with respect to living facilities

Notwithstanding anything to the contrary contained in this chapter, nothing contained herein shall be construed to prohibit any educational institution receiving funds under this Act, from maintaining separate living facilities for the different sexes....

## Section 1688. Neutrality with respect to abortion

Nothing in this chapter shall be construed to require or prohibit any person, or public or private entity, to provide or pay for any benefit or service, including the use of facilities, related to an abortion. Nothing in this section shall be construed to permit a penalty to be imposed on any person or individual because such person or individual is seeking or has received any benefit or service related to a legal abortion.

## Document Analysis

Although most people associate Title IX with athletics, the law says nothing directly about sports. The law is a "prohibition against discrimination" in education, based on a person's sex. In addition, it also has one section which prohibits discrimination based on "blindness or visual impairment." The basic law is simply stated in one sentence, with several paragraphs of exceptions following the prohibition against discriminatory policies in admission, participation, or benefits in educational programs or activities. Most exceptions seem to be based upon what it would take to assure skeptical members of Congress that certain traditional programs could continue. However, as exemplified by the law's impact on sports, the simplicity of the prohibition as law is deceptive due to the scope of its application upon educational institutions.

Title IX does not do away with single-sex colleges, for those that historically have had that admissions policy, or for those schools related to the military or merchant marines. Market forces (most students' desire coeducational institutions) or laws (a 1975 law opened the military academies) have caused most single-sex colleges to change their admission policies since that time. It should be noted that in Title IX, an exemption is not specifically given for single-sex elementary or high schools. Gender-based admission quotas, which had been common in many professional graduate programs, became illegal. Two results of the mandate that the treatment of male and female students be given equal opportunities has been the end of prohibitions against pregnant, or married, women's participation in the educational program and the use of Title IX to create institutional policies with the goal of ending instances of sexual violence or harassment.

The most visible change to the general public is the change to athletic programs. Many schools did, and do, complain that the impact of Title IX is to decrease opportunities for male athletes. However, overall the number of male athletes at the collegiate level has increased since 1972, although not as dramatically as the increase in women. Lists of programs which have been deleted have been compiled by various groups, with college wrestling as the sport most often cut. This is presented as the outcome of the law, rather than the new opportunities which are being given to female athletes. While some sports were definitely cut to balance athletic programs, the cost-benefit value of others was such that, even without Title IX, they would have been eliminated. The guidelines given for the implementation of Title IX is not that there must be total equality between programs for men and women, but rather that athletic opportunities, including facilities and scholarships, be substantially proportional.

The YMCA, YWCA, Boys State, Girls State, social fraternities, and "'beauty' pageant" scholarships exemptions are for things only loosely associated with formal educational institutions, however, they assisted in getting the bill passed. The mother-daughter/father-son exemption is the only thing that might be considered an activity specifically offered by some schools. The section on living facilities deals with a concern that many had, and to allay concerns, single-sex residence halls are legal, but need to be substantially equivalent. Thus, peripheral exemptions are allowed, but what it takes for an environment conducive to education must be gender-neutral.

## Essential Themes

The basic foundation for Title IX is equal opportunity for all students. While obviously this does not mean all students will take advantage of all opportunities, or be successful, Title IX simply dictates that there be essentially equal opportunities for both genders. In the more than four decades since Title IX was signed into law, higher education has had monumental changes as a result of Title IX and other social forces. In 1971–72, about 43 percent of the bachelor's degrees were earned by women, versus about 57 percent in 2011–12. Graduate and professional education has had an even larger change, with dental schools going from about 1 percent female to over 40 percent. Law schools and medical schools have moved from about 7 and 10 percent respectively, to women earning about 50 percent of the degrees. Within PhD programs, the increase has been from about 12 percent in 1970 to more than 50 percent of the new degrees being earned by women in 2012. Opening all programs to women on an equal basis has had a great, if less visible, impact on higher education.

The more visible aspect of Title IX, sports, has also had great changes for women. At the high school level, about ten times as many girls compete in sports as was the case before Title IX. At the collegiate level, which previously had a higher participation rate than at high schools, after more than forty years, about six times as many women participate in varsity athletics than was the case before Title IX. Even though there are more female undergraduates than male, there are still more opportunities for males to participate in varsity sports, and more money is expended on their programs. The increased physical activity created by girls' and young women's participation in sports has been credited with an overall increase in the quality of women's health.

The passage of this law was very much a part of the effort for greater equality within the general civil rights movement and, more specifically, what is known as second wave feminism. While most view the second wave as ending by the late 1980s, the concerns for equal opportunity remain. While the simple goal of true equality has not been fully attained, Title IX has been one major factor in the gains made by women.

*—Donald A. Watt, PhD*

**Bibliography and Additional Reading**

Chadband, Emma. "Nine Ways Title IX Has Helped Girls and Women in Education." *NEA Today.* National Education Association, 21 Jun. 2012. Web.

Department of Education. "Title 34 Education: Subtitle B, Part 106: Nondiscrimination on the Basis of Sex in Education Programs or Activities Receiving Federal Financial Assistance." *ED.gov.* US Department of Education, 2015. Web.

Hanson, Katherine, Vivian Guilfoy, & Sarita Pillai. *More than Title IX: How Equity in Education Has Shaped the Nation.* New York: Rowman & Littlefield Publishers, 2011. Print.

National Women's Law Center. *Titleix.info.* National Women's Law Center, 2015. Web.

Winslow, Barbara. "The Impact of Title IX." *History Now.* The Gilder Lehrman Institute of American History, 2015. Web.

# ■ *Roe v. Wade*

**Date:** January 22, 1973
**Author:** Justice Harry Blackmun, majority opinion; Justice William Rehnquist, dissenting
**Genre:** Court opinion

## Summary Overview

For about a decade prior to the Supreme Court ruling in *Roe v. Wade,* abortion laws had been changing in the United States. Whereas prior to that time the only legal abortions were to save the life of the mother, states were beginning to consider other reasons. During the 1960s, twelve states had loosened regulations on abortions, with four others putting virtually no restrictions on early term abortions in 1970. Texas, the state in which *Roe v. Wade* originated, was not one of these states. At the Supreme Court, Justice Blackmun, who had initially been considered a conservative, wrote the liberal-leaning opinion, overturning most restrictions on abortion. At first, the Catholic Church was the only group strongly opposing the ruling and pushing for change. While polls have indicated that a majority of Americans have always supported this ruling, opposition to it has spread to other religious groups and political conservatives, becoming a divisive electoral issue ever since the 1980s.

## Defining Moment

In 1821, Connecticut passed the first anti-abortion law in the United States. During the latter part of the century, all states passed laws prohibiting abortion, normally with an exception to save the mother's life. While the American Medical Association was a strong anti-abortion force during the latter half of the nineteenth century, in part because of the high mortality rate, by the mid-twentieth century the medical community was one of the central groups raising questions about the restrictions. This time, the focus was the high mortality rate from the hundreds of thousands of illegal abortions performed each year. Even with the introduction of oral contraceptives in the early 1960s, and a Supreme Court ruling in 1965 making them legal in all states, illegal abortions continued in large numbers. Within the civil rights movement, the women's liberation movement pushed for more control over an individual's own medical concerns, in addition to other aspects of life. Changes in lifestyle, advancements in medical procedures, and growing concern about the population explosion combined to increase the interest of women,

and couples, in various forms of birth control. While generally not the first choice, abortion was seen as one form among many.

In 1970, Jane Roe (Norma McCorvey) filed a suit seeking to have a legal abortion in Texas, although she did not fit any of the restrictive categories that would allow one to be performed. This case was combined in the judicial process with *Doe v. Bolton* from Georgia. Roe won her case at the district level and Doe lost hers, although Roe had to wait for the appeal process to be completed before she could legally obtain an abortion. (McCorvey had the baby long before the Supreme Court ruled on the issue.) The case was appealed directly to the Supreme Court, which took it shortly after ruling to uphold abortion restrictions in the District of Columbia.

Justice Blackmun, a Nixon appointee, was selected by Chief Justice Burger to write the majority opinion. Although the breadth of this 7–2 ruling was unexpected, it took several years for the political forces seeking to overturn it to coalesce. Much of the conservative anti-court sentiment, which had been unsuccessfully directed toward *Brown v. Board of Education* slowly began taking *Roe v. Wade* as its new target. As such, the majority opinion in *Roe v. Wade* has become a central point of contention in the political arena, with, over time, most Democrats desiring its retention and Republicans seeking to overturn it. Since the late 1980s, nominees for vacancies on the Supreme Court have been examined to try to determine their views of the *Roe v. Wade* opinion.

## Author Biography

Harry Andrew Blackmun (1908–1999) was born in Illinois, grew up in Minnesota (a childhood friend of Chief Justice Burger), and earned his law degree at Harvard University. He practiced and taught law in Minneapolis until 1950, when he became an attorney for the Mayo Clinic. In 1959, he was appointed to the Court of Appeals, and in 1970, President Nixon appointed him to be an associate justice on the Supreme Court. *Roe v. Wade* is his most well-known opinion and marked his move toward being one of the liberal members of the court.

William Hubbs Rehnquist (1924–2005), from Wisconsin, earned his law degree from Stanford University. Prior to joining the Supreme Court, he was in private practice until appointed assistant attorney general in 1969. In 1972, he became an associate justice (appointed by President Nixon), and in 1986, he was appointed chief justice by President Reagan.

## HISTORICAL DOCUMENT

No. 70-18
SUPREME COURT OF THE UNITED STATES
410 U.S. 113
January 22, 1973, Decided
Oral Argument (original) in *Roe v. Wade*

### MR. JUSTICE BLACKMUN delivered the opinion of the Court.

This Texas federal appeal and its Georgia companion, *Doe v. Bolton*, post, p. 179, present constitutional challenges to state criminal abortion legislation. The Texas statutes under attack here are typical of those that have been in effect in many States for approximately a century. The Georgia statutes, in contrast, have a modern cast and are a legislative product that, to an extent at least, obviously reflects the influences of recent attitudinal change, of advancing medical knowledge and techniques, and of new thinking about an old issue.

We forthwith acknowledge our awareness of the sensitive and emotional nature of the abortion controversy, of the vigorous opposing views, even among physicians, and of the deep and seemingly absolute convictions that the subject inspires. One's philosophy, one's experiences, one's exposure to the raw edges of human existence, one's religious training, one's attitudes toward life and family and their values, and the moral standards one establishes and seeks to observe, are all likely to influence and to color one's thinking and conclusions about abortion.

In addition, population growth, pollution, poverty, and racial overtones tend to complicate and not to simplify the problem.

Our task, of course, is to resolve the issue by constitutional measurement, free of emotion and of predilection. We seek earnestly to do this, and, because we do, we have inquired into, and in this opinion place some emphasis upon, medical and medical-legal history and what that history reveals about man's attitudes toward the abortion procedure over the centuries.

I

The Texas statutes that concern us here are Arts. 1191–1194 and 1196 of the State's Penal Code. These make it a crime to "procure an abortion," as therein defined, or to attempt one, except with respect to "an abortion procured or attempted by medical advice for the purpose of saving the life of the mother." Similar statutes are in existence in a majority of the States.

Texas first enacted a criminal abortion statute in 1854. This was soon modified into language that has remained substantially unchanged to the present time.

Jane Roe, a single woman who was residing in Dallas County, Texas, instituted this federal action in March 1970 against the District Attorney of the county. She sought a declaratory judgment that the Texas criminal abortion statutes were unconstitutional on their face, and an injunction restraining the defendant from enforcing the statutes.

Roe alleged that she was unmarried and pregnant; that she wished to terminate her pregnancy by an abortion "performed by a competent, licensed physician, under safe, clinical conditions"; that she was unable to get a "legal" abortion in Texas because her life did not appear to be threatened by the continuation of her pregnancy; and that she could not afford to travel to another jurisdiction in order to secure a legal abortion under safe conditions. She claimed that the Texas statutes were unconstitutionally vague and that they abridged her right of personal privacy, protected by the First, Fourth, Fifth, Ninth, and Fourteenth Amendments. By an amendment to her complaint Roe purported to sue "on behalf of herself and all other women" similarly situated.

James Hubert Hallford, a licensed physician, sought and was granted leave to intervene in Roe's action. In his complaint he alleged that he had been arrested previously for violations of the Texas abortion statutes and that two such prosecutions were pending against him. He described conditions of patients who came to him seeking abortions, and he claimed that for many cases he, as a physician, was unable to determine whether they fell within or outside the exception recognized by Article 1196. He alleged that, as a consequence, the statutes were vague and uncertain, in violation of the Fourteenth Amendment, and that they violated his own and his patients' rights to privacy in the doctor-patient relationship and his own right to practice medicine, rights he claimed were guaranteed by the First, Fourth, Fifth, Ninth, and Fourteenth Amendments.

John and Mary Doe, a married couple, filed a companion complaint to that of Roe. They also named the District Attorney as defendant, claimed like constitutional deprivations, and sought declaratory and injunctive relief. The Does alleged that they were a childless couple; that Mrs. Doe was suffering from a "neural-chemical" disorder; that her physician had "advised her to avoid pregnancy until such time as her condition has materially improved" (although a pregnancy at the present time would not present "a serious risk" to her life); that, pursuant to medical advice, she had discontinued use of birth control pills; and that if she should become pregnant, she would want to terminate the pregnancy by an abortion performed by a competent, licensed physician under safe, clinical conditions. By an amendment to their complaint, the Does purported to sue "on behalf of themselves and all couples similarly situated...."

IV

We are next confronted with issues of justiciability, standing, and abstention. Have Roe and the Does

established that "personal stake in the outcome of the controversy," that insures that "the dispute sought to be adjudicated will be presented in an adversary context and in a form historically viewed as capable of judicial resolution." Despite the use of the pseudonym, no suggestion is made that Roe is a fictitious person. For purposes of her case, we accept as true, and as established, her existence; her pregnant state, as of the inception of her suit in March 1970 and as late as May 21 of that year when she filed an alias affidavit with the District Court; and her inability to obtain a legal abortion in Texas.

Viewing Roe's case as of the time of its filing and thereafter until as late as May, there can be little dispute that it then presented a case or controversy and that, wholly apart from the class aspects, she, as a pregnant single woman thwarted by the Texas criminal abortion laws, had standing to challenge those statutes.

The appellee notes, however, that the record does not disclose that Roe was pregnant at the time of the District Court hearing on May 22, 1970, or on the following June 17 when the court's opinion and judgment were filed. And he suggests that Roe's case must now be moot because she and all other members of her class are no longer subject to any 1970 pregnancy. The usual rule in federal cases is that an actual controversy must exist at stages of appellate or certiorari review, and not simply at the date the action is initiated. But when, as here, pregnancy is a significant fact in the litigation, the normal 266-day human gestation period is so short that the pregnancy will come to term before the usual appellate process is complete. If that termination makes a case moot, pregnancy litigation seldom will survive much beyond the trial stage, and appellate review will be effectively denied. Our law should not be that rigid. Pregnancy often comes more than once to the same woman, and in the general population, if man is to survive, it will always be with us. Pregnancy provides a classic justification for a conclusion of nonmootness. It truly could be "capable of repetition, yet evading review."

We, therefore, agree with the District Court that Jane Roe had standing to undertake this litigation, that she presented a justiciable controversy, and that the termination of her 1970 pregnancy has not rendered her case moot....

V

The principal thrust of appellant's attack on the Texas statutes is that they improperly invade a right, said to be possessed by the pregnant woman, to choose to terminate her pregnancy. Appellant would discover this right in the concept of personal "liberty" embodied in the Fourteenth Amendment's Due Process Clause; or in personal, marital, familial, and sexual privacy said to be protected by the Bill of Rights or its penumbras, or among those rights reserved to the people by the Ninth Amendment. Before addressing this claim, we feel it desirable briefly to survey, in several aspects, the history of abortion, for such insight as that history may afford us, and then to examine the state purposes and interests behind the criminal abortion laws.

VI

It perhaps is not generally appreciated that the restrictive criminal abortion laws in effect in a majority of States today are of relatively recent vintage. Those laws, generally proscribing abortion or its attempt at any time during pregnancy except when necessary to preserve the pregnant woman's life, are not of ancient or even of common-law origin. Instead, they derive from statutory changes effected, for the most part, in the latter half of the 19th century....

The common law. It is undisputed that at common law, abortion performed before "quickening" —the first recognizable movement of the fetus in utero, appearing usually from the 16th to the 18th week of pregnancy—was not an indictable offense. The absence of a common-law crime for pre-quickening abortion appears to have developed from a confluence of earlier philosophical, theological, and civil and canon law concepts of when life begins. These disciplines variously approached the question in terms of the point at which the embryo or fetus became "formed" or recognizably human, or in terms of when a "person" came into being, that is,

infused with a "soul" or "animated." A loose consensus evolved in early English law that these events occurred at some point between conception and live birth. This was "mediate animation." Although Christian theology and the canon law came to fix the point of animation at 40 days for a male and 80 days for a female, a view that persisted until the 19th century, there was otherwise little agreement about the precise time of formation or animation. There was agreement, however, that prior to this point the fetus was to be regarded as part of the mother, and its destruction, therefore, was not homicide. Due to continued uncertainty about the precise time when animation occurred, to the lack of any empirical basis for the 40–80-day view, and perhaps to Aquinas' definition of movement as one of the two first principles of life, Bracton focused upon quickening as the critical point. The significance of quickening was echoed by later common-law scholars and found its way into the received common law in this country....

Gradually, in the middle and late 19th century the quickening distinction disappeared from the statutory law of most States and the degree of the offense and the penalties were increased. By the end of the 1950's, a large majority of the jurisdictions banned abortion, however and whenever performed, unless done to save or preserve the life of the mother. The exceptions, Alabama and the District of Columbia, permitted abortion to preserve the mother's health. Three States permitted abortions that were not "unlawfully" performed or that were not "without lawful justification," leaving interpretation of those standards to the courts. In the past several years, however, a trend toward liberalization of abortion statutes has resulted in adoption, by about one-third of the States, of less stringent laws, most of them patterned after the ALI Model Penal Code.

It is thus apparent that at common law, at the time of the adoption of our Constitution, and throughout the major portion of the 19th century, abortion was viewed with less disfavor than under most American statutes currently in effect. Phrasing it another way, a woman enjoyed a substantially broader right to terminate a pregnancy than she does in most States today. At least with respect to the early stage of pregnancy, and very possibly without such a limitation, the opportunity to make this choice was present in this country well into the 19th century. Even later, the law continued for some time to treat less punitively an abortion procured in early pregnancy....

VII

Three reasons have been advanced to explain historically the enactment of criminal abortion laws in the 19th century and to justify their continued existence.

It has been argued occasionally that these laws were the product of a Victorian social concern to discourage illicit sexual conduct. Texas, however, does not advance this justification in the present case, and it appears that no court or commentator has taken the argument seriously. The appellants and amici contend, moreover, that this is not a proper state purpose at all and suggest that, if it were, the Texas statutes are overbroad in protecting it since the law fails to distinguish between married and unwed mothers.

A second reason is concerned with abortion as a medical procedure. When most criminal abortion laws were first enacted, the procedure was a hazardous one for the woman. This was particularly true prior to the development of antisepsis. Antiseptic techniques, of course, were based on discoveries by Lister, Pasteur, and others first announced in 1867, but were not generally accepted and employed until about the turn of the century. Abortion mortality was high. Even after 1900, and perhaps until as late as the development of antibiotics in the 1940's, standard modern techniques such as dilation and curettage were not nearly so safe as they are today. Thus, it has been argued that a State's real concern in enacting a criminal abortion law was to protect the pregnant woman, that is, to restrain her from submitting to a procedure that placed her life in serious jeopardy.

Modern medical techniques have altered this situation. Appellants and various amici refer to medical data indicating that abortion in early pregnancy, that is, prior to the end of the first trimester, although not without its risk, is now relatively safe.

Mortality rates for women undergoing early abortions, where the procedure is legal, appear to be as low as or lower than the rates for normal childbirth. Consequently, any interest of the State in protecting the woman from an inherently hazardous procedure, except when it would be equally dangerous for her to forgo it, has largely disappeared. Of course, important state interests in the areas of health and medical standards do remain. The State has a legitimate interest in seeing to it that abortion, like any other medical procedure, is performed under circumstances that insure maximum safety for the patient. This interest obviously extends at least to the performing physician and his staff, to the facilities involved, to the availability of after-care, and to adequate provision for any complication or emergency that might arise. The prevalence of high mortality rates at illegal "abortion mills" strengthens, rather than weakens, the State's interest in regulating the conditions under which abortions are performed. Moreover, the risk to the woman increases as her pregnancy continues. Thus, the State retains a definite interest in protecting the woman's own health and safety when an abortion is proposed at a late stage of pregnancy.

The third reason is the State's interest—some phrase it in terms of duty—in protecting prenatal life. Some of the argument for this justification rests on the theory that a new human life is present from the moment of conception. The State's interest and general obligation to protect life then extends, it is argued, to prenatal life. Only when the life of the pregnant mother herself is at stake, balanced against the life she carries within her, should the interest of the embryo or fetus not prevail. Logically, of course, a legitimate state interest in this area need not stand or fall on acceptance of the belief that life begins at conception or at some other point prior to live birth. In assessing the State's interest, recognition may be given to the less rigid claim that as long as at least potential life is involved, the State may assert interests beyond the protection of the pregnant woman alone.

Parties challenging state abortion laws have sharply disputed in some courts the contention that a purpose of these laws, when enacted, was to protect prenatal life. Pointing to the absence of legislative history to support the contention, they claim that most state laws were designed solely to protect the woman. Because medical advances have lessened this concern, at least with respect to abortion in early pregnancy, they argue that with respect to such abortions the laws can no longer be justified by any state interest. There is some scholarly support for this view of original purpose. The few state courts called upon to interpret their laws in the late 19th and early 20th centuries did focus on the State's interest in protecting the woman's health rather than in preserving the embryo and fetus. Proponents of this view point out that in many States, including Texas, by statute or judicial interpretation, the pregnant woman herself could not be prosecuted for self-abortion or for cooperating in an abortion performed upon her by another. They claim that adoption of the "quickening" distinction through received common law and state statutes tacitly recognizes the greater health hazards inherent in late abortion and impliedly repudiates the theory that life begins at conception.

It is with these interests, and the weight to be attached to them, that this case is concerned.

VIII

The Constitution does not explicitly mention any right of privacy. In a line of decisions, however, the Court has recognized that a right of personal privacy, or a guarantee of certain areas or zones of privacy, does exist under the Constitution. In varying contexts, the Court or individual Justices have, indeed, found at least the roots of that right in the First Amendment, in the Fourth and Fifth Amendments, in the penumbras of the Bill of Rights, in the Ninth Amendment, or in the concept of liberty guaranteed by the first section of the Fourteenth Amendment. These decisions make it clear that only personal rights that can be deemed "fundamental" or "implicit in the concept of ordered liberty," are included in this guarantee of personal privacy. They also make it clear that the right has some extension to activities relating to marriage, procreation, contraception, family relationships, and child rearing and education.

This right of privacy, whether it be founded in the Fourteenth Amendment's concept of personal liberty and restrictions upon state action, as we feel it is, or, as the District Court determined, in the Ninth Amendment's reservation of rights to the people, is broad enough to encompass a woman's decision whether or not to terminate her pregnancy. The detriment that the State would impose upon the pregnant woman by denying this choice altogether is apparent. Specific and direct harm medically diagnosable even in early pregnancy may be involved. Maternity, or additional offspring, may force upon the woman a distressful life and future. Psychological harm may be imminent. Mental and physical health may be taxed by child care. There is also the distress, for all concerned, associated with the unwanted child, and there is the problem of bringing a child into a family already unable, psychologically and otherwise, to care for it. In other cases, as in this one, the additional difficulties and continuing stigma of unwed motherhood may be involved. All these are factors the woman and her responsible physician necessarily will consider in consultation.

On the basis of elements such as these, appellant and some amici argue that the woman's right is absolute and that she is entitled to terminate her pregnancy at whatever time, in whatever way, and for whatever reason she alone chooses. With this we do not agree. Appellant's arguments that Texas either has no valid interest at all in regulating the abortion decision, or no interest strong enough to support any limitation upon the woman's sole determination, are unpersuasive. The Court's decisions recognizing a right of privacy also acknowledge that some state regulation in areas protected by that right is appropriate. As noted above, a State may properly assert important interests in safeguarding health, in maintaining medical standards, and in protecting potential life. At some point in pregnancy, these respective interests become sufficiently compelling to sustain regulation of the factors that govern the abortion decision. The privacy right involved, therefore, cannot be said to be absolute. In fact, it is not clear to us that the claim asserted by some amici that one has an unlimited right to do with one's body as one pleases bears a close relationship to the right of privacy previously articulated in the Court's decisions. The Court has refused to recognize an unlimited right of this kind in the past.

We, therefore, conclude that the right of personal privacy includes the abortion decision, but that this right is not unqualified and must be considered against important state interests in regulation.

Where certain "fundamental rights" are involved, the Court has held that regulation limiting these rights may be justified only by a "compelling state interest," and that legislative enactments must be narrowly drawn to express only the legitimate state interests at stake.

## IX

The appellee and certain amici argue that the fetus is a "person" within the language and meaning of the Fourteenth Amendment. In support of this, they outline at length and in detail the well-known facts of fetal development. If this suggestion of personhood is established, the appellant's case, of course, collapses, for the fetus' right to life would then be guaranteed specifically by the Amendment. The appellant conceded as much on reargument. On the other hand, the appellee conceded on reargument that no case could be cited that holds that a fetus is a person within the meaning of the Fourteenth Amendment.

The Constitution does not define "person" in so many words. Section 1 of the Fourteenth Amendment contains three references to "person." The first, in defining "citizens," speaks of "persons born or naturalized in the United States." The word also appears both in the Due Process Clause and in the Equal Protection Clause. "Person" is used in other places in the Constitution: in the listing of qualifications for Representatives and Senators, Art. I, § 2, cl. 2, and § 3, cl. 3; in the Apportionment Clause, Art. I, § 2, cl. 3; in the Migration and Importation provision, Art. I, § 9, cl. 1; in the Emolument Clause, Art. I, § 9, cl. 8; in the Electors provisions, Art. II, § 1, cl. 2, and the superseded cl. 3; in the provision outlining qualifications for the office of President, Art. II, § 1, cl. 5; in the Extradition provisions, Art. IV, § 2, cl. 2, and the superseded

Fugitive Slave Clause 3; and in the Fifth, Twelfth, and Twenty-second Amendments, as well as in §§ 2 and 3 of the Fourteenth Amendment. But in nearly all these instances, the use of the word is such that it has application only postnatally. None indicates, with any assurance, that it has any possible pre-natal application.

All this, together with our observation, supra, that throughout the major portion of the 19th century prevailing legal abortion practices were far freer than they are today, persuades us that the word "person," as used in the Fourteenth Amendment, does not include the unborn.

This conclusion, however, does not of itself fully answer the contentions raised by Texas, and we pass on to other considerations. The pregnant woman cannot be isolated in her privacy. She carries an embryo and, later, a fetus, if one accepts the medical definitions of the developing young in the human uterus. The situation therefore is inherently different from marital intimacy, or bedroom possession of obscene material, or marriage, or procreation, or education, with which Eisenstadt and Griswold, Stanley, Loving, Skinner, and Pierce and Meyer were respectively concerned. As we have intimated above, it is reasonable and appropriate for a State to decide that at some point in time another interest, that of health of the mother or that of potential human life, becomes significantly involved. The woman's privacy is no longer sole and any right of privacy she possesses must be measured accordingly.

Texas urges that, apart from the Fourteenth Amendment, life begins at conception and is present throughout pregnancy, and that, therefore, the State has a compelling interest in protecting that life from and after conception. We need not resolve the difficult question of when life begins. When those trained in the respective disciplines of medicine, philosophy, and theology are unable to arrive at any consensus, the judiciary, at this point in the development of man's knowledge, is not in a position to speculate as to the answer.

It should be sufficient to note briefly the wide divergence of thinking on this most sensitive and difficult question.... Substantial problems for precise definition of this view are posed, however, by new embryological data that purport to indicate that conception is a "process" over time, rather than an event, and by new medical techniques such as menstrual extraction, the "morning-after" pill, implantation of embryos, artificial insemination, and even artificial wombs.

In areas other than criminal abortion, the law has been reluctant to endorse any theory that life, as we recognize it, begins before live birth or to accord legal rights to the unborn except in narrowly defined situations and except when the rights are contingent upon live birth. For example, the traditional rule of tort law denied recovery for prenatal injuries even though the child was born alive. That rule has been changed in almost every jurisdiction. In most States, recovery is said to be permitted only if the fetus was viable, or at least quick, when the injuries were sustained, though few courts have squarely so held. In a recent development, generally opposed by the commentators, some States permit the parents of a stillborn child to maintain an action for wrongful death because of prenatal injuries. Such an action, however, would appear to be one to vindicate the parents' interest and is thus consistent with the view that the fetus, at most, represents only the potentiality of life. Similarly, unborn children have been recognized as acquiring rights or interests by way of inheritance or other devolution of property, and have been represented by guardians ad litem. Perfection of the interests involved, again, has generally been contingent upon live birth. In short, the unborn have never been recognized in the law as persons in the whole sense.

X

In view of all this, we do not agree that, by adopting one theory of life, Texas may override the rights of the pregnant woman that are at stake. We repeat, however, that the State does have an important and legitimate interest in preserving and protecting the health of the pregnant woman, whether she be a resident of the State or a nonresident who seeks medical consultation and treatment there, and that it has still another important and legitimate interest in protecting the potentiality of human life. These interests are separate and distinct. Each grows in substantiality as the woman approaches term and, at a point during pregnancy, each becomes "compelling."

With respect to the State's important and legitimate interest in the health of the mother, the "compelling" point, in the light of present medical knowledge, is at approximately the end of the first trimester. This is so because of the now-established medical fact, that until the end of the first trimester mortality in abortion may be less than mortality in normal childbirth. It follows that, from and after this point, a State may regulate the abortion procedure to the extent that the regulation reasonably relates to the preservation and protection of maternal health. Examples of permissible state regulation in this area are requirements as to the qualifications of the person who is to perform the abortion; as to the licensure of that person; as to the facility in which the procedure is to be performed, that is, whether it must be a hospital or may be a clinic or some other place of less-than-hospital status; as to the licensing of the facility; and the like.

This means, on the other hand, that, for the period of pregnancy prior to this "compelling" point, the attending physician, in consultation with his patient, is free to determine, without regulation by the State, that, in his medical judgment, the patient's pregnancy should be terminated. If that decision is reached, the judgment may be effectuated by an abortion free of interference by the State.

With respect to the State's important and legitimate interest in potential life, the "compelling" point is at viability. This is so because the fetus then presumably has the capability of meaningful life outside the mother's womb. State regulation protective of fetal life after viability thus has both logical and biological justifications. If the State is interested in protecting fetal life after viability, it may go so far as to proscribe abortion during that period, except when it is necessary to preserve the life or health of the mother.

Measured against these standards, Art. 1196 of the Texas Penal Code, in restricting legal abortions to those "procured or attempted by medical advice for the purpose of saving the life of the mother," sweeps too broadly. The statute makes no distinction between abortions performed early in pregnancy and those performed later, and it limits to a single reason, "saving" the mother's life, the legal justification for the procedure. The statute, therefore, cannot survive the constitutional attack made upon it here.

This conclusion makes it unnecessary for us to consider the additional challenge to the Texas statute asserted on grounds of vagueness.

XI

To summarize and to repeat:

A state criminal abortion statute of the current Texas type, that excepts from criminality only a life-saving procedure on behalf of the mother, without regard to pregnancy stage and without recognition of the other interests involved, is violative of the Due Process Clause of the Fourteenth Amendment.

(a) For the stage prior to approximately the end of the first trimester, the abortion decision and its effectuation must be left to the medical judgment of the pregnant woman's attending physician.

(b) For the stage subsequent to approximately the end of the first trimester, the State, in promoting its interest in the health of the mother, may, if it chooses, regulate the abortion procedure in ways that are reasonably related to maternal health.

(c) For the stage subsequent to viability, the State in promoting its interest in the potentiality of human life may, if it chooses, regulate, and even proscribe, abortion except where it is necessary, in appropriate medical judgment, for the preservation of the life or health of the mother....

This holding, we feel, is consistent with the relative weights of the respective interests involved, with the lessons and examples of medical and legal history, with the lenity of the common law, and with the demands of the profound problems of the present day. The decision leaves the State free to place increasing restrictions on abortion as the period of pregnancy lengthens, so long as those restrictions are tailored to the recognized state interests. The decision vindicates the right of the physician to administer medical treatment according to his professional judgment up to the points where important state interests provide compelling justifications for intervention. Up to those points, the abortion decision in all its aspects is inherently, and primarily, a medical decision, and basic responsibility for it must rest with the physician....

It is so ordered.

**JUSTICE REHNQUIST, dissenting.**

The Court's opinion brings to the decision of this troubling question both extensive historical fact and a wealth of legal scholarship. While the opinion thus commands my respect, I find myself nonetheless in fundamental disagreement with those parts of it that invalidate the Texas statute in question, and therefore dissent.

The Court's opinion decides that a State may impose virtually no restriction on the performance of abortions during the first trimester of pregnancy. Our previous decisions indicate that a necessary predicate for such an opinion is a plaintiff who was in her first trimester of pregnancy at some time during the pendency of her lawsuit. While a party may vindicate his own constitutional rights, he may not seek vindication for the rights of others. The Court's statement of facts in this case makes clear, however, that the record in no way indicates the presence of such a plaintiff. We know only that plaintiff Roe at the time of filing her complaint was a pregnant woman; for aught that appears in this record, she may have been in her last trimester of pregnancy as of the date the complaint was filed.

Nothing in the Court's opinion indicates that Texas might not constitutionally apply its proscription of abortion as written to a woman in that stage of pregnancy. Nonetheless, the Court uses her complaint against the Texas statute as a fulcrum for deciding that States may impose virtually no restrictions on medical abortions performed during the first trimester of pregnancy. In deciding such a hypothetical lawsuit, the Court departs from the longstanding admonition that it should never "formulate a rule of constitutional law broader than is required by the precise facts to which it is to be applied."

Even if there were a plaintiff in this case capable of litigating the issue which the Court decides, I would reach a conclusion opposite to that reached by the Court. I have difficulty in concluding, as the Court does, that the right of "privacy" is involved in this case. Texas, by the statute here challenged, bars the performance of a medical abortion by a licensed physician on a plaintiff such as Roe. A transaction resulting in an operation such as this is not "private" in the ordinary usage of that word. Nor is the "privacy" that the Court finds here even a distant relative of the freedom from searches and seizures protected by the Fourth Amendment to the Constitution, which the Court has referred to as embodying a right to privacy.

If the Court means by the term "privacy" no more than that the claim of a person to be free from unwanted state regulation of consensual transactions may be a form of "liberty" protected by the Fourteenth Amendment, there is no doubt that similar claims have been upheld in our earlier decisions on the basis of that liberty. I agree with the statement of MR. JUSTICE STEWART in his concurring opinion that the "liberty," against deprivation of which without due process the Fourteenth Amendment protects, embraces more than the rights found in the Bill of Rights. But that liberty is not guaranteed absolutely against deprivation, only against deprivation without due process of law. The test traditionally applied in the area of social and economic legislation is whether or not a law such as that challenged has a rational relation to a valid state objective. *Williamson v. Lee Optical Co.*, 348 U.S. 483, 491 (1955). The Due Process Clause of the Fourteenth Amendment undoubtedly does place a limit, [***98] albeit a broad one, on legislative power to enact laws such as this. If the Texas statute were to prohibit an abortion even where the mother's life is in jeopardy, I have little doubt that such a statute would lack a rational relation to a valid state objective under the test stated in *Williamson*, supra. But the Court's sweeping invalidation of any restrictions on abortion during the first trimester is impossible to justify under that standard, and the conscious weighing of competing factors that the Court's opinion apparently substitutes for the established test is far more appropriate to a legislative judgment than to a judicial one.

The Court eschews the history of the Fourteenth Amendment in its reliance on the "compelling state interest" test. But the Court adds a new wrinkle to this test by transposing it from the legal considerations associated with the Equal Protection Clause of the Fourteenth Amendment to this case arising under the Due Process Clause of the Fourteenth Amendment. Unless I misapprehend the consequences of this transplanting of the "compelling state interest test," the Court's opinion will accomplish the seemingly impossible feat of leaving this area of the law more confused than it found it.

While the Court's opinion quotes from the dissent of Mr. Justice Holmes in *Lochner v. New York*, 198 U.S. 45, 74 (1905), the result it reaches is more closely attuned to the majority opinion of Mr. Justice Peckham in that case. As in *Lochner* and similar cases applying substantive due process standards to economic and social welfare legislation, the adoption of the compelling state interest standard will inevitably require this Court to examine the legislative policies and pass on the wisdom of these policies in the very process of deciding whether a particular state interest put forward may or may not be "compelling..."

For all of the foregoing reasons, I respectfully dissent.

## GLOSSARY

**eschew:** to avoid using

**penumbras:** implied rights from a constitution, such privacy

**supra:** an earlier part of the text, literally, above

## Document Analysis

Some anti-abortion activists consider *Roe v. Wade* the worst Supreme Court decision ever, causing grave harm upon individuals and society. Some who support the right to an abortion also see it as a very poorly written opinion, causing great societal harm because the weak arguments have created possible grounds for it being overturned. Whatever the view, all agree that it has been one of the most polarizing decisions in recent decades. The ruling relied upon the idea that there were no laws against abortion when the Constitution was written, as well as the concept of privacy taking precedence over any state interest. (Neither privacy nor the state's interest in private acts is directly outlined in the Constitution.) Using these ideas and concepts, the Court ruled that virtually all abortion laws in place at that time were unconstitutional. The ruling expands the understanding of privacy. It also clearly dictates that what is best for the woman is the deciding factor and that a fetus is not a person, in the normal sense of the law. Secondly, although of some importance, was the decision by the majority to allow the suit to proceed, since it broke the standard definition of what types of suits the Supreme Court will consider.

In his majority opinion, Blackmun argues that the state has no compelling interest in prohibiting early-term abortions. He asserts that the two people involved, the woman and her physician, have the right to privacy in their decisions regarding her health and medical care. Blackmun states that it is the physician's responsibility to give the women the best medical care possible. If they decide that an abortion is in the woman's best interest, Blackmun states that it is permissible for one to be performed. Dividing the period of pregnancy into thirds, Blackmun argues that it is not until sometime after the first trimester that the state's interest would take precedence over the woman's. Prior to the fetus becoming fully viable, in Blackmun's opinion, the state has no compelling interest in the situation. In opposition to this argument, Rehnquist, in his dissenting opinion, argues that there is no right of privacy in this situation, as the procedure causing the abortion is a public act, in that it takes place at a hospital or clinic. He also argues that the manner in which the state's interest is defined by Blackmun is new and based upon a shaky legal foundation. Rehnquist believes that while it is unreasonable to prohibit all abortions, denying that the state has an interest in the developing fetus is wrong.

Although it is a minor point in both opinions, the fact that the case was accepted by the Supreme Court is important. Normally, cases are only accepted if what is being appealed is something which is currently happening. Thus, the fact that the ruling was being issued in 1973 regarding something that existed in 1970, but not in 1973, was almost without precedence. However, recognizing how slowly the judicial system works, Blackmun and the majority understood that no case regarding pregnancy would ever get to the Supreme Court if an exception were not made. Only because they were willing to make this exception could this ruling be made.

## Essential Themes

For more than four decades, *Roe v. Wade* has caused great strife within American society. While the central point, that early-term abortions should not be restricted, has not been overturned, it has not been for lack of trying. Many states, as well as Congress, have passed laws attempting to decrease the time period or the manner in which abortions may be performed. This has resulted in hundreds of lawsuits. Some of these restrictions have been upheld in Supreme Court rulings, although most have not. Candidates for major offices, as well as judicial nominees, are often quizzed about their views on abortion. While abortions remain legal, as a result of the political and judicial efforts on both sides, there have been small to moderate movements in both directions. However, the net effect has been toward restricting access to abortions. However, neither side has been able to transform the situation enough that the other believes there is no point in continuing the struggle. Thus, it seems there is no end in sight to this political conflict.

In addition to political attempts to end legal abortions, there have been a number of violent incidents in which abortion clinics, or providers, were the targets. The first documented act of violence against an abortion facility occurred in 1976. Since that time, in the United States, at least eight deaths, more than three hundred bombings, or attempted bombings, and thousands of lesser crimes have been committed in an attempt to decrease the number of, or stop, abortions. This activity has been legally categorized as domestic terrorism. There has not been any large-scale organized violence against those opposing abortions.

Judicially, the manner in which privacy is viewed has been strengthened by this ruling. It is in line with many of the previous rulings, in which privacy could be expected in the areas of family, children, birth control, and procreation, although *Roe v. Wade* pushes out the limits. The emphasis that the state must have some compelling interest to restrict individual privacy is strengthened. Thus, the decision to terminate a pregnancy, for the court, falls within this expanded area of privacy. However, they make it clear that even with this expansion, the right and expectation of privacy has limits, when balanced against the state's interest as the fetus becomes viable. Part of the ongoing struggle has been where this line should be drawn, given modern medical technology.

—*Donald A. Watt, PhD*

**Bibliography and Additional Reading**

"57d. *Roe v. Wade* and Its Impact." *U.S. History: Pre-Columbian to the New Millennium.* USHistory.org/ Independence Hall Association, 2014. Web.

Greenhouse, Linda & Reva B. Siegel. "Before (and After) *Roe v. Wade*: New Questions About Backlash." *The Yale Law Journal.* The Yale Law Journal, 2011. Web.

Hillstrom, Laurie Collier. *Roe v. Wade.* Rpt. Detroit: Omnigraphics, Inc., 2008. Print.

Hull, N. E. H. & Peter Charles Hoffer. *Roe v. Wade: The Abortion Rights Controversy in American History.* 2nd ed. Lawrence, Kansas: University of Kansas Press, 2010. Print.

McBride, Alex. "Expanding Civil Rights: Landmark Cases: *Roe v. Wade* (1973)." *The Supreme Court.* PBS, 2006. Web.

# ■ Indira Gandhi: "What Educated Women Can Do"

**Date:** November 23, 1974
**Author:** Indira Gandhi
**Genre:** Speech

## Summary Overview

In this speech, Indira Gandhi expounds upon the capabilities of educated women. Gandhi was the first—and to date only—female Prime Minister of India. Although some at first viewed her as a weak leader, by the time of this speech Gandhi had consolidated her power and proven herself to be the most formidable force in Indian politics. She gave this speech to the Indraprastha College for Women at its fiftieth anniversary celebrations. She used the opportunity to talk about more than just women's education. She discussed India and its relationship with the outside world; she also offered glimpses at her own political acumen and worldview.

## Defining Moment

Indira Gandhi gave this speech at a critical period in both the history of India and the history of women's education in India.

The Indian subcontinent was not a unified political state until the twentieth century. Birthplace of two of the world's most popular religions, Hinduism and Buddhism, India has a long, rich, and mostly autonomous history. Western actors, particularly the British, increasingly infringed upon that autonomy in the seventeenth and eighteenth century; British control over India peaked in the nineteenth and early twentieth centuries. After helping the allied powers win the second world war, India gained independence in 1947. As the young nation's third Prime Minister, Indira Gandhi set India on the road to becoming the world power that it is today. Under her leadership, India's farming industry was revitalized and the nation became one of the world's few nuclear powers. Today India continues to expand, constituting a major geopolitical force and boasting one of the globe's fastest growing economies.

Women's education in India has been on the rise. Though there is evidence for the education of women during the Vedic period in the first and second millennia BCE, women's education subsequently all but disappeared from the subcontinent. British rule in the nineteenth century saw several firsts since the Vedic period. In 1818, schools first opened their doors to girls, and some secondary education became available to girls in 1849. In 1875, Madras Medical College became the first school in India to admit women into college courses, though they needed special permission. In 1879, Bethune College became the first school to admit full time female students, with the first female students graduating four years later in 1883. Indian independence brought a renewed focus on female education, as indicated by this document. In 1971 three years before this speech was given, the female literacy rate was at just twenty-two percent; three decades later in 2001, the female literacy rate had more than doubled to over fifty four percent. The male literacy rate also climbed during this period but not as quickly.

## Author Biography

Indira Gandhi served as Prime Minister to India and proved to be one of its most consequential figures. She was born Indira Priyadarshini Nehru on November 19, 1917 in the Allahabad province of British India. Her father, Jawaharlal Nehru, was a key player in India's push for independence, and after this goal was realized on August 15, 1947, he became the nation's first Prime Minister. She was well educated, including a stint at the University of Oxford. While in Great Britain she met her husband, Feroze Gandhi, who bears no relation to the famous Mahatma Gandhi. Upon returning to India, she served in the governments of India's first two Prime Ministers. For her father, Gandhi served as President of Congress; for his successor, Lal Bahadur Shastri, she served as Minister of Information and Broadcasting. She became India's third Prime Minister on January 24, 1966; as of this writing, she remains the only Prime Minister in India's history. Her two stints as Prime Minister (1966-1977 and 1980-1984) saw her evolve from being widely regarded as a puppet of other politicians to an iron-fisted ruler accused of tyranny. She achieved many significant successes, including helping Bangladesh win independence from Pakistan in 1971 , developing India's first nuclear weapons, and reviving India's

Indira Gandhi meeting President Lyndon B. Johnson in the Oval Office on 28 March 1966. by Yoichi Okamoto.

farming industry. Her first stint as Prime Minister ended when she was convicted of election malpractice in 1975, which led to her having to step down two years later. She won power back in 1980. Her second stint as Prime Minister was cut short by her assassination on October 31, 1984, when two of her own bodyguards, Sikhs enraged at recent Indian-Sikh relations, turned their service weapons on their leader.

## HISTORICAL DOCUMENT

An ancient Sanskrit saying says, woman is the home and the home is the basis of society. It is as we build our homes that we can build our country. If the home is inadequate—either inadequate in material goods and necessities or inadequate in the sort of friendly, loving atmosphere that every child needs to grow and develop—then that country cannot have harmony and no country which does not have harmony can grow in any direction at all.

That is why women's education is almost more important than the education of boys and men. We—and by "we" I do not mean only we in India but all the world—have neglected women's education. It is fairly recent. Of course, not to you but when I was a child, the story of early days of women's education in England, for instance, was very current. Everybody remembered what had happened in the early days.

I remember what used to happen here. I still remember the days when living in old Delhi even as a small child of seven or eight. I had to go out in a doli if I left the house. We just did not walk. Girls did not walk in the streets. First, you had your sari with which you covered your head, then you had another shawl or something with which you covered your hand and all the body, then you had a white shawl, with which every thing was covered again although your face was open fortunately. Then you were in the doli, which again was covered by another cloth. And this was in a family or community which did not observe purdah of any kind at all. In fact, all our social functions always were mixed functions but this was the atmosphere of the city and of the country.

Now, we have got education and there is a debate all over the country whether this education is adequate to the needs of society or the needs of our young people. I am one of those who always believe that education needs a thorough overhauling. But at the same time, I think that everything in our education is not bad, that even the present education has produced very fine men and women, specially scientists and experts in different fields, who are in great demand all over the world and even in the most affluent countries. Many of our young people leave us and go abroad because they get higher salaries, they get better conditions of work.

But it is not all a one-sided business because there are many who are persuaded and cajoled to go even when they are reluctant. We know of first class students, especially in medicine or nuclear energy for instance, they are approached long before they have passed out and offered all kinds of inducements to go out. Now, that shows that people do consider that they have a standard of knowledge and capability which will be useful anywhere in the world.

So, that is why I say that there is something worthwhile. It also shows that our own ancient philosophy has taught us that nothing in life is entirely bad or entirely good. Everything is somewhat of a mixture and it depends on us and our capability how we can extract the good, how we can make use of what is around us. There are people who through observation can learn from anything that is around them. There are others who can be surrounded by the most fascinating people, the most wonderful books, and other things and who yet remain quite closed in and they are unable to take anything from this wealth around them.

Our country is a very rich country. It is rich in culture, it is rich in many old traditions—old and even modern tradition. Of course, it has a lot of bad things too and some of the bad things are in the society—superstition, which has grown over the years and which sometimes clouds over the shining brightness of ancient thought and values, eternal values. Then, of course, there is the physical poverty of large numbers of our people. That is something which is ugly and that hampers the growth of millions of young boys and girls. Now, all these bad things we have to fight against and that is what we are doing since Independence.

But, we must not allow this dark side of the picture which, by the way, exists in every country in the world. Even the most rich country in the world has its dark side, but usually other people hide their dark sides and they try to project the shining side or the side of achievement. Here in India, we seem to want to project the worst side of society. Before anybody does anything, he has to have, of course, knowledge and capability, but along with it he has to have a certain amount of pride in what he or she is doing. He has to have self confidence in his own ability. If your teacher tells, "You cannot do this," even if you are a very bright student I think every time you will find, it will be more and more difficult for you to do it. But if your teacher encourages saying, "Go along you have done very good work, now try a little harder," then you will try a little harder and you will be able to do it. And it is the same with societies and with countries.

This country, India, has had remarkable achievements to its credit, of course in ancient times, but even in modern times, I think there are a few modern stories, success stories, which are as fascinating as the success story of our country. It is true that we have not banished poverty, we have not banished many of our social ills, but if you compare us to what we were just about 27 years ago, I think that you will not find a single other country that has been able to achieve so much under the most difficult circumstances.

Today, we are passing through specially dark days. But these are not dark days for India alone. Except for the countries which call themselves socialist and about which we do not really know very much, every other country has the same sort of economic problems, which we have. Only a few countries, which have very small populations, have no unemployment. Otherwise, the rich countries also today have unemployment. They have shortages of essential articles. They have shortages even of food.

I do not know how many of you know that the countries of Western Europe and Japan import 41 percent of their food needs, whereas India imports just under two percent. Yet, somehow we ourselves project an image that India is out with the begging bowl. And naturally when we ourselves say it, other people will say it much louder and much stronger. It is true, of course, that our two percent is pretty big because we are a very big country and we have a far bigger population than almost any country in the world with the exception of China. We have to see and you, the educated women, because it is great privilege for you to have higher education, you have to try and see our problems in the perspective of what has happened here in this country and what is happening all over the world.

There is today great admiration for certain things that have happened in other countries where the society is quite differently formed, where no dissent is allowed. The same people who admire that system or the achievements of that system are the ones who say there is dictatorship here even though, I think, nobody has yet been able to point out to me which country has more freedom of expression or action. So, something is said and a lot of people without thinking keep on repeating it with additions until an entirely distorted picture of the country and of our people is presented.

As I said, we do have many shortcomings, whether it is the government, whether it is the society. Some are due to our traditions because, as I said, not all tradition is good. And one of the biggest responsibilities of the educated women today is how to synthesise what has been valuable and timeless in our ancient traditions with what is good and valuable in modern thought. All that is modern is not good just as all that is old is neither all good nor all bad. We have to decide, not once and for all but almost every week, every month what is coming out that is good and useful to our country and what of the old we can keep and enshrine in our society. To be modern, most people think that it is something of a manner of dress or a manner of speaking or certain habits and customs, but that is not really being modern. It is a very superficial part of modernity.

For instance, when I cut my hair, it was because of the sort of life that I was leading. We were all in the movement. You simply could not have long hair and go in the villages and wash it every day. So, when you lead a life, a particular kind of life, your clothes, your everything has to fit into that life if you are to be efficient. If you have to go in the villages and you have to bother whether your clothes are going to be dirty, then you cannot be a good worker. You have to forget everything of that kind. That is why, gradually, clothes and so on have changed in some countries because of the changes in the lifestyle. Does it suit our life-style or what we want to do or not? If it does, maybe we have to adopt some of these things not merely because it is done in another country and perhaps for another purpose. But what clothes we wear is really quite unimportant. What is important is how we are thinking.

Sometimes, I am very sad that even people who do science are quite unscientific in their thinking and in their other actions—not what they are doing in the laboratories but how they live at home or their attitudes towards other people. Now, for India to become what we want it to become with a modern, rational society and firmly based on what is good in our ancient tradition and in our soil, for this we have to have a thinking public, thinking young women who are not content to accept what comes from any part of the world but are willing to listen to it, to analyse it and to decide whether it is to be accepted or whether it is to be thrown out and this is the sort of education which we want, which enables our young people to adjust to this changing world and to be able to contribute to it.

Some people think that only by taking up very high jobs, you are doing something important or you are doing national service. But we all know that the most complex machinery will be ineffective if one small screw is not working as it should and that screw is just as important as any big part. It is the same in national life. There is no job that is too small; there is no person who is too small. Everybody has something to do. And if he or she does it well, then the country will run well.

In our superstition, we have thought that some work is dirty work. For instance, sweeping has been regarded as dirty. Only some people can do it; others should not do it. Now we find that manure is the most valuable thing that the world has today and many of the world's economies are shaking because there is not enough fertilizer—and not just the chemical fertilizer but the ordinary manure, night-soil and all that sort of thing, things which were considered dirty.

Now it shows how beautifully balanced the world was with everything fitted in with something else. Everything, whether dirty or small, had a purpose. We, with our science and technology, have tried to—not purposely, but somehow, we have created an imbalance and that is what is troubling, on a big scale, the economies of the world and also people and individuals. They are feeling alienated from their societies, not only in India but almost in every country in the world, except in places where the whole purpose of education and government has to be to make the people conform to just one idea. We are told that people there are very happy in whatever they are doing. If they are told to clean the streets,

well, if he is a professor he has to clean the streets, if he is a scientist he has to do it, and we were told that they are happy doing it. Well, if they are happy, it is alright.

But I do not think in India we can have that kind of society where people are forced to do things because we think that they can be forced maybe for 25 years, maybe for 50 years, but sometime or the other there will be an explosion. In our society, we allow lots of smaller explosions because we think that that will guard the basic stability and progress of society and prevent it from having the kind of chaotic explosion which can retard our progress and harmony in the country.

So, I hope that all of you who have this great advantage of education will not only do whatever work you are doing keeping the national interests in view, but you will make your own contribution to creating peace and harmony, to bringing beauty in the lives of our people and our country. I think this is the special responsibility of the women of India. We want to do a great deal for our country, but we have never regarded India as isolated from the rest of the world. What we want to do is to make a better world. So, we have to see India's problems in the perspective of the larger world problems.

It has given me great pleasure to be with you here. I give my warm congratulations to those who are doing well and my very good wishes to all the others that they will also do much better. This college has had a high reputation but we must always see that we do better than those who were there before us. So, good luck and good wishes to you.

## Document Analysis

The document's title may have one believe that it is primarily about what educated women can accomplish. The speech does indeed cover this, but it also touches upon much more. It is about India and India's place within global relations. More than anything else, it is about seeing both the good and the bad in the world.

Indira Gandhi, the speaker, declaimed this speech at the Golden Jubilee—or fiftieth anniversary—celebration of the founding of the Indraprastha College For Women. The direct audience was the college's students, faculty, and staff. Yet as the Prime Minister of

India, Gandhi uses the speech to speak to all of India, and her audience is not limited to Indians alone. She connects India with the wider world both to universalize her comments and to widen her audience. For instance, at the beginning of her speech, Gandhi states that "We—and by 'we' I do not mean only we in India but all the world—have neglected women's education." By clarifying who is incorporated within the pronoun "we," Gandhi connects India's failure in women's education with that of the larger world. She makes a similar point at the end of the speech. She says that "We want to do a great deal for our country, but we have never regarded India as isolated from the rest of the world. What we want to do is to make a better world. So, we have to see India's problems in the perspective of the larger world problems." Viewing India as an integrated part of the larger world not only places the lack of women's education in its larger—and correct—context but also offers hope that what she and her audience accomplish can have a positive, global impact.

Throughout the speech, Gandhi repeatedly preaches moderation, pleading with her audience to recognize both the good and the bad in the world. A thesis statement of sorts comes when she argues that "Everything is somewhat of a mixture and it depends on us and our capability how we can extract the good, how we can make use of what is around us." As this sentence shows, seeing the world as a mixture of good and bad is not incompatible with an optimistic or positive outlook. Gandhi's moderation comes when she covers a variety of topics. In one example, while discussing the difference between ancient and modern, she states that "All that is modern is not good just as all that is old is neither all good nor all bad." In another example, she cuts a similarly middle-of-the-line tack when discussing education in India: "Now, we have got education and there is a debate all over the country whether this education is adequate to the needs of society or the needs of our young people. I am one of those who always believe that education needs a thorough overhauling. But at the same time, I think that everything in our education is not bad." This centrist tendency showcases one of the reasons Gandhi was successful as a politician. An example that highlights Gandhi's ability to use recognizing the mixture of good and bad to form a positive outlook comes when she discusses manure. Attempting to overturn her country's "superstitions," she explains how this material which is considered dirty is, in fact, extremely useful as fertilizer: "Now we find that manure is the most valuable thing that the world has today." Gandhi encourages her audience to recognize the good and the bad in the world and extract the good. This message is particularly relevant to women's education, a topic in which one can find many negatives as well as some positives.

## Essential Themes

Indira Gandhi discusses the theme of harmony at key points in the speech and connects it to the role of women in society. She begins her speech with a Sanskrit proverb which equates woman and the home and states that the home is the foundation of society. Gandhi continues, "If the home is inadequate—either inadequate in material goods and necessities or inadequate in the sort of friendly, loving atmosphere that every child needs to grow and develop—then that country cannot have harmony and no country which does not have harmony can grow in any direction at all." With this opening, she connects home life and society at large and makes women responsible for harmony in both realms. As a female Prime Minister, Gandhi stood as a living embodiment of her words. She returns to the theme of harmony at the end of her speech. Speaking directly to the members of the Indraprastha College For Women, she says, "So, I hope that all of you who have this great advantage of education will not only do whatever work you are doing keeping the national interests in view, but you will make your own contribution to creating peace and harmony, to bringing beauty in the lives of our people and our country." Just as before, she names women as capable of creating harmony. In this latter statement, she points to education as an aid for women in creating harmony.

—*Anthony Vivian, MA*

## Bibliography and Additional Reading

Dasgupta, Shahana. *Indira Gandhi: The Story of a Leader.* New Delhi: Rupa Publications, 2004. Print.

Frank, Katherine. *Indira: The Life of Indira Nehru Gandhi.* New York: Houghton Mifflin Harcourt, 2002. Print.

Gandhi, Indira. *My Truth.* New Delhi: Orient Paperbacks, 2013. Print.

Guha, Ramachandra. *India After Gandhi: The History of the World's Largest Democracy.* New Delhi: Harper Perennial, 2008. Print.

# ■ Shirley Chisholm: "The Black Woman in Contemporary America"

**Date:** 1974
**Author:** Shirley Chisholm
**Genre:** Address; Speech

## Summary Overview

Selected as the keynote speaker for a national conference on black women held at the University of Missouri in Kansas City, Shirley Chisholm enumerated the key issues facing African American women in her address "The Black Woman in Contemporary America." She pointedly reminded her audience that black women were not interested in being addressed as "Ms." or in gaining access to all-male social clubs. Rather, African American women's top priority was the welfare of their families and communities. Black and white women should unite around issues such as improved day-care facilities and increased job opportunities. At the same time that Chisholm was criticizing white feminists, she chided African American spokesmen who suggested that black women step aside to allow black men to monopolize leadership positions. Only by working together as equals could black men and women create the programs and policies needed by their communities. This speech typified Chisholm's fighting spirit, her willingness to confront contentious issues head on, and her rousing oratorical style.

As the first African American woman elected to Congress and a candidate for the 1972 Democratic presidential nomination, Chisholm was the most prominent black female political leader of the 1970s. An articulate and fiery public speaker, Chisholm was not afraid to challenge established power brokers or take a stand on controversial issues. Her arrival on the national stage coincided with growing African American political power and the emergence of the women's liberation movement. At a time when many women of color criticized white feminists for pursuing goals irrelevant to minority communities, Chisholm attempted to bridge the racial divide. She frequently claimed that she was more often discriminated against because she was a woman than because she was black.

## Defining Moment

As America entered the 1970s, the social movements that defined the tumultuous 1960s evolved and, in some cases, began to disintegrate. The civil rights movement that had been a powerful force for societal change a decade earlier no longer dominated the national agenda. Militant groups such as the Black Panther Party that had advocated armed revolution were forcefully suppressed. Other organizations concentrated their energies on developing black consciousness and building black studies programs on college and university campuses. As U.S. forces were withdrawn from Vietnam, the antiwar movement fell apart. Protest on college campuses receded, and the youthful counterculture began to wane.

In their place new forces appeared. The 1969 Stonewall Riots in New York City launched a gay pride movement that grew in strength during the next decade. A nascent environmental movement urged Americans to stop polluting the atmosphere and treat the earth with greater respect. The most potent inspiration for social change during the 1970s, however, came from the women's liberation movement. Influenced by the rhetoric of the civil rights struggle, American women began questioning their roles in the home, the economy, and the political system. The National Organization for Women, the foremost feminist organization of the 1960s, initially focused on legislative and economic goals such as ending discriminatory hiring practices and expanding educational opportunities. Across the country small groups of women gathered in "consciousness raising" sessions that critically examined relations between the sexes and encouraged women to seek fulfillment beyond their domestic roles. More young women sought higher education and delayed marriage and childbearing to pursue careers outside the home.

The emerging women's movement encompassed many interests and divergent ideological factions, but the most pronounced split was the racial divide. Since its origins in the early 1960s, its most articulate and visible figures had been college educated, middle-class white women. Betty Friedan's widely read book *The Feminine Mystique* (1963) identified "the problem without a name"—the lack of fulfillment felt by affluent suburban housewives whose status was defined by their husbands and whose lives revolved around child care and homemaking.

For many African American women this problem seemed inconsequential; they were preoccupied with more fundamental issues of family stability and economic survival. Although black feminists recognized the need for women of color to resist male chauvinism, they were reluctant to make common cause with white women. Mississippi civil rights icon Fannie Lou Hamer acidly observed that she was not interested in being liberated from a man—she liked her black husband just fine.

Young black women faced many challenging questions in the 1970s. Should they pursue newly opened career opportunities in the larger society or use their energies to build institutions within the black community? Should they take up the cause of gender equality or concentrate on eliminating racism from American society? Should unite in the call for gender equity with women of other races or form independent all-black organizations?

These were some of the contentious issues being debated when Shirley Chisholm appeared at the conference on black women in contemporary America. As one of the most prominent and outspoken African American women, Chisholm was an ideal choice to deliver the keynote address. In Congress she vigorously championed the interests of her mostly black and Latino constituents. At the same time, she maintained ties to the largely white women's movement. As a former teacher, Chisholm enjoyed speaking to youthful audiences, especially college students.

## Author Biography

Shirley Anita St. Hill was born in Brooklyn in 1924 to West Indian parents. She graduated from Girls High School and Brooklyn College and later earned a master's degree in education from Columbia University. After working as a day-care teacher, she became a supervisor of day-care centers for New York City. During the 1950s Chisholm entered Democratic politics and supported rising African American candidates. In 1964 she was elected to represent Bedford-Stuyvesant in the New York State Assembly. Four years later, she became the first African American woman elected to the U.S. House of Representatives. Outspoken and independent, she campaigned with the slogan, "Fighting Shirley Chisholm—Unbought and Unbossed." In the assembly and in Congress she championed the rights of women, children, and minorities and was a vocal opponent of the Vietnam War.

In January 1972 Chisholm announced that she was seeking the Democratic presidential nomination. Her candidacy was enthusiastically embraced by feminist activists but did not gain the backing of top party leaders, including many African American men. Because she lacked money and organization, her presidential bid was viewed as a largely symbolic effort. One of the most dynamic and colorful public speakers of her era, she was in demand as a lecturer, especially on college campuses. After serving seven terms in Congress, she announced in 1982 that she would not seek reelection. In retirement, she continued to lecture widely and taught politics and women's studies at Mount Holyoke College. She died in Ormond Beach, Florida, in 2005.

## HISTORICAL DOCUMENT

Ladies and gentlemen, and brothers and sisters all—I'm very glad to be here this evening. I'm very glad that I've had the opportunity to be the first lecturer with respect to the topic of the black woman in contemporary America. This has become a most talked-about topic and has caused a great deal of provocation and misunderstandings and misinterpretations. And I come to you this evening to speak on this topic not as any scholar, not as any academician, but as a person that has been out here for the past twenty years, trying to make my way as a black and a woman, and meeting all kinds of obstacles.

The black woman's role has not been placed in its proper perspective, particularly in terms of the current economic and political upheaval in America today. Since time immemorial the black man's emasculation resulted in the need of the black woman to assert herself in order to maintain some semblance of a family unit. And as a result of this historical circumstance, the black woman has developed perseverance; the black woman has developed strength; the black woman has developed tenacity of purpose and other attributes which today quite often are being looked upon negatively. She continues to be labeled a matriarch. And this is indeed a played-upon white sociological interpretation of the black woman's role that has been developed and perpetrated by Daniel Moynihan and other sociologists.

Black women by virtue of the role they have played in our society have much to offer toward the liberation of their people. We know that our men are coming forward, but the black race needs the collective talents and the collective abilities of black men and black women who have vital skills to supplement each other.

It is quite perturbing to divert ourselves on the dividing issue of the alleged fighting that absorbs the energies of black men and black women. Such statements as "the black woman has to step back while her black man steps forward" and "the black woman has kept back the black man" are grossly, historically incorrect and serve as a scapegoating technique to prevent us from coming together as human beings—some of whom are black men and some are black women.

The consuming interest of this type of dialogue abets the enemy in terms of taking our eyes off the ball, so that our collective talents can never redound in a beneficial manner to our ethnic group. The black woman who is educated and has ability cannot be expected to put said talent on the shelf when she can utilize these gifts side-by-side with her man. One does not learn, nor does one assist in the struggle, by standing on the sidelines, constantly complaining and criticizing. One learns by participating in the situation—listening, observing and then acting.

It is quite understandable why black women in the majority are not interested in walking and picketing a cocktail lounge which historically has refused to open its doors a certain two hours a day when men who have just returned from Wall Street gather in said lounge to exchange bits of business transactions that occurred on the market. This is a middle-class white woman's issue. This is not a pri-

ority of minority women. Another issue that black women are not overly concerned about is the "M-S" versus the "M-R-S" label. For many of us this is just the use of another label which does not basically change the fundamental inherent racial attitudes found in both men and women in this society. This is just another label, and black women are not preoccupied with any more label syndromes. Black women are desperately concerned with the issue of survival in a society in which the Caucasian group has never really practiced the espousal of equalitarian principles in America.

An aspect of the women's liberation movement that will and does interest many black women is the potential liberation, is the potential nationalization of daycare centers in this country. Black women can accept and understand this agenda item in the women's movement. It is important that black women utilize their brainpower and focus on issues in any movement that will redound to the benefit of their people because we can serve as a vocal and a catalytic pressure group within the so-called humanistic movements, many of whom do not really comprehend the black man and the black woman.

An increasing number of black women are beginning to feel that it is important first to become free as women, in order to contribute more fully to the task of black liberation. Some feel that black men—like all men, or most men—have placed women in the stereotypes of domestics whose duty it is to stay in the background—cook, clean, have babies, and leave all of the glory to men. Black women point to the civil rights movement as an example of a subtle type of male oppression, where with few exceptions black women have not had active roles in the forefront of the fight. Some like Coretta King, Katherine Cleaver, and Betty Shabazz have come only to their positions in the shadows of their husbands. Yet, because of the oppression of black women, they are strongest in the fight for liberation. They have led the struggle to fight against white male supremacy, dating from slavery times. And in view of these many facts it is not surprising that black women played a crucial role in the total fight for freedom in this nation. Ida Wells kept her newspaper free by walking the streets of Memphis, Tennessee, in the

1890s with two pistols on her hips. And within recent years, this militant condition of black women, who have been stifled because of racism and sexism, has been carried on by Mary McLeod Bethune, Mary Church Terrell, Daisy Bates, and Diane Nash.

The black woman lives in a society that discriminates against her on two counts. The black woman cannot be discussed in the same context as her Caucasian counterpart because of the twin jeopardy of race and sex which operates against her, and the psychological and political consequences which attend them. Black women are crushed by cultural restraints and abused by the legitimate power structure. To date, neither the black movement nor women's liberation succinctly addresses itself to the dilemma confronting the black who is female. And as a consequence of ignoring or being unable to handle the problems facing black women, black women themselves are now becoming socially and politically active.

Undoubtedly black women are cultivating new attitudes, most of which will have political repercussions in the future. They are attempting to change their conditions. The maturation of the civil rights movement by the mid '60s enabled many black women to develop interest in the American political process. From their experiences they learned that the real sources of power lay at the root of the political system. For example, black sororities and pressure groups like the National Council of Negro Women are adept at the methods of participatory politics—particularly in regard to voting and organizing. With the arrival of the '70s, young black women are demanding recognition like the other segments of society who also desire their humanity and their individual talents to be noticed. The tradition of the black woman and the Afro-American subculture and her current interest in the political process indicate the emergence of a new political entity.

Historically she has been discouraged from participating in politics. Thus she is trapped between the walls of the dominant white culture and her own subculture, both of which encourage deference to men. Both races of women have traditionally been limited to performing such tasks as opening envelopes, hanging up posters and giving teas. And the minimal involvement of black women exists because they have been systematically excluded from the political process and they are members of the politically dysfunctional black lower class. Thus, unlike white women, who escape the psychological and sociological handicaps of racism, the black woman's political involvement has been a most marginal role.

But within the last six years, the Afro-American subculture has undergone tremendous social and political transformation and these changes have altered the nature of the black community. They are beginning to realize their capacities not only as blacks, but also as women. They are beginning to understand that their cultural well-being and their social well-being would only be affirmed in connection with the total black struggle. The dominant role black women played in the civil rights movement began to allow them to grasp the significance of political power in America. So obviously black women who helped to spearhead the civil rights movement would also now, at this juncture, join and direct the vanguard which would shape and mold a new kind of political participation.

This has been acutely felt in urban areas, which have been rocked by sporadic rebellions. Nothing better illustrates the need for black women to organize politically than their unusual proximity to the most crucial issues affecting black people today. They have struggled in a wide range of protest movements to eliminate the poverty and injustice that permeates the lives of black people. In New York City, for example, welfare mothers and mothers of schoolchildren have ably demonstrated the commitment of black women to the elimination of the problems that threaten the well-being of the black family. Black women must view the problems of cities such as New York not as urban problems, but as the components of a crisis without whose elimination our family lives will neither survive nor prosper. Deprived of a stable family environment because of poverty and racial injustice, disproportionate numbers of our people must live on minimal welfare allowances that help to perpetuate the breakdown of family life. In the face of the increasing poverty besetting black communities, black women have a responsibility. Black women have a duty to bequeath a legacy to their children. Black women have a duty to move from the periphery of organized political activity into its main arena.

I say this on the basis of many experiences. I travel throughout this country and I've come in contact with thousands of my black sisters in all kinds of conditions in this nation. And I've said to them over and over again: it is not a question of competition against black men or brown men or red men or white men in America. It is a questions of the recognition that, since we have a tremendous responsibility in terms of our own families, that to the best of our ability we have to give everything that is within ourselves to give—in terms of helping to make that future a better future for our little boys and our little girls, and not leave it to anybody.

Francis Beal describes the black woman as a slave of a slave. Let me quote: "By reducing the black man in America to such abject oppression, the black woman had no protector and she was used—and is still being used—in some cases as the scapegoat for the evils that this horrendous system has perpetrated on black men. Her physical image has been maliciously maligned. She has been sexually molested and abused by the white colonizer. She has suffered the worst kind of economic exploitation, having been forced to serve as the white woman's maid and wet-nurse for white offspring, while her own children were more often starving and neglected. It is the depth of degradation to be socially manipulated, physically raped and used to undermine your own household—and then to be powerless to reverse this syndrome."

However, Susan Johnson notes a bit of optimism. Because Susan, a brilliant young black woman, has said that the recent strides made by the black woman in the political process is a result of the intricacies of her personality. And that is to say that as a political animal, she functions independently of her double jeopardy. Because confronted with a matrifocal past and present, she is often accused of stealing the black male's position in any situation beyond that of housewife and mother. And if that were not enough to burden the black woman, she

realizes that her political mobility then threatens the doctrine of white supremacy and male superiority so deeply embedded in the American culture.

So choosing not to be a victim of self-paralysis, the black woman has been able to function in the political spectrum. And more often than not, it is the subconsciousness of the racist mind that perceives her as less harmful than the black man and thus permits her to acquire the necessary leverage for political mobility. This subtle component of racism could prove to be essential to the key question of how the black woman has managed some major advances in the American political process.

It is very interesting to note that everyone—with the exception of the black woman herself—has been interpreting the black woman. It is very interesting to note that the time has come that black women can and must no longer be passive, complacent recipients of whatever the definitions of the sociologists, the psychologists and the psychiatrists will give to us. Black women have been maligned, misunderstood, misinterpreted—who knows better than Shirley Chisholm?

And I stand here tonight to tell to you, my sisters, that if you have the courage of your convictions, you must stand up and be counted. I hope that the day will come in America when this business of male versus female does not become such an overriding issue, so that the talents and abilities that the almighty God have given to people can be utilized for the benefit of humanity.

One has to recognize that there are stupid white women and stupid white men, stupid black women and stupid black men, brilliant white women and brilliant white men, and brilliant black women and brilliant black men. Why do we get so hung-up in America on this question of sex? Of course, in terms of the black race, we understand the historical circumstances. We understand, also, some of the subtle maneuverings and machinations behind the scenes in order to prevent black women and black men from coming together as a race of unconquerable men and women.

And I just want to say to you tonight, if I say nothing else: I would never have been able to make it in America if I had paid attention to all of the doomsday-criers about me. And I want to say in conclusion that as you have this conference here for the next two weeks, put the cards out on the table and do not be afraid to discuss issues that perhaps you have been sweeping under the rug because of what people might say about you. You must remember that once we are able to face the truth, the truth shall set all of us free.

In conclusion, I just want to say to you, black and white, north and east, south and west, men and women: the time has come in America when we should no longer be the passive, complacent recipients of whatever the morals or the politics of a nation may decree for us in this nation. Forget traditions! Forget conventionalisms! Forget what the world will say whether you're in your place or out of your place. Stand up and be counted. Do your thing, looking only to God—whoever your God is—and to your consciences for approval. I thank you.

## GLOSSARY

**Betty Shabazz:** the widow of slain civil rights leader Malcolm X

**Coretta King:** the widow of Martin Luther King, Jr.

**Daisy Bates:** a twentieth-century civil rights activist and journalist who served as an adviser to the black students who enrolled at Little Rock (Arkansas) High School under a court desegregation order in 1957

**Daniel Moynihan:** the author of the 1965 government report commonly called the Moynihan Report, which argued that the chief problem in the black community was the disintegration of the family

**Diane Nash:** a civil rights activist, cofounder of the Student Nonviolent Coordinating Committee, and a major figure in the Southern Christian Leadership Conference

**Francis Beal:** author of the 1969 pamphlet "Black Women's Manifesto"

**Katherine Cleaver:** probably a reference to Kathleen Cleaver, the wife of Black Panther Party activist Eldridge Cleaver and a civil rights activist in her own right

**Mary Church Terrell:** a late-nineteenth and early-twentieth-century activist, cofounder of the National Association of College Women, which later became the National Association of University Women, and one of the cofounders of the NAACP

**Mary McLeod Bethune:** an American educator who founded a Florida school that became Bethune-Cookman University

**matrifocal:** matriarchal, referring to a society in which women take the leading role

**"M-S" versus the "M-R-S" label:** a reference to the use of Ms. rather than Mrs. (or Miss) in addressing women, to take attention away from marital status

## Document Analysis

In 1974 Chisholm was invited to speak at a two-week symposium at the University of Missouri in Kansas City on the topic of black women in contemporary America. As the nation's most visible female African American leader and as one with a long history of advocacy for women's causes, Chisholm was the logical choice to deliver the keynote address. Drawing on a lifetime of personal experience as well as her twenty years of political involvement, she was well prepared to tackle this subject. Her starting point was the emasculation of the African American male during the years when slavery was prevalent in the South. Because black men were unable to provide for their children and protect their homes and because marriage was not recognized and men could be sold away from their families, black women were forced to take on nontraditional roles. Out of necessity, they developed the strength, perseverance, and tenacity to sustain their dependents. These attributes were often mistakenly described as *matriarchy* by such white social scientists as Daniel Patrick Moynihan, whose 1965 report, *The Negro Family: The Case for National Action*, was widely condemned by African American scholars and activists for its negative portrayal of the black family.

Rather than depicting black men and women as rivals in a contest for domination, Chisholm asserts that black women possessed valuable skills that could complement male contributions; each had vital abilities needed in the struggle for black liberation. Some leaders of black nationalist organizations suggested that African American women needed to step aside to allow men to claim their rightful place at the head of the family and community institutions. Chisholm rejects this proposal as a scapegoating technique; she emphasizes the need for both sexes to work together. Black women with skills and education could not be expected to retire from the scene and sit on the sidelines. This waste of badly needed talent would weaken rather than strengthen the African American cause. Only by working side by side would the common goal of liberation be achieved; only by participating in the struggle as equal partners with men would black women realize their full potential.

Chisholm next reviews the tensions between the mostly white women's liberation movement and African American women—an issue that troubled many feminists. Many of the disagreements between these two groups had their roots in differences in their class composition. The issues of most importance to working-class black women were not always the same as those that motivated middle-class white women. Controversies over symbolic questions, such as the exclusion of women from certain cocktail lounges or the use of the title "Ms." instead of "Mrs." were of little concern to blacks, who were preoccupied with issues of economic survival. However, this did not mean that black women rejected all proposals made by white feminists; in some areas their interests coincided. For example, the nationalization of day-care services, a cause that Chisholm championed, would be a great benefit for both black and white mothers and would be supported by working women of both races. By advocating policies and programs that directly addressed the needs of their community, African American women could act as a valuable pressure group within the largely white women's movement.

Chisholm asserts in her address that many black women had come to realize they had to be freed from traditional women's roles if they were going to contribute fully to the cause of black liberation. In the past, black women had been expected to stay in the background and let men monopolize positions of prominence. The civil rights movement was a case in point. Strong black women were the foundation of the movement, supplying a majority of the participants and organizing grassroots protests, but male chauvinism caused men to claim nearly all of the leadership positions and keep women out of the public spotlight. A few, such as Coretta King and Betty Shabazz, enjoyed celebrity because of the prominence of their husbands (Martin Luther King, Jr., and Malcolm X, respectively), but the list of African American women in the civil rights movement is much longer. Ida Wells, Mary McLeod Bethune, Mary Church Terrell, Daisy Bates, and Diane Nash all made important contributions to the southern freedom struggle but rarely received the recognition they deserved.

Chisholm claims that black women suffered a double discrimination because of their color and gender; for that reason, their problems could not be lumped together with those faced by white women. Neither the black movement nor the women's movement had been sensitive to this heavy burden. Thus, black women had had to cultivate attitudes and organizations to address their own unique issues. Their experience in the civil rights movement had produced a better understanding of the workings of the political system as well as the confidence to embark on new forms of political participation. This, she observes, had led to their growing interest in politics. Younger women were emerging as a force for change and demanding their rightful place in American society.

In the past, cultural norms had relegated black women to a minor role in politics and discouraged them from seeking elective office. As women and as members of the black lower class, they had been systematically disenfranchised. In the present, however, a fundamental change was under way. The liberation movement that had begun in the late 1960s had helped black women realize that their well-being was directly tied to the success of contests for political power. This was especially true in urban centers, where they daily confronted the issues most critical to the black community. Chisholm was encouraged by evidence from such areas as New York City, where black mothers had been at the forefront of movements to eliminate poverty and injustice. Rising poverty levels and minimal public assistance threatened the welfare of black families. Black women had a moral obligation to their children. They had no choice; they had to take a more active role in government. Chisholm notes that this movement to the center stage of politics should not be viewed as a threat to men; it was a question of survival. Black women, she says, must fully commit themselves to political struggle to assure their children a brighter future.

Chisholm concludes by urging the black women in her audience to "stand up and be counted." Americans, she observes, are hung up on questions of gender. These hang-ups have historical roots that prevent black men and women from working together effectively. She cites her career as an example of what is possible if people ignore criticism and squarely face difficult issues. She encourages everyone to look beyond differences of race and gender, to forget tradition and convention. Only by being true to their God and their consciences, she says, will they be able to create the kind of nation that will allow them to reach their full potential.

## Essential Themes

In an era when women are represented at all levels of government, when they occupy influential seats in the presidential cabinet and on the U.S. Supreme Court, and when they make up a growing portion of the nation' governors and senators, it is easy to forget that only a few decades ago a woman running for elective office was a rarity. Pioneering female politicians like Shirley Chisholm and Congresswoman Barbara Jordan overcame monumental barriers. Their success required enormous personal commitment and great sacrifice.

Chisholm was the first African American woman to be elected to Congress, but she was far from the last. By 2010 fourteen black women sat in the House of Representatives. Many accomplished female politicians took their inspiration from Chisholm's career. She was a role model for a generation of female activists.

Her victories proved that racism and sexism need not be insurmountable obstacles to political power.

Shirley Chisholm believed that she had a duty to spread the gospel of political empowerment. That is why, after her 1968 election, she devoted much of her time to public speaking. While it is difficult to accurately assess the impact of her Kansas City speech, there is no denying the cumulative effect of hundreds of similar addresses delivered to young women who packed college auditoriums to listen to her advice and learn from her example. All her life Chisholm fought against entrenched privilege to give a voice to those excluded from the corridors of power. Her courage and dedication remain an inspiration to all who hear her message.

—*Paul T. Murray, PhD*

## Bibliography and Additional Reading

Canson, Patricia E. "Shirley Chisholm." In *African American National Biography*, ed. Chisholm, Shirley. *Unbought and Unbossed*. Boston: Houghton Mifflin, 1970.

———. *The Good Fight*. New York: Harper & Row, 1973.

Henry Louis Gates, Jr., and Evelyn Brooks-Higginbotham. Vol. 2. New York: Oxford University Press, 2008.

Gallagher, Julie. "Waging 'The Good Fight': The Political Career of Shirley Chisholm, 1953–1982." *Journal of African American History* 92, no. 3 (2007): 393–416.

http://www.visionaryproject.org/chisholmshirley/.

Duffy, Susan. *Shirley Chisholm: A Bibliography of Writings by and about Her*. Metuchen, N.J.: Scarecrow Press, 1988.

Meehan, Thomas. "Moynihan of the Moynihan Report." New York Times "Books" Web site. http://www.nytimes.com/books/98/10/04/specials/moynihan-report.html.

Moynihan, Daniel Patrick. *The Negro Family: The Case for National Action*. Washington, D.C.: U.S. Government Printing Office, 1965.

Scheader, Catherine. *Shirley Chisholm: Teacher and Congresswoman*. Hillsdale, N.J.: Enslow Publishers, 1990.

"Shirley Chisholm." National Visionary Leadership Project Web site.

# ■ National Women's Conference Plan of Action

**Date:** 1977
**Author:** National Commission on the Observance of International Women's Year
**Genre:** Report

## Summary Overview

The 1977 National Women's Conference represented the apex of the feminist movement of the 1960s and 1970s. In 1975 President Ford issued an executive order creating the National Commission on the Observance of International Women's Year, with Jill Ruckelshaus as presiding officer. The commission undertook an investigation of women's inequality and issued its report *"...To Form a More Perfect Union..." Justice for Women* on July 1, 1976, just days before the nation's bicentennial. The report addressed issues such as equal pay, child care, violence against women, reproductive rights, women in elected office, media portrayals of women, the double-oppression of racism and sexism among minority women and issues facing homemakers. The commission also called for a National Women's Conference to formulate a Plan of Action. A bill by Congresswoman and feminist leader Bella Abzug (D-NY) mandated state conventions in all US states and territories to elect delegates and send resolutions to the National Conference. The state, territorial and national conferences were funded by a $5 million federal grant. The state conferences during the summer of 1977 were vigorously challenged by conservative anti-feminists led by right-wing activist Phyllis Shlafly, who denounced "federally funded feminism" and accused the events of promoting the Equal Rights Amendment (ERA), abortion and other measures they believed inimical to "traditional family values." In the end, the state conferences sent approximately 1,800 pro-women's rights delegates and 200 conservative delegates to Houston.

The Conference, convening in Houston's Albert Thomas Convention Hall, became a huge media event with a women's torch relay from Seneca Falls New York (site of the 1848 Women's Rights Conference) to Houston. It was led by new presiding officer Bella Abzug and featured feminist luminaries like Gloria Steinem, Betty Friedan, Congresswoman Barbara Jordan and other speakers such as Coretta Scott King and Margaret Mead. Notably, First Lady Rosalyn Carter was joined by former First Ladies Betty Ford and Lady Bird Johnson to open the ceremony. Divisions among the diverse delegates were addressed—especially concerns from minority women—and the delegates overcame deep divisions to endorse lesbian rights. The event was infused with high energy ("the Spirit of Houston") and has been described by Gloria Steinem years later as "... the most important event nobody knows about." The conference marked the culmination of the rising tide of feminism but also fueled an increasingly militant anti-feminist movement comprised of evangelicals, Catholics and Mormons that would be a key element in the rise of the New Right and the election of Ronald Reagan in 1980.

## Defining Moment

Th National Women's Conference of 1977 marked the culmination of the "Second Wave" Feminist movement that began with Betty Friedan's seminal 1963 book, *The Feminine Mystique*. Friedan's book coincided with the report of President John F. Kennedy's *President's Commission on the Status of Women*, chaired by former First Lady Eleanor Roosevelt, which documented widespread economic, legal and social discrimination against women. In 1966, Friedan and Catherine East spearheaded the formation of the National Organization for Women (NOW) to fight for women's legal and economic rights. NOW modeled itself on the NAACP and pursued a similar legal strategy while trying to appeal to the majority of mainstream American women.

As the turbulent 1960s progressed, a radical wing of the feminist movement emerged from younger activists rooted in the civil rights and anti-Vietnam War movements. These radical feminists criticized the liberal feminists of NOW as being too white, middle-class and focused on the interests of professional women. In contrast, the radicals sought to tie feminism into the movement for revolution, adding a gender critique of capitalism and imperialism into the class and race critiques of the New Left. For the radicals "the personal was political" and rather than focus on equal pay and professional opportunities like NOW, the radicals concentrated on issues such as rape, battering, and pornography. They established many of the nation's first battered women's shelters and sought to destigmatize intimate issues with books such as *Our Bodies,*

*Ourselves*. They also pioneered the "consciousness raising" sessions in which small groups of women shared personal experiences with sexism or the struggles with having an abortion, which was illegal in most of the United States. Radicals promoted women's solidarity with denunciations of male patriarchy and advocacy of "sisterhood." They also tended to be more engaged with the unique issues confronting minority women and the problems raised by an overwhelmingly white women's movement.

The radicals first came to national attention during the 1968 protests of the Miss America contest in Atlantic City, which they denounced for objectifying women. As the antiwar and civil rights movements passed their peaks, feminism emerged alongside the environmentalism and Gay Liberation as the dominant movements of the 1970s. A nationwide Women's Strike for Equality took place on August 26, 1970, which included marches of tens of thousands of women marching in cities from coast to coast. Women also made inroads into elected office, including New York's firebrand Congresswomen Bella Abzug (famous for her trademark hats), Patsy Matsu Takemoto Mink (D-HI), Elizabeth Holzman (D-NY) and Patricia Schroeder (D-CO). And in 1972 Congresswoman Shirley Chisholm (NY)—the first African American woman elected to Congress—made an historic run for the Democratic nomination for president. In 1971 and 1972 Congress passed the Equal Rights Amendment to the Constitution, declaring, "Equality of rights under the law shall not be denied or abridged by the United States or by any state on account of sex." The proposed Constitutional Amendment was sent to the states for ratification where, after a strong start, it eventually fell just short of ratification. Meanwhile the federal courts began enforcing Title VII of the 1964 Civil Rights Act that included a ban on sex discrimination as well as applying the equality clause of the 14th Amendment to women. Other victories followed such as Title IX of the 1973 Education amendments mandating sexual equality in education and the 1973 *Roe v. Wade* Supreme Court decision securing abortion rights.

By the 1975 IWY, the feminist movement had made deep inroads into the mainstream. However, these victories had sparked a powerful movement among predominantly religious women who saw the ERA bill as a threat to traditional family and abortion as a threat to the sanctity of life. The increasingly powerful "Pro-Family/Pro-Life Movement" contested the 1977 IWY state conventions and hoped to get the federally funded National Women's Conference canceled. The Houston Conference brought together all strands of the feminist movement, from moderate Republics through the liberals of NOW to more militant feminists, including a controversial but strong presence of lesbians demanding that they be included in the demands for equality. The conference passed 26 planks addressing many areas of women's rights and followed up by submitting a Plan of Action to President Jimmy Carter.

## Author Biography

On November 18-21, 1977, approximately 2,000 delegates and as many as 18,000 observers convened in Houston, Texas for the National Women's Conference, established by President Gerald Ford in 1975 as part of the United Nations' International Women's Year (IWY), which was later extended to the International Women's Decade, 1975-85. The conference brought together moderate, liberal and radical strands of the feminist movement and was attended by delegates from every U.S. state and territory, including, as mandated, women from a diversity of class and racial backgrounds. The conference was charged with coming up with a "Plan of Action" to move the United States toward full equality for women.

## HISTORICAL DOCUMENT

1977 National Women's Conference
Plan of Action

Declaration of American Women

    We are here to move history forward.
    We are women from every State and Territory in the Nation.

We are women of different ages, beliefs and lifestyles.
We are women of many economic, social, political, racial, ethnic, cultural,
educational and religious backgrounds.
We are married, single, widowed and divorced.
We are mothers and daughters.
We are sisters.

We speak in varied accents and languages but we share the common language and experience of American women who throughout our Nation's life have been denied the opportunities, rights, privileges and responsibilities accorded to men.

---

For the first time in the more than 200 years of our democracy, we are gathered in a National Women's Conference, charged under Federal law to assess the status of women in our country, to measure the progress we have made, to identify the barriers that prevent us from participating fully and equally in all aspects of national life, and to make recommendations to the President and to the Congress for means by which such barriers can be removed.

We recognize the positive changes that have occurred in the lives of women since the founding of our nation. In more than a century of struggle from Seneca Falls 1848 to Houston 1977, we have progressed from being non-persons and slaves whose work and achievements were unrecognized, whose needs were ignored, and whose rights were suppressed to being citizens with freedoms and aspirations of which our ancestors could only dream.

We can vote and own property. We work in the home, in our communities and in every occupation. We are 40 percent of the labor force. We are in the arts, sciences, professions and politics. We raise children, govern States, head businesses and institutions, climb mountains, explore the ocean depths and reach toward the moon.

Our lives no longer end with the childbearing years. Our lifespan has increased to more than 75 years. We have become a majority of the population, 51.3 percent, and by the 21st Century, we shall be an even larger majority.

But despite some gains made in the past 200 years, our dream of equality is still withheld from us and millions of women still face a daily reality of discrimination, limited opportunities and economic hardship.

Man-made barriers, laws, social customs and prejudices continue to keep a majority of women in an inferior position without full control of our lives and bodies.

From infancy throughout life, in personal and public relationships, in the family, in the schools, in every occupation and profession, too often we find our individuality, our capabilities, our earning powers diminished by discriminatory practices and outmoded ideas of what a woman is, what a woman can do, and what a woman must be.

Increasingly, we are victims of crimes of violence in a culture that degrades us as sex objects and promotes pornography for profit.

We are poorer than men. And those of us who are minority women...Blacks, Hispanic American, Native American and Asian Americans—must overcome the double burden of discrimination based on race and sex.

We lack effective political and economic power. We have only minor and insignificant roles in making, interpreting and enforcing our laws, in running our political parties, businesses, unions, schools and institutions, in directing the media, in governing our country, in deciding issues of war or peace.

We do not seek special privileges, but we demand as a human right a full voice and role for women in determining the destiny of our world, our nation, our families and our individual lives.

We seek these rights for all women, whether or not they choose as individuals to use them.

We are part of a worldwide movement of women who believe that only by bringing women into full partnership with men and respecting our rights as half the human race can we hope to achieve a world, our nation the whole human race—men, women and children—can live in peace and security.

Based on the views of women who have met in every State and Territory in the past year, the National Plan of Action is presented to the President and the Congress as our recommendations for implementing Public Law 94-167.

We are entitled to and expect serious attention to our proposals.

We demand immediate and continuing action on our National Plan by Federal, State, public and private institutions so that by 1985, the end of the international Decade for Women proclaimed by the United Nations, everything possible under the law will have been done to provide American women with full equality.

The rest will be up to the hearts, minds and moral consciences of men and women and what they do to make our society truly democratic and open to all.

We pledge ourselves with all the strength of our dedication to this struggle "to form a more perfect Union."

## Document Analysis

The document highlights the significance of the gathering in Houston and situates it in the grand sweep of American history, proclaiming it the first such gathering of women "in the more than 200 years of our democracy…" and invoking "more than a century of struggle from Seneca Falls 1848" (the founding of the women's suffrage movement and "first wave" feminism, led over the following decades by Susan B. Anthony, Elizabeth Cady Stanton, Lucy Stone, Carrie Chapman Catt, Ida B. Wells-Barnett, Mary Church Terrell and Alice Paul, among others, and culminating in the 1920 ratification of the 19th amendment granting women the vote.) Three important themes emerge from the document: the presentation of women's rights as mainstream and not radical, the diversity and unity of American women and the idea of women's equality as a natural outgrowth of American democracy. The anti-feminist movement led by Phyllis Schlafly had sought to portray the feminist movement as a radical challenge to traditional values. They denounced it as the embodiment of internationalism, secular humanism and collectivism, which would undermine religion, families, capitalism and individual liberty. The document avoids strident language and positions women's rights as the fulfillment of democracy by "bringing women into full partnership with men…" It counters charges that feminism sought to coerce traditional homemakers out of the home into the workplace by stating, "We seek these rights for all women, whether or not they choose as individuals to use them."

The document also addresses racial diversity among women, declaring, "And those of us who are minority women—Blacks, Hispanic American, Native American and Asian Americans—must overcome the double burden of discrimination based on race and sex." Furthermore, the declaration speaks to moderate, liberal and radical wings of the movement by addressing both economic and legal obstacles to equality and personal issues such as "crimes of violence in a culture that degrades us as sex objects and promotes pornography for profit."

Conspicuously absent, however, is any mention of lesbian or bi-sexual women (transgender women rarely entered mainstream discussions at the time) which was seen by many in the movement as a potentially divisive issue that might drive away more conventional straight women. As a whole, however, the declaration attempts to synthesize the goals and aspirations of different strands of the feminist movement and to package those demands as mainstream and a natural stage in the long trajectory of American democracy.

## Essential Themes

The leaders of the National Commission on the Observance of International Women's Year had expected a smooth journey from its establishment in 1975 under Republican President Gerald Ford through the convention in 1977 under the new Democratic President Jimmy Carter. Women's Liberation ("Women's Lib") had moved from a marginalized movement in the 1960s to a compelling one with widespread bi-partisan support. This trend was helped along by television shows such as *All in the Family* and *The Mary Tyler Moore Show* which highlighted feminist themes (Jean Stapleton, who played *All in the Family*'s Edith, was a prominent spokesperson for the National Woman's Conference as was actor Alan Alda, who played Hawkeye Pierce in the popular television show *M\*A\*S\*H\**).

However, building in the shadow of feminism's greatest gains in the first half of the 1970s was an anti-feminist movement comprised predominantly of conservative religious women determined to defeat the ERA and a fast-growing Pro-Life movement set on overturning the abortion rights. In response to the Gay Liberation Movement a strong anti-Gay movement led by Anita

Bryant emerged under the defamatory slogan, "Save our Children!" Opposition to "homosexuality" merged with anti-feminism into a powerful force in American politics. Just as the feminist movement had to bring together sometimes antagonistic groups, so too did the anti-feminist movement. Catholics, mobilized by opposition to abortion, had an historically tense relationship with Protestant evangelicals and both denominations looked upon Mormons as something of a cult. Nevertheless, the gains of the women's rights movement brought these groups together. Ironically, as conservative groups like National Right to Life, Women Who Want to Be Women (WWWW), the Eagle Forum and the IWY Citizens' Review Committee gained strength and employed particularly homophobic language to tar feminism as a whole, it compelled many radicals, who had regarded the IWY as too establishment, to join forces with liberals and moderates, and moved many of the latter to embrace the more radical demands of their lesbian sisters.

Galvanized by Phylis Schlafly's energetic and skillful leadership and support from conservative members of Congress such as Henry Hyde (R-Il) and Jesse Helms (R-NC), as well as ex-California governor Ronald Reagan, who nearly defeated Gerald Ford in the 1976 Republican presidential race, anti-feminists had gotten some states to rescind their ratification of the ERA and turned the state and territorial IWY conferences into ideological battlegrounds where parliamentary warfare often erupted into angry shouting matches.

Schlafly's leadership of the right was more than met by Abzug's strong and charismatic leadership from the left and the Houston National Women's Conference succeeded in mending many divisions in the feminist movement as well as convincing many non-committed women to proclaim themselves feminists. Many described themselves transformed by the "Spirit of Houston" and left the conference determined to fight until the triumph of full women's equality. Some of the delegates went on to successful careers in elective office such as future California Congresswoman Maxine Waters and future Texas Governor Ann Richards.

Despite the euphoria at the time, the Houston Conference represented what historian Marjorie J. Spruill has called "the Crest of the Second Wave." When the conference leaders passed along their final recommendations to President Carter, they were met with effusive praise but little action. The ERA remained stalled and despite a three-year extension, fell just shy of the three-quarters of US states needed for ratification.

Meanwhile, the conservative anti-feminist forces had gained experience in grass-roots organizing and were gaining influence. Anti-feminists became part of the newly formed Moral Majority and joined with free-market ideologues and militant anti-communists to comprise the New Right that would sweep Ronald Reagan into the White House in 1980 and reshape American politics for decades.

—*Robert Surbrug, PhD*

## Bibliography and Additional Readings

Echols, Alice. *Daring to be Bad: Radical Feminism in America, 1967-1975*. Minneapolis: University of Minnesota Press, 1989.

Levine, Suzanne Braun and Mary Thom (editors). *Bella Abzug: How One Tough Broad from the Bronx Fought Jim Crow and Joe McCarthy, Pissed Off Jimmy Carter, Battled for the Rights of Women and Workers, Rallied against War and for the Planet and Shook Up Politics along the Way (An Oral History)*. New York: Farrar, Straus and Giroux, 2007.

Spruill, Marjorie J. *Divided We Stand: The Battle over Women's Rights and Family Values that Polarized American Politics*. New York: Bloomsbury, 2017.

# THE PERSONAL IS POLITICAL

A Russian poster urging people to open their eyes about domestic violence against women. By Denitza Tchacarova [CC BY-SA 2.0 (https://creativecommons.org/licenses/by-sa/2.0)

# ■ *Webster v. Reproductive Health Services*

**Date:** July 3, 1989
**Author:** Sandra Day O'Connor; William Rehnquist
**Genre:** Court opinion

## Summary Overview

Ever since *Roe v. Wade*, abortion has been a major point of contention across American society. Those advocating more restrictions on, or the cessation of, abortions have sought to implement laws and regulations which would meet their goal, while being able to successfully defend these restrictions in court. When the state of Missouri sought to limit abortions in that state by outlawing the use of public facilities and prohibiting public employees from performing abortions, opponents of these restrictions took the case to court. The regulations also mandated greater pre-abortion counseling and tests on viability of the fetus. Those favoring the status quo created by *Roe v. Wade* believed that these restrictions would harm women and greatly restrict their freedom of choice.

The conservative majority on the Supreme Court agreed with the state of Missouri by upholding all the regulations established by the state. The Court ignored the definition of life beginning at conception, contained in the preamble to the law, as simply an introductory statement and not an applicable legal doctrine. At the time the ruling was issued, many on both sides believed it was the first step toward overturning *Roe v. Wade*.

## Defining Moment

*Webster v. Reproductive Health Services* was a Missouri abortion case. After 1973, when the Court's landmark ruling in *Roe v. Wade* essentially legalized abortion, Americans were sharply divided on the issue. In the years that followed, the abortion-related cases the courts heard did not necessarily bear directly on the constitutionality of *Roe v. Wade*. Rather, they turned on the extent to which any state could impose restrictions on abortion by, for example, specifying at what stage in the life of an unborn fetus abortions might be obtained or whether government funds or facilities could be used to perform abortions.

*Webster v. Reproductive Health Services* was just such a case. It arose from a Missouri law, referred to in the document as "§ 188.029," that imposed a number of restrictions on abortion in that state. Specifically, a preamble to the law stated that "unborn children have

protectable interests in life, health, and wellbeing." The law required Missouri to extend the same rights to unborn children as it did to other persons and to prohibit any government-employed doctor from aborting any fetus the doctor believed to be viable (able to sustain life outside the womb). Further, the law prohibited doctors from using state facilities or the assistance of state employees to perform abortions and prohibited the use of public funding to provide abortion counseling. After a U.S. district court in Missouri struck down these provisions, the Eighth Circuit Court of Appeals affirmed, holding that the provisions of the Missouri law were inconsistent with *Roe v. Wade* and therefore unconstitutional. Missouri's attorney general, William Webster, appealed the case to the U.S. Supreme Court, where it was argued on April 25, 1989. The Court issued its decision on July 3 of that year. The majority decision was written by Chief Justice William Rehnquist, but various justices wrote dissents and concurrences—and in some cases both—to various portions of the opinion.

## Author Biography

As chief justice of the United States, William Hubbs Rehnquist oversaw the Supreme Court's profound shift in a conservative direction after the more liberal leadership of his predecessor, Warren Burger. Rehnquist was born on October 1, 1924, in Milwaukee, Wisconsin. After serving in the U.S. Army Air Forces from 1943 to 1946, he attended Stanford University in California, earning bachelor's and master's degrees in political science. After two years at Harvard University, where he earned a second master's degree in government in 1950, he returned to Stanford to attend law school. There he graduated first in his class in 1952; one of his classmates was his future Supreme Court colleague Sandra Day O'Connor.

After serving as a judicial clerk for Supreme Court Justice Robert Jackson during the Court's 1952–1953 term, Rehnquist settled in Phoenix, Arizona, where he worked at a law firm and became active in Republican Party politics. From 1969 to 1971 he was assistant attorney general in the U.S. Justice Department's Office of Legal Counsel. In 1971 President Richard Nixon nominated him for a seat on the Supreme Court; after confirmation by the Senate, Rehnquist assumed his seat in 1972. In 1986 President Ronald Reagan nominated him to the position of chief justice, a position he held, despite ill health in his later years, until his death on September 3, 2005.

Sandra Day O'Connor holds the distinction of being the first woman to serve on the U.S. Supreme Court. She was born into a ranching family on March 26, 1930, in El Paso, Texas, though she grew up in Arizona, which would be her home state throughout most of her life. She earned a bachelor's degree in economics from Stanford University, in California, in 1950 and remained at Stanford to complete a law degree in 1952—taking two years rather than the normal three.

After completing her law degree, O'Connor was unable to find work as a lawyer in California because of her gender. Accordingly, she turned to the public sector. Her first job was as a deputy county attorney in California. She then accompanied her husband to Frankfurt, Germany, to work as a civilian attorney for the military. Returning to the United States, she opened her own law firm near Phoenix, Arizona, and then served four years as the state's assistant attorney general. In 1969, she was appointed to the Arizona State Senate,

and subsequently won two additional terms and served as the senate's majority leader. She joined Arizona's judiciary when she was elected judge of the Maricopa County Superior Court, and she was later appointed to the state's Court of Appeals.

On July 7, 1981, President Ronald Reagan nominated O'Connor to the Supreme Court to replace Justice Potter Stewart. Her nomination initially met with some skepticism. Conservatives were concerned that she did not have enough judicial experience, while liberals were concerned that, as an active member of the Republican Party, she was not committed to protecting abortion rights. Nonetheless, after being unanimously confirmed by the U.S. Senate, O'Connor took her seat on September 25, 1981. During her years on the Supreme Court, she proved moderately conservative, frequently voting with the more conservative Rehnquist. She was frequently the conservative swing vote on the nine-member Court in closely divided five-to-four decisions.

Unlike most Supreme Court justices, O'Connor retired from the bench in good health on January 31, 2006, primarily to spend more time with her husband, who was afflicted with Alzheimer's disease. In the years following her retirement, she became active as a public speaker, focusing on educating the public about the independence of the judiciary.

## HISTORICAL DOCUMENT

### William Rehnquist: Majority Opinion

CHIEF JUSTICE REHNQUIST announced the judgment of the Court...

This appeal concerns the constitutionality of a Missouri statute regulating the performance of abortions. The United States Court of Appeals for the Eighth Circuit struck down several provisions of the statute on the ground that they violated this Court's decision in *Roe v. Wade*, 410 U.S. 113 (1973), and cases following it. We noted probable jurisdiction, 488 U.S. 1003 (1989), and now reverse.

In June, 1986, the Governor of Missouri signed into law Missouri Senate Committee Substitute for House Bill No. 1596 (hereinafter Act or statute), which amended existing state law concerning unborn children and abortions. The Act consisted of 20 provisions, 5 of which are now before the

Court. The first provision, or preamble, contains "findings" by the state legislature that "[t]he life of each human being begins at conception," and that "unborn children have protectable interests in life, health, and wellbeing." ... The Act further requires that all Missouri laws be interpreted to provide unborn children with the same rights enjoyed by other persons, subject to the Federal Constitution and this Court's precedents. ... Among its other provisions, the Act requires that, prior to performing an abortion on any woman whom a physician has reason to believe is 20 or more weeks pregnant, the physician ascertain whether the fetus is viable by performing

such medical examinations and tests as are necessary to make a finding of the gestational age, weight, and lung maturity of the unborn child.

§ 188. 029. The Act also prohibits the use of public employees and facilities to perform or assist abortions not necessary to save the mother's life, and it prohibits the use of public funds, employees, or facilities for the purpose of "encouraging or counseling" a woman to have an abortion not necessary to save her life. ...

In July, 1986, five health professionals employed by the State and two nonprofit corporations brought this class action in the United States District Court for the Western District of Missouri to challenge the constitutionality of the Missouri statute. Plaintiffs, appellees in this Court, sought declaratory and injunctive relief on the ground that certain statutory provisions violated the First, Fourth, Ninth, and Fourteenth Amendments to the Federal Constitution. App. A9. They asserted violations of various rights, including the "privacy rights of pregnant women seeking abortions"; the "woman's right to an abortion"; the "righ[t] to privacy in the physician-patient relationship"; the physician's "righ[t] to practice medicine", the pregnant woman's "right to life due to inherent risks involved in childbirth"; and the woman's right to "receive ... adequate medical advice and treatment" concerning abortions. ...

\* \* \*

... The two nonprofit corporations are Reproductive Health Services, which offers family planning and gynecological services to the public, including abortion services up to 22 weeks "gestational age," and Planned Parenthood of Kansas City, which provides abortion services up to 14 weeks gestational age. ... The individual plaintiffs are three physicians, one nurse, and a social worker. All are "public employees" at "public facilities" in Missouri, and they are paid for their services with "public funds." ... The individual plaintiffs, within the scope of their public employment, encourage and counsel pregnant women to have nontherapeutic abortions. Two of the physicians perform abortions. ...

Several weeks after the complaint was filed, the District Court temporarily restrained enforcement of several provisions of the Act. Following a 3-day trial in December, 1986, the District Court declared seven provisions of the Act unconstitutional and enjoined their enforcement. ... These provisions included the preamble ...; the "informed consent" provision, which required physicians to inform the pregnant woman of certain facts before performing an abortion...; the requirement that post-16-week abortions be performed only in hospitals ...; the mandated tests to determine viability ...; and the prohibition on the use of public funds, employees, and facilities to perform or assist nontherapeutic abortions, and the restrictions on the use of public funds, employees, and facilities to encourage or counsel women to have such abortions. ...

The Court of Appeals for the Eighth Circuit affirmed, with one exception not relevant to this appeal. ... The Court of Appeals determined that Missouri's declaration that life begins at conception was "simply an impermissible state adoption of a theory of when life begins to justify its abortion regulations." ... Relying on *Colautti v. Franklin*, 439 U.S. 379, 388–389 (1979), it further held that the requirement that physicians perform viability tests was an unconstitutional legislative intrusion on a matter of medical skill and judgment. ... The Court of Appeals invalidated Missouri's prohibition on the use of public facilities and employees to perform or assist abortions not necessary to save the mother's life. ... It distinguished our decisions in *Harris v. McRae*, 448 U.S. 297 (1980), and *Maher v. Roe*, 432 U.S. 464 (1977), on the ground that

"[t]here is a fundamental difference between providing direct funding to effect the abortion decision and allowing staff physicians to perform abortions at an existing publicly owned hospital."

... The Court of Appeals struck down the provision prohibiting the use of public funds for "encouraging or counseling" women to have nontherapeutic abortions, for the reason that this provision was both overly vague and inconsistent with the right to an abortion enunciated in *Roe v. Wade*. ... The court also invalidated the hospitalization requirement for 16-week abortions ... and the prohibition on the use of public employees and facilities for abortion counseling, ... but the State has not appealed those parts of the judgment below. ...

II

Decision of this case requires us to address four sections of the Missouri Act: (a) the preamble; (b) the prohibition on the use of public facilities or employees to perform abortions; (c) the prohibition on public funding of abortion counseling; and (d) the requirement that physicians conduct viability tests prior to performing abortions. We address these *seriatim*.

A

The Act's preamble, as noted, sets forth "findings" by the Missouri legislature that "[t]he life of each human being begins at conception," and that "unborn children have protectable interests in life, health, and wellbeing." ... The Act then mandates that state laws be interpreted to provide unborn children with "all the rights, privileges, and immunities available to other persons, citizens, and residents of this state," . . . In invalidating the preamble, the Court of Appeals relied on this Court's dictum that "'a State may not adopt one theory of when life begins to justify its regulation of abortions.'" ... It rejected Missouri's claim that the preamble was "abortion-neutral," and "merely determine[d] when life begins in a nonabortion context, a traditional state prerogative."...

The State contends that the preamble itself is precatory, and imposes no substantive restrictions on abortions, and that appellees therefore do not have standing to challenge it. ... Appellees, on the other hand, insist that the preamble is an operative part of the Act intended to guide the interpretation of other provisions of the Act. ...

In our view, the Court of Appeals misconceived the meaning of the *Akron* dictum, which was only that a State could not "justify" an abortion regulation otherwise invalid under *Roe v. Wade* on the ground that it embodied the State's view about when life begins. Certainly the preamble does not, by its terms, regulate abortion or any other aspect of appellees' medical practice. The Court has emphasized that *Roe v. Wade* "implies no limitation on the authority of a State to make a value judgment favoring childbirth over abortion." ... The preamble can be read simply to express that sort of value judgment.

We think the extent to which the preamble's language might be used to interpret other state statutes or regulations is something that only the courts of Missouri can definitively decide.

... It will be time enough for federal courts to address the meaning of the preamble should it be applied to restrict the activities of appellees in some concrete way. Until then, this Court

is not empowered to decide ... abstract propositions, or to declare, for the government of future cases, principles or rules of law which cannot affect the result a to the thing in issue in the case before it.

... We therefore need not pass on the constitutionality of the Act's preamble.

B

Section 188.210 provides that it shall be unlawful for any public employee within the scope of his employment to perform or assist an abortion, not necessary to save the life of the mother, while § 188.215 makes it unlawful for any public facility to be used for the purpose of performing or assisting an abortion not necessary to save the life of the mother.

The Court of Appeals held that these provisions contravened this Court's abortion decisions. ... We take the contrary view.

As we said earlier this Term in *DeShaney v. Winnebago County Dept. of Social Services*, 489 U.S. 189, 196 (1989):

[O]ur cases have recognized that the Due Process Clauses generally confer no affirmative right to governmental aid, even where such aid may be necessary to secure life, liberty, or property interests of which the government itself may not deprive the individual.

In *Maher v. Roe, supra*, the Court upheld a Connecticut welfare regulation under which Medicaid recipients received payments for medical services related to childbirth, but not for nontherapeutic abortions. The Court rejected the claim that this unequal subsidization of childbirth and abortion was impermissible under *Roe v. Wade*. As the Court put it:

> The Connecticut regulation before us is different in kind from the laws invalidated in our previous abortion decisions. The Connecticut regulation places no obstacles—absolute or otherwise—in the pregnant woman's path to an abortion. An indigent woman who desires an abortion suffers no disadvantage as a consequence of Connecticut's decision to fund childbirth; she continues as before to be dependent on private sources for the service she desires. The State may have made childbirth a more attractive alternative, thereby influencing the woman's decision, but it has imposed no restriction on access to abortions that was not already there. The indigency that may make it difficult—and in some cases, perhaps, impossible—for some women to have abortions is neither created nor in any way affected by the Connecticut regulation...

More recently, in *Harris v. McRae*, 448 U.S. 297 (1980), the Court upheld "the most restrictive version of the Hyde Amendment," ... which withheld from States federal funds under the Medicaid program to reimburse the costs of abortions, "'except where the life of the mother would be endangered if the fetus were carried to term.'" ... As in *Maher and Poelker*, the Court required only a showing that Congress' authorization of "reimbursement for medically necessary services generally, but not for certain medically necessary abortions" was rationally related to the legitimate governmental goal of encouraging childbirth. ...

We think that this analysis is much like that which we rejected in *Maher, Poelker,* and *McRae*. As in those cases, the State's decision here to use public facilities and staff to encourage childbirth over abortion "places no governmental obstacle in the path of a woman who chooses to terminate her pregnancy." ... Just as Congress' refusal to fund abortions in *McRae* left an indigent woman with at least the same range of choice in deciding whether to obtain a medically necessary abortion as she would have had if Congress had chosen to subsidize no health care costs at all,... Missouri's refusal to allow public employees to perform abortions in public hospitals leaves a pregnant woman with the same choices as if the State had chosen not to operate any public hospitals at all. The challenged provisions only restrict a woman's ability to obtain an abortion to the extent that she chooses to use a physician affiliated with a public hospital. This circumstance is more easily remedied, and thus considerably less burdensome, than indigency, which "may make it difficult—and in some cases, perhaps, impossible—for some women to have abortions" without public funding. ... Having held that the State's refusal to fund abortions does not violate *Roe v. Wade*, it strains logic to reach a contrary result for the use of public facilities and employees. If the State may "make a value judgment favoring childbirth over abortion and ... implement that judgment by the allocation of public funds," ... surely it may do so through the allocation of other public resources, such as hospitals and medical staff.

The Court of Appeals sought to distinguish our cases on the additional ground that "[t]he evidence here showed that all of the public facility's costs in providing abortion services are recouped when the patient pays.".... We disagree.

"Constitutional concerns are greatest," we said in *Maher*, ...when the State attempts to impose its will by the force of law; the State's power to encourage actions deemed to be in the public interest is necessarily far broader.

Nothing in the Constitution requires States to enter or remain in the business of performing abortions. Nor, as appellees suggest, do private physicians and their patients have some kind of constitutional right of access to public facilities for the performance of abortions. ... Indeed, if the State does recoup all of its costs in performing abortions, and no state subsidy, direct or indirect, is available, it is difficult to see how any procreational choice is burdened by the State's ban on the use of its facilities or employees for performing abortions....

... Thus we uphold the Act's restrictions on the use of public employees and facilities for the performance or assistance of nontherapeutic abortions.

C

The Missouri Act contains three provisions relating to "encouraging or counseling a woman to have an abortion not necessary to save her life." Section 188.205 states that no public funds can be used for this purpose; § 188.210 states that public employees cannot, within the scope of their employment, engage in such speech; and § 188.215 forbids such speech in public facilities. The Court of Appeals did not consider § 188.205 separately from §§ 188.210 and 188.215. It held that all three of these provisions were unconstitutionally vague, and that the ban on using public funds, employees, and facilities to encourage or counsel a woman to have an abortion is an unacceptable infringement of the woman's fourteenth amendment right to choose an abortion after receiving the medical information necessary to exercise the right knowingly and intelligently.

\* \* \*

Missouri has chosen only to appeal the Court of Appeals' invalidation of the public funding provision, § 188.205. ... A threshold question is whether this provision reaches primary conduct, or whether it is simply an instruction to the State's fiscal officers not to allocate funds for abortion counseling. We accept, for purposes of decision, the State's claim that § 188.205 "is not directed at the conduct of any physician or health care provider, private or public," but "is directed solely at those persons responsible for expending public funds." ...

Appellees contend that they are not "adversely" affected under the State's interpretation of § 188.205, and therefore that there is no longer a case or controversy before us on this question. ... Plaintiffs are masters of their complaints, and remain so at the appellate stage of a litigation. ... A majority of the Court agrees with appellees that the controversy over § 188.205 is now moot, because appellees' argument amounts to a decision to no longer seek a declaratory judgment that § 188.205 is unconstitutional and accompanying declarative relief. ... We accordingly direct the Court

of Appeals to vacate the judgment of the District Court with instructions to dismiss the relevant part of the complaint. ...

Because this [dispute] was rendered moot in part by [appellees'] willingness permanently to withdraw their equitable claims from their federal action, a dismissal with prejudice is indicated.

\* \* \*

D

Section 188.029 of the Missouri Act provides:

Before a physician performs an abortion on a woman he has reason to believe is carrying an unborn child of twenty or more weeks gestational age, the physician shall first determine if the unborn child is viable by using and exercising that degree of care, skill, and proficiency commonly exercised by the ordinarily skillful, careful, and prudent physician engaged in similar practice under the same or similar conditions. In making this determination of viability, the physician shall perform or cause to be performed such medical examinations and tests as are necessary to make a finding of the gestational age, weight, and lung maturity of the unborn child and shall enter such findings and determination of viability in the medical record of the mother.

As with the preamble, the parties disagree over the meaning of this statutory provision. The State emphasizes the language of the first sentence, which speaks in terms of the physician's determination of viability being made by the standards of ordinary skill in the medical profession. ... Appellees stress the language of the second sentence, which prescribes such "tests as are necessary" to make a finding of gestational age, fetal weight, and lung maturity. ...

The Court of Appeals read § 188.029 as requiring that, after 20 weeks, "doctors *must* perform tests to find gestational age, fetal weight and lung maturity." ... The court indicated that the tests needed to determine fetal weight at 20 weeks are "unreliable and inaccurate," and would add $125 to $250 to the cost of an abortion. ... It also stated that

amniocentesis, the only method available to determine lung maturity, is contrary to accepted medical practice until 28–30 weeks of gestation, expensive, and imposes significant health risks for both the pregnant woman and the fetus.

\* \* \*

We must first determine the meaning of § 188.029 under Missouri law. Our usual practice is to defer to the lower court's construction of a state statute, but we believe the Court of Appeals has "fallen into plain error" in this case. ... "In expounding a statute, we must not be guided by a single sentence or member of a sentence, but look to the provisions of the whole law, and to its object and policy."

...The Court of Appeals' interpretation also runs "afoul of the well-established principle that statutes will be interpreted to avoid constitutional difficulties." ...

We think the viability testing provision makes sense only if the second sentence is read to require only those tests that are useful to making subsidiary findings as to viability.... It thus seems clear to us that the Court of Appeals' construction of § 188.029 violates well-accepted canons of statutory interpretation used in the Missouri courts. ...

The viability testing provision of the Missouri Act is concerned with promoting the State's interest in potential human life, rather than in maternal health. Section 188.029 creates what is essentially a presumption of viability at 20 weeks, which the physician must rebut with tests indicating that the fetus is not viable prior to performing an abortion. It also directs the physician's determination as to viability by specifying consideration, if feasible, of gestational age, fetal weight, and lung capacity. The District Court found that "the medical evidence is uncontradicted that a 20-week fetus is *not* viable," and that "23½ to 24 weeks gestation is the earliest point in pregnancy where a reasonable possibility of viability exists." ... But it also found that there may be a 4-week error in estimating gestational age, ... which supports testing at 20 weeks.

In *Roe v. Wade*, the Court recognized that the State has "important and legitimate" interests in protecting maternal health and in the potentiality of human life. ... During the second trimester, the State "may, if it chooses, regulate the abortion procedure in ways that are reasonably related to maternal health." ... After viability, when the State's interest in potential human life was held to become compelling, the State

may, if it chooses, regulate, and even proscribe, abortion except where it is necessary, in appropriate medical judgment, for the preservation of the life or health of the mother.

\* \* \*

In *Colautti v. Franklin*, ... upon which appellees rely, the Court held that a Pennsylvania statute regulating the standard of care to be used by a physician performing an abortion of a possibly viable fetus was void for vagueness. ... But in the course of reaching that conclusion, the Court reaffirmed its earlier statement in *Planned Parenthood of Central Mo. v. Danforth*, 428 U.S. 52, 64 (1976), that "the determination of whether a particular fetus is viable is, and must be, a matter for the judgment of the responsible attending physician."

... JUSTICE BLACKMUN, ... ignores the statement in *Colautti* that

neither the legislature nor the courts may proclaim one of the elements entering into the ascertainment of viability—be it weeks of gestation or fetal weight or any other single factor—as the determinant of when the State has a compelling interest in the life or health of the fetus.

... To the extent that § 188.029 regulates the method for determining viability, it undoubtedly does superimpose state regulation on the medical determination whether a particular fetus is viable. The Court of Appeals and the District Court thought it unconstitutional for this reason. ... To the extent that the viability tests increase the cost of what are in fact second-trimester abortions, their validity may also be questioned under *Akron*, 462 U.S. at 434–435, where the Court held that a requirement that second-trimester abortions must be performed in hospitals was invalid because it substantially increased the expense of those procedures.

We think that the doubt cast upon the Missouri statute by these cases is not so much a flaw in the statute as it is a reflection of the fact that the rigid trimester analysis of the course of a pregnancy enunciated in Roe has resulted in subsequent cases like *Colautti* and *Akron* making constitutional law in this area a virtual Procrustean bed. Statutes specifying elements of informed consent to be provided abortion patients, for example, were invalidated if they were thought to "structur[e] … the dialogue between the woman and her physician." … As the dissenters in *Thornburgh* pointed out, such a statute would have been sustained under any traditional standard of judicial review … or for any other surgical procedure except abortion. …

In the first place, the rigid *Roe* framework is hardly consistent with the notion of a Constitution cast in general terms, as ours is, and usually speaking in general principles, as ours does. The key elements of the *Roe* framework—trimesters and viability—are not found in the text of the Constitution, or in any place else one would expect to find a constitutional principle. Since the bounds of the inquiry are essentially indeterminate, the result has been a web of legal rules that have become increasingly intricate, resembling a code of regulations rather than a body of constitutional doctrine. AS JUSTICE WHITE has put it, the trimester framework has left this Court to serve as the country's *"ex officio* medical board with powers to approve or disapprove medical and operative practices and standards throughout the United States." …

In the second place, we do not see why the State's interest in protecting potential human life should come into existence only at the point of viability, and that there should therefore be a rigid line allowing state regulation after viability but prohibiting it before viability. The dissenters in *Thornburgh*, writing in the context of the *Roe* trimester analysis, would have recognized this fact by positing against the "fundamental right" recognized in *Roe* the State's "compelling interest" in protecting potential human life throughout pregnancy. "[T]he State's interest, if compelling after viability, is equally compelling before viability." …

The tests that § 188.029 requires the physician to perform are designed to determine viability.… But we are satisfied that the requirement of these tests permissibly furthers the State's interest in protecting potential human life, and we therefore believe § 188.029 to be constitutional.

JUSTICE BLACKMUN takes us to task for our failure to join in a "great issues" debate as to whether the Constitution includes an "unenumerated" general right to privacy as recognized in cases such as *Griswold v. Connecticut*, 381 U.S. 479 (1965), and *Roe*. But *Griswold v. Connecticut*, unlike *Roe*, did not purport to adopt a whole framework, complete with detailed rules and distinctions, to govern the cases in which the asserted liberty interest would apply. As such, it was far different from the opinion, if not the holding, of *Roe v. Wade*, which sought to establish a constitutional framework for judging state regulation of abortion during the entire term of pregnancy.… The experience of the Court in applying *Roe v. Wade* in later cases … suggests to us that there is wisdom in not unnecessarily attempting to elaborate the abstract differences between a "fundamental right" to abortion, as the Court described it in *Akron*, 462 U.S. at 420, n. 1, a "limited fundamental constitutional right," which JUSTICE BLACKMUN today treats *Roe* as having established … or a liberty interest protected by the Due Process Clause, which we believe it to be. The Missouri testing requirement here is reasonably designed to ensure that abortions are not performed where the fetus is viable—an end which all concede is legitimate—and that is sufficient to sustain its constitutionality.

JUSTICE BLACKMUN also accuses us, *inter alia*, of cowardice and illegitimacy in dealing with "the most politically divisive domestic legal issue of our time." … There is no doubt that our holding today will allow some governmental regulation of abortion that would have been prohibited under the language of cases such as *Colautti v. Franklin*, 439 U.S. 379 (1979), and *Akron v. Akron Center for Reproductive Health, Inc., supra*. But the goal of constitutional adjudication is surely not to remove inexorably "politically divisive" issues from the ambit of the legislative process, whereby the people through their elected representatives deal with matters of concern to them. The goal of constitutional adjudication is to hold true the balance between that which the Constitution puts beyond the reach of the democratic process and that which it does not. We think we have done that today. JUSTICE BLACKMUN's suggestion … that legislative bodies, in a Nation where more than half of our population is women, will treat our decision today as an invitation to enact abortion regulation reminiscent of the dark ages not only misreads our views but does scant justice to those who serve in such bodies and the people who elect them.

III

Both appellants and the United States as *Amicus Curiae* have urged that we overrule our decision in *Roe v. Wade*. … The facts of the present case, however, differ from those at issue in Roe. Here, Missouri has determined that viability is the point at which its interest in potential human life must be safeguarded. In *Roe*, on the other hand, the Texas statute criminalized the performance of *all* abortions, except when the mother's life was at stake. … This case therefore affords us no occasion to revisit the holding of *Roe*, which was that the Texas statute unconstitutionally infringed the right to an abortion derived from the Due Process Clause, … and we leave it undisturbed. To the extent indicated in our opinion, we would modify and narrow *Roe* and succeeding cases.

Because none of the challenged provisions of the Missouri Act properly before us conflict with the Constitution, the judgment of the Court of Appeals is

*Reversed.*

## Sandra Day O'Connor: Concurrence

The time when viability is achieved may vary with each pregnancy, and the determination of whether a particular fetus is viable is, and must be, a matter for the judgment of the responsible attending physician.

The 20-week presumption of viability in the first sentence of § 188.029, it could be argued (though,

I would think, unsuccessfully), restricts "the judgment of the responsible attending physician," by imposing on that physician the burden of overcoming the presumption. …

I do not think the second sentence of § 188.029, as interpreted by the Court, imposes a degree of state regulation on the medical determination of viability that in any way conflicts with prior decisions of this Court. As the plurality recognizes, the requirement that, where not imprudent, physicians perform examinations and tests useful to making subsidiary findings to determine viability "promot[es] the State's interest in potential human life, rather than in maternal health." No decision of this Court has held that the State may not directly promote its interest in potential life when viability is possible…. Thus, all nine Members of the *Thornburgh* Court appear to have agreed that it is not constitutionally impermissible for the State to enact regulations designed to protect the State's interest in potential life when viability is possible. That is exactly what Missouri has done in § 188.029.

Similarly, the basis for reliance by the District Court and the Court of Appeals below on *Colautti v. Franklin* disappears when § 188.029 is properly interpreted. In *Colautti*, the Court observed:

Because this point [of viability] may differ with each pregnancy, neither the legislature nor the courts may proclaim one of the elements entering into the ascertainment of viability—be it weeks of gestation or fetal weight or any other single factor—as the determinant of when the State has a compelling interest in the life or health of the fetus. Viability is the critical point.

The courts below, on the interpretation of § 188.029 rejected here, found the second sentence of that provision at odds with this passage from *Colautti*. On this Court's interpretation of § 188.029, it is clear that Missouri has not substituted any of the "elements entering into the ascertainment of viability" as "the determinant of when the State has a compelling interest in the life or health of the fetus." All the second sentence of § 188.029 does is to require, when not imprudent, the performance of "those tests that are useful to making *subsidiary* findings as to viability." Thus, consistent with *Colautti*, viability remains the "critical point" under § 188.029.

Finally, and rather half-heartedly, the plurality suggests that the marginal increase in the cost of an abortion created by Missouri's viability testing provision may make § 188.029, even as interpreted, suspect under this Court's decision in *Akron v. Akron Center for Reproductive Health, Inc.*, striking down a second-trimester hospitalization requirement. I dissented from the Court's opinion in *Akron* because it was my view that, even apart from *Roe*'s trimester framework, which I continue to consider problematic, the *Akron* majority had distorted and misapplied its own standard for evaluating state regulation of abortion which the Court had applied with fair consistency in the past: that, previability, "a regulation imposed on a lawful abortion is not unconstitutional unless it unduly burdens the right to seek an abortion."

It is clear to me that requiring the performance of examinations and tests useful to determining whether a fetus is viable, when viability is possible, and when it would not be medically imprudent

to do so, does not impose an undue burden on a woman's abortion decision.... the cost of examinations and tests that could usefully and prudently be performed when a woman is 20–24 weeks pregnant to determine whether the fetus is viable would only marginally, if at all, increase the cost of an abortion. ...

Moreover, the examinations and tests required by § 188.029 are to be performed when viability is possible. This feature of § 188.029 distinguishes it from the second-trimester hospitalization requirement struck down by the *Akron* majority. As the Court recognized in *Thornburgh*, the State's compelling interest in potential life postviability renders its interest in determining the critical point of viability equally compelling.... Accordingly, because the Court of Appeals misinterpreted § 188.029, and because, properly interpreted, § 188.029 is not inconsistent with any of this Court's prior precedents, I would reverse the decision of the Court of Appeals.

In sum, I concur in Parts I, II-A, II-B, and II-C of the Court's opinion and concur in the judgment as to Part II-D.

## GLOSSARY

**procrustean bed:** The use of arbitrary schemes to create uniformity.

**Roe v. Wade:** The case, decided in 1973, which determined abortion was legal throughout the United States. There could be no restrictions during the first trimester (0-12 weeks), while certain restrictions could be established for the second (13-28 weeks) and third trimesters (29 weeks to birth), balancing the state's and the woman's interests.

**viability:** Point at which a fetus could survive outside the womb.

## Document Analysis

Chief Justice William Rehnquist wrote the decision for the majority, but the Court's decision was a complicated one, with various justices writing dissents or concurrences—and in some cases both. Section I of Rehnquist's majority opinion, like the opening section of most Supreme Court decisions, reviewed the history of the case: who the litigants were, what the constitutional issues were, and how the case had found its way to the Supreme Court. Section II got to the heart of the matter by taking up the issues the case raised: the

preamble of the Missouri act, the prohibition on the use of public facilities to perform abortions and on the use of public funds for abortion counseling, and the requirement that doctors determine the viability of a fetus before performing an abortion.

Essentially, the Court reversed the decision of the Court of Appeals, ruling that the Missouri law was valid because it did not violate the due process clause of the Fourteenth Amendment to the Constitution. Specially, the majority ruled that the law's preamble was not unconstitutional because it was not used to justify any regulations or restrictions on abortions. Rehnquist presented the assertion that *Roe v. Wade* did not make a determination that either childbirth or abortion was preferable, therefore, a state was free to favor "childbirth over abortion," as this law did. Moreover, prohibiting the use of state facilities, funds, or employees was not seen as inconsistent with any of the Court's previous abortion rulings because no one had an "affirmative right" to state aid to have an abortion: "The State's decision here to use public facilities and staff to encourage childbirth over abortion 'places no governmental obstacle in the path of a woman who chooses to terminate her pregnancy.'"

Finally, the Court ruled that the law's provisions requiring doctors to perform tests to determine the viability of a fetus after twenty weeks of pregnancy were constitutional. Rehnquist argued that the state has an interest in "protecting potential human life," and therefore mandating viability tests during the second trimester was constitutional. The Court did, however, judge that limits on abortion that encompassed the entire second trimester of a pregnancy violated constitutional rights. In a final section, Rehnquist argued that the Court left "undisturbed" its decision in *Roe v. Wade*.

Justice Sandra Day O'Connor voted with the majority, but in addition to Rehnquist's opinion for the Court she wrote her own concurrence, clarifying her position on various portions of the decision. Her concurrence in *Webster* provided an example of her closely reasoned opinions and, perhaps more important, her painstaking efforts to square any given decision with previous Court rulings. In the section of her concurrence reproduced here, she took up the issue of the viability of a fetus and the question of whether the state has an interest in when this occurs. Put simply, the Missouri law under examination in this case placed restrictions on abortion by requiring physicians to perform tests to determine whether a fetus could survive outside the womb; if it could, then physicians could not legally abort it. The parties who contested the law argued that such a requirement placed an undue burden on a woman seeking an abortion, principally by increasing the cost because of the additional tests. O'Connor contended that this burden was not excessive.

O'Connor first took up the presumption of the Missouri law that a twenty-week-old fetus may be viable. She noted that the law's requirement that tests for viability be performed from that point onward on any woman seeking an abortion was not intended to substitute state regulation for a physician's judgment, as the court of appeals held. Rather, the provision in the Missouri law, O'Connor maintained, was merely a means to enable the presumption of viability at twenty weeks to be overcome. O'Connor went on to argue that the Missouri law and the Court's upholding of it were not in any way inconsistent with prior Court rulings. In this discussion, she cited two important cases in the history of abortion rights: *Thornburgh v. American College of Obstetricians and Gynecologists* (1986) and *Planned Parenthood Assn. of Kansas City, Mo., Inc. v. Ashcroft* (1983). O'Connor pointed out that in these cases, the Court upheld the principle that a state had a legitimate interest in "potential life" when "viability is certain"; she noted that in *Thornburgh* the Court struck down a Pennsylvania law only because the law failed to take into account emergency circumstances, not because the Court rejected the principle.

Further, in line with *Colautti v. Franklin*, O'Connor affirmed that the Missouri law under review still placed the judgment of fetal viability with the doctor and not with the state.

A key issue in the abortion debate concerned the question of whether a state could burden a pregnant woman's decision to have an abortion by, for example, increasing its cost or requiring a hospital stay. With respect to the Missouri law, O'Connor dismissed the objection to the added cost of testing as invalid. She argued that the cost of verifying whether or not a fetus was viable "does not impose an undue burden on a woman's abortion decision." She distinguished *Webster* from an earlier case, *Akron v. Akron Center for Reproductive Health, Inc.*, by noting that the latter case dealt with a requirement that a woman having an abortion at any time during the second trimester had to be hospitalized. This, in O'Connor's view, was an unreasonable burden. In contrast, the Missouri law, requiring "examinations and tests," with potential medical use during a five week period of the pregnancy was justified. She asserted that this would only "marginally, if at all, increase the cost of an abortion." Thus, the law does not unduly burden the pregnant woman.

O'Connor further noted that a fetus is not viable during much of the second trimester of pregnancy. Consequently, requiring tests for viability in weeks twenty through twenty-four is not the same as requiring a hospital stay at any time during the second trimester. On the basis of these arguments, O'Connor concluded that the Court's decision in *Webster*, contrary to the findings of the lower courts, is consistent with the Court's rulings in earlier cases. It was on this basis that she voted to reverse the judgment of the court of appeals and uphold the Missouri law.

## Essential Themes

Although Justice Scalia, in a strongly worded concurrence with the majority opinion, denounced the other members of the Court for not being willing to overturn *Roe v. Wade*, the other justices, especially the vital swing justice O'Connor, clearly indicated that it was unwilling to consider this drastic a step. However, they upheld all sections of the Missouri law which had been appealed, reversing the ruling by the Eighth Circuit Court of Appeals. The majority of the Court upheld the law by not directly addressing the subject of abortion, but rather by examining what could be considered necessary steps by the government relating to constitutional rights. They sidestepped the issue of life beginning at conception, by noting that this statement was in the preamble to the law, rather than in the law itself. Just as the preamble to the Constitution does not confer any legal rights or obligations, the preamble to the Missouri law had no standing as a legal document. In a slightly different approach, the Court ruled that the section of the law mandating counseling for women seeking an abortion was upheld as a non-controversial non-intrusive provision.

The rulings on the other sections of the law were based on what the obligations of the government were and what were not. The heart of the ruling was that although abortion was legal in the United States, no governmental entity, at any level, was obligated to provide the facilities in which, or personnel by which, abortions could be performed. In the minds of the five members who comprised the majority on the court, the prohibition against resources of various governmental agencies being used in the performance of abortions, was not an undue hardship upon the women seeking a legal abortion. Neither the woman's due process nor her right to privacy was infringed by the Missouri law. The other section of the law, fetal tests regarding viability, was seen as legal, since it was in the state's interest to "protect life." By allowing Missouri to place limits on the availability of abortions and to create hindrances in the process, the Supreme Court effectively narrowed the *Roe v. Wade* ruling, without ruling directly on the matter.

—*Michael J. O'Neal, PhD; and Donald A. Watt, PhD*

## Bibliography and Additional Reading

Biskupic, Joan. *Sandra Day O'Connor: How the First Woman on the Supreme Court Became Its Most Influential Justice.* New York: Ecco–HarperCollins Publishers, 2005. Print.

C-SPAN. "Supreme Court Oral Argument: Webster v. Reproductive Health Services: April 26, 1989." *Abortion & the Supreme Court.* Washington: National Cable Satellite Corporation, 2017. Web. 26 October 2017.

Estrich, Susan with Herman Schwartz ed. "The Politics of Abortion." *The Rehnquist Court: Judicial Activism on the Right.* New York: Hill and Wang, 2002. Print.

Hensley, Thomas R. with Kathleen Hale and Carl Snook. *The Rehnquist Court: Justices, Rulings and Legacy.* (ABC-CLIO Supreme Court Handbooks) Santa Barbara CA: ABC-CLIO Inc., 2006. Print.

Legal Information Institute. "Webster v. Reproductive Health Services." *Legal Information Institute.* Ithaca NY: Cornell Law School, 2017. Web. 27 October 2017.

# ■ Anita Hill: Opening Statement at the Senate Confirmation Hearing of Clarence Thomas

**Date:** October 11, 1991
**Author:** Anita Hill
**Genre:** Speech; Testimony

## Summary Overview

Anita Hill's Opening Statement at the Senate Confirmation Hearing of Clarence Thomas in 1991 was a bold and revealing account of sexual harassment in the workplace that also brought up issues related to gender discrimination and racism. During the course of the grueling proceedings conducted by the Senate Judiciary Committee regarding the nomination of Clarence Thomas to the U.S. Supreme Court, startling accusations of sexual harassment were raised by Hill against Thomas. A law professor at the University of Oklahoma who had been one of Thomas's coworkers, Hill only reluctantly came forward with detailed allegations. Her statement and subsequent testimony, which were broadcast on national television, provided a public glimpse into the confirmation process as well as the complex web of issues surrounding sexual harassment, gender discrimination, and racial stereotyping. Despite the controversy over his nomination, Thomas was confirmed by a close vote on the Senate floor, and he was sworn in as the 106th U.S. Supreme Court justice on October 23, 1991. He became only the second African American to hold the position, replacing the first African American Supreme Court justice, Thurgood Marshall.

Hill's opening statement was historically and culturally significant in a number of ways. It showed that as an issue, sexual harassment transcended considerations solely about race, and it exposed the profound damage that could be inflicted by verbal rather than physical sexual harassment. Moreover, Hill's account demonstrated that the "he said, she said" dilemma posed by many sexual harassment claims could be a difficult hurdle to overcome. Hill's statement also gave expression to the gender and racial discrimination she had endured and how they had been important factors in her decision to come forward. The statement was also significant because it pitted two African Americans against each other in the public eye and provoked widespread disagreement in the black community.

## Defining Moment

On June 27, 1991, Thurgood Marshall, the first African American justice to serve on the Supreme Court, announced that he was retiring. Marshall had been a prominent figure in the civil rights movement prior to his appointment to the nation's highest court. As chief counsel for the National Association for the Advancement of Colored People, Marshall had argued and won the landmark civil rights case *Brown v. Board of Education*. During his twenty-four-year tenure on the Supreme Court, the liberal Marshall championed constitutional protections of individual and civil rights. As a result of Marshall's resignation, President George H. W. Bush was charged with the difficult task of replacing him.

At the time of Marshall's pronouncement, the composition of the Supreme Court was shifting. During the administrations of both the elder Bush and Ronald Reagan, when a vacancy occurred at the Supreme Court, the presidents had chosen to fill it with a conservative justice. In 1987 President Reagan attempted to nominate Judge Robert Bork, a conservative, to the Supreme Court. However, key Democratic members of the Senate Judiciary Committee were concerned about Bork's views and vehemently opposed his nomination. As a result, Bork's nomination was easily defeated when it came to a vote in the Senate. Mindful of what had happened to Bork, President Bush did not want his nominee to be similarly defeated, but he also did not want to replace Marshall with a liberal-leaning justice.

Republicans felt that Judge Clarence Thomas, who had served on the federal court of appeals since 1990, was the best person to replace the retiring Marshall. Unlike Marshall, Thomas was a conservative African American male who had sharply critiqued affirmative action. Although Thomas was an anomaly among African American legal professionals, Republicans believed that by stressing his humble beginnings in Pin Point, Georgia, he would eventually gain African American support. Thomas was a Yale Law School graduate, who from 1981 to 1982 had been the assistant secretary for civil rights in the Department of Education and from 1982 to 1990 had served as chairman of the Equal Employment Opportunity Commission (EEOC). Conservative Washington insiders knew of Thomas from his government service and had suggested him to President Bush.

Civil right activists, leaders of civil rights groups, and liberal organizations were concerned about Thomas's disdain for affirmative action and other progressive causes. Members of the National Association for the Advancement of Colored People overwhelmingly opposed his nomination, and the National Abortion Rights Action League was concerned about his views on abortion, especially his take on the *Roe v. Wade* decision (1973), granting women wider rights to abortion. Moreover, Thomas's lack of judicial experience was a point of contention for the American Bar Association. Typically, the bar association rated Supreme Court justices "well qualified." Because of Thomas's limited experience on the federal court of appeals, however, the bar association gave Thomas only a "qualified" rating. In response, the White House obtained support from conservative groups to mount an attack against liberal groups that opposed Thomas. This campaign helped bolster Thomas's reputation in the right-wing community but did little to sway his many critics.

In August 1991, one month before the start of Thomas's Senate confirmation hearing, newspaper reporters and Washington insiders began to hear rumors that centered on Anita Hill, a former coworker of Thomas's, who claimed that she had been sexually harassed by him repeatedly. As the confirmation hearing neared, opponents of Thomas contacted Hill, a University of Oklahoma law professor, to determine the veracity of her claims. At first, Hill was hesitant to talk to reporters and staff members of the Senate Judiciary Committee, fearing that her anonymity would be jeopardized. She was first contacted by Gail Laster, counsel to the Judiciary Committee's Labor Subcommittee. Laster asked Hill generally about the rumors of sexual harassment; Hill did not tell Laster about the harassing behavior she herself had endured at the EEOC. Ricki Seidman, chief investigator of the Senate Labor and Human Resources Committee, twice communicated with Hill about the sexual harassment allegations. During her second conversation with Seidman, Hill told her some details of Thomas's behavior but also expressed her desire for confidentiality.

James Brudney, chief counsel to the Judiciary Committee's Labor Subcommittee, chaired by Senator Howard Metzenbaum, next contacted Hill about the rumors. After Hill explained the details of Thomas's conduct to Brudney, he spoke to Metzenbaum, who suggested contacting Harriet Grant of the office of Senator Joseph Biden, chairman of the Judiciary Committee. In the weeks prior to Hill's testimony before the Judiciary Committee, both Grant and Brudney spoke to Hill about revealing her information to the Federal Bureau of Investigation (FBI). Eventually, Hill agreed to be interviewed by the FBI and also submitted a written, notarized statement to the Senate Judiciary Committee memorializing her experiences with Thomas. Thereafter, the FBI report on Hill was submitted to some committee members.

Thomas began the confirmation process on September 10, 1991. Each senator on the Judiciary Committee gave an opening statement that either supported Thomas or expressed concerns about his past. For the most part, the committee, which consisted of seven Democrats and six Republicans, was divided along party lines. The committee's Democrats were much harder on Thomas than were their Republican counterparts, questioning him about his past speeches and articles, his views on natural law, decisions made while at the EEOC, and abortion rights. Typically, after a Democratic member finished questioning Thomas, a Republican member asked him an easier question in order to repair his credibility with the committee. During the initial confirmation hearing, Thomas was unaware of Hill's allegations. He endured the Senate Judiciary Committee's questioning for five days before other witnesses were called.

One of Thomas's key opponents was Sylvia Law, a professor of constitutional law in the areas of personal and privacy rights, who was concerned about Thomas's conservative views on women's reproductive rights. Other opponents included Molly Yard, president of the National Organization of Women; representatives from the American Federation of Labor and Congress of Industrial Organizations; Kate Michelman, executive director of the National Abortion Rights Action League; Faye Wattleton, president of the Planned Parenthood Federation of America; and Julius Chambers, from the National Association for the Advancement of Colored People's Legal Defense and Educational Fund. Speaking in support of Thomas, Guido Calabresi, then the dean of Yale Law School, praised his ability to remain independent and his potential to grow with the Supreme Court. Thomas's proponents also included Robert Woodson, president of the National Center for Neighborhood Enterprise; John E. Palmer, representing the Heartland Coalition for the Confirmation of Judge Clarence Thomas; and the Republican Black Caucus chair George C. Dumas.

Only days before the committee vote, Thomas was informed of the FBI report claiming that he had sexually harassed Hill when they both had worked at the Department of Education and EEOC. Thomas emphatically denied Hill's accusations, but the damage had been done. When the Judiciary Committee voted on the confirmation on September 27, the result was a seven-to-seven tie, and the nomination was sent to the Senate floor with no endorsement. Meanwhile, the news media took hold of the sexual harassment rumors and made Anita Hill a household name. The salacious details of the harassment were cast into the world of public opinion. In turn, the Senate, at the request of Thomas, delayed its confirmation vote. Finally, on October 11, 1991, Hill and Thomas appeared in front of the Senate Judiciary Committee to tell their sides of the story.

## Author Biography

The thirteenth child born to a poor farm family, Anita Faye Hill was born in 1956 in Okmulgee County, Oklahoma. Her father, Albert Hill, and mother, Erma Hill, both worked on the farm. From a young age, Anita Hill knew that hard work and dedication would be the keys to her success. She attended integrated schools and was shielded from racial tensions for much of her childhood. After she graduated from high school, Hill attended Oklahoma State University and graduated with honors in 1977. She received a JD degree from Yale Law School in 1980.

Hill's initial job out of law school was at the Washington, D.C., law firm Wald, Harkrader & Ross. While working for the law firm, she met Clarence Thomas. Soon afterward, in 1981, Thomas was appointed the assistant secretary for civil rights in the Department of Education, and he asked Hill if she would become his assistant. She accepted the job offer, and she followed Thomas to the EEOC when he became its chairman.

In 1983, Hill left the EEOC and took a position as an assistant law professor at the O.W. Colburn School of Law at Oral Roberts University. She subsequently became a professor at the College of Law at the University of Oklahoma, a position that she held at the time she appeared before the Senate Judiciary Committee. After testifying before the committee, she returned to her position at the University of Oklahoma. She was asked to speak at a number of events about her experience at the hearing and about sexual harassment. After controversy over a proposed and sponsored professorship in her name, she left the University of Oklahoma in 1996. As of 2010 she was employed at Brandeis University's Heller School for Social Policy and Management as a professor of social policy, law, and women's studies.

## HISTORICAL DOCUMENT

Mr. Chairman, Senator Thurmond, Members of the Committee, my name is Anita F. Hill, and I am a Professor of Law at the University of Oklahoma. I was born on a farm in Okmulge, Oklahoma, in 1956, the 13th child, and had my early education there. My father is Albert Hill, a farmer of that area. My mother's name is Erma Hill; she is also a farmer and housewife. My childhood was the childhood of both work and poverty; but it was one of solid family affection as represented by my parents who are with me as I appear here today. I was reared in a religious atmosphere in the Baptist faith and I have been a member of the Antioch Baptist Church in Tulsa since 1983. It remains a warm part of my life at the present time.

For my undergraduate work I went to Oklahoma State University and graduated in 1977. I am attaching to this statement my resume with further details of my education. I graduated from the university with academic honors and proceeded to the Yale Law School where I received my J.D. degree in 1980.

Upon graduation from law school I became a practicing lawyer with the Washington, D.C. firm of Wald, Harkrader & Ross. In 1981, I was introduced to now Judge Thomas by a mutual friend.

Judge Thomas told me that he anticipated a political appointment shortly and asked if I might be interested in working in that office. He was in fact appointed as Assistant Secretary of Education, in which capacity he was the Director of the Office for Civil Rights. After he was in that post, he asked if I would become his assistant and I did then accept that position. In my early period there I had two major projects. The first was an article I wrote for Judge Thomas' signature on "Education of Minority Students." The second was the organization of a seminar on high risk students, which was abandoned because Judge Thomas transferred to the EEOC before that project was completed.

During this period at the Department of Education, my working relationship with Judge Thomas was positive. I had a good deal of responsibility as well as independence. I thought that he respected my work and that he trusted my judgment. After approximately three months of working together, he asked me to go out with him socially. I declined and explained to him that I thought that it would only jeopardize what, at the time, I considered to be a very good working relationship. I had a normal social life with other men outside of the office and, I believed then, as now, that having a social relationship with a person who was supervising my work would be ill-advised. I was very uncomfortable with the idea and told him so.

I thought that by saying "no" and explaining my reasons, my employer would abandon his social suggestions. However, to my regret, in the following few weeks he continued to ask me out on several occasions. He pressed me to justify my reasons for saying "no" to him. These incidents took place in his office or mine. They were in the form of private conversations which would not have been overheard by anyone else.

My working relationship became even more strained when Judge Thomas began to use work situations to discuss sex. On these occasions he would call me into his office for reports on education issues and projects or he might suggest that because of time pressures we go to lunch at a government cafeteria. After a brief discussion of work, he would turn the conversation to discussion of sexual matters. His conversations were very vivid. He spoke about acts that he had seen in pornographic films involving such matters as women having sex with animals and films showing group sex or rape scenes. He talked about pornographic materials depicting individuals with large penises or large breasts involved in various sex acts. On several occasions Thomas told me graphically of his own sexual prowess.

Because I was extremely uncomfortable talking about sex with him at all and particularly in such a graphic way, I told him that I did not want to talk about those subjects. I would also try to change the subject to education matters or to nonsexual personal matters such as his background or beliefs. My efforts to change the subject were rarely successful.

Throughout the period of these conversations, he also from time-to-time asked me for social engagements. My reaction to these conversations was to avoid having them by eliminating opportunities for us to engage in extended conversations. This was difficult because I was his only assistant at the Office for Civil Rights. During the latter part of my time at the Department of Education, the social pressures and any conversations of this offensive kind ended. I began both to believe and hope that our working relationship could be on a proper, cordial and professional base.

When Judge Thomas was made Chairman of the EEOC, I needed to face the question of whether to go with him. I was asked to do so. I did. The work itself was interesting and at that time it appeared that the sexual overtures which had so troubled me had ended. I also faced the realistic fact that I had no alternative job. While I might have gone back to private practice, perhaps in my old firm or at another, I was dedicated to civil rights work and my first choice was to be in that field. Moreover, the Department of Education itself was a dubious venture; President Reagan was seeking to abolish the entire Department at that time.

For my first months at the EEOC, where I continued as an assistant to Judge Thomas, there were no sexual conversations or overtures. However, during the Fall and Winter of 1982, these began again. The comments were random and ranged from pressing me about why I didn't go out with him to remarks about my personal appearance. I remember his saying that someday I would have to give him the real reason that I wouldn't go out with him. He began to show real displeasure in his tone of voice, his demeanor and his continued pressure for an explanation. He commented on what I was wearing in terms of whether it made me more or less sexually attractive. The incidents occurred in his inner office at the EEOC.

One of the oddest episodes I remember was an occasion in which Thomas was drinking a Coke in his office. He got up from the table at which we were working, went over to his desk to get the Coke, looked at the can, and said, "Who has put pubic hair on my Coke?" On other occasions he referred to the size of his own penis as being larger than normal and he also spoke on some occasions of the pleasures he had given to women with oral sex.

At this point, late 1982, I began to feel severe stress on the job. I began to be concerned that Clarence Thomas might take it out on me by downgrading me or not giving me important assignments. I also thought that he might find an excuse for dismissing me. In January of 1983, I began looking for another job. I was handicapped because I feared that if he found out, he might make it difficult for me to find other employment and I might be dismissed from the job I had. Another factor that made my search more difficult was that this was a period of a government hiring freeze. In February, 1983, I was hospitalized for five days on an emergency basis for an acute stomach pain which I attributed to stress on the job. Once out of the hospital, I became more committed to find other employment and sought further to minimize my contact with Thomas. This became easier when Allyson Duncan became office director because most of my work was handled with her and I had contact with Clarence Thomas mostly in staff meetings.

In the Spring of 1983, an opportunity to teach law at Oral Roberts University opened up. I agreed to take the job in large part because of my desire to escape the pressures I felt at the EEOC due to Thomas. When I informed him that I was leaving in July, I recall that his response was that now I "would

no longer have an excuse for not going out with" him. I told him that I still preferred not to do so. At some time after that meeting, he asked if he could take me to dinner at the end of my term. When I declined, he assured me that the dinner was a professional courtesy only and not a social invitation. I reluctantly agreed to accept that invitation but only if it was at the very end of a workday. On, as I recall, the last day of my employment at the EEOC in the summer of 1983, I did have dinner with Clarence Thomas. We went directly from work to a restaurant near the office. We talked about the work I had done both at Education and at EEOC. He told me that he was pleased with all of it except for an article and speech that I done for him when we were at the Office for Civil Rights. Finally, he made a comment which I vividly remember. He said that if I ever told anyone about his behavior toward me it could ruin his career. This was not an apology nor was there any explanation. That was his last remark about the possibility of our going out or reference to his behavior.

In July 1983, I left the Washington, D.C. area and have had minimal contacts with Judge Clarence Thomas since.

I am of course aware from the press that some question has been raised about conversations I had with Judge Clarence Thomas after I left the EEOC. From 1983 until today I have seen Judge Clarence Thomas only twice. On one occasion I needed to get a reference from him and on another he made a public appearance in Tulsa. On one occasion he called me at home and we had an inconsequential conversation. On one other occasion he called me without reaching me and I returned the call without reaching him and nothing came of it. I have, on at least three occasions been asked to act as a conduit for others.

I knew his secretary, Diane Holt, well when I was with the EEOC. There were occasions on which I spoke to her and on some of those occasions undoubtedly I passed on some casual comment to Thomas.

There was a series of calls in the first three months of 1985 occasioned by a group in Tulsa which wished to have a civil rights conference; they wanted Thomas to be the speaker, and enlisted my assistance for this purpose. I did call in January and February to no effect and finally suggested to the person directly involved, Susan Cahall, that she put the matter back into her own hands and call directly. She did do that in March of 1985. In connection with that March invitation to Tulsa by Ms. Cahall, which was for a seminar conference some research was needed; I was asked to try to get the research work and did attempt to do so by a call to Thomas. There was another call about another possible conference in July of 1985.

In August of 1987, I was in Washington and I did call Diane Holt. In the course of this conversation she asked me how long I was going to be in town and I told her; she recorded it as August 15; it was in fact August 20. She told me about Thomas' marriage and I did say "congratulate him."

It is only after a great deal of agonizing consideration that I am able to talk of these unpleasant matters to anyone but my closest friends. Telling the world is the most difficult experience of my life. I was aware that he could affect my future career and did not wish to burn all my bridges. I may have used poor judgment; perhaps I should have taken angry or even militant steps both when I was in the agency or after I left it, but I must confess to the world that the course I took seemed to me to be the better as well as the easier approach. I declined any comment to newspapers, but later, when Senate staff asked me about these matters, I felt I had a duty to report. I have no personal vendetta against Clarence Thomas. I seek only to provide the Committee with information which it may regard as relevant. It would have been more comfortable to remain silent. I took no initiative to inform anyone. But when I was asked by a representative of this committee to report my experience, I felt that I had no other choice but to tell the truth.

## GLOSSARY

**EEOC:** Equal Employment Opportunity Commission

**Senator Thurmond:** Strom Thurmond, U.S. senator from South Carolina, at that time the ranking minority Republican on the Senate Judiciary Committee

## Document Analysis

This document contains four distinct topics: Hill's early life and career, the details of Thomas's harassing behavior, her decision not to come forward, and her subsequent decision to tell her story. Hill was also concerned about silently held biases against her as a result of the sexual harassment claim. It was important for her to make the members of the Senate Judiciary Committee, all of them white men, understand that women do not intentionally invite sexually harassing behavior. As a further obstacle to stating her case, Hill's legal career placed her, in the opinion of the committee, in a different category of women from those in many harassment cases, because, from a legal standpoint, she must have known right from wrong with respect to her professional relationship with Thomas.

### Early Life and Career

Hill's statement begins with a brief discussion of her educational experiences and her background, emphasizing her parents' struggles, her family ties, and her personal religious beliefs. She touches on her childhood poverty and her educational success at Oklahoma State University and Yale Law School. In addition, she notes her early work experiences at Wald, Harkrader & Ross, the Office for Civil Rights within the Department of Education, and the EEOC. All this background information was meant to demonstrate to the fourteen committee members that she was an intelligent, hardworking, and credible witness. Furthermore, Hill had to make herself appear first and foremost as an individual giving testimony, rather than emphasize being a woman or black. Indeed, she never mentions the words *gender discrimination* or *racism*; however, her background information reveals that she was concerned about both, specifically, the obstacles of poverty and racial prejudice that many African American women have had to overcome. Hill was thus portraying herself as someone who had overcome her disadvantaged childhood and become a successful lawyer.

### Details of Harassing Behavior

The second part of Hill's statement to the Senate Judiciary Committee focuses on explaining what constituted harassing behavior by Clarence Thomas. Hill starts with a discussion of the harassment that had occurred while she worked as Thomas's assistant in the Office for Civil Rights at the Department of Education. She states that at first Thomas did not exhibit such behavior toward her; however, she then observes that he began to harass her by repeatedly asking her to go out with him socially and even describing to her in detail pornographic films he had seen. After Hill provides these examples, she explains that she told Thomas that she did not want to jeopardize their working relationship and that sexual topics of conversation made her feel uncomfortable. Hill then notes how Thomas's harassing behavior ended before their transfer to the EEOC.

While he was chairman of the EEOC, Hill testifies, Thomas resumed making inappropriate overtures toward her. She describes how he started to make comments about her appearance and whether her clothes were "more or less sexually attractive." Again, she rebuffed Thomas's advances; however, he wanted an explanation as to why she would not go out with him. Hill then details specific episodes of Thomas's harassing behavior, including a conversation he had with her about his sexual prowess. As a result of Thomas's behavior, Hill felt severe stress while she was working at the EEOC.

Throughout her description of Thomas's behavior, Hill relates not only how she repeatedly declined Thomas's invitations but also how he continued to approach her and even questioned why she would not go out with him. These examples support Hill's allegations of workplace sexual harassment and, more important, show how she had become psychologically victimized—how she had come to blame herself for having been in such a situation. Indeed, she could have told the Senate Judiciary Committee only the details of Thomas's behavior, but that alone might not have been sufficient information to suggest sexual harassment. Thus, she takes the extra step of explaining that regardless of how she tried to ward off Thomas's advances, he

would not listen to her. Hill became both a victim and her own advocate in order to clarify her allegations to the male members of the Senate Judiciary Committee.

Incidentally, Hill's detailed account of Thomas's descriptions of pornographic films and his sexual prowess can be seen as perpetuating stereotypes about African Americans. It is possible that Hill had anticipated that some white male members of the Senate Judiciary Committee would not have given her statement the same weight if she had omitted these details. Although the vivid descriptions Hill gave to the committee could be perceived as reinforcing sexual myths about African Americans, she hardly could have been expected to withhold accurate testimony or make it less graphic for fear of contributing to racial stereotypes.

### Decision Not to Come Forward

The third section of Hill's statement focuses on her initial decision not to come forward. She begins by explaining her fear of reprisal from Thomas whenever she chose not to go out with him. These fears included being given less important work assignments and even the possibility of dismissal from her job. Because of these fears, Hill started to look for another job; however, the opportunities were minimal. She eventually found another position and informed Thomas. Hill then pointedly notes to the committee how she agreed to a final dinner with Thomas, during which "he said that if I ever told anyone about his behavior toward me it could ruin his career."

Hill's initial decision not to come forward and expose Thomas reflected a former trend in female reporting of workplace sexual harassment claims. In the early 1980s, sexual harassment claims by women were not prevalent, and these claims were often extremely difficult to prove. Although laws and regulations were already in place to prevent workplace sexual harassment, the support needed to provide credibility to a claim was difficult to obtain. The Civil Rights Act of 1964, signed by President Lyndon Johnson, was the first piece of legislation enacted to help prevent workplace sexual harassment. Title VII of that act prohibits discrimination based upon race, color, religion, national origin, or sex. In 1972 Congress passed the Equal Employment Opportunity Act, which amended the Civil Rights Act of 1964 and established the Equal Employment Opportunity Commission. The EEOC was given the authority to prevent persons from engaging in unlawful employment discrimination practices.

In 1980, the EEOC promulgated regulations titled *Guidelines on Discrimination Because of Sex*. These regulations helped to further define sexual harassment and what were considered acceptable workplace practices. By the mid-1980s, eighteen states had enacted legislation that specifically prohibited sexual harassment. In addition, as many as twenty-eight other states had laws that prohibited sex discrimination. An important decision by the U.S. Supreme Court, *Meritor Savings Bank v. Vinson* (1986), made it easier to prove sexual harassment under Title VII of the Civil Rights Act of 1964. Unfortunately for Hill, that case was decided after her experiences of sexual harassment, which had occurred during the early 1980s.

Hill's decision not to leave either the Department of Education or the EEOC—as well as to follow Thomas from the Department of Education to the EEOC—was likely the result of both gender and race discrimination. First, employment opportunities for female attorneys in the 1980s were not abundant. Female attorneys were often relegated to lower-level positions in comparison to those held by their male peers. Second, workplace racial discrimination was still an obstacle in the 1980s, despite laws and regulations that prohibited it. Hill was an African American female attorney working in a primarily white male world. In her statement she opines that at the time it would have been hard for her to find a position outside the Department of Education or EEOC. Thus, the possibility of being discriminated against when applying for other jobs was a significant factor not only in Hill's decision to follow Thomas to the EEOC but also in her delay in seeking other employment.

### Decision to Come Forward

The final section of Hill's statement explains her decision to testify about the sexual harassment claims. Hill concedes that she had not felt comfortable coming forward and making her allegations public to the Senate Judiciary Committee and the world. She also admits that her delay in coming forward might have been the result of poor judgment. Finally, Hill testifies that she eventually decided to come forward with the information because she had a duty to tell the truth.

### Essential Themes

Hill's opening statement and testimony became the focal point of Thomas's confirmation hearing, even though she appeared before the Senate Judiciary Committee toward the end of the hearing process, after the committee

had voted on whether to recommend Thomas's nomination. Once Hill made her opening statement, she spent the remainder of October 11, 1991, being grilled by the members of the committee. In particular, she was asked many questions about her personal life that had little to do with the sexual harassment claim. Senator Arlen Specter engaged in a concerted effort to discredit Hill. Referring to her statement to the FBI and her testimony to the Senate Judiciary Committee, he pointed out discrepancies between the two and questioned why certain facts were not included in the FBI report. He inquired further as to why Hill did not come forward with her sexual harassment claim until Thomas's confirmation hearing. In addition, Specter introduced an affidavit from John Doggett, a friend to both Hill and Thomas, in which Doggett claimed that Hill was unstable and had fantasized about him. Specter also asked Hill questions related to the number of times she and Thomas had spoken since she left the EEOC; in doing this, Specter attempted to insinuate that Hill was in contact with Thomas for more than professional reasons.

Among the others questioning Hill, Senator Howell Heflin, in order to call her testimony into doubt, accused her of fantasizing about Thomas. Some committee members intimated that her story should be presumed to be fictional because she had chosen to come forward late in the confirmation process. When Hill's testimony was complete, Thomas, angered by her accusations, testified and expressed his disdain for the proceedings as "high-tech lynching for uppity blacks." At that point, the confirmation hearing turned into a "he said, she said" nightmare for both Thomas and Hill, during which the purpose of the confirmation hearing, namely, to determine whether Thomas was the best person for the job, was lost. Eventually, Thomas was confirmed by a Senate vote of fifty-two to forty-eight, one of the narrowest such votes in U.S. history.

Hill's testimony before the committee captivated and educated audiences on issues surrounding sexual harassment in the workplace. Reporting of sexual harassment rose after Anita Hill came forward, as claims of sexual harassment began to be taken more seriously. Furthermore, her testimony made employers more aware of what constituted sexually harassing behavior, encouraging employers to monitor employee interactions more effectively and thus prevent sexually harassing behavior. In addition, many employers began to make it easier for victims of alleged sexual harassment to come forward without having to reveal their identities. This commitment to anonymity assuaged victims' fears of accuser retaliation and job dismissal. Many companies changed their personnel policies to ensure that all employees would comply with sexual harassment laws and regulations.

An unfortunate aspect of the Thomas confirmation hearing was that the process itself, which could have been relatively straightforward, turned into a public spectacle. Once the Senate Judiciary Committee had been informed that Thomas, a conservative African American, was President Bush's Supreme Court nominee, Democratic and Republican committee members set out to find information that would either help or hurt his chances of confirmation. Democrats on the committee had become aware of Hill's allegations before any Republicans had been informed; therefore, Thomas and Hill became engrossed in a political clash between Democrats and Republicans. The proceedings became unnecessarily acrimonious, as committee members tried to separate truth from lies with respect to Hill's charges of sexual harassment. As a result, the testimonies of both Thomas and Hill were not taken seriously, and the confirmation process was seen as a failure.

The proceedings had a massive impact on the African American community. Two successful African Americans were pitted against each other. On one hand was Clarence Thomas, a conservative who for the most part disliked affirmative action. On the other was Anita Hill, a law professor who some perceived as having turned on "one of her own." Indeed, the conflict over whom to believe created more questions than answers. Although Thomas was uncomfortable with affirmation action, he was nevertheless a nominee to the Supreme Court. Not many African Americans had been offered such a prestigious honor, and many believed that Thomas was a good model of what an African American man could achieve. In addition, many empathized with the struggle against racism and discrimination that Thomas had navigated successfully. Accordingly, some African Americans were willing to ignore Thomas's shortcomings in favor of what they thought his confirmation could do to promote positive views of African Americans.

Like Thomas, Hill had overcome racism and discrimination throughout her career. Notwithstanding, she did not fare as well as Thomas in African American public opinion. For example, there was a male-versus-female difference of opinion about her among African Americans. Some believed that Hill, as a black woman, should have remained quiet and not publicly revealed that she had been sexually harassed by a black man. Furthermore, Hill's accomplishments as a black woman were not accorded the same weight as Thomas's achievements. This caused confusion as to who, either Hill or Thomas, was best equipped to advance the interests of the African American community, and the two were inadvertently caught in a political nightmare that had both racial and gender ramifications. For these reasons, Hill's opening statement will have a lasting imprint on American history.

*—Colleen Ostiguy, MA, JD*

## Bibliography and Additional Reading

Brock, David. *The Real Anita Hill: The Untold Story.* New York: Free Press, 1993.

Chrisman, Robert, and Robert L. Allen, eds. Court of Appeal: the Black Community Speaks Out on the Racial and Sexual Politics of Clarence Thomas vs. Anita Hill. New York: Ballantine Books, 1992.

Danforth, John C. Resurrection: The Confirmation of Clarence Thomas. New York: Viking, 1994.

Foskett, Ken. *Judging Thomas: The Life and Times of Clarence Thomas.* New York: Harper Collins Publishers, 2004.

Garment, Suzanne. "Afterword: On Anita Hill and Clarence Thomas." In *Scandal: The Culture of Mistrust in American Politics.* New York: Times Books, 1992.

"Hearings before the Senate Committee on the Judiciary on the Nomination of Clarence Thomas to be Associate Justice of the Supreme Court of the United States, October 11, 12, and 13, 1991." GPO Access Web site. http://www.gpoaccess.gov/congress/senate/judiciary/sh102-1084pt4/browse.html.

Hill, Anita. *Speaking Truth to Power.* New York: Doubleday, 1997.

———, and Emma Coleman Jordan, eds. *Race, Gender, and Power in America: The Legacy of the Hill-Thomas Hearings.* New York: Oxford University Press, 1995.

Morrison, Toni, ed. Race-ing Justice, En-gendering Power: Essays on Anita Hill, Clarence Thomas, and the Construction of Social Reality. New York: Pantheon Books, 1992.

Phelps, Timothy M., and Helen Winternitz. Capitol Games: Clarence Thomas, Anita Hill, and the Story of a Supreme Court Nomination. New York: Hyperion, 1992.

Smith, Christopher E. Critical Judicial Nominations and Political Change: The Impact of Clarence Thomas. Westport, Conn.: Praeger, 1993.

# Planned Parenthood v. Casey

**Date:** June 29, 1992
**Authors:** Justices Sandra Day O'Connor, Anthony M. Kennedy, and David Souter
**Genre:** Court opinion

## Summary Overview

The Pennsylvania Abortion Control Act of 1982 contained provisions making it difficult for women to exercise their right to an abortion, as guaranteed by the Supreme Court ruling in *Roe v. Wade*. Planned Parenthood sued Governor Casey in an attempt to block enforcement of the law, and ultimately, the case made its way to the Supreme Court of the United States. Despite popular belief the Court would overturn the landmark *Roe* decision, the justices upheld a woman's right to an abortion. Despite the Court's decision to maintain abortion rights, the justices found only one of five Pennsylvania provisions, a wife's requirement to notify her spouse prior to an abortion, to be unconstitutional. The outcome of *Planned Parenthood v. Casey* was not considered by either pro-life or pro-choice groups to be a victory, and the arguments over a woman's right to have an abortion would wage on in America.

## Defining Moment

Prior to the 1973 landmark *Roe v. Wade* decision, which allowed women the right to an abortion, it was illegal in many states for women to access such a procedure. In states where abortion was legal, it was only allowed under certain circumstances, such as pregnancy as a result of rape or incest. Because of abortion restrictions in place prior to the *Roe* decision, women were undergoing illegal and often life-threatening procedures to terminate pregnancies. It is estimated prior to the passage of *Roe*, botched abortions were responsible for one in five maternal deaths. Once the Supreme Court ruled to allow women to legally access abortions in this country, laws began passing at the state level prohibiting women from exercising that right. After the decision in the *Roe* case made abortion legal, the debate in this country regarding a woman's right to choose was in a frenzy.

Regardless of the Court's decision in the matter, abortion was highly politicized and the argument over whether a women should be allowed to terminate a pregnancy caused social unrest. In the late 1980s, Ronald Reagan made it clear he wanted to see the *Roe* de-

cision overturned, and it momentarily looked as if this was a possibility when Reagan was almost successful in appointing an outspoken *Roe* dissenter to the Court. Anti-abortion supporters were doing their best to shut down abortion clinics by blocking entrances to facilities; heckling women attempting to access clinics; and, in some instances, resorting to violent protests. Despite restrictive laws being passed and attempts to change the ideology of the Court, public opinion at the time suggested eight out of ten citizens supported access to abortions, at least under some circumstances. Nonetheless, from 1973–1989 almost every state had passed some type of anti-abortion law; Pennsylvania alone was responsible for championing fourteen of the 306 laws passed in that time period.

The Pennsylvania Abortion Control Act of 1982 stated that, in order to receive an abortion, a woman must be provided with information, which many thought was designed to discourage women from going through with the procedure. Additionally, the law required: a twenty-four-hour waiting period, parental consent for unwed minors, informing spouses prior to the abortion, and certain reporting procedures. Opponents of the law believed it placed significant barriers in the way of a woman's ability to exercise her right to have an abortion. Planned Parenthood of Southeastern Pennsylvania sued Governor Casey in a court of law to have the Abortion Control Act overturned. Because two liberal Supreme Court justices had been replaced by more conservative justices, the nation anxiously waited to see if the Court would overturn a decision that had been crucial in the woman's rights movement.

## Author Biography

In a non-traditional move, the *Casey* opinion was written by three justices: O'Connor, Kennedy, and Souter. Sandra Day O'Connor was the first female appointed to the Supreme Court. Prior to her service on the Court, O'Connor attended Stanford Law, served as a two-term Arizona State senator, and was the attorney general of Arizona from 1965–1969. O'Connor served on the Supreme Court for twenty-four years before her retirement in 2006. Anthony M. Kennedy attended Harvard Law prior to serving as a constitutional law professor and a judge on the US Court of Appeals. Kennedy still serves on the Court today. David Souter attended Harvard for his undergraduate and law degrees and was a Rhodes Scholar at Magdalen College at Oxford. Prior to serving on the Court, Souter briefly had a private law practice and spent time as the attorney general for the state of New Hampshire. Souter retired from the Supreme Court in 2009.

## HISTORICAL DOCUMENT

PLANNED PARENTHOOD OF SOUTHEAST-
ERN PENNSYLVANIA
v.
ROBERT P. CASEY
No. 91–744
SUPREME COURT OF THE UNITED STATES
505 U.S. 833
June 29, 1992, Decided +

### JUSTICE O'CONNOR, JUSTICE KENNEDY, and JUSTICE SOUTER announced the judgment of the Court.

Liberty finds no refuge in a jurisprudence of doubt. Yet 19 years after our holding that the Constitution protects a woman's right to terminate her pregnancy in its early stages, *Roe v. Wade* (1973), that definition of liberty is still questioned. Joining the respondents as *amicus curiae*, the United States, as it has done in five other cases in the last decade, again asks us to overrule *Roe*. At issue in these cases are five provisions of the Pennsylvania Abortion Control Act of 1982. The Act requires that a woman seeking an abortion give her informed consent prior to the abortion procedure, and specifies that she be provided with certain information at least 24 hours before the abortion is performed. § 3205. For a minor to obtain an abortion, the Act requires the informed consent of one of her parents, but provides for a judicial bypass option if the minor does not wish to or cannot obtain a parent's consent. § 3206. Another provision of the Act requires that, unless certain exceptions apply, a married woman seeking an abortion must sign a statement indicating that she has notified her husband of her intended abortion. § 3209. The Act exempts compliance with these three requirements in the event of a "medical emergency," which is defined in § 3203 of the Act.

Before any of these provisions took effect, the petitioners, who are five abortion clinics and one physician representing himself as well as a class of physicians who provide abortion services, brought this suit seeking declaratory and injunctive relief. Each provision was challenged as unconstitutional on its face....

At oral argument in this Court, the attorney for the parties challenging the statute took the position that none of the enactments can be upheld without overruling *Roe v. Wade*. We disagree with that analysis; but we acknowledge that our decisions after *Roe* cast doubt upon the meaning and reach of its holding. Further, THE CHIEF JUSTICE admits that he would overrule the central holding of *Roe* and adopt the rational relationship test as the sole criterion of constitutionality. State and federal courts as well as legislatures throughout the Union must have guidance as they seek to address this subject in conformance with the Constitution. Given these premises, we find it imperative to review once more the principles that define the rights of the woman and the legitimate authority of the State respecting the termination of pregnancies by abortion procedures. After considering the fundamental constitutional questions resolved by *Roe*, principles of institutional integrity, and the rule of *stare decisis*, we are led to conclude this: the essential holding of *Roe v. Wade* should be retained and once again reaffirmed.

It must be stated at the outset and with clarity that *Roe*'s essential holding, the holding we reaffirm, has three parts. First is a recognition of the right of the woman to choose to have an abortion before viability and to obtain it without undue interference from the State. Before viability, the State's interests are not strong enough to support a prohibition of abortion or the imposition of a substantial obstacle to the woman's effective right to elect the procedure. Second is a confirmation of the State's power to restrict abortions after fetal viability, if the law contains exceptions for pregnancies which endanger the woman's life or health. And third is the principle that the State has legitimate interests from the outset of the pregnancy in protecting the health of the woman and the life of the fetus that may become a child. These principles do not contradict one another; and we adhere to each.

Constitutional protection of the woman's decision to terminate her pregnancy derives from the Due Process Clause of the Fourteenth Amendment. It declares that no State shall "deprive any person of life, liberty, or property, without due process of law." The controlling word in the cases before us is "liberty." Although a literal reading of the Clause might suggest that it governs only the procedures by which a State may deprive persons of liberty, for at least 105 years the Clause has been understood to contain a substantive component as well, one "barring certain government actions regardless of the fairness of the procedures used to implement them." Thus all fundamental rights comprised within the term liberty are protected by the Federal Constitution from invasion by the States."

The most familiar of the substantive liberties protected by the Fourteenth Amendment are those recognized by the Bill of Rights. We have held that the Due Process Clause of the Fourteenth Amendment incorporates most of the Bill of Rights against the States. It is tempting, as a means of curbing the discretion of federal judges, to suppose that liberty encompasses no more than those rights already guaranteed to the individual against federal interference by the express provisions of the first eight Amendments to the Constitution. But of course this Court has never accepted that view. It is also tempting, for the same reason, to suppose that the Due Process Clause protects only those practices, defined at the most specific level, that were protected against government interference by other rules of law when the Fourteenth Amendment was ratified. But such a view would be inconsistent with our law. It is a promise of the Constitution that there is a realm of personal liberty which the government may not enter. We have vindicated this principle before. Marriage is mentioned nowhere in the Bill of Rights and interracial marriage was illegal in most States in the 19th century, but the Court was no doubt correct in finding it to be an aspect of liberty protected against state interference by the substantive component of the Due Process Clause in *Loving v. Virginia*, 388 U.S. 1 (1967). Neither the Bill of Rights nor the specific practices of States at the time of the adoption of the Fourteenth Amendment marks the outer limits of the substantive sphere of liberty which the Fourteenth Amendment protects. See U.S. Const., Amdt. 9. As the second Justice Harlan recognized:

"The full scope of the liberty guaranteed by the Due Process Clause cannot be found in or limited by the precise terms of the specific guarantees elsewhere provided in the Constitution. This 'liberty' is not a series of isolated points pricked out in terms of the taking of property; the freedom of speech, press, and religion; the right to keep and bear arms; the freedom from unreasonable searches and seizures; and so on. It is a rational continuum which, broadly speaking, includes a freedom from all substantial arbitrary impositions and purposeless restraints,... and which also recognizes, what a reasonable and sensitive judgment must, that certain interests require particularly careful scrutiny of the state needs asserted to justify their abridgment." *Poe*

The inescapable fact is that adjudication of substantive due process claims may call upon the Court in interpreting the Constitution to exercise that same capacity which by tradition courts always have exercised: reasoned judgment. Its boundaries are not susceptible of expression as a simple rule. That does not mean we are free to invalidate state policy choices with which we disagree; yet neither does it permit us to shrink from the duties of our office....

Men and women of good conscience can disagree, and we suppose some always shall disagree, about the profound moral and spiritual implications of terminating a pregnancy, even in its earliest stage. Some of us as individuals find abortion offensive to our most basic principles of morality, but that cannot control our decision. Our obligation is to define the liberty of all, not to mandate our own moral code. The underlying constitutional issue is whether the State can resolve these philosophic questions in such a definitive way that a woman lacks all choice in the matter, except perhaps in those rare circumstances in which the pregnancy is itself a danger to her own life or health, or is the result of rape or incest.

It is conventional constitutional doctrine that where reasonable people disagree the government can adopt one position or the other. That theorem, however, assumes a state of affairs in which the choice does not intrude upon a protected liberty. Thus, while some people might disagree about whether or not the flag should be saluted, or disagree about the proposition that it may not be defiled, we have ruled that a State may not compel or enforce one view or the other.

Our law affords constitutional protection to personal decisions relating to marriage, procreation, contraception, family relationships, child rearing, and education. Our cases recognize "the right of the *individual*, married or single, to be free from unwarranted governmental intrusion into matters so fundamentally affecting a person as the decision whether to bear or beget a child." These matters, involving the most intimate and personal choices a person may make in a lifetime, choices central to personal dignity and autonomy, are central to the liberty protected by the Fourteenth Amendment. At the heart of liberty is the right to define one's own concept of existence, of meaning, of the universe, and of the mystery of human life. Beliefs about these matters could not define the attributes of personhood were they formed under compulsion of the State.

These considerations begin our analysis of the woman's interest in terminating her pregnancy but cannot end it, for this reason: though the abortion decision may originate within the zone of conscience and belief, it is more than a philosophic exercise. Abortion is a unique act. It is an act fraught with consequences for others: for the woman who must live with the implications of her decision; for the persons who perform and assist in the procedure;

for the spouse, family, and society which must confront the knowledge that these procedures exist, procedures some deem nothing short of an act of violence against innocent human life; and, depending on one's beliefs, for the life or potential life that is aborted. Though abortion is conduct, it does not follow that the State is entitled to proscribe it in all instances. That is because the liberty of the woman is at stake in a sense unique to the human condition and so unique to the law. The mother who carries a child to full term is subject to anxieties, to physical constraints, to pain that only she must bear. That these sacrifices have from the beginning of the human race been endured by woman with a pride that ennobles her in the eyes of others and gives to the infant a bond of love cannot alone be grounds for the State to insist she make the sacrifice. Her suffering is too intimate and personal for the State to insist, without more, upon its own vision of the woman's role, however dominant that vision has been in the course of our history and our culture. The destiny of the woman must be shaped to a large extent on her own conception of her spiritual imperatives and her place in society....

While we appreciate the weight of the arguments made on behalf of the State in the cases before us, arguments which in their ultimate formulation conclude that *Roe* should be overruled, the reservations any of us may have in reaffirming the central holding of *Roe* are outweighed by the explication of individual liberty we have given combined with the force of *stare decisis*. We turn now to that doctrine.

The obligation to follow precedent begins with necessity, and a contrary necessity marks its outer limit. With Cardozo, we recognize that no judicial system could do society's work if it eyed each issue afresh in every case that raised it. Indeed, the very concept of the rule of law underlying our own Constitution requires such continuity over time that a respect for precedent is, by definition, indispensable. At the other extreme, a different necessity would make itself felt if a prior judicial ruling should come to be seen so clearly as error that its enforcement was for that very reason doomed.

Even when the decision to overrule a prior case is not, as in the rare, latter instance, virtually foreordained, it is common wisdom that the rule of *stare decisis* is not an "inexorable command," and certainly it is not such in every constitutional case. Rather, when this Court reexamines a prior holding, its judgment is customarily informed by a series of prudential and pragmatic considerations designed to test the consistency of overruling a prior decision with the ideal of the rule of law, and to gauge the respective costs of reaffirming and overruling a prior case. Thus, for example, we may ask whether the rule has proven to be intolerable simply in defying practical workability; whether the rule is subject to a kind of reliance that would lend a special hardship to the consequences of overruling and add inequity to the cost of repudiation; whether related principles of law have so far developed as to have left the old rule no more than a remnant of abandoned doctrine; or whether facts have so changed, or come to be seen so differently, as to have robbed the old rule of significant application or justification.

So in this case we may enquire whether *Roe*'s central rule has been found unworkable; whether the rule's limitation on state power could be removed without serious inequity to those who have relied upon it or significant damage to the stability of the society governed by it; whether the law's growth in the intervening years has left *Roe*'s central rule a doctrinal anachronism discounted by society; and whether *Roe*'s premises of fact have so far changed in the ensuing two decades as to render its central holding somehow irrelevant or unjustifiable in dealing with the issue it addressed.

Although *Roe* has engendered opposition, it has in no sense proven "unworkable," representing as it does a simple limitation beyond which a state law is unenforceable. While *Roe* has, of course, required judicial assessment of state laws affecting the exercise of the choice guaranteed against government infringement, and although the need for such review will remain as a consequence of today's decision, the required determinations fall within judicial competence.

The inquiry into reliance counts the cost of a rule's repudiation as it would fall on those who have relied reasonably on the rule's continued application. Abortion is customarily chosen as an unplanned response to the consequence of unplanned activity or to the failure of conventional birth control, and except on the assumption that no intercourse would have occurred but for *Roe*'s holding, such behavior may appear to justify no reliance claim. Even if reliance could be claimed on that unrealistic assumption, the argument might run, any reliance interest would be *de minimis*.

To eliminate the issue of reliance that easily, however, one would need to limit cognizable reliance to specific instances of sexual activity. But to do this would be simply to refuse to face the fact that for two decades of economic and social developments, people have organized intimate relationships and made choices that define their views of themselves and their places in society, in reliance on the availability of abortion in the event that contraception should fail. The ability of women to participate equally in the economic and social life of the Nation has been facilitated by their ability to control their reproductive lives. The Constitution serves human values, and while the effect of reliance on *Roe* cannot be exactly measured, neither can the certain cost of overruling *Roe* for people who have ordered their thinking and living around that case be dismissed.

No evolution of legal principle has left *Roe*'s doctrinal footings weaker than they were in 1973. No development of constitutional law since the case was decided has implicitly or explicitly left *Roe* behind as a mere survivor of obsolete constitutional thinking.

It will be recognized, of course, that *Roe* stands at an intersection of two lines of decisions, but in whichever doctrinal category one reads the case, the result for present purposes will be the same. The *Roe* Court itself placed its holding in the succession of cases most prominently exemplified by *Griswold v. Connecticut* (1965). When it is so seen, *Roe* is clearly in no jeopardy, since subsequent constitutional developments have neither disturbed, nor do they threaten to diminish, the scope of recognized protection accorded to the liberty relating to intimate relationships, the family, and decisions about whether or not to beget or bear a child.

*Roe*, however, may be seen not only as an exemplar of *Griswold* liberty but as a rule (whether or not mistaken) of personal autonomy and bodily integrity, with doctrinal affinity to cases recognizing limits on governmental power to mandate medical treatment or to bar its rejection. If so, our cases since *Roe* accord with *Roe*'s view that a State's interest in the protection of life falls short of justifying any plenary override of individual liberty claims.

Finally, one could classify *Roe* as *sui generis*. If the case is so viewed, then there clearly has been no erosion of its central determination....

Nor will courts building upon *Roe* be likely to hand down erroneous decisions as a consequence. Even on the assumption that the central holding of *Roe* was in error, that error would go only to the strength of the state interest in fetal protection, not to the recognition afforded by the Constitution to the woman's liberty. The soundness of this prong of the *Roe* analysis is apparent from a consideration of the alternative. If indeed the woman's interest in deciding whether to bear and beget a child had not been recognized as in *Roe*, the State might as readily restrict a woman's right to choose to carry a pregnancy to term as to terminate it, to further asserted state interests in population control, or eugenics, for example. Yet *Roe* has been sensibly relied upon to counter any such suggestions.

We have seen how time has overtaken some of *Roe*'s factual assumptions: advances in maternal health care allow for abortions safe to the mother later in pregnancy than was true in 1973, and advances in neonatal care have advanced viability to a point somewhat earlier. But these facts go only to the scheme of time limits on the realization of competing interests, and the divergences from the factual premises of 1973 have no bearing on the validity of *Roe*'s central holding, that viability marks the earliest point at which the State's interest in fetal life is constitutionally adequate to justify a legislative ban on nontherapeutic abortions. The soundness or unsoundness of that constitutional judgment in no sense turns on whether viability occurs at approximately 28 weeks, as was usual at the time of *Roe*, at 23 to 24 weeks, as it sometimes does today, or at some moment even slightly earlier in pregnancy, as it may if fetal respiratory capacity can somehow be enhanced in the future. Whenever it may occur, the attainment of viability may continue to serve as the critical fact, just as it has done since *Roe* was decided; which is to say that no change in *Roe*'s factual underpinning has left its central holding obsolete, and none supports an argument for overruling it.

The sum of the precedential enquiry to this point shows *Roe*'s underpinnings unweakened in any way affecting its central holding. While it has engendered disapproval, it has not been unworkable. An entire generation has come of age free to assume *Roe*'s concept of liberty in defining the capacity of women to act in society, and to make reproductive decisions; no erosion of principle going to liberty or personal autonomy has left *Roe*'s central holding a doctrinal remnant; *Roe* portends no developments at odds with other precedent for the analysis of personal liberty; and no changes of fact have rendered viability more or less appropriate as the point at which the balance of interests tips. Within the bounds of normal *stare decisis* analysis, then, and subject to the considerations on which it customarily turns, the stronger argument is for affirming *Roe*'s central holding, with whatever degree of personal reluctance any of us may have, not for overruling it.

In a less significant case, *stare decisis* analysis could, and would, stop at the point we have reached. But the sustained and widespread debate *Roe* has provoked calls for some comparison between that case and others of comparable dimension that have responded to national controversies and taken on the impress of the controversies addressed.... Only two such decisional lines from the past century present themselves for examination, and in each instance the result reached by the Court accorded with the principles we apply today.

The first example is that line of cases identified with *Lochner v. New York*, 198 U.S. 45 (1905), which imposed substantive limitations on legislation limiting economic autonomy in favor of health and welfare regulation, adopting, in Justice Holmes's view, the theory of laissez-faire. The second comparison that 20th century history invites is with the cases employing the separate-but-equal rule for applying the Fourteenth Amendment's equal protection guarantee. They began with *Plessy v. Ferguson*, 163 U.S. 537 (1896), holding that legislatively mandated racial segregation in public transportation works no denial of equal protection, rejecting the argument that racial separation enforced by the legal machinery of American society treats the black race as inferior.

*West Coast Hotel* and *Brown* [overruling *Lochner* and *Plessy*] each rested on facts, or an understanding of facts, changed from those which furnished the claimed justifications for the earlier constitutional resolutions. Each case was comprehensible as the Court's response to facts that the country could understand, or had come to understand already, but which the Court of an earlier day, as its own declarations disclosed, had not been able to perceive. As the decisions were thus comprehensible they were also defensible, not merely as the victories of one doctrinal school over another by dint of numbers (victories though they were), but as applications of constitutional principle to facts as they had not been seen by the Court before. In constitutional adjudication as elsewhere in life, changed circumstances may impose new obligations, and the thoughtful part of the Nation could accept each decision to overrule a prior case as a response to the Court's constitutional duty.

Because the cases before us present no such occasion it could be seen as no such response. Because neither the factual underpinnings of *Roe*'s central holding nor our understanding of it has changed (and because no other indication of weakened precedent has been shown), the Court could not pretend to be reexamining the prior law with any justification beyond a present doctrinal disposition to come out differently from the Court of 1973. To overrule prior law for no other reason than that would run counter to the view repeated in our cases, that a decision to overrule should rest on some special reason over and above the belief that a prior case was wrongly decided....

In two circumstances, however, the Court would almost certainly fail to receive the benefit of the doubt in overruling prior cases. There is, first, a point beyond which frequent overruling would overtax the country's belief in the Court's good faith. Despite the variety of reasons that may inform and justify a decision to overrule, we cannot forget that such a decision is usually perceived (and perceived correctly) as, at the least, a statement that a prior decision was wrong. There is a limit to the amount of error that can plausibly be imputed to prior Courts. If that limit should be exceeded, disturbance of prior rulings would be taken as evidence that justifiable reexamination of principle had given way to drives for particular results in the short term. The legitimacy of the Court would fade with the frequency of its vacillation....

The country's loss of confidence in the Judiciary would be underscored by an equally certain and equally reasonable condemnation for another failing in overruling unnecessarily and under pressure. Some cost will be paid by anyone who approves or implements a constitutional decision where it is unpopular, or who refuses to work to undermine the decision or to force its reversal. The price may be criticism or ostracism, or it may be violence. An extra price will be paid by those who themselves disapprove of the decision's results when viewed outside of constitutional terms, but who nevertheless struggle to accept it, because they respect the rule of law. To all those who will be so tested by following, the Court implicitly undertakes to remain steadfast, lest in the end a price be paid for nothing. The promise of constancy, once given, binds its maker for as long as the power to stand by the decision survives and the understanding of the issue has not changed so fundamentally as to render the commitment obsolete.

The Court's duty in the present cases is clear. In 1973, it confronted the already-divisive issue of governmental power to limit personal choice to undergo abortion, for which it provided a new resolution based on the due process guaranteed by the Fourteenth Amendment. Whether or not a new social consensus is developing on that issue, its divisiveness is no less today than in 1973, and pressure to overrule the decision, like pressure to retain it, has grown only more intense. A decision to overrule *Roe*'s essential holding under the existing circumstances would address error, if error there was, at the cost of both profound and unnecessary damage to the Court's legitimacy, and to the Nation's commitment to the rule of law. It is therefore imperative to adhere to the essence of *Roe*'s original decision, and we do so today.

From what we have said so far it follows that it is a constitutional liberty of the woman to have some freedom to terminate her pregnancy. We conclude that the basic decision in *Roe* was based on a constitutional analysis which we cannot now repudiate. The woman's liberty is not so unlimited, however, that from the outset the State cannot show its concern for the life of the unborn, and at a later point in fetal development the State's interest in life has sufficient force so that the right of the woman to terminate the pregnancy can be restricted.

That brings us, of course, to the point where much criticism has been directed at *Roe*, a criticism that always inheres when the Court draws a specific rule from what in the Constitution is but a general standard. We conclude, however, that the urgent claims of the woman to retain the ultimate control over her destiny and her body, claims implicit in the meaning of liberty, require us to perform that function. Liberty must not be extinguished for want of a line that is clear. And it falls to us to give some real substance to the woman's liberty to determine whether to carry her pregnancy to full term.

We conclude the line should be drawn at viability, so that before that time the woman has a right to choose to terminate her pregnancy. We adhere to this principle for two reasons. First, as we have said, is the doctrine of *stare decisis*. The second reason is that the concept of viability, as we noted in *Roe*, is the time at which there is a realistic possibility of maintaining and nourishing a life outside the womb, so that the independent existence of the second life can in reason and all fairness be the object of state protection that now overrides the rights of the woman...

Yet it must be remembered that *Roe v. Wade* speaks with clarity in establishing not only the woman's liberty but also the State's "important and legitimate interest in potential life." That portion of the decision in *Roe* has been given too little acknowledgment and implementation by the Court in its subsequent cases. Those cases decided that any regulation touching upon the abortion decision must survive strict scrutiny, to be sustained only if drawn in narrow terms to further a compelling state

interest. Not all of the cases decided under that formulation can be reconciled with the holding in *Roe* itself that the State has legitimate interests in the health of the woman and in protecting the potential life within her. In resolving this tension, we choose to rely upon *Roe*, as against the later cases.

*Roe* established a trimester framework to govern abortion regulations. Under this elaborate but rigid construct, almost no regulation at all is permitted during the first trimester of pregnancy; regulations designed to protect the woman's health, but not to further the State's interest in potential life, are permitted during the second trimester; and during the third trimester, when the fetus is viable, prohibitions are permitted provided the life or health of the mother is not at stake.

The trimester framework no doubt was erected to ensure that the woman's right to choose not become so subordinate to the State's interest in promoting fetal life that her choice exists in theory but not in fact. We do not agree, however, that the trimester approach is necessary to accomplish this objective. A framework of this rigidity was unnecessary and in its later interpretation sometimes contradicted the State's permissible exercise of its powers...

These considerations of the nature of the abortion right illustrate that it is an overstatement to describe it as a right to decide whether to have an abortion "without interference from the State." All abortion regulations interfere to some degree with a woman's ability to decide whether to terminate her pregnancy. The Court's experience applying the trimester framework has led to the striking down of some abortion regulations which in no real sense deprived women of the ultimate decision. Those decisions went too far because the right recognized by *Roe* is a right "to be free from unwarranted governmental intrusion into matters so fundamentally affecting a person as the decision whether to bear or beget a child." Not all governmental intrusion is of necessity unwarranted; and that brings us to the other basic flaw in the trimester framework: even in *Roe*'s terms, in practice it undervalues the State's interest in the potential life within the woman.

*Roe v. Wade* was express in its recognition of the State's "important and legitimate interests in preserving and protecting the health of the pregnant woman [and] in protecting the potentiality of human life." The trimester framework, however, does not fulfill *Roe*'s own promise that the State has an interest in protecting fetal life or potential life.

The very notion that the State has a substantial interest in potential life leads to the conclusion that not all regulations must be deemed unwarranted. Not all burdens on the right to decide whether to terminate a pregnancy will be undue. In our view, the undue burden standard is the appropriate means of reconciling the State's interest with the woman's constitutionally protected liberty. Because we set forth a standard of general application to which we intend to adhere, it is important to clarify what is meant by an undue burden.

A finding of an undue burden is a shorthand for the conclusion that a state regulation has the purpose or effect of placing a substantial obstacle in the path of a woman seeking an abortion of a nonviable fetus. A statute with this purpose is invalid because the means chosen by the State to further the interest in potential life must be calculated to inform the woman's free choice, not hinder it. And a statute which, while furthering the interest in potential life or some other valid state interest, has the effect of placing a substantial obstacle in the path of a woman's choice cannot be considered a permissible means of serving its legitimate ends. To the extent that the opinions of the Court or of individual Justices use the undue burden standard in a manner that is inconsistent with this analysis, we set out what in our view should be the controlling standard. In our considered judgment, an undue burden is an unconstitutional burden. Understood another way, we answer the question, left open in previous opinions discussing the undue burden formulation, whether a law designed to further the State's interest in fetal life which imposes an undue burden on the woman's decision before fetal viability could be constitutional. The answer is no.

Some guiding principles should emerge. What is at stake is the woman's right to make the ultimate decision, not a right to be insulated from all others in doing so. Regulations which do no more than create a structural mechanism by which the State,

or the parent or guardian of a minor, may express profound respect for the life of the unborn are permitted, if they are not a substantial obstacle to the woman's exercise of the right to choose. Unless it has that effect on her right of choice, a state measure designed to persuade her to choose childbirth over abortion will be upheld if reasonably related to that goal. Regulations designed to foster the health of a woman seeking an abortion are valid if they do not constitute an undue burden.

The Court of Appeals applied what it believed to be the undue burden standard and upheld each of the provisions except for the husband notification requirement. We agree generally with this conclusion...

We next consider the informed consent requirement. Except in a medical emergency, the statute requires that at least 24 hours before performing an abortion a physician inform the woman of the nature of the procedure, the health risks of the abortion and of childbirth, and the "probable gestational age of the unborn child." The physician or a qualified nonphysician must inform the woman of the availability of printed materials published by the State describing the fetus and providing information about medical assistance for childbirth, information about child support from the father, and a list of agencies which provide adoption and other services as alternatives to abortion. An abortion may not be performed unless the woman certifies in writing that she has been informed of the availability of these printed materials and has been provided them if she chooses to view them.

Our prior decisions establish that as with any medical procedure, the State may require a woman to give her written informed consent to an abortion. In this respect, the statute is unexceptional. Petitioners challenge the statute's definition of informed consent because it includes the provision of specific information by the doctor and the mandatory 24-hour waiting period....

Our analysis of Pennsylvania's 24-hour waiting period between the provision of the information deemed necessary to informed consent and the performance of an abortion under the undue burden standard requires us to reconsider the premise behind the decision in *Akron I* invalidating a parallel requirement. In *Akron I* we said: "Nor are we convinced that the State's legitimate concern that the woman's decision be informed is reasonably served by requiring a 24-hour delay as a matter of course." We consider that conclusion to be wrong. The idea that important decisions will be more informed and deliberate if they follow some period of reflection does not strike us as unreasonable, particularly where the statute directs that important information become part of the background of the decision. The statute, as construed by the Court of Appeals, permits avoidance of the waiting period in the event of a medical emergency and the record evidence shows that in the vast majority of cases, a 24-hour delay does not create any appreciable health risk. In theory, at least, the waiting period is a reasonable measure to implement the State's interest in protecting the life of the unborn, a measure that does not amount to an undue burden.

Whether the mandatory 24-hour waiting period is nonetheless invalid because in practice it is a substantial obstacle to a woman's choice to terminate her pregnancy is a closer question. The findings of fact by the District Court indicate that because of the distances many women must travel to reach an abortion provider, the practical effect will often be a delay of much more than a day because the waiting period requires that a woman seeking an abortion make at least two visits to the doctor. These findings are troubling in some respects, but they do not demonstrate that the waiting period constitutes an undue burden. In light of the construction given the statute's definition of medical emergency by the Court of Appeals, and the District Court's findings, we cannot say that the waiting period imposes a real health risk....

The spousal notification requirement is thus likely to prevent a significant number of women from obtaining an abortion. It does not merely make abortions a little more difficult or expensive to obtain; for many women, it will impose a substantial obstacle. We must not blind ourselves to the fact that the significant number of women who fear for their safety and the safety of their children are likely to be deterred from procuring an abortion as surely as if the Commonwealth had outlawed abortion in all cases....

### JUSTICE STEVENS, concurring in part and dissenting in part....
### JUSTICE BLACKMUN, concurring in part, concurring in the judgment in part, and dissenting in part....

Three years ago, in *Webster v. Reproductive Health Services*, 492 U.S. 490(1989), four Members of this Court appeared poised to "cast into darkness the hopes and visions of every woman in this country" who had come to believe that the Constitution guaranteed her the right to reproductive choice. All that remained between the promise of *Roe* and the darkness of the plurality was a single, flickering flame. Decisions since *Webster* gave little reason to hope that this flame would cast much light. But now, just when so many expected the darkness to fall, the flame has grown bright.

I do not underestimate the significance of today's joint opinion. Yet I remain steadfast in my belief that the right to reproductive choice is entitled to the full protection afforded by this Court before *Webster*. And I fear for the darkness as four Justices anxiously await the single vote necessary to extinguish the light.

Make no mistake, the joint opinion of JUSTICES O'CONNOR, KENNEDY, and SOUTER is an act of personal courage and constitutional principle. In contrast to previous decisions, the authors of the joint opinion today join JUSTICE STEVENS and me in concluding that "the essential holding of *Roe v. Wade* should be retained and once again reaffirmed." In brief, five Members of this Court today recognize that "the Constitution protects a woman's right to terminate her pregnancy in its early stages...."

### JUSTICE SCALIA, with whom THE CHIEF JUSTICE, JUSTICE WHITE, and JUSTICE THOMAS join, concurring in the judgment in part and dissenting in part.

My views on this matter are unchanged from those I set forth in my separate opinions in *Webster v. Reproductive Health Services* (1989) (opinion concurring in part and concurring in judgment). The States may, if they wish, permit abortion on demand, but the Constitution does not *require* them to do so. The permissibility of abortion, and the limitations upon it, are to be resolved like most important questions in our democracy: by citizens trying to persuade one another and then voting. As the Court acknowledges, "where reasonable people disagree the government can adopt one position or the other..."

The joint opinion frankly concedes that the amorphous concept of "undue burden" has been inconsistently applied. Because the three Justices now wish to "set forth a standard of general application," the joint opinion announces that "it is important to clarify what is meant by an undue burden." I certainly agree with that, but I do not agree that the joint opinion succeeds in the announced endeavor. To the contrary, its efforts at clarification make clear only that the standard is inherently manipulable and will prove hopelessly unworkable in practice.....

The ultimately standardless nature of the "undue burden" inquiry is a reflection of the underlying fact that the concept has no principled or coherent legal basis. As THE CHIEF JUSTICE points out, *Roe*'s strict-scrutiny standard "at least had a recognized basis in constitutional law at the time *Roe* was decided," while "the same cannot be said for the 'undue burden' standard, which is created largely out of whole cloth by the authors of the joint opinion...." The appropriate analogy, therefore, is that of a state law requiring purchasers of religious books to endure a 24-hour waiting period, or to pay a nominal additional tax of 1 [cent]. The joint opinion cannot possibly be correct in suggesting that we would uphold such legislation on the ground that it does not impose a "substantial obstacle" to the exercise of First Amendment rights. The "undue burden" standard is not at all the generally applicable principle the joint opinion pretends it to be; rather, it is a unique concept created specially for these cases, to preserve some judicial foothold in this ill-gotten territory. In claiming otherwise, the three Justices show their willingness to place all constitutional rights at risk in an effort to preserve what they deem the "central holding in *Roe*...."

The Court's reliance upon *stare decisis* can best be described as contrived. It insists upon the necessity of adhering not to all of *Roe*, but only to what it calls the "central holding." It seems to me that *stare decisis* ought to be applied even to the doctrine of *stare decisis*, and I confess never to have heard of this new, keep-what-you-want-and-throw-away-the-rest version....

The Court's description of the place of *Roe* in the social history of the United States is unrecognizable. Not only did *Roe* not, as the Court suggests, *resolve* the deeply divisive issue of abortion; it did more than anything else to nourish it, by elevating it to the national level where it is infinitely more difficult to resolve. National politics were not plagued by abortion protests, national abortion lobbying, or abortion marches on Congress before *Roe v. Wade* was decided. Profound disagreement existed among our citizens over the issue—as it does over other issues, such as the death penalty—but that disagreement was being worked out at the state level. As with many other issues, the division of sentiment within each State was not as closely balanced as it was among the population of the Nation as a whole, meaning not only that more people would be satisfied with the results of state-by-state resolution, but also that those results would be more stable. Pre-*Roe*, moreover, political compromise was possible.

*Roe*'s mandate for abortion on demand destroyed the compromises of the past, rendered compromise impossible for the future, and required the entire issue to be resolved uniformly, at the national level. At the same time, *Roe* created a vast new class of abortion consumers and abortion proponents by eliminating the moral opprobrium that had attached to the act. ("If the Constitution *guarantees* abortion, how can it be bad?"—not an accurate line of thought, but a natural one.) Many favor all of those developments, and it is not for me to say that they are wrong. But to portray *Roe* as the statesmanlike "settlement" of a divisive issue, a jurisprudential Peace of Westphalia that is worth preserving, is nothing less than Orwellian. *Roe* fanned into life an issue that has inflamed our national politics in general, and has obscured with its smoke the selection of Justices to this Court in particular, ever since. And by keeping us in the abortion-umpiring business, it is the perpetuation of that disruption, rather than of any *Pax Roeana*, that the Court's new majority decrees. The Imperial Judiciary lives.

I cannot agree with, indeed I am appalled by, the Court's suggestion that the decision whether to stand by an erroneous constitutional decision must be strongly influenced—*against* overruling, no less—by the substantial and continuing public opposition the decision has generated. The Court's judgment that any other course would "subvert the Court's legitimacy" must be another consequence of reading the error-filled history book that described the deeply divided country brought together by *Roe*....

But whether it would "subvert the Court's legitimacy" or not, the notion that we would decide a case differently from the way we otherwise would have in order to show that we can stand firm against public disapproval is frightening. It is a bad enough idea, even in the head of someone like me, who believes that the text of the Constitution, and our traditions, say what they say and there is no fiddling with them. But when it is in the mind of a Court that believes the Constitution has an evolving meaning, that the Ninth Amendment's reference to "other" rights is not a disclaimer, but a charter for action, and that the function of this Court is to "speak before all others for [the people's] constitutional ideals" unrestrained by meaningful text or tradition—then the notion that the Court must adhere to a decision for as long as the decision faces "great opposition" and the Court is "under fire" acquires a character of almost czarist arrogance. We are offended by these marchers who descend upon us, every year on the anniversary of *Roe*, to protest our saying that the Constitution requires what our society has never thought the Constitution requires. These people who refuse to be "tested by following" must be taught a lesson. We have no Cossacks, but at least we can stubbornly refuse to abandon an erroneous opinion that we might otherwise change— to show how little they intimidate us.

Of course, as THE CHIEF JUSTICE points out, we have been subjected to what the Court calls "'political pressure'" by *both* sides of this issue. Maybe today's decision *not* to overrule *Roe* will be seen as buckling to pressure from *that* direction. Instead of engaging in the hopeless task of predicting public perception—a job not for lawyers but for political campaign managers—the Justices should do what

is *legally* right by asking two questions: (1) Was *Roe* correctly decided? (2) Has *Roe* succeeded in producing a settled body of law? If the answer to both questions is no, *Roe* should undoubtedly be overruled.

What makes all this relevant to the bothersome application of "political pressure" against the Court are the twin facts that the American people love democracy and the American people are not fools. As long as this Court thought (and the people thought) that we Justices were doing essentially lawyers' work up here—reading text and discerning our society's traditional understanding of that text—the public pretty much left us alone. Texts and traditions are facts to study, not convictions to demonstrate about. But if in reality our process of constitutional adjudication consists primarily of making *value judgments;* if we can ignore a long and clear tradition clarifying an ambiguous text, as we did, for example, five days ago in declaring unconstitutional invocations and benedictions at public high school graduation ceremonies, *Lee v. Weisman,* 505 U.S. 577 (1992); If, as I say, our pronouncement of constitutional law rests primarily on value judgments, then a free and intelligent people's attitude towards us can be expected to be (*ought* to be) quite different. The people know that their value judgments are quite as good as those taught in any law school—maybe better. If, indeed, the "liberties" protected by the Constitution are, as the Court says, undefined and unbounded, then the people *should* demonstrate, to protest that we do not implement *their* values instead of *ours.* Not only that, but confirmation hearings for new Justices *should* deteriorate into question-and-answer sessions in which Senators go through a list of their constituents' most favored and most disfavored alleged constitutional rights, and seek the nominee's commitment to support or oppose them. Value judgments, after all, should be voted on, not dictated; and if our Constitution has somehow accidently committed them to the Supreme Court, at least we can have a sort of plebiscite each time a new nominee to that body is put forward.

There is a poignant aspect to today's opinion. Its length, and what might be called its epic tone, suggest that its authors believe they are bringing to an end a troublesome era in the history of our Nation and of our Court. "It is the dimension" of authority, they say, to "call the contending sides of national controversy to end their national division by accepting a common mandate rooted in the Constitution."

There comes vividly to mind a portrait by Emanuel Leutze that hangs in the Harvard Law School: Roger Brooke Taney, painted in 1859, the 82d year of his life, the 24th of his Chief Justiceship, the second after his opinion in *Dred Scott*. He is all in black, sitting in a shadowed red armchair, left hand resting upon a pad of paper in his lap, right hand hanging limply, almost lifelessly, beside the inner arm of the chair. He sits facing the viewer and staring straight out. There seems to be on his face, and in his deep-set eyes, an expression of profound sadness and disillusionment. Perhaps he always looked that way, even when dwelling upon the happiest of thoughts. But those of us who know how the lustre of his great Chief Justiceship came to be eclipsed by *Dred Scott* cannot help believing that he had that case—its already apparent consequences for the Court and its soon-to-be-played-out consequences

for the Nation—burning on his mind. I expect that two years earlier he, too, had thought himself "calling the contending sides of national controversy to end their national division by accepting a common mandate rooted in the Constitution."

It is no more realistic for us in this litigation, than it was for him in that, to think that an issue of the sort they both involved—an issue involving life and death, freedom and subjugation—can be "speedily and finally settled" by the Supreme Court, as President James Buchanan in his inaugural address said the issue of slavery in the territories would be. Quite to the contrary, by foreclosing all democratic outlet for the deep passions this issue arouses, by banishing the issue from the political forum that gives all participants, even the losers, the satisfaction of a fair hearing and an honest fight, by continuing the imposition of a rigid national rule instead of allowing for regional differences, the Court merely prolongs and intensifies the anguish.

We should get out of this area, where we have no right to be, and where we do neither ourselves nor the country any good by remaining.

## GLOSSARY

**viability:** ability to live

## Document Analysis

The first task facing the Court in deciding this case was determining whether to uphold the *Roe* decision, which resulted in a very divided Court. Citing the idea of liberty found under the Due Process Clause of the Fourteenth Amendment, Justices O'Connor, Kennedy, and Souter, co-authoring the opinion, reaffirmed the prior ruling in the *Roe* case. According to the opinion, the Court found women should be free from government intrusion when making decisions regarding reproduction, and women have the right to define their "own concept of existence." It was the majority opinion of the Court that women should be free to dictate the scope and direction of their own lives, and making choices regarding reproduction was vital to ensuring women's liberty. With a bare majority, the Court reaffirmed the

*Roe* decision and ruled abortion was still legal in the United States.

States did have the authority to prohibit abortion after viability unless the health or life of the mother was in question. The justices reexamined the definition of viability established in *Roe,* and because of certain medical advancements offering more sophisticated information, they found it necessary to update the previous definition of viability. The Court established viability was not twenty-eight weeks as previously thought, but instead should be set at twenty-three to twenty-four weeks to reflect more recent medical information. In addition to reevaluating viability, the justices decided to apply the notion of undue burden to abortion rights. Undue burden refers to placing obstacles in a woman's way that would make it difficult, or prevent her from getting an abortion. The Court also used the undue burden language to help make a judgement on a provision found within the Pennsylvania Abortion Control Act.

The second major task before the Court was to examine the five provisions established in the Pennsylvania law: informed consent, twenty-four hour waiting period, parental consent, reporting requirements, and spousal notification. The Court upheld all of the provisions, considered to be some of the most restrictive abortion provisions, except for spousal notification. Citing the undue burden language, it was believed that to make a woman notify her spouse prior to an abortion was to place obstacles in the way of a woman's right to choose. The spousal notification law seemed to situate a husband in a position of power over his wife or imply that the husband was in a position to grant permission to his wife. The issue of domestic violence was also discussed, with justices noting that forcing women who were in abusive marriages to discuss abortion with a husband could make domestic situations worse. It was noted in the opinion that "women do not lose their constitutionally protected liberty when they marry" and, as such, requiring women to notify their spouse was deemed a rights violation.

## Essential Themes

The Court was faced with a difficult decision: overturn *Roe* and disappoint pro-choice advocates, or uphold the previous decision keeping women's reproductive rights intact and devastating pro-life proponents. While it is evident heated debate regarding a woman's right to choose is still an issue we face today, the war over abortion was at an all-time high when the *Planned Parenthood v. Casey* case was emerging. Overturning *Roe* had the potential to stimulate even more contention in the nation than the previous two decades of abortion discussion. While the ruling in *Planned Parenthood v. Casey* reaffirmed *Roe*, it also upheld some of the most impeding abortion regulations the country had seen since before the original *Roe* ruling. The ruling itself, while of obvious importance, is perhaps not as interesting as the way the Court went about making the overall decision. What was unique about the case was the Court chose to examine the issue of abortion by

viewing women as individuals who were equal to men. In *Roe*, the right to privacy meant the government must essentially leave women alone to make their choice. In *Casey*, women are discussed as individuals who have an equal place in society and, as such, have rights that are protected by the Constitution. The court considered a woman's role in society and went so far as to highlight women's educational pursuits, contributions to the economy, and progressive social placement. The Court was not simply addressing abortion as a medical issue, but instead was looking at women as individuals, who have the right to choose the course of their own lives. The ruling in *Casey* did not particularly please either side of the abortion debate. Pro-choice advocates were disappointed in the restrictive provisions upheld by the Court, and pro-life supporters were devastated the Court did not overturn *Roe*. The Court, at the time of the *Casey* ruling, was more conservative than during *Roe*, but the justices were evaluating a woman's right to choose from the progressive mindset that women have an equal place in society and, as such, deserve to have their fundamental rights protected.

—*Amber R. Dickinson, PhD*

## Bibliography and Additional Reading

Biskupic, Joan. Sandra Day O'Connor: How the First Woman on the Supreme Court Became its Most Influential Justice. New York: ECCO, 2005.

Daly, Erin. "Reconsidering Abortion Law: Liberty, Equality, and the New Rhetoric of Planned Parenthood v. Casey." Am. UL Rev. 45 (1995): 77.

Devins, Neal. "How Planned Parenthood v. Casey (Pretty Much) Settled the Abortion Wars." The Yale Law Journal (2009): 1318–1354.

Irons, Peter. A People's History of the Supreme Court. New York: Penguin Books, 2000.

Linton, Paul Benjamin. "Planned Parenthood v. Casey: The Flight from Reason in the Supreme Court." Louis U. Pub L. Rev. 13 (1993): 15.

O'Brien, Michael. John F. Kennedy: a Biography. Macmillan, 2005.

Yarbrough, Tinsley E. David Hackett Souter: Traditional Republican on the Rehnquist Court. Oxford, UK: Oxford University Press, 2005.

# ■ Vice President Joseph Biden on Combating Violence against Women

**Date:** December 10, 2014
**Author:** Joseph Biden
**Genre:** Speech

## Summary Overview

Every year at the Solidarity Awards, Vital Voices recognizes men who have advocated for the rights of women and girls domestically and internationally. The honorees in 2014 were the actor Sir Patrick Stewart, South African activist Bafana Khumalo, athlete Don McPherson, and Vice President Joe Biden. Vital Voices honored Vice President Biden on the twentieth anniversary of the passage of the Violence Against Women Act, which he drafted and succeeded in passing when he was a senator. In this speech, Biden reflects on the people who influenced him to be concerned about violence against women. Then, he goes over the process of passing this landmark legislation in 1994; finally, he expands his focus to the international situation and concludes that much more work is necessary in order to eradicate gendered violence. Biden shows in this speech how resistant governments have been to changing misogynistic statutes. It was difficult for him to pass VAWA in 1994, and there is still much work that the international community has to accomplish to provide safety globally.

## Defining Moment

Joe Biden called the Violence Against Women Act (VAWA) the "single most significant legislation that I've crafted during my 35-year tenure in the Senate." The beginnings of this landmark legislation go back to concerns in the 1960s and 1970s about the rising crime rate in the United States. During this time, several organizations were formed and laws passed with a focus on women's rights. For example, the National Organization for Women was founded in 1966; the decision of

the Supreme Court in *Roe v. Wade* reaffirmed the right of women to have access to abortions, and the Equal Rights Amendment was nearly ratified in 1979.

Still, a troubling situation remained. In the 1980s, researchers studied the influence of family violence on national crime ratings. The data collected suggested a connection. Researchers found that women were statistically more likely to suffer violence related to their gender than were men; they found that women were more likely to suffer violence at the hands of an intimate partner, too. Additionally, attacks by an intimate partner were likely to be more dangerous to women than attacks by a stranger. One survey found that women were ten times more likely than men to experience sexual assault. As a senator at the time, Joe Biden and his colleague Barbara Boxer sought to highlight the hypocrisy of a country that was tough on crime, but considered domestic violence a private issue to be dealt with at home.

VAWA increased punishments for certain gendered violent crimes and created or improved programs that supported victims of such crimes. Among other provisions, VAWA was responsible for creating a "rape shield law," which prevents a victim's past sexual conduct from being used against them in court, and the National Domestic Violence Hotline, a confidential and toll-free hotline to provide support and information for people looking for help. In the twenty years since Congress first passed VAWA, intimate partner violence and homicide has decreased, more crimes are being reported and resulting in arrests than before, and protection orders against must be recognized across all state lines. Yet, as Biden recognizes in this speech, VAWA only addresses issues specific to judicial administration in the United States: a larger cultural problem needs to be addressed in the way men and women approach gendered violence domestically and abroad.

## Author Biography

Vice President Joseph Biden was born in 1942 and raised primarily in Delaware. Later in his career, his love of his home state endeared him to his constituents and defined his 2008 presidential campaign. However, before he entered politics, Biden was a practicing lawyer, varying between criminal and corporate law practice. He was elected at the age of thirty to the US Senate as a Democrat in 1972. As a senator, he worked on drafting several crime laws and became involved in foreign affairs (particularly the Yugoslav Wars in the early 1990s and resisting military involvement in the Gulf and Iraq Wars). In 1994, he drafted and succeeded in passing the Violence Against Women Act, which made measures to protect women from domestic violence. Biden failed to gain the Democratic presidential nomination in 1988 and 2008; he did become Barack Obama's running mate in the 2008 elections and then vice president of the United States. Biden continued to work on the same issues that concerned him as senator. While Biden was vice president for a second term, his Violence Against Women Act was reauthorized in 2013.

## HISTORICAL DOCUMENT

Thank you very much. Sir Patrick [Stewart, also honored], I learned a while ago, you are exactly right: That until people are brave enough to step forward, to pull the Band-Aid off, shed light on this dirty little secret, nothing will happen. And Don [Don McPherson, another honoree], you're a good man. You get it. You're also a hell of an athlete. But you reflect what my dad thought was the definition of a man: someone with the courage to stand up whenever any injustice occurs. And Bafana [South African Bafana Khumalo, another honoree], I need your help. I drafted years ago the International Violence Against Women Act. The president and I have been trying to get that passed for some time. It does cut off foreign aid and assistance to countries that engage in practices that are just inhumane. And Diane [von Furstenberg], thank you very, very much for you, personally, for presenting this honor to me. It means a lot.

The fact of the matter is that if you've hung around as long as I have, you're given awards. But I measure the value of an award based on the consequence of the organization giving the award. And this award means a lot to me. You are an incredible group of people. I've had the opportunity to work with Vital Voices since its inception, and you've done so much good for so many people. And on behalf of my sister and I, my sister Valerie, my closest friend in life, that's here with me today, I want to thank her as well. Diane and I were sitting there beforehand, and she said, "Men learn from their mothers." Well, men do learn, boys learn, from their mothers, their sisters. I've had a great, great—this is not hyperbole—a great honor to be surrounded by women with backbones like ramrods. I mean that sincerely. With profound intellects, accomplished women. And women like my sister, who have excelled and exceeded in everything she's done, and excelled and exceeded more than I have.

Look, let me just say it straight: Violence against women is a stain on the moral character of a society, in any society in which it occurs. It's an obligation of all societies, particularly the men in society, to stand up and do all in their power to eradicate that stain. And it is a stain on the conscience of a country. This is an issue, that has been made repeatedly tonight, of basic human rights.

My dad said it differently. He said, "Everyone is entitled to be treated with dignity." That was my dad's favorite word, the one we heard most often. We should be attacking this virus, this stain, with a profound sense of urgency. Urgency. For as I speak, there are thousands of women around the world being brutalized. Mutilated. Killed at the hands of those who allegedly love them and care about them.

I'm often asked, because I've been doing this for so long, why am I so passionate about this. Everyone assumes that because of my passion, it must be that my mother, or a woman in my family, was brutalized. Thank god, they have not been. But I was raised by a decent, graceful man, my dad; our dad. And he thought, and from the time we can remember, all of my siblings, this is the god's truth, my word is the bible, he raised us to understand the greatest sin a man or woman could commit is the abuse of power. And the ultimate abuse of power, the cardinal sin, was for a man to raise his hand against a woman or a child.

But unlike most people of my dad's generation, he went further. He was a gentle man, but he raised us to intervene. He taught us, where we saw it, the definition of our manhood was not what a great football player, baseball player me or any of my brothers or sister were, it was to stand up and do the right thing.

I remember when my sister, my younger sister, was beat up by a young boy when she was in seventh grade. I'm older than my sister, I was two years ahead of her. I remember coming back from mass on Sunday, always the big treat was we would get to stop at a doughnut shop at a strip shopping center. We went in, and we would get doughnuts, and my dad would wait in the car. As I was coming out, my sister tugged on me and said, 'That's the boy who kicked me off my bicycle.'

So I went home, and we only lived about a quarter mile away. So I got on my bicycle and rode back, and he was in the doughnut shop with his parents, leaning down on those slanted counters, you know, those slanted counters in pastry shops. And I walked up behind him, and smashed his head against the glass. Now, I'm not recommending this. But I want to tell you about my father. His father grabbed me, and I looked at his father, and I said, "If you ever touch my sister again, I'll come back and I will kill your son."

Now, that was a euphemism. And I thought I was really, really in trouble. I thought I was going to be arrested. I went home. My father had never once raised his hand to any one of his children, never once. I thought I was in real trouble. He pulled me aside, and said, "Joey, you shouldn't do that. And I'm proud of you, son. I'm proud of you." The point was, the way we were raised, the definition of who we were, was whether we speak up. Whether it's physically engaging, because so many men are cowards, they have the physical capacity to intervene, but they're cowards, thinking they're men. Whatever it is, just speak up, and speak out.

I began focusing on this issue as a young senator, more than three decades ago, because we were largely a nation of bystanders. Our legal system at the state and local level still reflective—excuse me, Sir Patrick [Stewart], English common law, which we inherited. Which was not until the 14th century did the English common law court say, because so many women died because they were being beaten by their spouses to death, that a man could no longer beat a woman, his wife, with a rod bigger than the circumference of his thumb. The rule of thumb.

This notion that women are chattels is a central part of our culture, inherited from our Anglo-Saxon ancestry, but also in many other cultures, and our law. I asked my staff, when I started to write the law, two men and four brilliant women, one of whom is here today, and went on to be a distinguished professor of law for 10 or 12 years, I asked her to come back and be my council. And I asked them to go out and do a survey of the laws on the books in the states to determine where and whether or not this implicit bias that somehow it's the woman's fault, somehow it's a man's right, are written in the laws.

They wrote a paper, and I'm happy to send it to any of you who are interested, because you may be. It's over 23 years old. We listed in almost every state in the nation, the application of law was different. In the state of Delaware, my home state, if you consented to go out with me, if you were a voluntary partner, no matter what I did to you, no matter how brutally I raped you, I could not be convicted of first-degree rape. If I jumped out of an alley and brutally raped you, I could be convicted of first-degree rape.

Think of the premise: You must have done something. You must have somehow, inexplicably consented somehow, to something. I could not be convicted of first-degree rape.

I could go on *ad nauseum* and list the laws that are changed now. But the fact is that no one at that time denied that kicking your wife in the stomach, or smashing her face against the wall, or throwing her down the steps in public was repugnant. But society basically turned a blind eye. Hardly anyone ever directly intervened, as my father taught us, and as he did. Almost no one called it a crime. It was a family affair. A religious matter. A cultural issue. It was none of our business.

And indeed, when I began to draft the Violence Against Women legislation, the reason why it didn't work out at first, I physically drafted it myself, because no one wanted to be part of it. There are a lot of you out there who are working like the devil to do something, but getting nowhere. Because of the incredibly talented staff I had, we put together the Violence Against Women Act. And when we did, our opponents said that what Biden was doing—I could give you all the quotes—was "undermining the solidarity of the family." Seriously. That it would impact on the cohesion, bring about the disintegration of the American family. When we championed, and [they] now exist, women's shelters, and housing, and transitional housing, they were characterized "as indoctrination centers for runaway wives." This is 1989. 1990. 1991. 1992.

Senator Birch Bayh, you may remember from Indiana, back in the early '80s introduced in the Judiciary Committee, and got a law passed saying that a man, a husband, could be convicted for raping his wife. In the markup of that bill, the deceased senator from Alabama said on the record in frustration, "My young friend just doesn't understand, sometimes a man has to use force with his wife." On the record.

Even some in this audience did not support the Violence Against Women Act in the beginning, to tell the truth. No women's organization stepped forward and supported it, until Ellie Smeal spoke about it. It was characterized as "This is just a fad on Biden's part." That was the phrase used. Others said that it was important but did not deserve the national response.

I had written into the law a civil-rights cause of action, which eventually was struck down by the court, that I was going too far, equating violence against women with violence against the very organization I came out of, the civil-rights movement. Everyone seemed satisfied to either keep this dirty little secret in the background, or worried that it would trump other issues, like gender equality, the right to choose, and other issues.

Finally, we had a meeting in my office, at my conference table. I can name the people there, they all remember, and I called in every major women's organization, including the civil-rights groups. And finally Ellie Smeal spoke up, that's why I love her. She said, "What are we doing? What are we doing? Why aren't we supporting this?" And they all came around because of Ellie, not because of me. And everything began to change.

Because the one thing I was absolutely convinced about, and I know I am referred to in the White House as "The White House optimist," I believe in the basic decency of human beings. And I believe

part of the reason people don't react is they think they're not supposed to react. This cultural norm that had been imposed upon us. I was convinced we could change attitudes and gain the support of the American people if we forced them to look this epidemic in the eye. And that's what we did with extensive hearings.

Brave women came forward, and before the whole world, in over a thousand hours of hearings, said, "This is what happened to me." Remember that young model here in New York, whose face was slashed because she wouldn't go out with her landlord? She and others stepped forward, so no one could pretend, no woman or man could pretend that it wasn't happening. I was convinced once that happened, the American public would have to react. They would react. Because so many of you in this room took part in that cause, and led the cause, and were there before I and others were there, we were able to pass the Violence Against Women Act 20 years ago. But it took four years.

And between 1993 and 2010, the rate dropped by 64 percent. But there's still so much more to do. Now, the reason I raised this with you now is because I'm convinced when we rip the Band-Aid off and force the world to look this in the eye, we can succeed. But that's what it takes. Because the same arguments we heard at home, I'm now hearing abroad.

I've now traveled a million miles as vice-president, and so many more as chairman of the Foreign Relations Committee. And those of you who are involved know there's not a country I go in I do not raise this issue. Not a single country I go in. But I'm told: It's a family affair, or you don't understand our culture, you don't understand our religious practices, you don't understand we're different. You have no right to trespass on our culture. Let me make something absolutely clear to everyone here: There is NEVER, never, a religious, a cultural, a societal, justification for inhumanity. Period. Never. Never. And don't be intimidated when you are told that you don't understand our culture. You're right, I don't understand it. They're wrong. They're simply wrong.

And we have an obligation to speak out, and be just as forceful on the world stage as we were in

America for the last 30 years. In every country I visit, this is a matter of discussion. The significant measure of decency of any society is the extent to which they tolerate this abuse of power in violence against women. Those nations which continue to tolerate honor killings, genital mutilation, rape as punishment. My wife Jill just got back—I think she's the only Westerner to go into the East—the Democratic Republic of the Congo in the East—visit hospitals where over 100,000 women overall, 1,000 of them in one hospital, where rape is used as a weapon of war, and then the women are mutilated with bayonets. An uncomfortable thing to say at a dinner, but that's what happens.

Not only are these societies backward, and we should not apologize for saying what they are, they will never be able to enjoy the benefits of economic growth and stability unless they begin to empower women. What these societies have to understand is that old Chinese proverb is correct: Women hold up half the sky. And they deserve as much protection and dignity as any man.

My sister, Valerie, said in a speech she recently made, "We are all made weaker when in the name or the guise of culture, in the guise of righteousness, in the name of religion, any woman, anywhere is discounted, disenfranchised, disrespected; when one is sold, berated, beaten, we're all less." And that's the god's truth. That's the reality.

And what we're focused on now, here in the United States, and I agree what you should be focused on around the world, is to take away the excuses, the rationalizations, the justifications on the part of men who lack the moral courage, or moral center, to intervene. Too many crimes continue to be committed, too much brutality inflicted, too much pain endured, under the guise of culture. More than 120 million women, today, around the world suffer from genital mutilation. As many as 50 percent of women in Pakistan are beaten by their husbands. Dowry killings account for more than 25 percent of all the violent deaths in India. More than 5,000 honor killings occur around the world each year.

In the Democratic Republic of Congo, 1,100 rapes are reported each month, an average of 36 women and girls raped every day. A total of 200,000

since the recent conflict began. Since 2009, at least 500 women and girls from northern Nigeria have been abducted by Boko Haram. And we are acting in the United States. It's the African Union, the Africans are not acting.

We, the president, have offered everything from our special forces to all that we have available. Right here in America, an average of three women a day are murdered by abusive partners. Across the globe, nearly one in three women has experienced physical or sexual violence at the hand of an intimate partner. As many as 38 percent of murdered women are killed by an intimate partner.

Just imagine—imagine if all that was happening to men. The mutilations, the beatings, the rapes, the murders. How many men are absolutely outraged when you hear about the rape of a man? The indignity that it causes at the hands of another man. It's time for men to speak up, to stand up, to put themselves in the way. In the way.

Freedom from fear of violence is a basic human right. And the obligation to intervene is a basic moral obligation for every man, one that transcends national boundaries, and religious concerns, and cultural differences. This change is not beyond our capacity, for god's sake. Especially in the world of communication today, instant communications.

Now that we have spoken up as a nation, we have much more to do, because of all the pressure you have placed on your government. All of you in this room have applied, and continue to apply, significant pressure, and now the world is beginning to respond. Just like early on in the fight here, just beginning to respond.

At the United Nations, Ban Ki-moon, the secretary general, made the UNITE to End Violence Against Women campaign a top priority, organizing a network of men and leaders to highlight the important role men can play in changing the culture of this issue. In Ireland, Edward Kenny, a fine man, recently helped launch an action campaign to reduce violence against women, calling on his fellow countrymen to "challenge any cultural acceptance of or blindness to the violence in all sectors of our society." In the heart of the Balkans, the Croatian president has called together a national summit to urge men to fight against domestic violence. In Sudan, where 88 percent of the women and girls, 15 to 18, are reported to be subject to genital mutilation, 74-year-old Sheik Mohamed Saeed is calling for an end to the practice. "How can a man be a leader," he asked, "without taking such a challenge and fighting for positive change?"

I'm taking too long, I apologize. I will end by saying I accept this award in the hope, and the expectation, that the person you give this award to ten years from now will be able to talk to you about the progress. How many women have been saved around the world because of the action you've taken between now and the next ten years. That we will have made significant progress through the fundamental change in attitude that must take place if we are to win.

Don [McPherson], I'm always asked, What constitutes victory? Because there will always be violent crime, throughout all societies, like a wave, a wave moves on, but priorities remain the same. But what constitutes success? Success will occur when the day comes that no woman in the world who has been beaten, brutalized, raped, ever, ever, ever, consciously or subconsciously asks what so many women ask today: What did I do? What did I do to deserve this?

When I was a young lawyer, I was a public defender. I was told by a senior trial lawyer, picking my first jury in a rape case that I was assigned, "Pick men, don't pick women." I thought that was counterintuitive. Because women blame women. Young Marla, whose face was slashed, was asked, "What

did they say, your mother, your friends?" And they learned, they said, "Why were you in a bar? What were you wearing? What did you have on?"

It's not only the culture of men in America we have to change, we have to change the culture of our daughters. My daughter, my sister, have been raised to understand that it is never, never, never, never, never, never, your fault. I got in trouble in the hearing, when I was doing this hearing 20 years ago, I said, "If a woman got up stark naked, walked out of this room, and walked across to the Capitol, she'd be arrested for indecent exposure. But no man, no man, would have a right to lay a hand upon her." I got more hate mail than you can imagine. No man, no man, has a right, and no woman should ever question what did she do to deserve this?

And the second cultural change that has to take place is when no man in America, or the world, thinks that he ever has the right to raise a hand to a woman in anything other than self-defense. Never. Never, never, never. It's that simple. It's that absolute. It will still happen, but we have to end the ability to rationalize that I had some right, that was my woman, that was my wife. You never, ever, have the right.

Ladies and gentlemen, until the whole world accepts that no means no, or even more, that ONLY yes means yes. Only yes means yes. Ladies and gentlemen, I mean this when I say it, with your help, and your continued passion, we can actually change the cultures around the world, and continue to change our culture. Our civilization, the measure of our civility, depends on us doing a whole hell of a lot more. Thank you all, and may God bless you.

## Document Analysis

Vice President Biden is not only known for his work on the Violence Against Women Act in 1994, but also for his distinctive speech-giving style. This speech is an example of Biden's gregarious and folksy way of speaking when he is engaged in political events. Since Biden can and has used a speechwriter, this choice of style must be deliberate. This style has been helpful for Biden in his many senatorial and presidential campaigns when he needs average Americans to support him; he also uses this same method of persuasion at the 2014 Vital

Voices, so as to encourage more action for social justice from his listeners. In this speech, it is possible to isolate Biden's specific style for campaigning for important issues through his use of personal memories.

First, Biden often draws on his own history in order to create familiarity between himself and the audience. This rhetoric of familiarity is meant to instill pathos in the audience and make Biden appear more trustworthy. After Biden thanks the appropriate people and introduces the subject of gendered violence, he immediately delves into his personal history. He poses to the audience the supposition that he must be related to a woman who was the victim of violence to be so passionate about eradicating it; he says: "everyone assumes that because of my passion, it must be that my mother, or a woman in my family, was brutalized. Thank god, they have not been. But I was raised by a decent, graceful man, my dad; our dad." Biden could have elected a different rhetorical strategy; for example, he could have said that a person did not need to experience tragedy to have empathy. Instead, Biden begins an anecdote about how he, as a young boy, stood up for his sister who was kicked by another boy. He continues by outlining all the opposition he faced when he was drafting VAWA; in the process, he offers several anecdotes where he remembers the direct speech of an aide or opponent offering advice or criticism to him. Biden also refers to his experiences as a lawyer and a speech he heard his sister recently make. Biden's custom of referring to his own personal experiences is used to persuade his audience emotionally that violence against women is still an endemic cultural problem.

Finally, it is possible to understand why Biden would choose to tie his own experiences closely to his argument by considering the following: why should an audience listen to what Biden, a man, has to say about women's safety? Biden, a habitual political campaigner as well, recognizes this gulf could hamper his connection to the audience. Consequently, he uses his personal history to create familiarity and trust with his audience. By constantly referring to his own emotions about VAWA and international gender violence, Biden reveals his true purpose in making this speech. He is not simply thanking the crowd for an award. He is urging the audience not to become complacent and continue fighting for women's rights.

## Essential Themes

The Violence Against Women Act was first ratified in 1994; it was reauthorized again in 2000, 2005, and 2013. This act is noteworthy for increasing the punishment for acts of gendered violence in the United States as well as creating several services to support victims of such crimes. Biden's VAWA was among the first pieces of legislation to make a substantive difference in the way the criminal justice system approached crime between intimate partners. VAWA made crimes against women a responsibility of the state and federal government rather than the domestic sphere. Finally, it was written law: women and girls were not supposed to bear responsibility for being beaten, assaulted, or stalked.

Although the version of VAWA that the government enacted in 1994 reduced national crime levels, this legislation was not a universal solution for all women's issues. Biden recognizes this limitation in this document at the same time as he recognizes that VAWA created an improvement in many women's lives. The first version of VAWA was not detailed enough to encompass the different issues that affect different ages, races, and sexualities, but future reauthorizations attempted to increase protection. Biden's draft of VAWA covered protection of women based on gender, but increasing recognition of intersectionality (the study of how different oppressive institutions like racism, sexism, and homophobia interrelate) has improved the original version of the legislation. When Congress reauthorized VAWA in 2000, provisions were added to protect foreign nationals, disabled, and elderly women. In 2005, VAWA strengthened penalties for repeat offenders and was offered more protection to Native American women. When it was proposed to extend VAWA's protection to same-sex couples in 2013, the reauthorization of VAWA experienced more trouble in Congress; this version of VAWA was eventually passed in its extended form.

The expansion of VAWA's provisions can offer protection to men who suffer intimate partner violence, individuals in same-sex relationships, and transgender people. Additionally, local police forces and judicial systems still have issues in prosecuting crimes against women, especially those who come from minority backgrounds. Biden's speech stresses the need to continue working towards protecting those who cannot protect themselves.

—*Ashleigh Fata, MA*

## Bibliography and Additional Reading

Biden, Joseph. "20 Years of Change: Joe Biden on the Violence Against Women Act." Time. Time, Inc., 10 Sept. 2014. Web.

Crowell, Nancy A. & Ann W. Burgess, eds. Understanding Violence Against Women. Washington, DC: National Academy Press, 1996. Print.

Harding, Kate. Asking for It: The Alarming Rise of Rape Culture—and What We Can Do About It. Philadelphia: Da Capo, 2015. Print.

Osnos, Evan. "The Biden Agenda." The New Yorker. Condé Nast, 28 Jul. 2014. Web.

# ■ *United States v. Virginia*

**Date:** June 26, 1996
**Author:** Justice Ruth Bader Ginsburg
**Genre:** Court opinion

## Summary Overview

Although throughout the twentieth century the majority of colleges and universities were co-educational, virtually all institutions of higher education were co-educational by the 1990s. Among the public schools, only two with unique curricula were not coeducational, the Virginia Military Institute (VMI) and the Citadel (South Carolina). Both used a form of military training for the men who were accepted to the corps of cadets, and by the mid-1990s both were facing legal pressure to admit women. When the Fourth Circuit Court of Appeals ruled in favor of allowing Virginia to create a "substantively comparable" school for women, the United States appealed to the Supreme Court. Justice Ruth Bader Ginsburg, one of the Supreme Court's strongest advocates for gender equality, wrote the majority opinion which mandated the inclusion of both men and women among the student body of VMI. She, and the other six justices who voted for gender integration, not only ended legal gender discrimination in public higher education, but they strengthened the legal affirmation that "separate but equal" was not possible.

## Defining Moment

Beginning in the 1950s, discrimination in educational facilities and systems was addressed by a variety of legislative and judicial means. These changes dealt with not only racial/ethnic segregation, but also with separation by gender in publicly supported educational facilities/systems. In the 1970s two landmark pieces of legislation were passed supporting an end to discrimination against women. In 1972, Title IX was passed, which mandated that no person be excluded from federally funded educational opportunities "on the basis of sex." In 1976, a combination of legislation and an executive order by President Gerald Ford opened U. S. service academies to women. Beginning that fall, the first women cadets entered all three major service academies. Although that legislation/executive order did not bear directly on this case, the twenty years' worth of evidence that gender inclusive military training could succeed made some of the arguments put forward by Virginia less effective. Women desiring this type of

higher education were no longer willing to be denied, and obtained the assistance of the federal government in pursuing this goal.

For private single-sex schools, as well as for VMI, a major argument was that the exclusion of the other gender was an important aspect of their mission. Thus, Virginia proposed opening the Virginia Women's Institute for Leadership (VWIL) to offer women an opportunity for a unique experience in higher education. The commonwealth argued that the two institutions together would offer equal protection to all its citizens. However, the currents of history were against Virginia, as the "substantively comparable" version of "separate but equal" was decades out of date. By not offering any "exceedingly persuasive justification" for the exclusion of women from VMI, the majority of the Court mandated an end to publically-supported single-sex institutions of higher education. (The Citadel dropped the defense of its policy in the courts when the ruling on this case made it clear that there was no chance of successfully defending its male-only admissions policy.)

Although VMI swiftly moved to move into compliance with this ruling, accepting women for the admissions class of 1997, the first women entering VMI were in a difficult position due to VMI's traditional views of women and the social views of some of the new students' classmates. However, the fact that the superintendent of VMI (Josiah Bunting 1995-2003), during judicial proceedings regarding the Citadel, had called women "a toxic kind of virus" indicated the resistance the women would face once they were admitted. VMI did consider becoming private, with the governing board deciding by a 9-8 vote to remain commonwealth-related. With that decision, there was no turning back. Single gender public higher education, in the United States, had come to an end.

## Author Biography

Ruth Bader was born on March 15, 1933, in Brooklyn, New York. She graduated from Cornell University in 1954 and that year married Martin Ginsburg, a classmate. She enrolled at Harvard Law School, but after her husband found employment with a New York City law firm, she transferred to Columbia University, where she graduated tied for first in her class in 1959. That year she accepted a two-year clerkship for U.S. District Court Judge Edmund L. Palmieri in New York. After working on the Columbia Law School Project on International Procedure from 1961 to 1963, Ginsburg accepted a post as a law professor at Rutgers University, where she taught until 1972. She also served as volunteer counsel to the New Jersey chapter of the American Civil Liberties Union (ACLU). At the ACLU, Ginsburg litigated sex discrimination cases and cofounded the Women's Rights Project. Ironically, during her time at Rutgers she became pregnant with her son, James, and because she was not tenured, she concealed her pregnancy with oversized clothes. In 1972 Ginsburg accepted a position at Columbia University, the law school's first woman with the rank of full professor.

In 1980 President Jimmy Carter nominated Ginsburg as a justice on the U.S. Court of Appeals for the District of Columbia. Then, in 1993, President Bill Clinton nominated her to replace Justice Byron White on the U.S. Supreme Court. Ginsburg's reputation as a moderate on the U.S. Court of Appeals was helpful to her confirmation. In her years on the Supreme Court, her written decisions in numerous key cases made her a leading voice in the judicial branch for sex equality, thus expanding the rights of the American public, including both women and men.

## HISTORICAL DOCUMENT

Founded in 1839, VMI is today the sole single-sex school among Virginia's 15 public institutions of higher learning. VMI's distinctive mission is to produce "citizen-soldiers," men prepared for leadership in civilian life and in military service. VMI pursues this mission through pervasive training of a kind not available anywhere else in Virginia. Assigning prime place to character development, VMI uses an "adversative method" modeled on English public schools and once characteristic of military instruction. VMI constantly endeavors to instill physical and mental discipline in its cadets and impart to them a strong moral code. The school's graduates leave VMI with heightened comprehension of their capacity to deal with duress and stress, and a large sense of accomplishment for completing the hazardous course....

Neither the goal of producing citizen-soldiers nor VMI's implementing methodology is inherently unsuitable to women. And the school's impressive record in producing leaders has made admission desirable to some women. Nevertheless, Virginia has elected to preserve exclusively for men the advantages and opportunities a VMI education affords. ...

VMI produces its "citizen-soldiers" through "an adversative, or doubting, model of education" which features "[p]hysical rigor, mental stress, absolute equality of treatment, absence of privacy, minute regulation of behavior, and indoctrination in desirable values." As one Commandant of Cadets described it, the adversative method "dissects the young student," and makes him aware of his "limits and capabilities," so that he knows "how far he can go with his anger,... how much he can take under stress,... exactly what he can do when he is physically exhausted."

VMI cadets live in spartan barracks where surveillance is constant and privacy nonexistent; they wear uniforms, eat together in the mess hall, and regularly participate in drills. Entering students are incessantly exposed to the rat line, "an extreme form of the adversative model," comparable in intensity to Marine Corps boot camp. Tormenting and punishing, the rat line bonds new cadets to their fellow sufferers and, when they have completed the 7-month experience, to their former tormentors....

In the two years preceding the lawsuit, the District Court noted, VMI had received inquiries from 347 women, but had responded to none of them. "[S]ome women, at least," the court said, "would want to attend the school if they had the opportunity." The court further recognized that, with recruitment, VMI could "achieve at least 10&percent; female enrollment"—a sufficient 'critical mass' to provide the female cadets with a positive educational experience." And it was also established that "some women are capable of all of the individual activities required of VMI cadets." In addition, experts agreed that if VMI admitted women, "the VMI ROTC experience would become a better training program from the perspective of the armed forces, because it would provide training in dealing with a mixed-gender army."

The District Court ruled in favor of VMI, however, and rejected the equal protection challenge pressed by the United States.... The District Court reasoned that education in "a single-gender environment, be it male or female," yields substantial benefits. VMI's school for men brought diversity to an otherwise coeducational Virginia system, and that diversity was "enhanced by VMI's unique method of instruction." If single-gender education for males ranks as an important governmental objective, it becomes obvious, the District Court concluded, that the only means of achieving the objective "is to exclude women from the all-male institution-VMI."...

The Court of Appeals for the Fourth Circuit disagreed and vacated the District Court's judgment. The appellate court held: "The Commonwealth of Virginia has not ... advanced any state policy by which it can justify its determination, under an announced policy of diversity, to afford VMI's unique type of program to men and not to women."...

The parties agreed that "some women can meet the physical standards now imposed on men," and the court was satisfied that "neither the goal of producing citizen soldiers nor VMI's implementing methodology is inherently unsuitable to women." The Court of Appeals, however, accepted the District Court's finding that "at least these three aspects of VMI's program—physical training, the absence of privacy, and the adversative approach—would be materially affected by coeducation." Remanding the case, the appeals court assigned to Virginia, in the first instance, responsibility for selecting a remedial course. The court suggested these options for the State: Admit women to VMI; establish parallel institutions or programs; or abandon state support, leaving VMI free to pursue its policies as a private institution....

In response to the Fourth Circuit's ruling, Virginia proposed a parallel program for women: Virginia Women's Institute for Leadership (VWIL).

The 4-year, state-sponsored undergraduate program would be located at Mary Baldwin College, a private liberal arts school for women, and would be open, initially, to about 25 to 30 students. Although VWIL would share VMI's mission-to produce "citizen-soldiers"—the VWIL program would differ, as does Mary Baldwin College, from VMI in academic offerings, methods of education, and financial resources.

The average combined SAT score of entrants at Mary Baldwin is about 100 points lower than the score for VMI freshmen. Mary Baldwin's faculty holds "significantly fewer Ph.D.'s than the faculty at VMI," and receives significantly lower salaries. While VMI offers degrees in liberal arts, the sciences, and engineering, Mary Baldwin, at the time of trial, offered only bachelor of arts degrees. A VWIL student seeking to earn an engineering degree could gain one, without public support, by attending Washington University in St. Louis, Missouri, for two years, paying the required private tuition....

Virginia represented that it will provide equal financial support for in-state VWIL students and VMI cadets, and the VMI Foundation agreed to supply a $5.4625 million endowment for the VWIL program. Mary Baldwin's own endowment is about $19 million; VMI's is $131 million. Mary Baldwin will add $35 million to its endowment based on future commitments; VMI will add $220 million. The VMI Alumni Association has developed a network of employers interested in hiring VMI graduates. The Association has agreed to open its network to VWIL graduates, but those graduates will not have the advantage afforded by a VMI degree....

The court recognized that, as it analyzed the case, means merged into end, and the merger risked "bypass[ing] any equal protection scrutiny." The court therefore added another inquiry, a decisive test it called "substantive comparability." The key question, the court said, was whether men at VMI and women at VWIL would obtain "substantively comparable benefits at their institution or through other means offered by the [S]tate." Although the appeals court recognized that the VWIL degree "lacks the historical benefit and prestige" of a VMI degree, it nevertheless found the educational opportunities at the two schools "sufficiently comparable."...

The Fourth Circuit denied rehearing en banc.... Judge Motz agreed with Judge Phillips that Virginia had not shown an "'exceedingly persuasive justification'" for the disparate opportunities the State supported....

We note, once again, the core instruction of this Court's pathmarking decisions in *J. E. B. v. Alabama ex rel. T. B.*, and *Mississippi Univ. for Women*: Parties who seek to defend gender-based government action must demonstrate an "exceedingly persuasive justification" for that action....

In 1971, for the first time in our Nation's history, this Court ruled in favor of a woman who complained that her State had denied her the equal protection of its laws. Since *Reed*, the Court has repeatedly recognized that neither federal nor state government acts compatibly with the equal protection principle when a law or official policy denies to women, simply because they are women, full citizenship stature—equal opportunity to aspire, achieve, participate in and contribute to society based on their individual talents and capacities.

Without equating gender classifications, for all purposes, to classifications based on race or national origin, the Court, in post-*Reed* decisions, has carefully inspected official action that closes a door or denies opportunity to women (or to men). To summarize the Court's current directions for cases of official classification based on gender: Focusing on the differential treatment or denial of opportunity for which relief is sought, the reviewing court must determine whether the proffered justification is "exceedingly persuasive." The burden of justification is demanding and it rests entirely on the State. The State must show "at least that the [challenged] classification serves 'important governmental objectives and that the discriminatory means employed' are 'substantially related to the achievement of those objectives.'" The justification must be genuine, not hypothesized or invented post hoc in response to litigation. And it must not rely on overbroad generalizations about the different talents, capacities, or preferences of males and females.

The heightened review standard our precedent establishes does not make sex a proscribed classification. Supposed "inherent differences" are no longer accepted as a ground for race or national origin classifications. Physical differences between men and women, however, are enduring: "[T]he two sexes are not fungible; a community made up exclusively of one [sex] is different from a community composed of both."

"Inherent differences" between men and women, we have come to appreciate, remain cause for celebration, but not for denigration of the members of either sex or for artificial constraints on an individual's opportunity. Sex classifications may be used to compensate women "for particular economic disabilities [they have] suffered," to "promot[e] equal employment opportunity," to advance full development of the talent and capacities of our Nation's people. But such classifications may not be used, as they once were, to create or perpetuate the legal, social, and economic inferiority of women.

Measuring the record in this case against the review standard just described, we conclude that Virginia has shown no "exceedingly persuasive justification" for excluding all women from the citizen-soldier training afforded by VMI....

Single-sex education affords pedagogical benefits to at least some students, Virginia emphasizes, and that reality is uncontested in this litigation. Similarly, it is not disputed that diversity among public educational institutions can serve the public good. But Virginia has not shown that VMI was established, or has been maintained, with a view to diversifying, by its categorical exclusion of women, educational opportunities within the State. In cases of this genre, our precedent instructs that "benign" justifications proffered in defense of categorical exclusions will not be accepted automatically; a tenable justification must describe actual state purposes, not rationalizations for actions in fact differently grounded....

Ultimately, in 1970, "the most prestigious institution of higher education in Virginia," the University of Virginia, introduced coeducation and, in 1972, began to admit women on an equal basis with men. A three-judge Federal District Court confirmed: "Virginia may not now deny to women, on the basis of sex, educational opportunities at the Charlottesville campus that are not afforded in other institutions operated by the [S]tate."...

VMI, too, offers an educational opportunity no other Virginia institution provides, and the school's "prestige"—associated with its success in developing "citizen-soldiers"—is unequaled. Virginia has closed this facility to its daughters and, instead, has devised for them a "parallel program," with a faculty less impressively credentialed and less well paid, more limited course offerings, fewer opportunities for military training and for scientific specialization. VMI, beyond question, "possesses to a far greater degree" than the VWIL program "those qualities which are incapable of objective measurement but which make for greatness in a … school," including "position and influence of the alumni, standing in the community, traditions and prestige." Women seeking and fit for a VMI-quality education cannot be offered anything less, under the State's obligation to afford them genuinely equal protection.

## GLOSSARY

**en banc:** literally, "on the bench"; refers to a case heard with the judges sitting together.

**endowment:** the reserve of money and investments used to help fund an institution such as a college or university.

**fungible:** interchangeable.

**proscribed:** prohibited.

***Reed***: *Reed v. Reed*, a 1971 Supreme Court ruling overturning an Idaho law giving men preference over women as estate administrators.

**remanding:** sending back to a lower court for further consideration.

**spartan:** barren, primitive.

## Document Analysis

In this highly publicized 1996 case, Ginsburg, writing the majority opinion, had the opportunity to apply her knowledge and passion for gender equality to the postsecondary education context. This case involved a Fourteenth Amendment equal protection challenge by the United States to the Commonwealth of Virginia and the Virginia Military Institute, a public all-male military college. It was prompted by a complaint filed with the United States' Attorney General by a female high-school student seeking admission to VMI. In her majority opinion, Ginsburg was very clear that Virginia had not met either of the possible criteria which might allow the existence of VMI as a single sex institution. Virginia did not demonstrate that the "diversity" created by VMI contributed to the commonwealth's system of higher education (or even that VMI was intended to promote diversity), nor that there was any "persuasive justification" for VMI's current single-gender status.

VMI was the only single-sex public institution of higher education in Virginia. Established in 1839, the school has the mission to create "citizen soldiers" and, as Ginsburg described it, as a place which was intended to strengthen a student physically, mentally, and morally. Ginsburg wrote, in her opinion, that the challenges which composed the VMI educational experience allowed the graduate to understand their limits, as well as to have pride in what was accomplished in the four years at VMI. This type of education, was based on the English public school model, and once was common to military instruction. Ginsburg described it as being similar to the environment of a boot camp, VMI argued that this was not suitable to a co-educational environment in general, and specifically to female cadets.

The U.S. Attorney General, representing the woman who desired to attend VMI, was unsuccessful at the district court level. However, after this ruling for VMI, an appeal to the U.S. Court of Appeals for the Fourth Circuit reversed the decision and ordered the Commonwealth of Virginia to remedy the constitutional violation. Virginia responded with plans to create a school for women, the VWIL. The district and appeals courts then found the proposed remedy to be constitutional. At that point, the case was appealed to the U.S. Supreme Court, by the Attorney General.

Ginsburg noted that the attributes needed to succeed in an environment such as VMI, were not limited to males. From testimonies given by individuals on both sides of the case, she understood that VMI's goal of producing leaders and the means by which this was attained, was suitable for men and women, and that there were individuals from both sexes who desired to participate in this opportunity. Nonetheless, Ginsburg continued on, "Virginia has elected to preserve exclusively for men the advantages and opportunities a VMI education affords." She noted that at the district court level, experts testified that since the army had become much more inclusive of women, having women attend VMI would help train future leaders for this type of environment.

VMI argued that a single-sex, all-male public college (the only one in Virginia) provided diversity to an otherwise co-educational Virginia system, and served an important governmental interest. The Commonwealth of Virginia proposed a parallel program for women, which Ginsburg asserted was akin to the all-black colleges proposed by segregated southern universities in the 1940s and early 1950s in response to equal protection challenges. Virginia proposed the creation of the Virginia Women's Institute for Leadership, to be located at Mary Baldwin College, a private liberal arts school for women. The district court, treating VMI deferentially, found that Virginia's proposal satisfied the Constitution's equal protection requirement. The Fourth Circuit affirmed, applying the test of whether VMI and Virginia Women's Institute for Leadership students would receive "substantively comparable" benefits. The U.S. Supreme Court, disagreed with the Fourth Circuit, and held that the appropriate standard when a sex-based classification was used is, as Ginsburg states, "an exceedingly persuasive justification."

Ginsburg emphasized that substantively speaking, the parallel program did not compare with that of VMI. She noted that the program's curriculum was limited in comparison with VMI's. At least initially, the women's institute would offer only the Bachelor of Arts degree, while VMI could offer degrees in the arts, sciences, and engineering. In addition, the resources which were to be committed to the women's school were much less, as illustrated that even after the transfer of some funds from VMI to VWIL, the VWIL endowment would be about 100 million dollars less than that of VMI. The students already at the proposed location of VWIL statistically were not as strong academically, and the faculty (due to lower salaries) did not have as much graduate training as the faculty at VMI. Ginsburg argued that the proposal that female applicants to Virginia Women's Institute for Leadership would have a "substantively comparable" experience and degree was not supported by the numbers or by history. Virginia argued that VMI's all-male student body was an important source of diversity, for it gave the state's students an alternative type of institution to attend. Ginsburg, however, emphasized that recent history undermined this argument. It was the standard until relatively recently to segregate women from male university students and that after decades of slow change, Virginia's most prestigious institution of higher education, the University of Virginia, introduced co-education and in 1972, began to admit women on an equal basis with men.

Referring to precedent, Ginsburg cited *Reed v. Reed*, a 1971 case in which the Court struck down an Idaho law that said that males must be preferred to females where several equally entitled persons are claiming to administer a decedent's estate. For Ginsburg and the majority of the court, this ruling, in favor of the woman, demonstrated that women could not arbitrarily be denied equal protection under a state's laws. Ginsburg noted that the heightened level of scrutiny used for Court review of gender classifications did not equate for all purposes with other forms of discrimination, such as that based on race or ethnicity. However, denial of equal opportunity based on gender had been an ongoing concern of the courts. Ginsburg did recognize that there are differences between men and women, but these should not be used to "to create or perpetuate the legal, social, and economic inferiority of women."

Ginsburg agreed with Virginia that there have been benefits demonstrated pedagogically for single-sex education, but that was not the issue under review. She argued, though, that legal precedent required that Virginia's reasons for using a gender-based classification not be accepted automatically but must be shown to have a "tenable justification" that described a real purpose for the single-sex institute. She argued that on this important element of the law, Virginia's rationale for the benefits of single-sex education was not tenable and thus was discriminatory in violation of the equal protection clause.

Ginsburg understood and emphasized that VMI had a tradition and educational experience different from any other institution of higher education in Virginia. But, she also understood and wrote that historically, Virginia had not allowed women to participate in this educational opportunity. In addition, she asserted that the proposed educational experience at the VWIL would be quite inferior to that offered by VMI, at least in the foreseeable future. Thus, she concluded, "Women seeking and fit for a VMI-quality education cannot be offered anything less, under the State's obligation to afford them genuinely equal protection."

When Ginsburg analyzed the case, as the justice writing the majority opinion, there were several steps necessary in considering whether or not keeping VMI a single-sex institution was legal. In the minds of the majority of the Court members, none of these things created a situation justifying allowing VMI to remain all male. While the style of the educational experience was extreme, within the scope of U.S. higher education, being a woman did not automatically keep a woman from being able to achieve the goals. Some women have expressed interest in being a part of the VMI educational community, which gave them standing to pursue the case. For Ginsburg, and the others, there was no overriding benefit to the commonwealth, or its citizens, which justified the discriminatory status of not allowing women to attend VMI. The alternative proposed by Virginia was not a realistic comparable experience, nor was it going to be supported in a manner equal to VMI. Finally, a situation in which a woman was denied entry because she is a woman, meant that the educational opportunity which this admission entailed could never be achieved. All of these combined to demonstrate to Ginsburg that VMI should be open to both men and women as a matter of law, as well as social equality.

## Essential Themes

The basic underlying question before the Supreme Court in the *United States v. Virginia* was, given the 14th Amendment, is it possible for higher education supported with public funds to automatically exclude individuals who were not of a specific gender, in this instance, not men? Related to this was the question of whether the answer to the basic question could be altered if an opportunity for a similar educational experience were given to those excluded. In this case, Virginia was offering to establish the VWIL, if the commonwealth was allowed to keep VMI all male.

The fact that all other publically-funded institutions of higher education (with the exception of the Citadel which had a concurrent case in the federal judiciary) had become coeducational more than a decade prior to this, gave an indication as to how the court might rule. Although judicial decisions do not always seem to be straightforward, the final sentence of Section 1 of the 14th Amendment was the foundation for the majority opinion. It reads, "No State shall . . . deny to any person within its jurisdiction the equal protection of the laws." In the *United States v. Virginia* this was interpreted to mean that both men and women had to be admitted as students to VMI.

Virginia had argued that, as with certain other amendments, the 14th Amendment did not have to be interpreted in such an absolute manner. It had suggested the creation of the VWIL as a means to grant an equal educational possibility for women. While Ginsburg outlined ways in which the proposed institute would not have been equal to VMI, that was only a secondary support to one of the main arguments in her opinion. For Ginsburg, and the others supporting the majority opinion, the VWIL was unnecessary, because it was possible for women to meet the standards for admission and for the successful completion of the educational program at VMI. Given this, "equal protection of the laws" was clearly interpreted as allowing all individuals who qualified the opportunity to be a part of the student body at VMI.

Justice Anthony Scalia, the only one of the eight participating justices issuing a dissenting opinion, rejected the majority opinion because he rejected change forced upon institutions by the courts. (Scalia accepted the changes at the federal military institutions because it had been based on legislation.) He also accepted the argument that Virginia had an "important state interest" in having an all-male school, which in this case, overrode a literal reading of "equal protection of the laws." However, it is clear that the 7-1 vote by the members of the Court demonstrated that they accepted Ginsburg's interpretation rather than Scalia's. Thus, the discussion of "equal protection" in terms of public higher education was decided in favor of inclusiveness. The automatic exclusion of individuals from this type of publically-funded educational program, due solely to their gender, was found to be unconstitutional.

*—Donald A. Watt, PhD*

## Bibliography and Additional Readings

Bartlett, Katherine T. "Unconstitutionally Male? The Story of United States v. Virginia." *Duke Law Working Paper*. Paper 12. Durham: Duke Law School, 2010. Web. 8 August 2017.

Brodie, Laura Fairchild. *Breaking Out: VMI and the Coming of Women*. New York: Vintage Books, 2001. Print.

Diamond, Diane and Michael Kimmel. "'Toxic Virus' or Lady Virtue." *Going Coed: Women's Experiences in Formerly Men's Colleges and Universities, 1950-2000*. Leslie Miller-Bernal and Susan L. Poulson, eds. Nashville: Vanderbilt University Press, 2004. Print and Web. (Google Books) 8 August 2017.

Huffman, Brian. "United States v. Virginia Case Summary." *UH Law Library*. Honolulu: William S. Richardson School of Law Law Library, 2017. Web. 7 August 2017.

Legal Law Institute. "United States v. Virginia et al. (94-1941), 518 U.S. 515 (1996)." *Legal Law Institute*. Ithaca: Cornell University Law School, 2017. Web. 8 August 2017.

Oyez. "United States v. Virginia." *Oyez*. Chicago: Cornell's Legal Information Institute, Justia, and Chicago-Kent College of Law, 2017. Web. 7 August 2017.

Strum, Philippa. *Women in the Barracks: The VMI Case and Equal Rights*. Lawrence: University of Kansas Press. 2002. Print.

# ■ Ruth Bader Ginsburg: Concurrence in *Stenberg, Attorney General of Nebraska, v. Carhart*

**Date:** June 28, 2000
**Author:** Ruth Bader Ginsburg
**Genre:** Court opinion

## Summary Overview

The case of *Stenberg, Attorney General of Nebraska, v. Carhart* dealt with a Nebraska law that made it illegal to perform a second-trimester abortion, except when it was deemed necessary to save the life of the mother. It was one of a number of cases which came before the federal courts during the 1990s, as "right-to-life" groups pushed state legislatures to pass a variety of laws which they hoped would limit the freedom of women to choose to have an abortion, or overturn the legality of abortions completely. Their goal was to find a law limiting abortion which would be ruled constitutional and become the template for laws in other jurisdictions.

As with many other attempts, Justice Stephen Breyer, writing for the majority, stated that any abortion law that imposed an undue burden on a woman's "right to choose" (abortion) was unconstitutional. In writing this, he included this Nebraska law. On the issue of abortion rights, Ginsburg had been critical of the Court's decision in the landmark 1973 case, *Roe v. Wade*, arguing that the decision contributed to divisiveness about abortion in the ensuing decades. However, she sided with the majority in *Stenberg*, writing in her concurrence that the state was not interested in saving the life of the fetus, but rather in limiting a woman's right to choose. Her disagreement with the wording of *Roe v. Wade* was not a disagreement with the legal precedent establishing abortion as a legal right for women.

## Defining Moment

In 1973, the Supreme Court finally ruled on *Roe v. Wade*, which recognized a woman's right to abortion under the right to privacy, as developed by previous court rulings. Dividing pregnancy into trimesters, the court allowed for certain, but undefined, regulations and restrictions for the second and third trimesters. Guidance was given in the 1992 ruling in *Planned Parenthood of Southeast Pennsylvania v. Casey*, when the idea of placing an "undue burden," or a "substantial obstacle," became the test to be imposed on any abortion regulations proposed by a state. The Nebraska legislature sought to regulate second trimester abortions when it passed a law prohibiting "partial birth abortions." The statute included a definition of what constituted a "partial birth abortion," although in some sections of the law, including defining the terms used in defining "partial birth abortion," there was a lack of clarity. The law only allowed an exception if the mother's life was in danger.

*Stenberg v. Carhart* became the test case for very restrictive abortion, which essentially outlawed an abortion procedure used in some second trimester abortions. It was understood that throughout the whole range of health care not all medical procedures are equally as effective for the variety of patients/clients in need of medical attention. In the majority opinion, the fact that the vast number of abortions were not "partial birth abortions" did not affect the merits of the case. Justice Ginsburg, as a member of the majority, supported the concept that outlawing one form of abortion, even if it were rarely used, was taking away a constitutional right from the few women in need of this procedure. Thus, Ginsburg ruled that the law was unconstitutional and emphasized her support for this position by writing a concurring opinion. This ruling continued to uphold the legally of abortion and forced anti-abortion legislators to seek other ways in which to limit the practice. However, by upholding the "undue burden" principle, the legislators' task became much more difficult.

## Author Biography

Ruth Bader was born on March 15, 1933, in Brooklyn, New York. She graduated from Cornell University in 1954 and that year married Martin Ginsburg, a classmate. She enrolled at Harvard Law School, but after her husband found employment with a New York City law firm, she transferred to Columbia University, where she graduated tied for first in her class, in 1959. That year she accepted a two-year clerkship for U.S. District

Commissioned portrait of Ginsburg in 2000. By Simmie Knox, under commission of the United States Supreme Court.

Court Judge Edmund L. Palmieri in New York. After working on the Columbia Law School Project on International Procedure from 1961 to 1963, Ginsburg accepted a post as a law professor at Rutgers University, where she taught until 1972. She also served as volunteer counsel to the New Jersey chapter of the American Civil Liberties Union (ACLU). At the ACLU, Ginsburg litigated sex discrimination cases and cofounded the Women's Rights Project. Ironically, during her time at Rutgers she became pregnant with her son, James, and because she was not tenured, she concealed her pregnancy with oversized clothes. In 1972 Ginsburg accepted a position at Columbia University, the law school's first woman with the rank of full professor.

Ruth Bader Ginsburg's early commitment to women's rights and equality was perhaps forged when the dean of Harvard Law School asked her and her eight female classmates why they were taking up seats at the school that rightly should be occupied by men. If that were not enough, she was unable to win a clerkship for a U.S.

Supreme Court justice because of her gender, and she did not receive a job offer from the New York City firm where she clerked during the summer before her final year in law school. Then, after she took a teaching position at the Rutgers University Law School, she discovered that she was being paid less than male colleagues with the same rank. These circumstances motivated Ginsburg's preoccupation with civil rights generally and the rights of women in particular.

In 1980, President Jimmy Carter nominated Ginsburg as a justice on the U.S. Court of Appeals for the District of Columbia. Then, in 1993, President Bill Clinton nominated her to replace Justice Byron White on the U.S. Supreme Court. Ginsburg's reputation as a moderate on the U.S. Court of Appeals was helpful to her confirmation. In her years on the Supreme Court, her written decisions in numerous key cases made her a leading voice for gender equality in the judicial branch, thus expanding the rights of the American public, including both women and men.

## HISTORICAL DOCUMENT

I write separately only to stress that amidst all the emotional uproar caused by an abortion case, we should not lose sight of the character of Nebraska's "partial birth abortion" law. As the Court observes, this law does not save any fetus from destruction, for it targets only "a *method* of performing abortion." Nor does the statute seek to protect the lives or health of pregnant women. Moreover, as Justice Stevens points out, the most common method of performing previability second trimester abortions is no less distressing or susceptible to gruesome description. Seventh Circuit Chief Judge Posner correspondingly observed, regarding similar bans in Wisconsin and Illinois, that the law prohibits the D & X procedure "not because the procedure kills the fetus, not because it risks worse complications for the woman than alternative procedures would do, not because it is a crueler or more painful or more

disgusting method of terminating a pregnancy." Rather, Chief Judge Posner commented, the law prohibits the procedure because the State legislators seek to chip away at the private choice shielded by *Roe v. Wade*, even as modified by *Casey*.

A state regulation that "has the purpose or effect of placing a substantial obstacle in the path of a woman seeking an abortion of a nonviable fetus" violates the Constitution. Such an obstacle exists if the State stops a woman from choosing the procedure her doctor "reasonably believes will best protect the woman in [the] exercise of [her] constitutional liberty." Again as stated by Chief Judge Posner, "if a statute burdens constitutional rights and all that can be said on its behalf is that it is the vehicle that legislators have chosen for expressing their hostility to those rights, the burden is undue."

---

## GLOSSARY

**D & X procedure:** dilation and extraction, a method of performing abortion, generally between the twentieth and twenty-fourth weeks after conception, consisting of expansion of the cervix and removal of the fetus in sections; also a method used to remove a deceased fetus from the uterus of the mother

**Previability:** with respect to a fetus, the state of not yet being able to sustain life outside the womb

**Seventh Circuit Chief Judge Posner:** Richard Posner (1939–), a judge of the Seventh Circuit Court of Appeals (Chicago) from 1991 and chief judge from 1993 to 2000

---

### Document Analysis

Justice Ginsburg wrote her concurring opinion to emphasize the aspects of the case which she believed needed to be the central points of the legal opinion. Although she did not contradict any portion of the majority opinion written by Justice Stephen Breyer, Ginsburg believed that it needed to be clearly stated that the only reason the law was passed by the Nebraska legislator, in her opinion, was as an attempt to open courts to the possibility of narrowing the rights upheld in *Roe v. Wade*. She believed, and wrote in her concurrence, that there were no medical reasons for the law; it was only an attempt at social engineering. Not allowing a woman and her doctor to choose the best procedure for terminating her pregnancy was an unacceptable limitation.

In this case, the Court revisited abortion, an issue important to Ginsburg's concern with gender equality. The case addressed the right of states to ban a particular type of abortion procedure called a "partial-birth" abortion. This phrase has been widely used in the media to refer to a procedure that medical practitioners call an "intact dilation and extraction." It refers to one form by which late-term abortions are performed. As such, the matter has been highly controversial, with opponents of "partial-birth" abortion seeing it as akin to infanticide. This appeal challenged a Nebraska law that outlawed partial-birth abortions. Justice Stephen Breyer, writing for the five-to-four majority, struck down the Nebraska law. The core of his argument was that the law criminalized "partial-birth" abortions in violation of the due process clause of the Fourteenth Amendment to the Constitution. Citing such precedent-setting cases as *Roe v. Wade* (1973) and *Planned Parenthood v. Casey* (1993), the Court majority maintained that Nebraska law placed an "undue burden" on a woman's right to an abortion.

Ginsburg voted with the majority, but in addition, she wrote a concurrence with the majority's decision because she wanted "only to stress that amidst all the emotional uproar caused by an abortion case, we should not lose sight of the character of Nebraska's 'partial birth abortion' law." She stated that a faithful reading of the law made it clear that it would not necessarily stop an abortion, since it was only a specific medical procedure which was being outlawed. This, in her understanding, would not improve the woman's health, nor was the procedure being outlawed more likely to cause a woman's death. Ginsburg asserted that the important issue in this case was not that this form of abortion was any more gruesome than other forms of abortion but rather that with such bans, states sought to *limit* a woman's choice. She added that any type of second trimester abortion could be seen as a "gruesome" procedure. As Ginsburg wrote, any abortion in the second trimester could cause "distress," not just those performed with the procedure which Nebraska sought to outlaw. Thus, underlying her opinion was the understanding that if this form of abortion was limited, it was quite probable that laws outlawing more common forms of abortion would quickly follow.

Ginsburg was careful to use the important term "previability" when describing the fetus in partial-birth abortions. She referred to *Planned Parenthood v. Casey*, when she reaffirmed that states could not constitutionally impose a "substantial obstacle" to a woman seeking to have an abortion. Similar to her own use of the term "previability", Ginsburg's quotation from the previous decision included its use of the term "nonviable fetus." Noting the importance of choice, and in particular deference to the judgment of medical professionals, she wrote that limiting the types of procedures which could be used in the abortion, was limiting the woman's right to the best possible medical care and her constitutional rights. Ginsburg's careful jurisprudence was apparent here as she took care to emphasize a particular aspect of the majority opinion in order to ensure that it did not get lost in the broader ruling.

Ginsburg sought to put state legislatures on notice, that any attempt to limit the availability of abortions would be opposed by her. Any law touching on the subject, which did not have a strong medical foundation would be understood by Ginsburg as an attempt to limit the constitutional rights of women. Although she believed that *Roe v. Wade* had some flaws, the basic rights affirmed in that case were, for Ginsburg, to be protected from all encroachment.

## Essential Themes

Ginsburg's advocacy on behalf of gender equality represents the common role that civil rights activists have played in American law. Advocating on behalf of those on the margins American society, individuals, such as Ginsburg, sought to extend basic rights to the mainstream of American society. The chief impact of her tenure on the Court of Appeals and on the Supreme Court was to extend the due process and equal protection clauses of the Fourteenth Amendment to matters of gender equality; prior to Ginsburg's efforts, there had been little effort to extend these kinds of constitutional protections to women.

Ginsburg's concern with the civil rights of women extended to other groups. She generally has been regarded as a liberal judge on a wide range of social and criminal issues. She has widely been noted for the deference she has shown to the legal systems and laws of other nations, arguing that U.S. law, where possible, should harmonize with international law. She believes that the laws of other nations—on such issues as the war against terrorism, the treatment of enemy combatants, or the use of torture in interrogating terrorism suspects—has contributed to evolving standards of what is morally, ethically, and legally right and that the United States can and should be at least in part guided by these standards.

In *Stenberg v. Carhart*, Ginsburg voted, and wrote, about the importance of not limiting a woman's freedom of choice in one particular medical procedure, an abortion. After this ruling, states which wanted to limit women's access to abortion, had to use other means to do this. A secondary result of the ruling was that appointments to the Supreme Court became even more politicized than in the past. The hope of many anti-abortion groups has been that eventually the membership on the Court would change enough that the justices would vote to limit or outlaw abortions. Thus, deducing a nominee's position on this issue has become a focal point in the appointment process. Such a change occurred prior to hearing a case involving a federal law similar to his one, and in *Gonzales v. Carhart*, the Supreme Court held that the law was constitutional. Whether or not further changes are ever made to the constitutional protection of a woman's right to an abortion, Justice Ginsburg has made her position on the subject very clear, and has offered strong guidance for future courts as they examined legislation dealing with medical procedures.

—*Michael Chang, Michael J. O'Neal, PhD, and Donald A. Watt, PhD*

## Bibliography and Additional Reading

C SPAN. "Supreme Court Oral Argument: Stenberg v. Carhart, April 25, 2000." *C-SPAN*. Washington: National Cable Satellite Corporation, 2017. Web. 24 October 2017.

Ginsburg, Ruth Bader with Mary Hartnett and Wendy W. Williams. *My Own Words: Ruth Bader Ginsburg*. New York: Simon & Schuster, 2016. Print.

Hirshman, Linda. *Sisters in Law: How Sandra Day O'Connor and Ruth Bader Ginsburg Went to the Supreme Court and Changed the World*. New York: HarperCollins, 2015. Print.

Justia. "Stenberg v. Carhart: 530 U.S. 914 (2000)." *Justia*. Mountain View: Justia, 2017. Web. 24 October 2017.

Oyez. *Body Politic: The Supreme Court and Abortion Law*. Chicago: Oyez and the Institute on the Supreme Court of the United States, 2017. Web. 22 October 2017.

# ■ European Union: Summary of Directive on Gender Equality

**Date:** July 5, 2006
**Author:** European Parliament and Council of the European Union
**Genre:** Legislation

## Summary Overview

Gender inequality is a pervasive problem in Europe, as it is in the United States. The directive that is summarized in this entry is an attempt by the European Union to combat this problem. The EU issued this directive in 2006. Its stated goal was to coordinate and simplify previous directives on gender equality, as well as provide a more comprehensive vision for achieving this elusive end. The directive was written by the European Parliament and the Council of the European Union, the two major decision making bodies of the European Union. The directive outlines the areas in which gender equality is to be sought. It also puts forward procedures for empowering victims of gender discrimination, as well as bodies to oversee and manage all of these efforts.

## Defining Moment

The European Union has long made gender equality a priority. In 1957, the Treaty of Rome established the predecessor to the European Union, the European Economic Community, made up of Belgium, France, Italy, Luxembourg, the Netherlands and West Germany. The Treaty of Rome itself included the principle of equal pay for equal work. A number of directives aimed at curbing gender discrimination followed. A 1978 directive aimed to secure equality for women and men in the matter of social security. A 1992 directive introduced measures to help keep pregnant, recently pregnant, and nursing women safe in the workplace. After the official founding of the European Union, more directives followed. In 2004, a directive codified the principle of equality "in the access to and supply of goods and services."

The 2006 directive featured in this chapter sought to consolidate these previous measures and provide a more comprehensive approach to gender equality. After this landmark directive, other directives have attempted to shore up details. One 2010 directive strove to standardize parental leave policies, and another one from the same year took on gender discrimination among self-employed individuals. The results have been mixed. For example, the European Union began issuing yearly reports on the gender pay gap, the difference in pay that a man and a woman receive for doing the same work. The close monitoring of this statistic and the European Union's commitment to decreasing this gap are promising signs, as is the modest decline in the estimated rate. Despite these positives, according to the European Union itself the pay gap as of January 2017 was still at 16.3 percent. The stubborn persistence of the pay gap shows the difficulty in combating both this specific form of inequality as well as other, similar entrenched types of gender discrimination.

## Author Biography

The official authors of this legislative document are the European Parliament and the Council of the European Union, two official bodies of the EU. The Parliament consists of seven-hundred-and-fifty-one members elected by direct election every five years; the Council of the European Union is made up of ministers sent from all of the member nations. Together the Parliament and the Council comprise the two main decision making bodies of the European Union, and both bodies predate the European Union itself. The European Parliament was established in 1952 as the Common Assembly of the European Coal and Steel Community. It became the European Parliament in 1962 and held its first elections in 1979. The Council was formed in 1958 as the Council of the European Economic Community, one year after the Treaty of Rome formed this predecessor to the European Union. Not until 1993 did the Maastricht Treaty officially form the European Union. The European Union has since expanded its membership. The issuing of Euro banknotes starting in 2002 has further consolidated its members. Great Britain's vote to leave the European Union on June 23, 2016 has challenged but not fatally harmed the EU's strength.

Anti-dowry poster in Bangalore, India. According to Amnesty International, "[T]he ongoing reality of dowry-related violence is an example of what can happen when women are treated as property." By tara hunt from San Francisco, USA (Say no to dowry) [CC BY-SA 2.0 (https://creativecommons.org/licenses/by-sa/2.0)]

## HISTORICAL DOCUMENT

Summary of DIRECTIVE 2006/54/EC OF THE EUROPEAN PARLIAMENT AND OF THE COUNCIL

of 5 July 2006

on the implementation of the principle of equal opportunities and equal treatment of men and women in matters of employment and occupation (recast)

The objective of this Directive is to consolidate several directives on gender equality by simplifying, modernising and improving EU legislation in the area of equal treatment for men and women in employment.

### SUMMARY

Equality between men and women is a fundamental principle of EU law which applies to all aspects of life in society, including to the world of work.

**Equality in employment and working conditions**
This Directive prohibits direct* or indirect discrimination* between men and women concerning the conditions of:

recruitment, access to employment and self-employment;
dismissals;
vocational training and promotion;
membership of workers' or employers' organisations.

In addition, Article 157 of the Treaty on the Functioning of the EU prohibits discrimination on grounds of sex on matters of pay for the same work or work of equal value. This principle also applies to job classification systems used for determining pay.

However, different treatment for men and women may be justified by reason of the nature of the particular occupational activity, if the measures taken are legitimate and proportionate.

EU countries must encourage employers and vocational trainers to act against discrimination (both direct and indirect) on grounds of sex, and particularly against harassment* and sexual harassment*.

**Equality in social protection**
Women and men are treated equally under occupational social security schemes, particularly concerning:

the scope and conditions of access to the schemes;
the contributions;
the calculation of benefits, including supplementary benefits, and the conditions governing the duration and retention of entitlement.

This principle applies to the whole working population, including:

self-employed workers, however for this category EU countries may provide for different treatment, in particular concerning the age of retirement;
workers whose activity is interrupted by illness, maternity, accident or involuntary unemployment;
persons seeking employment, retired and disabled workers, and those claiming under them.

**Maternal, paternal and adoption leave**
At the end of maternal, paternal or adoption leave, employees have the right to:

return to their jobs or to equivalent posts on conditions which are no less favourable to them;
benefit from any improvement in working conditions to which they would have been entitled during their absence.

**Defence of rights**
EU countries must put in place remedies for employees who have been victims of discrimination, such as conciliation and judicial procedures. In addition, they shall take the necessary measures to protect employees and their representatives against

adverse treatment as a reaction to a complaint within the company or to any legal proceedings.

Lastly, they shall establish penalties and reparation or compensation possibilities in relation to the damage sustained.

In the case of legal proceedings, the burden of proof is on the party accused of discrimination who must prove that there has been no breach of the principle of equal treatment.

**Promoting equal treatment**
EU countries appoint bodies whose role it is to promote, analyse and monitor equal treatment, to ensure that the legislation is followed and also to provide independent support to victims of discrimination.

In addition, enterprises must promote the principle of gender equality and strengthen the role of social partners and non-governmental organisations.

## GLOSSARY

**Direct discrimination:** where one person is treated less favourably on grounds of sex than another is, has been or would be treated in a comparable situation.

**Indirect discrimination:** where an apparently neutral provision, criterion or practice would put persons of one sex at a particular disadvantage compared with persons of the other sex, unless that provision, criterion or practice is objectively justified by a legitimate aim, and the means of achieving that aim are appropriate and necessary.

**Harassment:** where unwanted conduct related to the sex of a person occurs with the purpose or effect of violating the dignity of a person, and of creating an intimidating, hostile, degrading, humiliating or offensive environment.

**Sexual harassment:** where any form of unwanted verbal, non-verbal or physical conduct of a sexual nature occurs, with the purpose or effect of violating the dignity of a person, in particular when creating an intimidating, hostile, degrading, humiliating or offensive environment.

## Document Analysis

This document is the European Union's summary of its 2006 directive. Despite it's brevity, the document outlines what the directive hope to enact and explains how it intends to do so.

The opening of the document includes a programmatic statement clearly laying out the intent of the directive: "The objective of this Directive is to consolidate several directives on gender equality by simplifying, modernising and improving EU legislation in the area of equal treatment for men and women in employment." This statement indicates that this is not the first directive on gender equality but that the previous directives were not sufficient. The next section, titled "SUMMARY," continues to specify what the directive will enact. It reads "Equality between men and women is a fundamental principle of EU law which applies to all aspects of life in society, including to the world of

work." This latter statement underscores the importance which the European Union places on gender equality and also specifies that this directive will focus on gender equality in the workplace.

Following this opening, the document is divided into five main sections, followed by background, and key terms sections as well as a reiteration of the act's title and number. The first three main sections outline the areas that the directive covers. The first requires equal treatment "in employment and working conditions." This includes recruitment, dismissal, and training. The authors cite a previous treaty which prohibits pay discrimination; this directive clarifies that this article also applies to job classification systems which dictate pay. The second section calls or equal treatment "in social protection," which is in reference to "occupational social security schemes." The third section aims to ensure that men and women going on parental leave do not receive unfair discrimination while they are gone or upon their return.

The final two main sections seek to set effective mechanisms for the enforcement of the first three sections. The fourth section requires countries in the European Union to establish systems of recourse for victims of gender discrimination, "such as conciliation and judicial procedures." The directive goes further, attempting to shield victims who speak out from retaliation: "In addition, they shall take the necessary measures to protect employees and their representatives against adverse treatment as a reaction to a complaint within the company or to any legal proceedings." This section further includes a call for countries to set penalties and compensation, and it even places the burden of proof on the party accused. The fifth and final section complements the fourth. It calls for countries to appoint bodies that can promote and oversee gender equality. These bodies can "ensure that the legislation is followed and also to provide independent support to victims of discrimination." These two sections reveal the authors' understanding that victims of gender discrimination face an uphill battle if they attempt to seek justice. The authors hope that these standardized systems can help lessen the burden placed on victims of gender discrimination and help to further promote gender equality.

## Essential Themes

The two themes of equality and enforcement come up throughout the document The former is the ideal which the direct strives to enact; the inclusion of the latter is a tacit acknowledgement that the attainment of that ideal will take serious effort.

The theme of equality is explicitly developed throughout the document, straight from the title which names "the principle of equal opportunities and equal treatment" between the genders in the workplace. Both "equality" and "equal treatment" are mentioned in the programmatic statement—or abstract—directly after the subject. Showcasing the centrality of the theme to the directive, the one sentence summary begins with the word "Equality," as do the next two section titles "Equality in employment and working conditions" and "Equality in social protection." Of course, the development of the theme of equality runs deeper then these mentions. The two sections whose titles begin with

"Equality" are devoted to promoting this concept within their given realms. Other sections that do not explicitly mention the theme are focused on promoting it. For example, the section entitled "Maternal, paternal and adoption leave" is no less concerned with equality than the two sections that precede it. It states that "At the end of maternal, paternal or adoption leave, employees have the right to: return to their jobs or to equivalent posts on conditions which are no less favourable to them." In other words, this section of the directive aims to ensure equal treatment for workers despite the disruption caused by parental leave.

While the theme of equality is the ideal for which the directive strives, the theme of enforcement stands as a stark reminder that the directive is operating in reality. The word enforcement does not appear in the document but stands as a blanket term for the procedures which the document sets up to attempt to achieve gender equality. One example comes in the "Defence of rights" section. It reads, "EU countries must put in place remedies for employees who have been victims of discrimination, such as conciliation and judicial procedures." Another example follows in the next section: "EU countries appoint bodies whose role it is to promote, analyse and monitor equal treatment, to ensure that the legislation is followed and also to provide independent support to victims of discrimination." As these two examples exhibit, enforcement procedures can differ broadly in form, yet they have the same goal: to help the ideal of gender equality materialize in the real world.

—*Anthony Vivian, MA*

## Bibliography and Additional Reading

Bohnet, Iris. *What Works: Gender Equality by Design*. Cambridge, MA: Belknap Press, 2016. Print.

European Union. "Directive 2006/54/EC of the European Parliament and of the Council." European Union.   http://eur-lex.europa.eu/legal-content/EN/TXT/?qid=1435216807215&uri=CELEX:32006L0054. Retrieved October 29, 2017. Web.

Kantola, J. *Gender and the European Union*. New York: Palgrave Macmillan, 2010. Print.

McClain, Linda C. & Joanna L. Grossman, eds. *Gender Equality: Dimensions of Women's Equal Citizenship*. Cambridge: Cambridge University Press, 2009. Print.

# ■ Malala Yousafzai: Address at the UN "Youth Takeover" Event

**Date:** July 12, 2013
**Author:** Malala Yousafzai
**Genre:** Address, political tract, petition

## Summary Overview

This speech, given by the teenage activist Malala Yousafzai, was part of a larger event hosted and promoted by the United Nations (the UN). This speech in particular focuses on the need for education, especially in childhood, in order to build a better world. Yousafzai focuses on several main points in order to make her argument: the desperate need to equal access to education around the world and across gender lines; the role of women independently and the role of government in the promotion of equal rights; the perversion of Islam by terrorists; and the need for love in place of hate regardless of boundaries created by gender, age, race, nationality, and faith. This UN event was called the "Youth Takeover" and gave a platform to the largest under 25 population the world has ever seen. This speech was one part of a larger idea to give voice to the younger generation in an attempt to better the world for the future.

## Defining Moment

This speech and the event "Youth Takeover of the UN" came at a pivotal time in world history, but is also modern enough to be considered part of current events. For the last three decades, especially intensifying around the turn of the century, radicalism and faith- and race-based divides have intensified in many places around the world. Many of these divides have turned to violent conflict, oftentimes based on misunderstandings or hatred of something different. As Malala Yousafzai states in her speech that a lack of education has drastic and terrible results. Specifically, she says, "Poverty, ignorance, injustice, racism and the deprivation of basic rights are the main problems faced by both men and women." By championing education for boys and girls everywhere, many world leaders believe that the future can have more understanding between people of different backgrounds, as well as more equality and opportunity.

This event included over 600 teenaged activists from around the world, including countries where activism and the education of girls is banned and punishable by death. The main goal was to urge the 193 countries of the United Nations to take decisive action and find ways to get education to children currently denied access. The United Nations was originally developed after World War II in order to prevent any other catastrophes of that size and scope, however, war is not the only peril for the world as a whole. According to many, the prohibition of education and the resulting ignorance could cause nearly as much damage. These teenagers came together at the United Nations building in New York City in order to share their own experiences and lay out ideas for the betterment of their world.

While it is not possible to tell, in the intervening few years, how much of a direct impact the Youth Takeover has had on international policy and governmental regulations concerning education, the very fact that such an event found a place in the homebase of the United Nations speaks volumes to the impact that young activists are having on the world. Even a decade ago, it would have been nearly impossible for a group of children (in the eyes of many legal institutions) to speak about issues so openly and powerfully.

## Author Biography

Malala Yousafzai is one of the world's most famous (and youngest) women's rights and child's rights activists. She was born in Mingora, Pakistan on July 12, 1997. She spent much of her childhood advocating for childhood education and defying the Taliban's ban on education for girls. This defiance led to the incident which brought her to popular international attention in 2012. On her way home from school, a Taliban soldier shot Malala in the head, attempting to carry out the death warrant sworn out on her. She fortunately survived and continues her struggle against inequality today.

Yousafzai at Women of the World Festival, 2014.

Due to her courage and unfailing spirit, Yousafzai was awarded Pakistan's National Youth Peace Prize in 2011 and the Nobel Peace Prize in 2014. In addition, she holds the distinction for youngest recipient of a Nobel Peace Award. She has since also published a book entitled *I Am Malala: The Girl Who Stood Up for Education and Was Shot by the Taliban*. Yousafzai gave this speech before the United Nations on her sixteenth birthday.

## HISTORICAL DOCUMENT

There are hundreds of Human rights activists and social workers who are not only speaking for human rights, but who are struggling to achieve their goals of education, peace and equality. Thousands of people have been killed by the terrorists and millions have been injured. I am just one of them.

So here I stand... one girl among many.

I speak—not for myself, but for all girls and boys.

I raise up my voice—not so that I can shout, but so that those without a voice can be heard.

Those who have fought for their rights:

- Their right to live in peace.

- Their right to be treated with dignity.

- Their right to equality of opportunity.

- Their right to be educated.

Dear Friends, on the 9th of October 2012, the Taliban shot me on the left side of my forehead. They shot my friends too. They thought that the bullets would silence us. But they failed. And then, out of that silence came, thousands of voices. The terrorists thought that they would change our aims and stop our ambitions but nothing changed in my life except this: Weakness, fear and hopelessness died. Strength, power and courage was born. I am the same Malala. My ambitions are the same. My hopes are the same. My dreams are the same.

Dear sisters and brothers, I am not against anyone. Neither am I here to speak in terms of personal revenge against the Taliban or any other terrorists group. I am here to speak up for the right of education of every child. I want education for the sons and the daughters of all the extremists especially the Taliban.

I do not even hate the Talib who shot me. Even if there is a gun in my hand and he stands in front of me. I would not shoot him. This is the compassion that I have learnt from Muhammad-the prophet of mercy, Jesus Christ and Lord Buddha. This is the legacy of change that I have inherited from Martin Luther King, Nelson Mandela and Muhammad Ali Jinnah. This is the philosophy of non-violence that I have learnt from Gandhi Jee, Bacha Khan and Mother Teresa. And this is the forgiveness that I have learnt from my mother and father. This is what my soul is telling me, be peaceful and love everyone.

Dear sisters and brothers, we realise the importance of light when we see darkness. We realise the importance of our voice when we are silenced. In the same way, when we were in Swat, the north of Pakistan, we realised the importance of pens and books when we saw the guns.

The wise saying, "The pen is mightier than sword" was true. The extremists are afraid of books and pens. The power of education frightens them. They are afraid of women. The power of the voice of women frightens them. And that is why they killed 14 innocent medical students in the recent attack in Quetta. And that is why they killed many female teachers and polio workers in Khyber Pukhtoon Khwa and FATA. That is why they are blasting schools every day. Because they were and they are

afraid of change, afraid of the equality that we will bring into our society.

I remember that there was a boy in our school who was asked by a journalist, "Why are the Taliban against education?" He answered very simply. By pointing to his book he said, "A Talib doesn't know what is written inside this book." They think that God is a tiny, little conservative being who would send girls to the hell just because of going to school. The terrorists are misusing the name of Islam and Pashtun society for their own personal benefits. Pakistan is peace-loving democratic country. Pashtuns want education for their daughters and sons. And Islam is a religion of peace, humanity and brotherhood. Islam says that it is not only each child's right to get education, rather it is their duty and responsibility.

Honourable Secretary General, peace is necessary for education. In many parts of the world especially Pakistan and Afghanistan; terrorism, wars and conflicts stop children to go to their schools. We are really tired of these wars. Women and children are suffering in many parts of the world in many ways. In India, innocent and poor children are victims of child labour. Many schools have been destroyed in Nigeria. People in Afghanistan have been affected by the hurdles of extremism for decades. Young girls have to do domestic child labour and are forced to get married at early age. Poverty, ignorance, injustice, racism and the deprivation of basic rights are the main problems faced by both men and women.

Dear fellows, today I am focusing on women's rights and girls' education because they are suffering the most. There was a time when women social activists asked men to stand up for their rights. But, this time, we will do it by ourselves. I am not telling men to step away from speaking for women's rights rather I am focusing on women to be independent to fight for themselves.

Dear sisters and brothers, now it's time to speak up.

So today, we call upon the world leaders to change their strategic policies in favour of peace and prosperity.

We call upon the world leaders that all the peace deals must protect women and children's rights.

A deal that goes against the dignity of women and their rights is unacceptable.

We call upon all governments to ensure free compulsory education for every child all over the world.

We call upon all governments to fight against terrorism and violence, to protect children from brutality and harm.

We call upon the developed nations to support the expansion of educational opportunities for girls in the developing world.

We call upon all communities to be tolerant—to reject prejudice based on cast, creed, sect, religion or gender. To ensure freedom and equality for women so that they can flourish. We cannot all succeed when half of us are held back.

We call upon our sisters around the world to be brave—to embrace the strength within themselves and realise their full potential.

Dear brothers and sisters, we want schools and education for every child's bright future. We will continue our journey to our destination of peace and education for everyone. No one can stop us. We will speak for our rights and we will bring change through our voice. We must believe in the power and the strength of our words. Our words can change the world.

Because we are all together, united for the cause of education. And if we want to achieve our goal, then let us empower ourselves with the weapon of knowledge and let us shield ourselves with unity and togetherness.

Dear brothers and sisters, we must not forget that millions of people are suffering from poverty, injustice and ignorance. We must not forget that millions of children are out of schools. We must not forget that our sisters and brothers are waiting for a bright peaceful future.

So let us wage a global struggle against illiteracy, poverty and terrorism and let us pick up our books and pens. They are our most powerful weapons.

One child, one teacher, one pen and one book can change the world.

Education is the only solution. Education First.

## Document Analysis

This core text from Malala Yousafzai's speech to the United Nations in 2013, focuses on several main ideas within her larger argument. She calls for women to work for the improvement of the lives of other women and girls, not to wait for anyone else to aid them. She calls for governments to be a driving force for change and to aid in areas where terrorism and instability prevents children from going to school or living normal lives. She also calls attention to the true nature of Islam--not a religion of hate and violence, but a religion that promotes brotherhood and unity.

Yousafzai straddles a delicate line in her speech. She calls on women to work for themselves and the improvement of their own gender. "There was a time when women social activists asked men to stand up for their rights. But, this time, we will do it by ourselves." But at the same time, she is asking for governmental assistance with these goals. "So today, we call upon the world leaders to change their strategic policies in favour of peace and prosperity." It could be seen as confusing--this seeming play on words in calling for independence then immediately asking for governments to step in. But Yousafzai is not naive. She knows that women must make strides forward. She knows that the teen activists to whom she is speaking must make strides forward. But she also knows that it is not enough to desire and work for change without the re-enforcement of governmental policy and strict implementation of laws. And that seems to be her main reason for coming before the UN--to ask the governmental heads of over 190 nations to find ways to help the world through promoting education for children, boy and girl alike.

Yousafzai also takes this opportunity to address, somewhat indirectly, the misconceptions that many people have about Islam and the main tenants of the religion. She openly states that terrorists pervert the true nature of Islam and use that perversion as a tool to create fear. In her own words, without terrorism, "Pakistan is peace-loving democratic country. Pashtuns want education for their daughters and sons. And Islam is a religion of peace, humanity and brotherhood. Islam says that it is not only each child's right to get education, rather it is their duty and responsibility." Terrorists, such as the Taliban, feed on ignorance and fear. They fear education, because it draws out the illogic and misrepresentation in their own actions. Yousafzai and others like her intend to end such barbarity by providing access to the greater world-history, politics, mathematics, and even art-letting no child be forced away from their potential.

## Essential Themes

The lasting significance of this speech has yet to be determined, but the main themes are enduring. Inclusivity. Education. Progress. Change, both on a micro- and a macro- level. This speech also functions as a call to arms, for Malala Yousafzai strongly encourages individuals to work for change and progress. But, unlike some activists, she does so without undermining the importance of working with governments and other groups which are able to influence the course of global politics. This mix of personal empowerment alongside institutional change and development seems to be the only way to make lasting progress on many of the world's problems.

Furthermore, she calls for multi-country, cross-race, cross-religion, unified work for the betterment of all--girls in Nigeria, Pakistan, India, and many other nations which are often left out of conversations or, at least, seriously underrepresented at such meetings. By working to break down barriers put up through politics and geography, Yousafzai attempts to encourage the world's youth to unite in their goals. This type of unification could be one of the only ways that freedom and equality can be inclusive. Through our modern age, social and civil rights have been highly dependant on race, wealth, and their attendant privilege. Any attempt to work through these barriers, to provide real equality, could bring promising change to the world as a whole.

The influence of Malala Yousafzai and the hundreds of teen activists who stood alongside her cannot be underestimated. As stated above, only within the last few years have such opportunities opened up for young activists. But through the impressive attendance and coverage by media networks, this influence can only continue to grow. Hopefully, this allows for a continuing change in the perspective of institutions, such as the UN, which will contribute to it taking the voices and experiences of young men and women into account and working to improve their lives in the coming years.

—*Anna Accettola, MA*

## Bibliography and Additional Resources

"At UN, Malala Yousafzai Rallies Youth to Stand up for Universal Education." UN News Center, United Nations, 12 July 2013, www.un.org/apps/news/story.asp?NewsID–45395#.WcGGrUuGPrc.

Fartyal, Sonu, and Poonam Prajapati. "Woman Empowerment through Education." Saving Humanity, G. B. Pant University, 2012, pp. 315–320.

Kettler, Sara. "Malala Yousafzai." Biography.com, A&E Networks Television, 17 Aug. 2017, www.biography.com/people/malala-yousafzai-21362253.

Sahni, Urvashi. Reaching for the Sky: Empowering Girls through Education. Brookings Institution Press, 2017.

Yousafzai, Malala, and Christina Lamb. I Am Malala: the Girl Who Stood up for Education and Was Shot by the Taliban. Weidenfeld & Nicolson, 2016.

# ■ Women in the Service Implementation Plan

**Date:** January 9, 2013
**Author:** Chairman of the Joint Chiefs of Staff General Martin E. Dempsey
**Genre:** Memorandum

## Summary Overview

In this document, General Martin Dempsey, chairman of the Joint Chiefs of Staff, recommends to Secretary of Defense Leon Panetta that the United States military's prohibition on women in combat roles should be lifted. In some capacity or another, women have served in every war that the United States of America has ever fought. Though restrictions limited women from many combat roles, those restrictions continued to shrink as female soldiers asserted themselves in new roles. Less than two weeks after General Dempsey sent this memorandum to Secretary of Defense Leon Panetta, the latter lifted the exclusion of women from combat. In the document, General Dempsey outlines the unanimous consensus of the Joint Chiefs of Staff for this policy-shift and their plan for moving forward.

## Defining Moment

Women have played a pivotal role in the military throughout America's history, though limitations imposed upon them often constricted their opportunities. Women have served in every war this country has ever fought, in numerous roles, particularly as nurses. Though restrictions have kept women from participating in combat, there are numerous examples of American women shirking these limitations in order to fight for their country, extending as far back as Deborah Sampson's contributions in the Revolutionary War. In the 1970s, restrictions on women in the armed forces began to see significant loosening. In 1976, the US finally allowed women to enroll in the US Military Academy at West Point, the Naval Academy at Annapolis, and the Air Force Academy. Starting in 1978, women were allowed to serve on noncombat ships as technicians, nurses, and officers; this right was extended to combat ships in 1993. Two years before that, in 1991, women were officially allowed to fly combat missions. Despite these advancements and the long record of service among American women, gender-based restrictions on some combat positions remained in place well into the twenty-first century.

This document reveals an instance when shifts in legislation trailed change in the real world. Women were deployed to the combat zone in the First and Second Gulf Wars and often faced the thick of the fray alongside their male counterparts. Shortages of troops, regulation loopholes, and the changing nature of war all contributed to women serving in these roles, despite the existing legal limitations. In early 2012, gender restrictions on some positions within the military were lifted, but the vast majority of restrictions remained in place. Finally, in late January 2013, about two weeks after this memorandum was sent, Secretary of Defense Leon Panetta, the recipient of this memo, lifted the official exclusion of women from combat. This shift marked a notable policy victory for women's rights in America, yet a shift in policy that was simply catching up to reality. Women had been serving in combat zones for years, and their service ultimately muted any serious opposition to the lifting of these restrictions.

## Author Biography

Martin Edward Dempsey was born on March 14, 1952. He graduated in 1974 from the United States Military Academy at West Point, and later, studying the Irish literary revival, he obtained a master's degree in literature from Duke University. Dempsey served in commanding roles in both Gulf Wars. He continued to rise through the ranks of the United States Army until he became the army chief of staff in early 2011 and the chairman of the Joint Chiefs of Staff in August of that same year. After a long, distinguished career, he retired in September 2015. All three of his children also served in the army, including his two daughters.

Four American F-15 Eagle pilots from the 3d Wing walk to their jets at Joint Base Elmendorf-Richardson. By U.S. Air Force photo by Tech. Sgt. Keith Brown.

## HISTORICAL DOCUMENT

CHAIRMAN OF THE JOINT CHIEFS OF STAFF
WASHINGTON, DC 20318–9999
CM-0017-13
INFO MEMO                         9 January 2013

FOR: SECRETARY OF DEFENSE
FROM: General Martin E. Dempsey, CJCS
SUBJECT: Women in the Service Implementation Plan

The time has come to rescind the direct combat exclusion rule for women and to eliminate all unnecessary gender-based barriers to service. The Joint Chiefs of Staff unanimously join me in proposing that we move forward with the full intent to integrate women into occupational fields to the maximum extent possible. To implement these initiatives successfully and without sacrificing our warfighting capability or the trust of the American people, we will need time to get it right.

We recognize the bravery and contributions of women in combat. We have made tremendous progress in expanding service opportunities for women since your February 2012 announcement, which officially notified Congress of the Department's intent to rescind the co-location restriction and to implement Exceptions to Policy (ETP) allowing women to be assigned to select positions in ground combat units at the battalion level. Recently, the Services opened 13,139 positions under co-location and an additional 1,186 positions under Exceptions to Policy.

Guiding Principles. To successfully integrate women into the remaining restricted occupational fields within our military, we must keep our guiding principles at the forefront. We are driven by:

Ensuring the success of our Nation's warfighting forces by preserving unit readiness, cohesion, and morale.

Ensuring all Service men and women are given the opportunity to succeed and are set up for success with viable career paths.

Retaining the trust and confidence of the American people to defend this Nation by promoting policies that maintain the best quality and most qualified people.

Validating occupational performance standards, both physical and mental, for all military occupational specialties (MOSs), specifically those that remain closed to women.

Eligibility for training and development within designated occupational fields should consist of qualitative and quantifiable standards reflecting the knowledge, skills, and abilities necessary for each occupation. For occupational specialties open to women, the occupational performance standards must be gender-neutral as required by Public Law 103–160, Section 542 (1993).

Ensuring that a sufficient cadre of midgrade/senior women enlisted and officers are assigned to commands at the point of introduction to ensure success in the long run. This may require an adjustment to our recruiting efforts, assignment processes, and personnel policies. Assimilation of women into heretofore "closed units" will be informed by continual in-stride assessments and pilot efforts.

Goals and Milestones. The following goals and milestones will support the elimination of unnecessary gender-based barriers to service:

Services will expand the number of units and number of women assigned to those units—based on ETP—and provide periodic updates on progress each quarter beginning in 3rd quarter, FY 2013.

The Navy will continue to assign women to afloat units as: (1) technical changes and modifications for reasonable female privacy and appropriate female berthing arrangements are completed; (2) female officer and enlisted leadership assignments can be implemented; and (3) ships' schedules permit Integration will be expeditiously implemented considering good order and judicious use of fiscal resources.

Services will continue to develop, review, and validate individual occupational standards. Validated gender-neutral occupational standards will be used to assess and assign Service members not later than September 2015.

The Services and U.S. Special Operations Command (USSOCOM) will proceed in a deliberate, measured and responsible way to assign women to currently closed MOSs as physical standards and operational assessments are completed and as it becomes possible to introduce cadres as described above. The Services and USSOCOM must complete all studies by 1st quarter, FY 2016, and provide periodic updates each quarter beginning in 3rd quarter, FY 2013.

If we find that the assignment of women to a specific position or occupational specialty is in conflict with our stated principles, we will request an exception to policy.

This deliberate approach to reducing gender-based barriers to women's service will provide the time necessary to institutionalize these important changes and to integrate women into occupational fields in a climate where they can succeed and flourish. Ultimately, we will ensure the success of our military forces and maintain the trust of the American people.

## Document Analysis

This memorandum has two distinct yet related goals. General Martin Dempsey aims to justify the imminent lifting of the exclusion of women from combat, and he strives to outline a blueprint for moving forward. This section will analyze these two authorial motives in turn.

Dempsey strikes a positive tone in both the introduction and conclusion to help justify the proposed lifting of gender-based restrictions. His positive tone reveals his confidence that this step towards equality will benefit the US military. This positivity is established from the very outset; he begins, "The time has come to rescind the direct combat exclusion rule for women and to eliminate all unnecessary gender-based barriers to service." The line as a whole introduces and summarizes the memorandum; the first four words express the sense that these changes are overdue. His justification continues in the following line, as he establishes his specific authority. As chairman of the Joint Chiefs of Staff, General Dempsey is the highest ranking military advisor to the president and the secretary of defense; he bolsters that authority by citing the unanimous support of the entire Joint Chiefs of Staff. In the first line of the second paragraph, Dempsey states, "We recognize the bravery and contributions of women in combat." As outlined in the Defining Moment section above, by January 2013, women had already been playing a large role in combat, which facilitated this shift in policy. Here, the author directly cites women's service to help justify the proposed change.

In addition to justifying the lifting of these restrictions, the author begins to map a path forward. In the final line of the opening paragraph, he measures his positive tone by acknowledging, "we will need time to get it right." Similarly, in the conclusion he qualifies the proposed approach as "deliberate." This mindful approach does not undermine the author's enthusiasm to achieve the proposed changes, but instead, it confirms and underlines his seriousness. The "Goals and Milestones" section highlights five specific steps to be taken to help with the imminent shift in policy. For example, the third bullet point in this section reads, "Services will continue to develop, review, and validate individual occupational standards. Validated gender-neutral occupational standards will be used to assess and assign Service members not later than September 2015." This step attempts to limit the continuation of gender discrimination in job assignment after the restrictions are lifted. General Dempsey names a specific date by which he hopes this step will be accomplished; the setting of this deadline immediately creates accountability. The blueprinting of the road ahead lends gravity to the proposal, in turn helping the author's other primary motive: justifying the proposed policy shift.

## Essential Themes

Opportunity is a theme that General Dempsey develops as an important aspect of the proposed lifting of the combat restrictions for women. The term is first mentioned in the second paragraph as a previous expansion of opportunities for women is mentioned. However, the concept gets fully developed as a theme a little bit later in the "Guiding Principles" section. The second bullet point of this section reads, "Ensuring all Service men and women are given the opportunity to succeed and are set up for success with viable career paths." The author claims that opportunity is crucial for the military's success. Finally, the last bullet point from the same section does not mention the term directly, but continues to develop the concept. It begins, "Ensuring that a sufficient cadre of midgrade/senior women enlisted and officers are assigned to commands at the point of introduction to ensure success in the long run." Moving from the abstract to the concrete, General Dempsey calls for an immediate enlistment of women to ensure the continued success of the policy and future opportunity for women.

Trust is another theme that General Dempsey develops throughout the document. The concept first comes up in the last line of the opening paragraph, which states, "To implement these initiatives successfully and without sacrificing our warfighting capability or the trust of the American people, we will need time to get it right." In this line, the author calls for patience so that the changes can be implemented without losing the American people's trust. However, over the next two iterations of the theme, the usage shifts: The author still discusses the trust of the American people, but keeping this trust becomes a reason to enact the proposed policy shift in first place, not just the grounds for implementing it patiently. Among the "Guiding Principles," the author includes, "Retaining the trust and confidence of the American people to defend this Nation by promoting policies that maintain the best quality and most qualified people." In this principle, it is clear that the author believes that the equality and fairness inherent to the policy shift will help the US military retain the trust of the American populace. Similarly, the document concludes with a final invocation of the theme of trust, "Ultimately, we will ensure the success of our military forces and maintain the trust of the American people." This sentence succinctly summarizes the author's justification for the proposed shift in policy which he has developed throughout the document. By showing that the American people's trust is contingent not only on maintaining war-readiness, but on promoting fairness, General Dempsey helps solidify his argument for the proposed shift in policy.

—*Anthony Vivian*

## Bibliography and Additional Reading

Biank, Tanya. Undaunted: The Real Story of America's Servicewomen in Today's Military. New York: NAL Caliber, 2014. Print.

Holmstedt, Kirsten. Band of Sisters: American Women at War in Iraq. Mechanicsburg, PA: Stackpole Books, 2008. Print.

Lemmon, Gayle Tzemach. Ashley's War: The Untold Story of a Team of Women Soldiers on the Special Ops Battlefield. New York: HarperCollins Publishers, 2015. Print.

Thorpe, Helen. Soldier Girls: The Battles of Three Women at Home and at War. New York: Scribner, 2014. Print.

# Hillary Clinton's Acceptance Speech at the 2016 Democratic National Convention

**Date:** July 28, 2016
**Author:** Hillary Rodham Clinton
**Genre:** Speech

## Summary Overview

On the last night of the Democratic National Convention, Hillary Rodham Clinton finally took the stage to accept formally her nomination as the Democratic candidate for the United States presidential election in 2016. After a tense primary campaign between herself and challenger Senator Bernie Sanders, as well as a previous presidential run in 2008, this moment represented a culmination of many years of work by Clinton and her supporters. This moment also represented the first time a major national political party in the United States nominated a woman to be its presidential candidate, and was an important milestone for many women who had anticipated seeing a woman run for the highest office in the country. Clinton's speech shows a candidate ready to approach the next phase of the election cycle by establishing her vision for the United States and uniting her party and other supporters against her opponent, Republican Donald J. Trump.

## Defining Moment

Speculation swirled for months around whether Hillary Clinton would run for president again before she officially announced her campaign in April 2015. She was one of the most notable and experienced women in politics in addition to the fact that she had run a formidable earlier campaign for the presidency during the 2008 Democratic primaries against President Obama. When she formally suspended her presidential campaign in 2008, she said to a crowd of supporters: "I am a woman and, like millions of women, I know there are still barriers and biases out there, often unconscious, and I want to build an America that respects and embraces the potential of every last one of us." After she stepped down from her role as President Obama's secretary of state in 2013, many suspected that she was preparing to capitalize on this earlier assertion and build a new campaign for 2016.

Hillary Clinton's second presidential campaign was not just a result of her deciding that she finally had the right support and sufficient experience to run success-fully. The 2008 Democratic primary election between a woman and an African-American man was a radical moment in American history, which had largely been a narrative of white male political actors. The 2008 primaries, and Obama's successful presidential campaigns in 2008 and 2012, redefined who could plausibly run for and be elected to the highest political offices.

However, Clinton's path to the Democratic nomination was not a certainty despite her political experience and number of connections. Independent Senator Bernie Sanders of Vermont ran a competitive campaign against the former Secretary of State during the primaries between 2015 and 2016. Compared to the perspective of Clinton as an "establishment" politician," the Sanders campaign particularly excited young voters, utilized grassroots organizing, and raised millions through small donations. Although there were fears of widening internal divisions between progressive voters, ultimately Sanders suspended his campaign after it was clear that Clinton received more votes. Although Clinton practically clinched her nomination by June 2016, the Democratic National Convention at the end of July 2016 was the official venue for recognizing this feat and strengthening party bonds around the contender whom it would send to fight against the Republicans in the main presidential election in November of the same year.

## Author Biography

Hillary Rodham was born in Chicago on October 26, 1947. She was politically active from an early age and continued to have an active political career over the years. She gained renown for her commencement ceremony speech as valedictorian at Wellesley College in 1969, in which she eloquently supported the student activist movements. As a student at Yale Law School, she not only met her future husband, Bill Clinton, who was then a student from Arkansas with a similar dedication to liberal politics; she also worked for the Children's Defense Fund and participated on the staff for the House Judiciary Committee investigating the Watergate scandal.

Clinton's 2016 presidential campaign logo. By Hillary Clinton campaign team.

After she married Bill Clinton in 1975 and moved to Arkansas, Hillary Rodham, who had not yet taken her husband's last name, agreed to subordinate her own political ambitions for his in a southern state with conservative norms. Still, she continued to pursue her career and the policy goals that interested her. She became the first female partner at Rose Law Firm and actively advocated for children's health, education, and better medical care for poor people. After Bill Clinton was elected president of the United States in 1992 and 1996, she, now as Hillary Rodham Clinton, continued to take a more active political role than previous political spouses; she continued in this capacity to pursue the same interests that motivated her as a student and as First Lady of Arkansas. Although her efforts to pass universal healthcare reform were not successful, she did play a critical role in passing the Children's Healthcare Initiative Program.

After her husband's two terms, she began a political career in her own name. She was elected senator of New York in 2000. While senator, she was conspicuously present at the World Trade Center site after the terrorist attack of September 11, comforting victims and praising clean-up efforts. On the other hand, she voted in 2002 to give the Bush administration the prerogative to invade Iraq, a vote she later came to regret. In 2008 she decided to run for president, but was outpolled by fellow senator Barack Obama. Upon Obama's election to the presidency, she agreed to become his Secretary of State. As diplomat, she continued her active work, which included disaster relief efforts in Haiti and helping the president to send a Navy SEAL team to kill the terrorist leader Osama bin Laden, as well as continuing to pursue issues related to women and children.

However, political opponents have often capitalized on her and her husband's personal lives and professional careers to foment controversy. Her husband's infidelity, her use of a private e-mail server, and the attack at a US embassy in Benghazi while she was Secretary of State are a few of the most notable scandals that threatened to derail her second presidential run in 2016. Despite a hard-fought primary battle with Senator Bernie Sanders of Vermont, she won the Democratic nomination and excited many Americans with the possibility that she might become the United States' first female president, but she was still dogged by controversy, which only intensified in the media as hacked e-mails were published online by internet vigilante group Wikileaks. This speculation over e-mails may have cost her the general election of November 2016, in which she won the popular vote but was still defeated based on electoral college votes by Republican Donald Trump in one of the most stunning upsets in American electoral history.

## HISTORICAL DOCUMENT

Thank you! Thank you for that amazing welcome. And Chelsea, thank you. I'm so proud to be your mother and so proud of the woman you've become. Thanks for bringing Marc into our family, and Charlotte and Aidan into the world. And Bill, that conversation we started in the law library 45 years ago is still going strong. It's lasted through good times that filled us with joy, and hard times that tested us. And I've even gotten a few words in along the way. On Tuesday night, I was so happy to see that my Explainer-in-Chief is still on the job. I'm also grateful to the rest of my family and the friends of a lifetime.

To all of you whose hard work brought us here tonight. And to those of you who joined our campaign this week. And what a remarkable week it's been.

We heard the man from Hope, Bill Clinton. And the man of Hope, Barack Obama. America is stronger because of President Obama's leadership, and I'm better because of his friendship.

We heard from our terrific vice president, the one-and-only Joe Biden, who spoke from his big heart about our party's commitment to working people.

First Lady Michelle Obama reminded us that our children are watching, and the president we elect is going to be their president, too.

And for those of you out there who are just getting to know Tim Kaine—you're soon going to understand why the people of Virginia keep promoting him: from City Council and mayor, to Governor, and now Senator. He'll make the whole country proud as our Vice President.

And...I want to thank Bernie Sanders. Bernie, your campaign inspired millions of Americans, particularly the young people who threw their hearts and souls into our primary. You've put economic and social justice issues front and center, where they belong. And to all of your supporters here and around the country: I want you to know, I've heard you. Your cause is our cause.

Our country needs your ideas, energy, and passion. That's the only way we can turn our progressive platform into real change for America. We wrote it together—now let's go out there and make it happen together.

My friends, we've come to Philadelphia—the birthplace of our nation—because what happened in this city 240 years ago still has something to teach us today. We all know the story. But we usually focus on how it turned out—and not enough on how close that story came to never being written at all.

When representatives from 13 unruly colonies met just down the road from here, some wanted to stick with the King. Some wanted to stick it to the king, and go their own way. The revolution hung in the balance. Then somehow they began listening to each other ... compromising ... finding common purpose. And by the time they left Philadelphia, they had begun to see themselves as one nation. That's what made it possible to stand up to a King.

That took courage. They had courage.

Our Founders embraced the enduring truth that we are stronger together. America is once again at a moment of reckoning. Powerful forces are threatening to pull us apart. Bonds of trust and respect are fraying. And just as with our founders, there are no guarantees. It truly is up to us. We have to decide whether we all will work together so we all can rise together.

Our country's motto is *e pluribus unum*: out of many, we are one. Will we stay true to that motto? Well, we heard Donald Trump's answer last week at his convention. He wants to divide us—from the rest of the world, and from each other. He's betting that the perils of today's world will blind us to its unlimited promise. He's taken the Republican Party a long way … from "Morning in America" to "Midnight in America." He wants us to fear the future and fear each other.

Well, a great Democratic President, Franklin Delano Roosevelt, came up with the perfect rebuke to Trump more than eighty years ago, during a much more perilous time. "The only thing we have to fear is fear itself."

Now we are clear-eyed about what our country is up against. But we are not afraid. We will rise to the challenge, just as we always have. We will not build a wall. Instead, we will build an economy where everyone who wants a good paying job can get one. And we'll build a path to citizenship for millions of immigrants who are already contributing to our economy! We will not ban a religion. We will work with all Americans and our allies to fight terrorism.

There's a lot of work to do. Too many people haven't had a pay raise since the crash. There's too much inequality. Too little social mobility. Too much paralysis in Washington. Too many threats at home and abroad.

But just look at the strengths we bring to meet these challenges. We have the most dynamic and diverse people in the world. We have the most tolerant and generous young people we've ever had. We have the most powerful military. The most innovative

entrepreneurs. The most enduring values. Freedom and equality, justice and opportunity.

We should be so proud that these words are associated with us. That when people hear them—they hear … America.

So don't let anyone tell you that our country is weak. We're not.

Don't let anyone tell you we don't have what it takes. We do.

And most of all, don't believe anyone who says: "I alone can fix it."

Those were actually Donald Trump's words in Cleveland. And they should set off alarm bells for all of us. Really? I alone can fix it? Isn't he forgetting? Troops on the front lines. Police officers and fire fighters who run toward danger. Doctors and nurses who care for us. Teachers who change lives. Entrepreneurs who see possibilities in every problem. Mothers who lost children to violence and are building a movement to keep other kids safe.

He's forgetting every last one of us.

Americans don't say: "I alone can fix it." We say: "We'll fix it together."

Remember: Our Founders fought a revolution and wrote a Constitution so America would never be a nation where one person had all the power. Two hundred and forty years later, we still put our faith in each other.

Look at what happened in Dallas after the assassinations of five brave police officers. Chief David Brown asked the community to support his force, maybe even join them. And you know how the community responded? Nearly 500 people applied in just 12 days. That's how Americans answer when the call for help goes out.

20 years ago I wrote a book called "It Takes a Village." A lot of people looked at the title and asked, what the heck do you mean by that? This is what I mean. None of us can raise a family, build a business, heal a community or lift a country totally alone. America needs every one of us to lend our energy, our talents, our ambition to making our nation better and stronger. I believe that with all my heart.

That's why "Stronger Together" is not just a lesson from our history. It's not just a slogan for our campaign. It's a guiding principle for the country we've always been and the future we're going to build. A country where the economy works for everyone, not just those at the top. Where you can get a good job and send your kids to a good school, no matter what ZIP code you live in. A country where all our children can dream, and those dreams are within reach. Where families are strong … communities are safe. And yes, love trumps hate.

That's the country we're fighting for. That's the future we're working toward. And so it is with humility … determination … and boundless confidence in America's promise … that I accept your nomination for President of the United States!

Now, sometimes the people at this podium are new to the national stage. As you know, I'm not one of those people. I've been your first lady. Served 8 years as a Senator from the great state of New York. I ran for President and lost. Then I represented all of you as Secretary of State.

But my job titles only tell you what I've done. They don't tell you why. The truth is, through all these years of public service, the "service" part has always come easier to me than the "public" part. I get it that some people just don't know what to make of me. So let me tell you.

The family I'm from … well, no one had their name on big buildings. My family were builders of a different kind. Builders in the way most American families are. They used whatever tools they had—whatever God gave them—and whatever life in America provided—and built better lives and better futures for their kids. My grandfather worked in the same Scranton lace mill for 50 years. Because he believed that if he gave everything he had, his children would have a better life than he did. And he was right.

My dad, Hugh, made it to college. He played football at Penn State and enlisted in the Navy after Pearl Harbor. When the war was over he started his own small business, printing fabric for draperies. I remember watching him stand for hours over silk screens. He wanted to give my brothers and me opportunities he never had. And he did.

My mother, Dorothy, was abandoned by her parents as a young girl. She ended up on her own at 14, working as a house maid. She was saved by the kindness of others. Her first grade teacher saw she had nothing to eat at lunch, and brought extra food to share. The lesson she passed on to me years later stuck with me: No one gets through life alone. We have to look out for each other and lift each other up. She made sure I learned the words of our Methodist faith: "Do all the good you can, for all the people you can, in all the ways you can, as long as ever you can."

I went to work for the Children's Defense Fund, going door-to-door in New Bedford, Massachusetts on behalf of children with disabilities who were denied the chance to go to school. I remember meeting a young girl in a wheelchair on the small back porch of her house. She told me how badly she wanted to go to school—it just didn't seem possible. And I couldn't stop thinking of my mother and what she went through as a child. It became clear to me that simply caring is not enough.

To drive real progress, you have to change both hearts and laws. You need both understanding and action. So we gathered facts. We built a coalition. And our work helped convince Congress to ensure access to education for all students with disabilities. It's a big idea, isn't it? Every kid with a disability has the right to go to school. But how do you make an idea like that real? You do it step-by-step, year-by-year … sometimes even door-by-door.

And my heart just swelled when I saw Anastasia Somoza on this stage, representing millions of young people who—because of those changes to our laws—are able to get an education. It's true … I sweat the details of policy—whether we're talking about the exact level of lead in the drinking water in Flint, Michigan, the number of mental health facilities in Iowa, or the cost of your prescription drugs.

Because it's not just a detail if it's your kid—if it's your family. It's a big deal. And it should be a big deal to your president.

Over the last three days, you've seen some of the people who've inspired me. People who let me into their lives, and became a part of mine. People like Ryan Moore and Lauren Manning. They told their stories Tuesday night. I first met Ryan as a seven-year old. He was wearing a full body brace that must have weighed forty pounds. Children like Ryan kept me going when our plan for universal health care failed … and kept me working with leaders of both parties to help create the Children's Health Insurance Program that covers 8 million kids every year.

Lauren was gravely injured on 9/11. It was the thought of her, and Debbie St. John, and John Dolan and Joe Sweeney, and all the victims and survivors, that kept me working as hard as I could in the Senate on behalf of 9/11 families, and our first responders who got sick from their time at Ground Zero.

I was still thinking of Lauren, Debbie and all the others ten years later in the White House Situation Room when President Obama made the courageous decision that finally brought Osama bin Laden to justice.

In this campaign, I've met so many people who motivate me to keep fighting for change. And, with your help, I will carry all of your voices and stories with me to the White House. I will be a President for Democrats, Republicans, and Independents. For the struggling, the striving and the successful. For those who vote for me and those who don't. For all Americans.

Tonight, we've reached a milestone in our nation's march toward a more perfect union: the first time that a major party has nominated a woman for President. Standing here as my mother's daughter, and my daughter's mother, I'm so happy this day has come. Happy for grandmothers and little girls and everyone in between. Happy for boys and men, too—because when any barrier falls in America, for anyone, it clears the way for everyone. When there are no ceilings, the sky's the limit.

So let's keep going, until every one of the 161 million women and girls across America has the opportunity she deserves. Because even more important than the history we make tonight, is the history we will write together in the years ahead.

Let's begin with what we're going to do to help working people in our country get ahead and stay ahead.

Now, I don't think President Obama and Vice President Biden get the credit they deserve for saving us from the worst economic crisis of our lifetimes. Our economy is so much stronger than when they took office. Nearly 15 million new private-sector jobs. Twenty million more Americans with health insurance. And an auto industry that just had its best year ever. That's real progress. But none of us can be satisfied with the status quo. Not by a long shot.

We're still facing deep-seated problems that developed long before the recession and have stayed with us through the recovery. I've gone around our country talking to working families. And I've heard from so many of you who feel like the economy just isn't working. Some of you are frustrated—even furious. And you know what? You're right. It's not yet working the way it should. Americans are willing to work—and work hard. But right now, an awful lot of people feel there is less and less respect for the work they do. And less respect for them, period.

Democrats are the party of working people. But we haven't done a good enough job showing that we get what you're going through, and that we're going to do something about it. So I want to tell you tonight how we will empower Americans to live better lives.

My primary mission as President will be to create more opportunity and more good jobs with rising wages right here in the United States. From my first day in office to my last! Especially in places that for too long have been left out and left behind. From our inner cities to our small towns, from Indian Country to Coal Country. From communities ravaged by addiction to regions hollowed out by plant closures.

And here's what I believe.

I believe America thrives when the middle class thrives. I believe that our economy isn't working the way it should because our democracy isn't working the way it should. That's why we need to appoint Supreme Court justices who will get money out of politics and expand voting rights, not restrict them. And we'll pass a constitutional amendment to overturn Citizens United!

I believe American corporations that have gotten so much from our country should be just as patriotic in return. Many of them are. But too many aren't. It's wrong to take tax breaks with one hand and give out pink slips with the other. And I believe Wall Street can never, ever be allowed to wreck Main Street again.

I believe in science. I believe that climate change is real and that we can save our planet while creating millions of good-paying clean energy jobs.

I believe that when we have millions of hard-working immigrants contributing to our economy, it would be self-defeating and inhumane to kick them out. Comprehensive immigration reform will grow our economy and keep families together—and it's the right thing to do.

Whatever party you belong to, or if you belong to no party at all, if you share these beliefs, this is your campaign. If you believe that companies should share profits with their workers, not pad executive bonuses, join us.

If you believe the minimum wage should be a living wage … and no one working full time should have to raise their children in poverty … join us.

If you believe that every man, woman, and child in America has the right to affordable health care … join us.

If you believe that we should say "no" to unfair trade deals … that we should stand up to China … that we should support our steelworkers and auto-workers and homegrown manufacturers … join us.

If you believe we should expand Social Security and protect a woman's right to make her own health care decisions … join us.

And yes, if you believe that your working mother, wife, sister, or daughter deserves equal pay … join us.

Let's make sure this economy works for everyone, not just those at the top. Now, you didn't hear any of this from Donald Trump at his convention. He spoke for 70-odd minutes—and I do mean odd. And he offered zero solutions. But we already know he doesn't believe these things. No wonder he doesn't like talking about his plans. You might have noticed, I love talking about mine.

In my first 100 days, we will work with both parties to pass the biggest investment in new, good-paying jobs since World War II. Jobs in manufacturing, clean energy, technology and innovation, small business, and infrastructure. If we invest in infrastructure now, we'll not only create jobs today, but lay the foundation for the jobs of the future. And we will transform the way we prepare our young people for those jobs.

Bernie Sanders and I will work together to make college tuition-free for the middle class and debt-free for all! We will also liberate millions of people who already have student debt. It's just not right that Donald Trump can ignore his debts, but students and families can't refinance theirs.

And here's something we don't say often enough: College is crucial, but a four-year degree should not be the only path to a good job. We're going to help more people learn a skill or practice a trade and make a good living doing it.

We're going to give small businesses a boost. Make it easier to get credit. Way too many dreams die in the parking lots of banks. In America, if you can dream it, you should be able to build it.

We're going to help you balance family and work. And you know what, if fighting for affordable child care and paid family leave is playing the "woman card," then Deal Me In!

*(Oh, you've heard that one?)*

Now, here's the thing, we're not only going to make all these investments, we're going to pay for every single one of them. And here's how: Wall Street, corporations, and the super rich are going to start paying their fair share of taxes. Not because we resent success. Because when more than 90 percent of the gains have gone to the top 1 percent, that's where the money is. And if companies take tax breaks and then ship jobs overseas, we'll make them pay us back. And we'll put that money to work where it belongs … creating jobs here at home!

Now I know some of you are sitting at home thinking, well that all sounds pretty good. But how are you going to get it done? How are you going to break through the gridlock in Washington? Look at my record. I've worked across the aisle to pass laws and treaties and to launch new programs that help millions of people. And if you give me the chance, that's what I'll do as President. But Trump, he's a businessman. He must know something about the economy.

Well, let's take a closer look. In Atlantic City, 60 miles from here, you'll find contractors and small businesses who lost everything because Donald Trump refused to pay his bills. People who did the work and needed the money, and didn't get it—

not because he couldn't pay them, but because he wouldn't pay them.

That sales pitch he's making to be your president? Put your faith in him—and you'll win big? That's the same sales pitch he made to all those small businesses. Then Trump walked away, and left working people holding the bag. He also talks a big game about putting America First. Please explain to me what part of America First leads him to make Trump ties in China, not Colorado. Trump suits in Mexico, not Michigan. Trump furniture in Turkey, not Ohio. Trump picture frames in India, not Wisconsin. Donald Trump says he wants to make America great again—well, he could start by actually making things in America again.

The choice we face is just as stark when it comes to our national security. Anyone reading the news can see the threats and turbulence we face. From Baghdad and Kabul, to Nice and Paris and Brussels, to San Bernardino and Orlando, we're dealing with determined enemies that must be defeated. No wonder people are anxious and looking for reassurance. Looking for steady leadership.

You want a leader who understands we are stronger when we work with our allies around the world and care for our veterans here at home. Keeping our nation safe and honoring the people who do it will be my highest priority. I'm proud that we put a lid on Iran's nuclear program without firing a single shot—now we have to enforce it, and keep supporting Israel's security. I'm proud that we shaped a global climate agreement—now we have to hold every country accountable to their commitments, including ourselves. I'm proud to stand by our allies in NATO against any threat they face, including from Russia.

I've laid out my strategy for defeating ISIS. We will strike their sanctuaries from the air, and support local forces taking them out on the ground. We will surge our intelligence so that we detect and prevent attacks before they happen. We will disrupt their efforts online to reach and radicalize young people in our country. It won't be easy or quick, but make no mistake—we will prevail.

Now Donald Trump says, and this is a quote, "I know more about ISIS than the generals do." No, Donald, you don't.

He thinks that he knows more than our military because he claimed our armed forces are "a disaster." Well, I've had the privilege to work closely with our troops and our veterans for many years, including as a senator on the Armed Services Committee. I know how wrong he is. Our military is a national treasure.

We entrust our commander-in-chief to make the hardest decisions our nation faces. Decisions about war and peace. Life and death. A president should respect the men and women who risk their lives to serve our country—including the sons of Tim Kaine and Mike Pence, both Marines.

Ask yourself: Does Donald Trump have the temperament to be Commander-in-Chief? Donald Trump can't even handle the rough-and-tumble of a presidential campaign. He loses his cool at the slightest provocation. When he's gotten a tough question from a reporter. When he's challenged in a debate. When he sees a protester at a rally. Imagine him in the Oval Office facing a real crisis. A man you can bait with a tweet is not a man we can trust with nuclear weapons.

I can't put it any better than Jackie Kennedy did after the Cuban Missile Crisis. She said that what worried President Kennedy during that very dangerous time was that a war might be started—not by big men with self-control and restraint, but by little men—the ones moved by fear and pride.

America's strength doesn't come from lashing out. Strength relies on smarts, judgment, cool resolve, and the precise and strategic application of power. That's the kind of Commander-in-Chief I pledge to be.

And if we're serious about keeping our country safe, we also can't afford to have a President who's in the pocket of the gun lobby. I'm not here to repeal the Second Amendment. I'm not here to take away your guns. I just don't want you to be shot by someone who shouldn't have a gun in the first place. We should be working with responsible gun owners to pass common-sense reforms and keep guns out of the hands of criminals, terrorists and all others who would do us harm.

For decades, people have said this issue was too hard to solve and the politics were too hot to touch.

But I ask you: How can we just stand by and do nothing? You heard, you saw, family members of people killed by gun violence. You heard, you saw, family members of police officers killed in the line of duty because they were outgunned by criminals. I refuse to believe we can't find common ground here.

We have to heal the divides in our country. Not just on guns. But on race. Immigration. And more. That starts with listening to each other. Hearing each other. Trying, as best we can, to walk in each other's shoes. So let's put ourselves in the shoes of young black and Latino men and women who face the effects of systemic racism, and are made to feel like their lives are disposable. Let's put ourselves in the shoes of police officers, kissing their kids and spouses goodbye every day and heading off to do a dangerous and necessary job.

We will reform our criminal justice system from end-to-end, and rebuild trust between law enforcement and the communities they serve. We will defend all our rights—civil rights, human rights and voting rights … women's rights and workers' rights … LGBT rights and the rights of people with disabilities! And we will stand up against mean and divisive rhetoric wherever it comes from.

For the past year, many people made the mistake of laughing off Donald Trump's comments—excusing him as an entertainer just putting on a show. They think he couldn't possibly mean all the horrible things he says like when he called women "pigs." Or said that an American judge couldn't be fair because of his Mexican heritage. Or when he mocks and mimics a reporter with a disability. Or insults prisoners of war like John McCain—a true hero and patriot who deserves our respect.

At first, I admit, I couldn't believe he meant it either. It was just too hard to fathom—that someone who wants to lead our nation could say those things. Could be like that. But here's the sad truth: There is no other Donald Trump … This is it. And in the end, it comes down to what Donald Trump doesn't get: that America is great—because America is good.

So enough with the bigotry and bombast. Donald Trump's not offering real change. He's offering empty promises. What are we offering? A bold agenda to improve the lives of people across our country—to keep you safe, to get you good jobs, and to give your kids the opportunities they deserve.

The choice is clear. Every generation of Americans has come together to make our country freer, fairer, and stronger. None of us can do it alone. I know that at a time when so much seems to be pulling us apart, it can be hard to imagine how we'll ever pull together again. But I'm here to tell you tonight progress is possible. I know because I've seen it in the lives of people across America who get knocked down and get right back up. And I know it from my own life. More than a few times, I've had to pick myself up and get back in the game.

Like so much else, I got this from my mother. She never let me back down from any challenge. When I tried to hide from a neighborhood bully, she literally blocked the door. "Go back out there," she said. And she was right. You have to stand up to bullies. You have to keep working to make things better, even when the odds are long and the opposition is fierce. We lost my mother a few years ago. I miss her every day. And I still hear her voice urging me to keep working, keep fighting for right, no matter what.

That's what we need to do together as a nation. Though "we may not live to see the glory," as the song from the musical Hamilton goes, "let us gladly join the fight." Let our legacy be about "planting seeds in a garden you never get to see." That's why we're here … not just in this hall, but on this Earth. The Founders showed us that. And so have many others since. They were drawn together by love of country, and the selfless passion to build something better for all who follow.

That is the story of America. And we begin a new chapter tonight. Yes, the world is watching what we do. Yes, America's destiny is ours to choose. So let's be stronger together. Looking to the future with courage and confidence. Building a better tomorrow for our beloved children and our beloved country. When we do, America will be greater than ever.

Thank you and may God bless the United States of America!

## Document Analysis

During important occasions in the 2016 presidential election, Hillary Rodham Clinton often wore outfits specifically designed to communicate a message. As she delivered her speech to a large crowd on July 28, 2016, she was dressed in a white pantsuit in homage to the color suffragettes in the early twentieth century commonly wore. In her convention speech, however, Clinton devotes only a few sentences to the historical gravity of the moment, as she was the first woman nominated by a major party as their presidential candidate. Instead, she focuses her speech much more on her campaign's motto, "Stronger Together," than on the gendered implications of her nomination. The theme of unity emphasizes that Clinton is a candidate who represents the core principles of the country, as well as it implies that Trump represents the direct opposite.

Clinton begins her speech by framing it around people other than herself who have worked together to accomplish a great feat. She first thanks many of the previous speakers and supporters at the convention, and then transitions into an overview of American history. Her review focuses on the collaborative efforts of the thirteen original colonies against one British king. Since she describes their fight against a king, Clinton is clearly describing the Founders as they came together to write the Declaration of Independence rather than another moment, like the Constitutional Convention, when she says: "somehow they began listening to each other … compromising … finding common purpose. And by the time they left Philadelphia, they had begun to see themselves as one nation." She continues to reinforce the ideals of compromise and collaboration as defining characteristics of the United States by citing the country's motto, *e pluribus unum*. Clinton translates this as "out of many, we are one," but she has included "we" into the translation where it does not exist in the Latin. This slight addition contributes to Clinton's depiction of the United States as a unified community built on cooperation.

After she transitions to introduce herself, Clinton similarly presents herself as practicing the same values as the Founders. Her family instilled in her the idea of service on behalf of others, and her career reflects the subordination of the self for a greater community good. After meeting one girl who was unable to go to school, she says that she was determined to change this. She does not put the emphasis on herself, but includes herself in a larger process: "We built a coalition. And our work helped convince Congress to ensure access to education for all students with disabilities." She completes this characterization of herself by saying finally: "I will be a President for Democrats, Republicans, and Independents. For the struggling, the striving and the successful. For those who vote for me and those who don't. For all Americans." Her opponent, on the other hand, she characterizes as more self-centered. Donald Trump uses the pronoun "I," as in "I alone can fix it," compared to Clinton, who repeatedly stresses the pronoun "we." Donald Trump, as she explains, mocks and attacks people for their identities, rather than working together with different people. He, she says, does not represent the "story of America," but she does.

This "story of America," of course, leaves out the many examples of hardship and division in the country's history. Clinton focuses on the positive aspects of American history, instead of, for example, on the great obstacles the women's rights movement had to combat to make her speech even conceivable. Clinton's focus on unity and history shows a politician hoping to present herself as a traditional candidate as well as a politician pivoting away from interparty divisions and towards a harder fight ahead.

## Essential Themes

In her concession speech on November 9, 2016, Hillary Clinton alluded to her 2008 concession speech and said: "Now, I know we have still not shattered that highest and hardest glass ceiling, but someday someone will—and hopefully sooner than we might think right now." Although Hillary Clinton's stunning defeat meant that she would not be the first female president of the United States, her electoral college loss to Donald Trump inspired many women to follow her lead in running for office. Groups like Emerge America and Ready to Run which train women to run for office noticed a surge of women signing up and expressing interest in seeking political office in the wake of Clinton's defeat. Some of these new potential political candidates expressed that they were driven by Donald Trump's sexism, others by Clinton's loss. This surge in women running for political office may start to resolve eventually the imbalance in gender representation in U.S. politics. In 2017 women represented roughly twenty percent of the U.S. Congress; only six women held governorships out of fifty states; and women held only twenty five percent of the seats in state legislatures.

Increased female representation in positions of political power is not just a matter of symbolic importance. Research shows that women govern differently than men. In Congress, women sponsor and co-sponsor more bills, they bring more federal money to their districts, and they drive policies that support women, children, social welfare, and national security. Female politicians also tend to be more bipartisan and build coalitions, both of which qualities can be essential behind the scenes tactics to getting bills passed. Female legislators tend to bring both their experience as women to the bills they write and they tend to work in collaborative ways to pass those bills. Hillary Clinton's acceptance speech and her career as a whole support this model of female governing. A firm believer that "women's rights are human rights," she advocated for children and women from the time she was a student at Yale Law, and she ran her presidential campaign on the idea that the country was stronger working together than divided by partisan rhetoric.

—*Ashleigh Fata, MA*

## Bibliography and Additional Reading

Clinton, Hillary Rodham. *What Happened*. New York: Simon & Schuster, 2017.

*Center for American Women and Politics*. Eagleton Institute of Politics at Rutgers U, 2017, http://www.cawp.rutgers.edu/. Accessed Nov. 1. 2017.

Miller, Claire Cain. "Women Actually Do Govern Differently." *The New York Times*, 10 Nov. 2016, https://www.nytimes.com/2016/11/10/upshot/women-actually-do-govern-differently.html.

Orr, Katie and Megan Kamerick. "Trump's Election Drives More Women to Consider Running for Office." *NPR*, 23 Feb. 2017, http://www.npr.org/2017/02/23/515438978/trumps-election-drives-more-women-to-consider-running-for-office.

# ■ *Whole Woman's Health v. Hellerstedt*

**Date:** June 27, 2016
**Author:** Stephen Breyer
**Genre:** Court opinion

## Summary Overview

On June 27, 2016 the Supreme Court of the United States issued its opinion in *Whole Woman's Health v. Hellerstedt*, a suit involving a challenge to a Texas law regulating abortion. The Court reversed the lower Federal court's ruling and held that two provisions in the law—requiring physicians who perform abortions to have admitting privileges at a nearby hospital and requiring abortion clinics in Texas to have facilities that were comparable to an ambulatory surgical center—placed a substantial obstacle in the path of women in the state seeking an abortion, constituted an undue burden on abortion access, and thus violated the U.S. Constitution.

## Defining Moment

The history of abortion rulings from the U.S. Supreme Court spans over forty years. The Supreme Court has repeatedly tested the ability of the states to regulate, through a variety of means, a woman's right to abortion. Since the Court's January 1973 ruling in *Roe v. Wade*, which granted women the constitutional right to terminate a pregnancy, the Supreme Court has carefully analyzed the ability of states to place regulations on abortion and further clarified the constitutional protections afforded to women wishing to terminate a pregnancy.

Prior to *Roe v. Wade*, and indeed throughout much of American history, states had banned or placed severe restrictions on abortion. Many of these laws, enacted in the nineteenth century, acted to restrict those who performed abortions rather than pregnant women. In general, the stated goal of these laws was to protect pregnant women from medical malpractice or injury from inadequately performed procedures. In the early twentieth century there was an almost total ban on abortion across the United States. However, changes in the social climate, including women's suffrage and the burgeoning feminist movement, saw changes in attitudes regarding a woman's right to make decisions regarding her reproductive health.

In 1967 Colorado became the first state to recognize and expand the right of a woman to seek a legal abortion. By 1970 twelve states had made changes to their abortion laws. Moreover, New York, Washington, Hawaii and Alaska acted to decriminalize abortion entirely during the early stages of a pregnancy. As the abortion rights movement began to take hold, many advocates began to challenge the existing state abortion laws, arguing that they were overly broad, violated equal protection under the U.S. Constitution, and restricted a woman's right to determine their own reproductive health. Many early challenges to these state laws were rejected by state and federal courts.

In *Roe v. Wade,* the Supreme Court considered a challenge to a Texas law outlawing abortion in all cases except those in which the life of the mother was at risk. In a 7-2 decision, the Court concluded that constitutional rights to privacy and liberty protected a woman's right to decide to terminate a pregnancy. Writing for the majority, Justice Harry Blackmun noted that while "the Constitution does not explicitly mention any right to privacy" a number of prior Court decisions found "a guarantee of certain areas or zones of privacy." This guarantee was grounded in the 14th Amendment's guarantee of liberty and the Bill of Rights which together created a zone of privacy in the areas of society such as marriage, contraception and family relationships. Earlier Court decisions such as *Griswold v. Connecticut*, a decision which struck down Connecticut's anti-contraception law for intruding on marital privacy, paved the way for recognizing such privacy rights in *Roe*. In *Griswold*, Justice William Douglas, writing for the majority, asserted, "zones" of personal privacy were guaranteed by the U.S. Constitution and that personal privacy was fundamental to liberty under "the protected prenumbra of specific guarantees of the Bill of Rights."

In *Roe* the Court held that access to abortion is a fundamental right and that only a "compelling state interest" could justify a state law that limited that right. The Court recognized in *Roe* that a state has an "important and legitimate interest" in protecting a mother's health and "the potentiality of human life" in her womb. The Court created a three-tiered legal framework, based on the nine months of pregnancy, in which the state gained a greater compelling interest with each successive trimester of the pregnancy.

In the years following *Roe,* the Supreme Court addressed a number of issues which arose from that decision including informed consent, parental consent, spousal consent and waiting periods imposed on women seeking an abortion. In these cases, the Court affirmed *Roe* and its three-tiered framework.

In 1992, the Court granted certiorari to hear *Planned Parenthood of Southeastern Pennsylvania v. Casey. Casey* involved a challenge to a broad abortion law enacted which required informed consent as well as a 24-hour waiting period for women seeking an abortion. The law also required a minor to obtain consent from at least one parent or guardian as well as for a wife to obtain consent from her husband. Waivers to both consents could be obtained for certain limited circumstances.

The Court's decision in *Casey* demonstrated the fractured ideologies among the justices. The Court's three centrist Justices, Kennedy, O'Connor and Souter, issued a joint opinion, a highly unusual practice. These three justices were joined by the more liberal wing of the Court—Justices Blackmun and Stevens—in upholding *Roe's* core holding that a state may not prohibit pre-viability abortions. However, the three centrists were joined by the Court's conservative wing—Justices Rehnquist, Scalia, White and Thomas—in affirming the Pennsylvania law's requirements with the exception of the spousal notification.

The Court affirmed *Roe* and asserted the importance of maintaining the status quo on the rights to liberty and privacy. However, the three-tiered framework in *Roe* was substantially modified. Notably, under *Casey,* states could regulate abortion during the entire period before fetal viability and for reasons beyond protecting the health of the mother. The Court also dismantled *Roe's* prohibition on the regulation of abortion during the first trimester of pregnancy and the limitation of regulation between the end of the first trimester and the point of fetal viability. Thus, a state's interest in and regulation of abortion could potentially extend throughout pregnancy. Finally, the *Casey* holding also established a less rigorous standard for determining the constitutionality of state abortion laws. In *Roe* the Court held that abortion was a fundamental right and that states could only regulate it before fetal viability if there was a "compelling state interest." This triggered a "strict scrutiny" standard, the highest legal standard for determining whether a law is constitutional. The

*Casey* Court replaced strict scrutiny with the less rigorous "undue burden" standard, meaning the regulation of abortion before the point of fetal viability would be unconstitutional only if it imposed an undue burden on a woman's right to terminate her pregnancy.

Although it dismantled portions of *Roe, Casey* gave states wide latitude to regulate abortion before fetal viability but, in turn, by ultimately affirming *Roe,* the court solidified the strength of the right to privacy for abortion and created a stronger legal precedent.

The Supreme Court dealt with the "partial-birth abortion" issue in *Stenberg v. Carhart,* striking down a Nebraska ban on partial-birth abortion which invalidated similar laws in 30 other states. Partial-birth refers to a procedure known in medicine as "dilation and extraction" which is performed late in the second trimester. The Nebraska law made it a felony to perform the procedure. The Supreme Court held that the statute lacked an exception for the health of the woman and stated that a state can promote but not endanger a woman's health when regulating abortion. In 2003 Congress passed and President George W. Bush signed the Federal Partial Birth Abortion Ban Act, the first federal law that banned the dilation and extraction procedure. Abortion rights advocates challenged the Act and lower courts ultimately struck in down, citing *Stenberg.* In 2007 the Supreme Court heard *Gonzales v. Carhart,* which reversed precedent and upheld the federal ban by a 5-4 vote in what was considered a major victory for abortion opponents.

After *Carhart,* several states began enacting more vigorous abortion laws with more requirements to be met by physicians performing abortions. Known as the "Trap Law" strategy ("Targeted Regulation of Abortion Providers"), these laws imposed more regulations on abortions than on other procedures posing similar or greater medical risks.

It is within this climate that the Supreme Court granted certiorari to hear *Whole Woman's Health v. Hellerstedt* and reversed and remanded the 5th Circuit Court by a 5-4 decision, in a major ruling on abortion. Justice Breyer delivered the opinion of the Court, in which Justices Kennedy, Ginsburg, Sotomayor, and Kagan joined. Justice Ginsburg filed a concurring opinion. Justice Thomas filed a dissenting opinion. Justice Alito filed a dissenting opinion in which Chief Justice Roberts and Justice Thomas joined.

In this latest challenge to state abortion regulation, Justice Stephen Breyer, writing for the Court majority, held that two provisions in a Texas law—requiring physicians who perform abortions to have admitting privileges at a nearby hospital and requiring abortion clinics in the state to have facilities comparable to an ambulatory surgical center—place a substantial obstacle in the path of women seeking an abortion, constitute an undue burden on abortion access, and therefore violate the Constitution.

## About the Author

Stephen Breyer is an Associate Justice on the Supreme Court. He was born on August 15, 1938 in San Francisco, California. Breyer studied philosophy at Stanford University and attended Oxford University's Magdalen College as a Marshall Scholar before attending Harvard Law School, graduating magna cum laude in 1964. Breyer was a law clerk for Supreme Court Associate Justice Arthur J. Goldberg for the 1964-65 term, before becoming special assistant to the U.S. Attorney General for Antitrust. In 1967 he began his tenure as a law professor at Harvard University. Breyer served on the Watergate Special Prosecution Force in 1973 and was appointed special counsel to the Senate Judiciary Committee and then chief counsel to the Committee.

President Carter nominated Breyer to serve on the U.S. Court of Appeals for the First Circuit and, after Senate confirmation, he took the bench in December 1980. He joined the U.S. Sentencing Commission in 1985 and was named chief judge of the Court of Appeals in 1990. Breyer was initially considered for a seat on the U.S. Supreme Court upon the retirement of Justice Byron White in 1993 but was ultimately nominated by President Clinton to replace Justice Harry Blackmun. Breyer was approved by the Senate and assumed his position as Associate Justice on August 3, 1994.

During his tenure on the Supreme Court, Breyer has earned a reputation for his pragmatism and was often in opposition to the more conservative Justices on the Court. However, Breyer sided with his conservative colleagues most notably in a 2014 decision upholding a Michigan constitutional amendment banning affirmative action in the state's public universities. Breyer sided with the court's more liberal wing in the 2015 rulings that upheld federal tax subsidies of the Affordable Care Act and in *Obergefell v. Hodges* that made same sex marriage legal in all 50 states.

## HISTORICAL DOCUMENT

WHOLE WOMAN'S HEALTH et al. *v.* HELLERSTEDT, COMMISSIONER, TEXAS DEPARTMENT OF STATE HEALTH SERVICES, et al.

No. 15–274.
Argued March 2, 2016—Decided June 27, 2016

A "State has a legitimate interest in seeing to it that abortion… is performed under circumstances that insure maximum safety for the patient." *Roe* v. *Wade*, 410 U. S. 113 . But "a statute which, while furthering [a] valid state interest, has the effect of placing a substantial obstacle in the path of a woman's choice cannot be considered a permissible means of serving its legitimate ends," *Planned Parenthood of Southeastern Pa.* v. *Casey*, 505 U. S. 833 (plurality opinion), and "[u]nnecessary health regulations that have the purpose or effect of presenting a substantial obstacle to a woman seeking an abortion impose an undue burden on the right," *id.*, at 878.

In 2013, the Texas Legislature enacted House Bill 2 (H. B. 2), which contains the two provisions challenged here. The "admitting-privileges requirement" provides that a "physician performing or inducing an abortion… must, on the date [of service], have active admitting privileges at a hospital… located not further than 30 miles from the" abortion facility. The "surgical-center requirement" requires an "abortion facility" to meet the "minimum standards… for ambulatory surgical centers" under Texas law. Before the law took effect, a group of Texas abortion providers filed the *Abbott* case, in which they lost a facial challenge to the constitutionality of the admitting-privileges provision. After the law went into effect, petitioners, another group of abortion providers (including some *Abbott* plaintiffs), filed this suit, claiming that both the admitting-privileges and the surgical-center provisions violated the Fourteenth Amendment, as interpreted in *Casey*. They sought injunctions preventing enforcement of the admitting-privileges provision as applied to physicians at one abortion facility in McAllen and one in El Paso and prohibiting enforcement of the surgical-center provision throughout Texas.

Based on the parties' stipulations, expert depositions, and expert and other trial testimony, the District Court made extensive findings, including, but not limited to: as the admitting-privileges requirement began to be enforced, the number of facilities providing abortions dropped in half, from about 40 to about 20; this decrease in geographical distribution means that the number of women of reproductive age living more than 50 miles from a clinic has doubled, the number living more than 100 miles away has increased by 150%, the number living more than 150 miles away by more than 350%, and the number living more than 200 miles away by about 2,800%; the number of facilities would drop to seven or eight if the surgical-center provision took effect, and those remaining facilities would see a significant increase in patient traffic; facilities would remain only in five metropolitan areas; before H. B. 2's passage, abortion was an extremely safe procedure with very low rates of complications and virtually no deaths; it was also safer than many more common procedures not subject to the same level of regulation; and the cost of compliance with the surgical-center requirement would most likely exceed $1.5 million to $3 million per clinic. The court enjoined enforcement of the provisions, holding that the surgical-center requirement imposed an undue burden on the right of women in Texas to seek previability abortions; that, together with that requirement, the admitting-privileges requirement imposed an undue burden in the Rio Grande Valley, El Paso, and West Texas; and that the provisions together created an "impermissible obstacle as applied to all women seeking a previability abortion."

The Fifth Circuit reversed in significant part. It concluded that res judicata barred the District Court from holding the admitting-privileges requirement unconstitutional statewide and that res

judicata also barred the challenge to the surgical-center provision. Reasoning that a law is "constitutional if (1) it does not have the purpose or effect of placing a substantial obstacle in the path of a woman seeking an abortion of a nonviable fetus and (2) it is reasonably related to... a legitimate state interest," the court found that both requirements were rationally related to a compelling state interest in protecting women's health.

*Held*:

1. Petitioners' constitutional claims are not barred by res judicata. Pp. 10–18.

(a) Res judicata neither bars petitioners' challenges to the admitting-privileges requirement nor prevents the Court from awarding facial relief. The fact that several petitioners had previously brought the unsuccessful facial challenge in *Abbott* does not mean that claim preclusion, the relevant aspect of res judicata, applies. Claim preclusion prohibits "successive litigation of the very same claim," *New Hampshire* v. *Maine*, 532 U. S. 742 , but petitioners' as-applied postenforcement challenge and the *Abbott* plaintiffs' facial preenforcement challenge do not present the same claim. Changed circumstances showing that a constitutional harm is concrete may give rise to a new claim. *Abbott* rested upon facts and evidence presented before enforcement of the admitting-privileges requirement began, when it was unclear how clinics would be affected. This case rests upon later, concrete factual developments that occurred once enforcement started and a significant number of clinics closed.

Res judicata also does not preclude facial relief here. In addition to requesting as-applied relief, petitioners asked for other appropriate relief, and their evidence and arguments convinced the District Court of the provision's unconstitutionality across the board. Federal Rule of Civil Procedure 54(c) provides that a "final judgment should grant the relief to which each party is entitled, even if the party has not demanded that relief in its pleadings," and this Court has held that if the arguments and evidence show that a statutory provision is unconstitutional on its face, an injunction prohibiting its enforcement is "proper," *Citizens United* v. *Federal Election Comm'n*, 558 U. S. 310. Pp. 10–15.

(b) Claim preclusion also does not bar petitioners' challenge to the surgical-center requirement. In concluding that petitioners should have raised this claim in *Abbott*, the Fifth Circuit did not take account of the fact that the surgical-center provision and the admitting-privileges provision are separate provisions with two different and independent regulatory requirements. Challenges to distinct regulatory requirements are ordinarily treated as distinct claims. Moreover, the surgical-center provision's implementing regulations had not even been promulgated at the time *Abbott* was filed, and the relevant factual circumstances changed between the two suits. Pp. 16–18.

2. Both the admitting-privileges and the surgical-center requirements place a substantial obstacle in the path of women seeking a previability abortion, constitute an undue burden on abortion access, and thus violate the Constitution. Pp. 19–39.

(a) The Fifth Circuit's standard of review may be read to imply that a district court should not consider the existence or nonexistence of medical benefits when deciding the undue burden question, but *Casey* requires courts to consider the burdens a law imposes on abortion access together with the benefits those laws confer, see 505 U. S., at 887–898. The Fifth Circuit's test also mistakenly equates the judicial review applicable to the regulation of a constitutionally protected personal liberty with the less strict review applicable to, *e.g.*, economic legislation. And the court's requirement that legislatures resolve questions of medical uncertainty is inconsistent with this Court's case law, which has placed considerable weight upon evidence and argument presented in judicial proceedings when determining the constitutionality of laws regulating abortion procedures. See *id.*, at 888–894. Explicit legislative findings must

be considered, but there were no such findings in H. B. 2. The District Court applied the correct legal standard here, considering the evidence in the record—including expert evidence—and then weighing the asserted benefits against the burdens. Pp. 19–21.

(b) The record contains adequate legal and factual support for the District Court's conclusion that the admitting-privileges requirement imposes an "undue burden" on a woman's right to choose. The requirement's purpose is to help ensure that women have easy access to a hospital should complications arise during an abortion procedure, but the District Court, relying on evidence showing extremely low rates of serious complications before H. B. 2's passage, found no significant health-related problem for the new law to cure. The State's record evidence, in contrast, does not show how the new law advanced the State's legitimate interest in protecting women's health when compared to the prior law, which required providers to have a "working arrangement" with doctors who had admitting privileges. At the same time, the record evidence indicates that the requirement places a "substantial obstacle" in a woman's path to abortion. The dramatic drop in the number of clinics means fewer doctors, longer waiting times, and increased crowding. It also means a significant increase in the distance women of reproductive age live from an abortion clinic. Increased driving distances do not always constitute an "undue burden," but they are an additional burden, which, when taken together with others caused by the closings, and when viewed in light of the virtual absence of any health benefit, help support the District Court's "undue burden" conclusion. Pp. 21–28.

(c) The surgical-center requirement also provides few, if any, health benefits for women, poses a substantial obstacle to women seeking abortions, and constitutes an "undue burden" on their constitutional right to do so. Before this requirement was enacted, Texas law required abortion facilities to meet a host of health and safety requirements that were policed by inspections and enforced through administrative, civil, and criminal penalties. Record evidence shows that the new provision imposes a number of additional requirements that are generally unnecessary in the abortion clinic context; that it provides no benefit when complications arise in the context of a medical abortion, which would generally occur after a patient has left the facility; that abortions taking place in abortion facilities are safer than common procedures that occur in outside clinics not subject to Texas' surgical-center requirements; and that Texas has waived no part of the requirement for any abortion clinics as it has done for nearly two-thirds of other covered facilities. This evidence, along with the absence of any contrary evidence, supports the District Court's conclusions, including its ultimate legal conclusion that requirement is not necessary. At the same time, the record provides adequate evidentiary support for the District Court's conclusion that the requirement places a substantial obstacle in the path of women seeking an abortion. The court found that it "strained credulity" to think that the seven or eight abortion facilities would be able to meet the demand. The Fifth Circuit discounted expert witness Dr. Grossman's testimony that the surgical-center requirement would cause the number of abortions performed by each remaining clinic to increase by a factor of about 5. But an expert may testify in the "form of an opinion" as long as that opinion rests upon "sufficient facts or data" and "reliable principles and methods." Fed. Rule Evid. 702. Here, Dr. Grossman's opinion rested upon his participation, together with other university researchers, in research tracking the number of facilities providing abortion services, using information from, among other things, the state health services department and other public sources. The District Court acted within its legal authority in finding his testimony admissible. Common sense also suggests that a physical facility that satisfies a certain physical demand will generally be unable to meet live times that demand without expanding physically or otherwise incurring significant costs. And Texas presented no evidence at trial suggesting that expansion was possible. Finally, the District Court's finding that a currently licensed abortion facility would have to incur considerable costs to meet the surgical-center requirements supports the conclusion that more surgical centers will not soon fill the gap left by closed facilities. Pp. 28–36.

(d) Texas' three additional arguments are unpersuasive. Pp. 36–39.

*790 F. 3d 563 and 598, reversed and remanded.*

## GLOSSARY

**judicial review:** a constitutional doctrine which allows a court to review legislative or executive acts to determine whether they are constitutional

**rational basis:** the most lenient form of judicial review; a test courts may utilize to determine the constitutionality of a law. To pass rational basis review, the challenged law must be rationally related to a legitimate government interest; generally used when no fundamental rights or suspect classifications are at issue.

**strict scrutiny:** the highest level of judicial review, applied by the Supreme Court to a law that is alleged to violate equal protection rights under the U.S. Constitution and to determine if the law is narrowly tailored to serve a compelling state interest

**undue burden:** in the field of reproductive rights, having the effect of placing a substantial obstacle in the path of a woman seeking to have an abortion of a fetus that is not yet viable. Laws that place an undue burden on a fundamental right are unconstitutional.

## Document Analysis

*Whole Woman's Health* is, as of this writing, the U. S. Supreme Court's most recent abortion decision. The Court held two restrictions contained within a Texas law unconstitutional under the undue burden standard which the Court set forth as a balancing test. With this approach, the Court resolved the uncertainty that had plagued the undue burden standard but also allowed for continued judicial discretion in instances where abortion restrictions fit less easily into this type of cost-benefit analysis.

In July 2013, Texas enacted House Bill 2 ("HB 2"), which introduced two abortion restrictions. First, it required every physician performing an abortion to have admitting privileges at a hospital within 100 miles of the abortion site. Second, it subjected the abortion facility to enacting the same standards as those applied to ambulatory surgical centers. A group of abortion providers in the state sued Texas seeking invalidation of the admitting privileges requirement. The providers argued that the restriction unduly burdened a woman's fundamental right to terminate her pregnancy. The federal district court agreed and enjoined enforcement of the admitting privileges requirement. The Fifth Circuit Court of Appeals reversed the district court on the merits. It accepted the state's argument that the admitting privileges requirement improved the health outcomes of women seeking abortions.

A second group of providers, including some from the prior case, later sought relief from the admitting privileges requirement and sought to invalidate the surgical center requirement. The district court held both requirements imposed an undue burden on women seeking abortions. It concluded that the admitting privileges requirements caused almost half of the state's abortion clinics to close and the costs of complying with the surgical center requirement would lead to more closures. Moreover, the court concluded the few remaining clinics would be unable to meet the demand for abortion services and the closures would require women to travel long distances to receive care. The district court also held that abortion procedures in Texas were already relatively safe and that neither requirement would lower the risk associated with abortion.

The Fifth Circuit reversed the district court rejecting the district court's legal standard used to invalidate the law. The Fifth Circuit set forth a test that a law is valid if it (1) "does not have the purpose or effect of placing a substantial obstacle in the path of a woman seeking an abortion or a nonviable fetus" and (2) "is reasonably related to (or designed to further) a legitimate state interest." Using this test the Fifth Circuit concluded both parts of the law were "rationally related" to the state's legitimate interest in protecting the health of the woman.

The Supreme Court reversed the Fifth Circuit and concluded that both provisions "place[d] a substantial obstacle in the path of women seeking a previability abortion, each constitute[d] an undue burden on abortion access, and each violate[d] the Federal Constitution." The Court concluded that neither of the two provisions in the law offered any actual benefit to a woman's health. The evidence showed that complications from abortion are rare and most occurred after the woman left the facility when neither of the two provisions would be of any assistance. The Court also found substantial obstacles to the two provisions: notably, that 75 percent of the clinics in Texas closed because of the law, causing a severe limitation to access. Also, the court found that the shortage of clinics would cause a drastic decline in the quality of service provided at the remaining clinics. Moreover, the number of women forced to travel long distances would also cause an undue burden.

Justices Thomas, Alito and Chief Justice Roberts dissented. Justice Thomas disagreed with an earlier decision that allowed abortion providers to be able to raise the constitutional rights of their patients and disagreed with it here, thus claiming that the providers had no legal standing to bring the case. He also disagreed that a woman has a constitutional right to an abortion and with the majority's application of the undue burden standard. Justice Alito argued that the clinics may have closed for other reasons other than the law and chastised the majority for not giving more deference to the state.

In rejecting a rational basis test, the *Whole Woman's Health* decision gave abortion jurisprudence much needed guidance on how to apply the undue burden standard by establishing a clear balancing test between any obstacle to a woman's access to the fundamental right of abortion and the state's stated interest in promoting the health of the woman. The Court importantly noted that a careful review of the lower court findings, the evidence, and the amici's briefs is needed to determine what the actual health benefits of a law are as well as what the actual burdens of each provision on women are. This tightened up the analysis to avoid future loopholes or manipulation of the undue burden test.

## Essential Themes

*Whole Woman's Health* is a key decision that further developed and defined what constitutes a substantial obstacle to a woman's control over the abortion decision. The Court demonstrated attention to the constitutional values at stake in the abortion right. The Court scrutinized the facts and identified and balanced the benefits and burdens framework originally set forth in *Planned Parenthood v. Casey*. The Court applied a close scrutiny to the rationale behind the Texas law that purported to protect women's health but had the practical effect of obstructing access to abortion.

—*Michele McBride Simonelli, JD*

## Bibliography and Additional Reading

Hartman, Gary R., Roy M. Mersky, Cindy L. Tate, *Landmark Supreme Court Cases: The Most Influential Decisions of the Supreme Court of the United States*. New York: Facts on File, Inc., 2014.

Linda Greenhouse & Reva B. Siegel, "*Casey* and the Clinic Closings: When "Protecting Health" Obstructs Choice, *Yale Law Journal*, 1428 (2016).

*Planned Parenthood of Southeastern Pa. v. Casey*, 112 S.Ct. 2791 (1992). Justia: US Supreme Court https://supreme.justia.com/cases/federal/us/505/833/case.html [accessed October 31, 2017].

Shapiro, Ian, editor. *Abortion: The Supreme Court Decisions 1965-2000*. Indianapolis: Hackett Publishing Co., Inc., 2001.

Steven R. Morrison, "Personhood Amendments After Whole Woman's Health v. Hellerstedt," *Case Western Reserve Law Review*, 67 (2016): 447-499.

*Whole Woman's Health v. Hellerstedt*, 136 S.Ct. 2292 (2016). Justia: US Supreme Court https://supreme.justia.com/cases/federal/us/579/15-274/ [accessed October 31, 2017].

# ■ Angela Davis: Women's March on Washington

**Date:** January 21, 2017
**Author:** Angela Davis
**Genre:** Speech

## Summary Overview

Controversial, world-renowned scholar and activist Angela Davis delivered this speech on September 21, 2017 during the Women's March on Washington. This event, organized in response and opposition to the incoming presidential administration of Donald J. Trump, was accompanied by marches around the United States as well as protests around the world and was the largest political demonstration in the nation's capital city since the protests of the Vietnam War era.

There are a number of important concepts and ideas in Davis's speech that give us some insight into the concerns of progressive activists in the second decade of the twenty-first century. One of the most important concepts is that of the "intersectional" aspects of feminism. Both Davis and the organizers of the march recognized that the structural aspects of American society, politics, economics and culture that placed women at a disadvantage also had similar effects on racial, ethnic, and religious minorities, people with disabilities, immigrants, and others in the United States. Thus, Davis's speech not only addresses issues of gender equality but homophobia and transphobia, economic inequality, environmental justice—particularly access to safe water—and other issues that "intersect" with feminist concerns.

In this speech, Angela Davis also calls for continued resistance throughout the coming years of the Trump administration, emphasizing that opposition to the proposed policies of the Trump White House (and the ideological and cultural factors that had contributed to his election) should not end with this post-inauguration event.

## Defining Moment

The 2016 US Presidential election between Democrat Hillary Clinton and Republican Donald Trump was remarkably divisive. With heated rhetoric, Trump targeted immigrants (particularly Muslims and immigrants from Mexico) and promised severe restrictions on immigration. Numerous Trump comments surfaced that many considered to be degrading to women. While some were alienated by Trump's words, other Americans saw his forthrightness as a welcome response to what they considered to be a growing atmosphere of "political correctness." Donald Trump's Vice Presidential running mate, Indiana governor Mike Pence had supported legislation in Indiana that his critics charged limited women's access to reproductive health care as well as signing into law the 2015 Religious Freedom Restoration Act, which opponents asserted opened the door to discrimination against members of the LGBT community being protected as a "religious liberty." Trump's rhetoric and Pence's gubernatorial record proved troubling to civil rights advocates.

Following Trump's election, a number of activists organized nationwide protests and marches to take place on January 21, 2017, following Trump's inauguration. While the main march occurred in Washington, D.C., similar demonstrations were organized not only throughout the United States but around the world. The organizers, in their "Mission & Vision" statement, characterized the circumstances which inspired the protest as resulting from "he rhetoric of the past election cycle" which "insulted, demonized, and threatened many of us—immigrants of all statuses, Muslims and those of diverse religious faiths, people who identify as LGBTQIA, Native people, Black and Brown people, people with disabilities, survivors of sexual assault—and our communities are hurting and scared." While having as a starting point the concerns about women's rights under the new administration, the communities and causes addressed by the march broadened beyond gender, with the group's "Unity Principles" citing the following issues:

Ending violence
  Reproductive rights
  LGBTQIA [Lesbian, Gay, Bisexual, Transgender and Transsexual, Queer, Intersex, Asexual] rights
    Worker's rights
    Civil rights
    Disability rights
    Immigrant rights
    Environmental justice

This broadened vision of concerns and causes illustrates the notion of, as Angela Davis says in her speech, of a feminism that is "inclusive and intersectional" and provides a window into the wide community of progressive activism in the twenty-first century.

## Author Biography

Angela Y. Davis was born on January 26, 1944 in Alabama. As a child in Birmingham, Davis got involved in civil rights issues, taking part in anti-segregation marches. Her mother as involved in an organization called the Southern Negro Youth Congress, which was a civil rights organization that, from its inception in 1937, was suspected of some connection with the Communist Party. During the 1940s and 1950s, in fact, the organization was under surveillance by the FBI. In a 1989 interview, Davis recalled how she became acquainted with the Communist Party as a child through friends of her parents. This connection would continue when Davis was in high school. She earned a place in a program that provided for African American students from the south to attend school in the north. Davis attended school in Greenwich Village, New York City and became involved in a Communist-affiliated student organization called Advance.

Davis's political activism would continue as a student at Brandeis University, leading to her being interviewed about her attendance at a Communist-organized youth festival. Graduating from Brandeis, Davis continued her schooling at the University of Frankfurt in Germany, and the University of California, San Diego where she earned a Master's degree, and Humboldt University in East Berlin, where she earned a doctorate in philosophy. She began teaching in the philosophy department of the University of California at Los Angeles in 1969, where she was known for her radical feminist activism and membership in the Communist Party USA. She was briefly removed from the position by the University's ruling board—at the suggestion of Governor Ronald Reagan—because of her Communist Party membership. While rehired, she was fired again in 1970 for speeches in which, among other things, she referred to the police as "pigs."

In August, 1970, a California court house hostage situation resulted in the deaths of a judge and three others. Davis was put on the FBI most-wanted fugitive list due to charges of aggravated kidnapping and first degree murder for her role in the situation, alleged to be purchasing the guns used in the hostage taking. Davis was apprehended in October of that year. After a highly publicized trial, Davis was acquitted in June, 1972. Throughout the decade she visited Cuba, the Soviet Union, and East Germany delivering public speeches. During the 1980s and 1990s and into the twenty-first century, Davis continued her academic career teaching and writing at various institutions as well as her progressive political activism.

## HISTORICAL DOCUMENT

At a challenging moment in our history, let us remind ourselves that we the hundreds of thousands, the millions of women, trans-people, men and youth who are here at the Women's March, we represent the powerful forces of change that are determined to prevent the dying cultures of racism, hetero-patriarchy from rising again.

We recognize that we are collective agents of history and that history cannot be deleted like web pages. We know that we gather this afternoon on indigenous land and we follow the lead of the first peoples who despite massive genocidal violence have never relinquished the struggle for land, water, culture, their people. We especially salute today the Standing Rock Sioux.

The freedom struggles of black people that have shaped the very nature of this country's history cannot be deleted with the sweep of a hand. We cannot be made to forget that black lives do matter. This is a country anchored in slavery and colonialism, which means for better or for worse the very history of the United States is a history of immigration and enslavement. Spreading xenophobia, hurling accusations of murder and rape and building walls will not erase history.

No human being is illegal.

The struggle to save the planet, to stop climate change, to guarantee the accessibility of water from the lands of the Standing Rock Sioux, to Flint, Michigan, to the West Bank and Gaza. The struggle to save our flora and fauna, to save the air—this is ground zero of the struggle for social justice.

This is a women's march and this women's march represents the promise of feminism as against the pernicious powers of state violence. And inclusive and intersectional feminism that calls upon all of us to join the resistance to racism, to Islamophobia, to anti-Semitism, to misogyny, to capitalist exploitation.

Yes, we salute the fight for 15. We dedicate ourselves to collective resistance. Resistance to the billionaire mortgage profiteers and gentrifiers. Resistance to the health care privateers. Resistance to the attacks on Muslims and on immigrants. Resistance to attacks on disabled people. Resistance to state violence perpetrated by the police and through the prison industrial complex. Resistance to institutional and intimate gender violence, especially against trans women of color.

Women's rights are human rights all over the planet and that is why we say freedom and justice for Palestine. We celebrate the impending release of Chelsea Manning. And Oscar López Rivera. But we also say free Leonard Peltier. Free Mumia Abu-Jamal. Free Assata Shakur.

Over the next months and years we will be called upon to intensify our demands for social justice to become more militant in our defense of vulnerable populations. Those who still defend the supremacy of white male hetero-patriarchy had better watch out.

The next 1,459 days of the Trump administration will be 1,459 days of resistance: Resistance on the ground, resistance in the classrooms, resistance on the job, resistance in our art and in our music.

This is just the beginning and in the words of the inimitable Ella Baker, 'We who believe in freedom cannot rest until it comes.' Thank you.

## GLOSSARY

**Ella Baker:** African American civil rights activist who lived from 1903 to 1986.

**ground zero:** a point of impact or origination

**hetero-patriarchy:** the dominance of maleness and heterosexuality in the socio-political hierarchy

**misogyny:** hatred, fear, and oppression of women

**"the fight for 15":** the movement to increase the federal minimum wage to $15 per hour

## Document Analysis

Davis begins her speech by highlighting the large number of participants at the march, which she numbers as "hundreds of thousands" and "millions." The Washington Post estimated the number of Marchers in Washington as around half a million, but the number who participated around the United States as between 3.3 and 4.6 million. Davis point out the diverse group of "women, trans-people, men and youth" participating in the march and points to both the numbers and the make-up of the marchers as the force that will ensure the continued decline of "racism, hetero-patriarchy."

Davis then describes herself and the marchers as "agents of history" and that history cannot be erased or "deleted." She invokes the indigenous, Native American

possession of the land on which Washington, D.C. is located. Davis then draws a parallel between the centuries-long resistance of Native American groups to White American encroachment on land and resources and the goals and persistence of the marchers. Davis also takes this opportunity to recognize the efforts of the Standing Rock Sioux who had been protesting—both on the scene and through the court system—the construction of the Dakota Access oil pipeline as a danger to their religious sites as well as their drinking water supply.

In the third paragraph, Davis uses the rallying cry of the Black Lives Matter movement, which emerged in 2013 after George Zimmerman was acquitted in the death of Trayvon Martin, as a reminder that the United States has its roots in "slavery and colonialism" and explains that the history of the country "is a history of immigration and enslavement." Building on this theme of immigration, she asserts that "Spreading xenophobia, hurling accusations of murder and rape and building walls will not erase history." This is a reference to several comments and proposals from Donald Trump during the 2016 Presidential campaign, in which he alleged that immigrants—particularly from Mexico—were rapists and murders and his pledge to build "a wall" to prevent further illicit immigration. Her next statement, that human beings are not "illegal" is a broader condemnation of anti-immigration sentiment in the United States.

Davis then, again broadening the scope of the activism she sees represented by those marching and the causes for which they stand, addresses environmental concerns such as climate change but also narrower environmental concerns. She again mentions the Standing Rock protest, but also invokes the water crisis in Flint, Michigan where government mismanagement led to water contaminated with lead and other harmful substances. Her water concerns—which are also political issues—extend to issues of water access in Gaza and the West Bank, part of the ongoing Israeli-Palestinian conflict. In the next paragraph, Davis discusses the "inclusive and intersectional" nature of the feminism represented at the march; a feminism that recognizes the connections between feminism and racism as well as other issues.

She goes on to address issues of economic equality, such as the drive to raise the federal minimum wage, opposition to corporate profiteering—including that going in the health care sector. Davis then adds to the abuses the marchers will resist, scubas violent attacks on immigrants and the disabled. She also condemns the police and prison structures of the United States and promotes continued resistance to violence based on gender. She speaks to issues of gender and violence outside the United States, calling for "freedom and justice" for Palestine. She praises the release of Chelsea Manning (a transgender women convicted by court-martial in 2013 of violating the Espionage Act, and Oscar López Rivera, the Puerto Rican independence activist convicted of seditious conspiracy in 1981. Davis urges the release of others in prison for controversial, politically-charged reasons such as American Indian Movement activist Leonard Peltier and African American activists Mumia Abu-Jamal and Assata Shakur.

Davis closes her speech by calling for an intensification of protest and foresees an increased militancy as well. She declares that the entirety of the Trump administration will be focused on resistance in all areas of American life, culture, and society.

## Essential Themes

In her 2017 speech to the Women's March on Washington, Angela Davis highlights the persistent and important theme that the march, as well as the resistance to the ideology and goals of the incoming Trump administration that the march symbolizes, is not a fight only by and for women. The march, rather, represents a wide array of progressive causes. This connection between feminism and other struggles, such as those against racism, economic inequality, homophobia or other is what Davis means when she discusses the feminism presented at the march as being "inclusive and intersectional." As discussed in "Defining Moment," above, the concerns of women in the face of the challenges presented by the Trump administration in areas such as reproductive rights, access to medical care, and economic equality, including the gender gap in pay, hiring, and benefits are central to the march organizers. Other issues of social justice, however, are also part of the unifying principles behind the march. Davis takes the opportunity bring the marchers' (and the world's) attention to a number of social justice issues that focused not only on gender but also on economic equality. Discussing causes like a $15 minimum wage, concerns about urban gentrification, and "billionaire mortgage profiteers" is in keeping with Davis's long-standing concerns, reaching back to the 1960s and 1970s as well.

—*Aaron Gulyas, MA*

## Bibliography and Additional Reading

Bhavnani, Kum-Kum, and Angela Y. Davis. "Complexity, Activism, Optimism: An Interview with Angela Y. Davis." *Feminist Review*, no. 31, 1989, pp. 66–81.

Davis, Angela Y. *Angela Davis: An Autobiography* (New York: International Publishers, 2013).

—— Freedom Is a Constant Struggle: Ferguson, Palestine, and the Foundations of a Movement (Chicago: Haymarket Books, 2016).

Ferree, Myra Marx and Alli Mari Tripp, eds., *Global Feminism: Transnational Women's Activism, Organizing, and Human Rights* (New York: New York University Press, 2006).

"Mission and Vision," Women's March on Washington https://www.womensmarch.com/mission/

"Unity Principles," Women's March on Washington https://www.womensmarch.com/principles/

# APPENDIXES

# Chronological List

# Web Resources

http://www.pbslearningmedia.org/collection/the-womens-movement/

PBS Learning Media's site on The Women's Movement.

http://history.house.gov/Exhibitions-and-Publications/WIC/Historical-Essays/No-Lady/Womens-Rights/

From the U.S. House of Representatives "History, Art & Archives" website, an overview of the early women's rights movement in the United States.

https://www.archives.gov/research/alic/reference/womens-history.html

The National Archives offers a range of resources on the topic of women's history generally and more specifically on women's suffrage and related topics.

http://now.org/

The website of the National Organization for Women (NOW).

http://www.sewallbelmont.org/learn/womens-history-in-the-u-s/

https://www.fawcettsociety.org.uk/

Home page of the Fawcett Society, a leading organization for gender equality and women's rights in the United Kingdom.

The Sewell-Belmont House and Museum provides resources on "the history of women's progress toward equality."

http://loc.gov/rr/program/bib/civilrights/external.html

From the Library of Congress, a fine list of web resources on the subject of African American civil rights.

https://www.bl.uk/sisterhood/timeline

From the British Library, a "Timeline of the Women's Liberation Movement," 1960s thru 1980s.

http://libguides.msubillings.edu/c.php?g=242203&p=1610129

From Montana State University, a small but useful collection of websites covering women's rights and women's history.

http://www.jstor.org/stable/10.1086/588436?seq=1#page_scan_tab_contents

A scholarly essay on the topic of third-wave feminism.

# Bibliography

"19th Amendment to the U.S. Constitution: Women's Right to Vote (1920)." National Archives "Our Documents" Web site. http://www.ourdocuments.gov/doc.php?flash=true&doc=63. Accessed on January 15, 2008.

"57d. *Roe v. Wade* and Its Impact." *U.S. History: Pre-Columbian to the New Millennium.* USHistory.org/ Independence Hall Association, 2014. Web.

"Abigail Smith Adams." *The White House*, The United States Government, 8 Mar. 2017, www.whitehouse. gov/1600/first-ladies/abigailadams.

"African American Women." Duke University Library "Digitized Collections" Web site. http://library.duke. edu/specialcollections.

"At UN, Malala Yousafzai Rallies Youth to Stand up for Universal Education." UN News Center, United Nations, 12 July 2013, www.un.org/apps/news/story. asp?NewsID=45395#.WeGGrUuGPrc.

"Betty Friedan." History.com, A&E Television Networks, 2009, www.history.com/topics/womens-history/betty-friedan.

"Elizabeth Cady Stanton." History.com, A&E Television Networks, 2009, www.history.com/topics/womens-history/elizabeth-cady-stanton.

"Hearings before the Senate Committee on the Judiciary on the Nomination of Clarence Thomas to be Associate Justice of the Supreme Court of the United States, October 11, 12, and 13, 1991." GPO Access Web site. http://www.gpoaccess.gov/congress/senate/judiciary/sh102-1084pt4/browse.html.

"History of the National Association of Colored Women's Clubs, Inc." National Association of Colored Women's Clubs Web Site. http://www.nacwc.org.

"Josephine St. Pierre Ruffin." Mass Humanities Statehouse Women's Leadership Project Web Site. http:// www.masshumanities.org

"Josephine St. Pierre Ruffin." National Women's Hall of Fame "Women of the Hall" Web Site. http://www. greatwomen.org .

"Liberty, Equality, Fraternity: Exploring the French Revolution." George Mason University Web site. http://chnm.gmu.edu/revolution.

"Mission and Vision," Women's March on Washington https://www.womensmarch.com/mission/

"Ongoing Struggle for Human Rights." Universal Declaration of Human Rights Web site. http://www.udhr. org/history/timeline.htm.

"The First Women's Rights Convention." National Park Service Web site. http://www.nps.gov/wori/historyculture/the-first-womens-rights-convention.htm. Accessed on January 15, 2008.

"Unity Principles," Women's March on Washington https://www.womensmarch.com/principles/

"Votes for Women: Selections from the National American Woman Suffrage Association Collection, 1848–1921." The Library of Congress American Memory Web site. http://memory.loc.gov/ammem/naw/nawshome.html. Accessed on January 15, 2008.

"Women's Fight for the Vote: The Nineteenth Amendment." Exploring Constitutional Conflicts Web site. http://www.law.umkc.edu/faculty/projects/ftrials/conlaw/nineteentham.htm. Accessed on January 15, 2008.

Adams, John, et al. *The Adams-Jefferson Letters The Complete Correspondence Between Thomas Jefferson and Abigail and John Adams.* The University of North Carolina Press, 2012.

Adams, Katherine H.; Keene, Michael L. *Alice Paul and the American Suffrage Campaign.* University of Illinois Press, 2008.

Adiletta, Dawn C. *Elizabeth Cady Stanton: Women's Suffrage and the First Vote.* Rosen/PowerPlus Books, 2005.

*African American Women Writers of the 19th Century.* Schomburg Center for Research in Black Culture's "Digitial Schomburg African American Women Writers of the 19th Century" Web site. http://digital.nypl.org.

Alice Paul Institute. Web site. http://www.alicepaul. org/. Accessed on March 4, 2008.

Amnesty International. *Human Rights Are Women's Rights.* New York: Amnesty International, 1995.

Anna Howard Shaw Center. "About Anna Howard Shaw." *Boston University School of Theology.* Boston: Boston University, 2017. Web. 29 October 2017.

Ashworth, Georgina. *Of Violence and Violation: Women and Human Rights.* London: CHANGE, 1986.

Bagge, Peter. Woman Rebel. *The Margaret Sanger Story.* Montreal: Drawn and Quarterly, 2013.

Bair, Deirdre. 1990. *Simone de Beauvoir: A Biography.* New York: Summit Books.

Baker, Jean H. *Margaret Sanger: A Life of Passion.* New York: Hill and Wang, 2011.

_____. *Sisters: The Lives of America's Suffragists.* Hill and Wang, 2005.

_____. *Votes for Women: The Struggle for Suffrage Revisited*. New York: Oxford University Press, 2002.

Baker, Keith Michael. *The Old Regime and the French Revolution*. Chicago: University of Chicago Press, 1987.

Barakso, Maryann. *Governing NOW: Grassroots Activism in the National Organization for Women*. Ithaca, N.Y.: Cornell University Press, 2004.

Barber, Lucy G. *Marching on Washington: the Forging of an American Political Tradition*. Berkeley: University of California Press, 2002. Print.

Barry, Kathleen. *Susan B. Anthony: A Biography of a Singular Feminist*. New York: New York University Press, 1988.

Bartlett, Katherine T. "Unconstitutionally Male? The Story of United States v. Virginia." *Duke Law Working Paper*. Paper 12. Durham: Duke Law School, 2010. Web. 8 August 2017.

Bausum, Ann. *With Courage and Cloth: Winning the Fight for a Woman's Right to Vote*. National Geographic, 2004

Bederman, Gail. *Manliness and Civilization: A Cultural History of Gender and Race in the United States, 1880-1917* (Women in Culture and Society). University of Chicago Press, 1995.

Berry, Mary Frances. *Why the ERA Failed: Politics, Women's Rights, and the Amending Process of the Constitution*. New York: Indiana UP, 1988. Print.

Best, Geoffrey, ed. *The Permanent Revolution: The French Revolution and Its Legacy, 1789–1989*. London: Fontana Press, 1988.

Bhavnani, Kum-Kum, and Angela Y. Davis. "Complexity, Activism, Optimism: An Interview with Angela Y. Davis." *Feminist Review*, no. 31, 1989, pp. 66–81.

Biank, Tanya. Undaunted: The Real Story of America's Servicewomen in Today's Military. New York: NAL Caliber, 2014. Print.

Biden, Joseph. "20 Years of Change: Joe Biden on the Violence Against Women Act." *Time*. Time, Inc., 10 Sept. 2014. Web.

Biskupic, Joan. *Sandra Day O'Connor: How the First Woman on the Supreme Court Became Its Most Influential Justice*. New York: Ecco–HarperCollins Publishers, 2005. Print.

Black, Edwin. *War against the Weak: Eugenics and America's Campaign to Create a Master Race*. Washington, DC: Dialog Press, 2012.

Bohnet, Iris. *What Works: Gender Equality by Design*. Cambridge, MA: Belknap Press, 2016. Print.

Bradley, Patricia. *Mass Media and the Shaping of American Feminism, 1963-1975*. University Press of Mississippi, 2004.

Branch, Taylor. *Parting the Waters: America in the King Years, 1954–63*. New York: Simon and Schuster, 1988. Print.

Brock, David. *The Real Anita Hill: The Untold Story*. New York: Free Press, 1993.

Brodie, Laura Fairchild. *Breaking Out: VMI and the Coming of Women*. New York: Vintage Books, 2001. Print.

Bronski, Michael. *A Queer History of the United States*. Boston: Beacon Press, 2011.

Brooks, Pamela E. *Boycotts, Buses, and Passes: Black Women's Resistance in the U.S. South and South Africa*. Amherst, MA: University of Massachusetts Press, 2008. Print.

Buechler, Steven M. *Women's Movements in the United States: Woman Suffrage, Equal Rights, and Beyond*. New Brunswick, NJ: Rutgers University Press, 1990.

Bullough, Vern L., ed. *Encyclopedia of Birth Control*. Santa Barbara: ABC-CLIO, 2001.

Bunch, Charlotte, Noeleen Heyzer, Sushma Kapoor, and Joanne Sandler. "Women's Human Rights and Development: A Global Agenda for the 21st Century." In *A Commitment to the World's Women: Perspectives on Development for Beijing and Beyond*, ed. Noeleen Heyzer. New York: UNIFEM, 1995.

Burns, Ken and Paul Barnes. "United States vs. Anthony." *Not for Ourselves Alone*. Washington: PBS and WETA, 1999. Web. 25 October 2017.

Burns, Stewart. *Daybreak of Freedom: The Montgomery Bus Boycott*. Chapel Hill, NC: UNC Press, 1997. Print.

Butler, Amy E. *Two Paths to Equality: Alice Paul and Ethel M. Smith in the ERA Debate, 1921–1929*. Albany: State University of New York Press, 2002.

Cahill, Bernadette. *Alice Paul, the National Women's Party and the Vote*. Jefferson, NC: McFarland & Company, 2015. Print.

Carby, Hazel. *Reconstructing Womanhood: The Emergence of the Afro-American Woman Novelist*. New York: Oxford University Press, 1987.

Castro, Ida L. and Alexis M. Herman. *Equal Pay: A Thirty-Five Year Perspective*. Washington: US Dept. of Labor, Women's Bureau, 1998. Print and Online. 14 November 2017.

*Center for American Women and Politics*. Eagleton Institute of Politics at Rutgers U, 2017, http://www.cawp.rutgers.edu/. Accessed Nov. 1. 2017.

Chadband, Emma. "Nine Ways Title IX Has Helped Girls and Women in Education." *NEA Today*. National Education Association, 21 Jun. 2012. Web.

Chafe, William H. *The Paradox of Change: American Women in the Twentieth Century*. New York: Oxford University Press, 1991.

_____. *The American Woman: Her Changing Social, Economic, and Political Roles, 1920–1970*. New York: Oxford University Press, 1972.

Chemerinsky, Erwin. "Rediscovering Brandeis's Right to Privacy." *Brandeis LJ* 45 (2006): 643.

Chrisman, Robert, and Robert L. Allen, eds. Court of Appeal: the Black Community Speaks Out on the Racial and Sexual Politics of Clarence Thomas vs. Anita Hill. New York: Ballantine Books, 1992.

Clinton, Hillary Rodham. *What Happened*. New York: Simon & Schuster, 2017.

Clissold, Stephen. *St. Teresa of Avila*. New York: Seabury Press, 1982.

Cobble, Dorothy Sue and Julia Bowes. ""Esther Peterson." *American National Biography Online*. New York: Oxford University Press/The American Council of Learned Societies, 2005. Web. 15 November 2017.

Collins, Gail. *When Everything Changed: The Amazing Journey of American Women from 1960 to the Present*. New York: Little Brown, 2009. Print.

Collins, Patricia Hill. *Black Feminist Thought: Knowledge, Consciousness, and the Politics of Empowerment*. 2nd ed. New York: Routledge, 2000.

Conway, Jill. "Jane Addams: An American Heroine." *Daedalus* 93.2 (1964): 761–780.

Cook, Blanche Wiesen. *Eleanor Roosevelt, Volume 1: The Early Years, 1884-1933*. New York: Penguin Books, 1993. Print.

Cooper, Anna Julia. *A Voice from the South*, ed. Mary Helen Washington. New York: Oxford University Press, 1990.

Cott, Nancy F. *The Grounding of Modern Feminism*. New Haven, Conn.: Yale University Press, 1987.

Craig, Layne. *When Sex Changed Birth Control Politics and Literature between the World Wars*. City: Rutgers University Press, 2013.

Crowell, Nancy A. & Ann W. Burgess, eds. Understanding Violence Against Women. Washington, DC: National Academy Press, 1996. Print.

C-SPAN. "Supreme Court Oral Argument: *Stenberg v. Carhart*, April 25, 2000." *C-SPAN*. Washington: National Cable Satellite Corporation, 2017. Web. 24 October 2017.

_____. "Supreme Court Oral Argument: *Webster v. Reproductive Health Services*: April 26, 1989." *Abortion & the Supreme Court*. Washington: National Cable Satellite Corporation, 2017. Web. 26 October 2017.

Daly, Erin. "Reconsidering Abortion Law: Liberty, Equality, and the New Rhetoric of Planned Parenthood v. Casey." Am. UL Rev. 45 (1995): 77.

Danforth, John C. Resurrection: The Confirmation of Clarence Thomas. New York: Viking, 1994.

Danieli, Yael, Elsa Stamatopoulou, and Clarence J. Dias, eds. *The Universal Declaration of Human Rights: Fifty Years and Beyond*. New York: Baywood, 1998.

Dasgupta, Shahana. *Indira Gandhi: The Story of a Leader*. New Delhi: Rupa Publications, 2004. Print.

Davis, Angela Y. *Angela Davis: An Autobiography* (New York: International Publishers, 2013).

_____. *Freedom Is a Constant Struggle: Ferguson, Palestine, and the Foundations of a Movement*. Chicago: Haymarket Books. 2016)

Davis, Elizabeth Lindsay. *Lifting as They Climb*, ed. Henry Louis Gates, Jr. New York: G. K. Hall, 1996.

Day, Elizabeth. "#BlackLivesMatter: the birth of a new civil rights movement." *The Guardian*. The Guardian Media Limited, 19 Jul. 2015. Web.

Department of Education. "Title 34 Education: Subtitle B, Part 106: Nondiscrimination on the Basis of Sex in Education Programs or Activities Receiving Federal Financial Assistance." *ED.gov*. US Department of Education, 2015. Web.

Devins, Neal. "How Planned Parenthood v. Casey (Pretty Much) Settled the Abortion Wars." *The Yale Law Journal* (2009): 1318–1354.

Diamond, Diane and Michael Kimmel. "'Toxic Virus' or Lady Virtue." *Going Coed: Women's Experiences in Formerly Men's Colleges and Universities, 1950-2000*. Leslie Miller-Bernal and Susan L. Poulson, eds. Nashville: Vanderbilt University Press, 2004. Print and Web. (Google Books) 8 August 2017.

Dicken, E. W. Trueman. *The Crucible of Love: A Study of the Mysticism of St. Teresa of Jesus and St. John of the Cross*. New York: Sheed and Ward, 1963.

Douglas, William O. *The Court Years, 1939–1975: The Autobiography of William O. Douglas*. New York: Vintage Books, 1981.

Doyle, William. *The French Revolution: A Very Short Introduction*. Oxford, U.K.: Oxford University Press, 2001.

Dray, Philip. *At the Hands of Persons Unknown: The Lynching of Black America*. New York: Random House, 2002.

Dubois, Ellen Carol. 1992. *The Elizabeth Cady Stanton-Susan B. Anthony Reader*. Boston: Northeastern University Press.

_____. *Feminism and Suffrage: The Emergence of an Independent Women's Movement in America, 1848-1869*. Cornell University Press, 1999.

_____. *Woman Suffrage and Women's Rights*. New York: New York University Press, 1998.

Dunbar-Nelson, Alice. *Give Us Each Day: The Diary of Alice Dunbar-Nelson*, ed. Gloria T. Hull. New York: W. W. Norton, 1984.

Echols, Alice. *Daring to Be Bad: Radical Feminism in America, 1967–1975*. Minneapolis: University of Minnesota Press, 1989.

Eleanor Roosevelt Papers Project. "Biographical Essay." *Eleanor Roosevelt Papers Project*. Washington: George Washington University, 2017. Web. 25 October 2017.

Estrich, Susan with Herman Schwartz ed. "The Politics of Abortion." *The Rehnquist Court: Judicial Activism on the Right*. New York: Hill and Wang, 2002. Print.

European Union. "Directive 2006/54/EC of the European Parliament and of the Council." European Union. http://eur-lex.europa.eu. Retrieved October 29, 2017. Web.

Evans, Sara M. *Tidal Wave: How Women Changed America at Century's End*. New York: Free Press, 2003.

_____. *Born for Liberty: A History of Women in America*. New York: Free Press, 1989.

Fartyal, Sonu, and Poonam Prajapati. "Woman Empowerment through Education." Saving Humanity, G. B. Pant University, 2012, pp. 315–320.

Fawcett, Millicent. *What I Remember*. Honolulu, HI: University Press of the Pacific, 2004. Print.

Ferguson, Kathy E. 2011. "Gender and Genre in Emma Goldman." University of Chicago Press: *Signs* 36.3 (Spring), 733-757.

Ferree, Myra Marx and Alli Mari Tripp, eds., *Global Feminism: Transnational Women's Activism, Organizing, and Human Rights* (New York: New York University Press, 2006).

Fisher, Louis. *American Constitutional Law*. 5th ed. Vol. 2. Durham, NC: Carolina Academic Press, 2003.

Flexner, Eleanor & Ellen Fitzpatrick. *Century of Struggle: The Woman's Rights Movement in the United States*. Boston: Belknap Press, 1996. Print.

Foner, Philip S., and Robert James Branham, eds. *Lift Every Voice: African-American Oratory 1787–1900*. Tuscaloosa: University of Alabama Press, 1998.

Ford, Linda G. *Iron-Jawed Angels: The Suffrage Militancy of the National Women's Party, 1912-1920*. Lanham, NY: University Press of America, 1991. Print.

Foskett, Ken. *Judging Thomas: The Life and Times of Clarence Thomas*. New York: Harper Collins Publishers, 2004.

Fradin, Dennis B., and Judith Bloom Fradin. *Fight On! Mary Church Terrell's Battle for Integration*. New York: Clarion Books, 2003.

Fradin, Judith Bloom and Dennis Brindell Fradin. *Jane Addams: Champion of Democracy*. New York: Clarion, 2006.

Fraioli, Deborah. *Joan of Arc and the Hundred Years War*. Westport, CT: Greenwood Press, 2005. Print.

Frank, Katherine. *Indira: The Life of Indira Nehru Gandhi*. New York: Houghton Mifflin Harcourt, 2002. Print.

Franklin, Cary. "Griswold and the Public Dimension of the Right to Privacy." *The Yale LJ Forum*. The Yale Law Journal, 2 Mar. 2015. Web.

Franzen, Trisha. *Anna Howard Shaw: the Work of Woman Suffrage*. (Women in American History) Champaign IL: University of Illinois Press, 2014. Print.

Freedman, Estelle. *The essential feminist reader*. New York: Modern Library, 2007.

Friedan, Betty. *The Feminine Mystique* (50th Anniversary Edition). Norton Press, 2001.

_____. *It Changed My Life: Writings on the Women's Movement*. Cambridge, MA: Harvard UP, 1998. Print.

Frisken, Amanda. *Victoria Woodhull's Sexual Revolution: Political Theater and the Popular Press in Nineteenth-Century America*. Philadelphia: University of Pennsylvania Press, 2004.

Gandhi, Indira. *My Truth*. New Delhi: Orient Paperbacks, 2013. Print.

Garment, Suzanne. "Afterword: On Anita Hill and Clarence Thomas." In *Scandal: The Culture of Mistrust in American Politics*. New York: Times Books, 1992.

Gelles, Edith Belle. *Portia: the World of Abigail Adams*. Indiana University Press, 2010.

Giddings, Paula. When and Where I Enter: The Impact of Black Women on Race and Sex in America. New York: Bantam, 1984.

Ginsburg, Ruth Bader with Mary Hartnett and Wendy W. Williams. *My Own Words: Ruth Bader Ginsburg*. New York: Simon & Schuster, 2016. Print.

Ginzberg, Lori D. 2009. *Elizabeth Cady Stanton: An American Life*. New York: Hill and Wang.

_____. *Untidy Origins: A Story of Woman's Rights in Antebellum New York*. Chapel Hill: University of North Carolina Press, 2005.

Glendon, Mary Ann. *A World Made New: Eleanor Roosevelt and the Universal Declaration of Human Rights*. New York: Random House, 2001.

Godwin, William. *Memoirs of the Author of The Vindication of the Rights of Woman*. London, J. Johnson, 1798.

Goldsmith, Barbara. *Other Powers: The Age of Suffrage, Spiritualism, and the Scandalous Victoria Woodhull*. New York: Knopf Books, 1998.

Gordon Linda. *Women's Body, Women's Right: A Social History of Birth Control in America*. New York: Grossman, 1976.

Gordon, Ann D. ed. *The Elizabeth Cady Stanton & Susan B. Anthony Papers Project*. New Brunswick NJ: Rutgers, The State University of New Jersey, 2012. Web. 25 October 2017.

_____. *African American Women and the Vote, 1837–1965*. Amherst: University of Massachusetts Press, 1997.

Gordon, Charlotte. *Romantic Outlaws: The Extraordinary Lives of Mary Wollstonecraft and Mary Shelley*. New York, Random House, 2015.

Gordon, Lyndall. *Vindication: A Life of Mary Wollstonecraft*. New York, Harper Perennial, 2006.

Gornick, Vivian. 2013. *Revolution as a Way of Life*. Yale University Press.

Greenhouse, Linda & Reva B. Siegel. "Before (and After) *Roe v. Wade*: New Questions About Backlash." *The Yale Law Journal*. The Yale Law Journal, 2011. Web.

Griffith, Elisabeth. *In Her Own Right: The Life of Elizabeth Cady Stanton*. New York: Oxford University Press, 1985.

Guha, Ramachandra. *India After Gandhi: The History of the World's Largest Democracy*. New Delhi: Harper Perennial, 2008. Print.

Gura, Philip F. 2008. *American Transcendentalism: A History*. Hill and Wang.

Hamington, Maurice. *The Social Philosophy of Jane Addams*. Chicago: University of Illinois Press, 2009.

Hanson, Katherine, Vivian Guilfoy, & Sarita Pillai. *More than Title IX: How Equity in Education Has Shaped the Nation*. New York: Rowman & Littlefield Publishers, 2011. Print.

Harding, Kate. Asking for It: The Alarming Rise of Rape Culture—and What We Can Do About It. Philadelphia: Da Capo, 2015. Print.

Harrison, Kathryn. *Joan of Arc: A Life Transfigured*. New York: Doubleday, 2014. Print.

Harrison, Patricia Greenwood. *Connecting Links: The British and American Woman Suffrage Movements, 1900-1914*. Westport CT: Greenwood Press, 2000. Print.

Hartman, Gary R., Roy M. Mersky, Cindy L. Tate, *Landmark Supreme Court Cases: The Most Influential Decisions of the Supreme Court of the United States*. New York: Facts on File, Inc., 2014.

Heilbrun, Carolyn G. *Education of a Woman: The Life of Gloria Steinem*. New York: Ballantine Books, 1996. Print.

Hensley, Thomas R. with Kathleen Hale and Carl Snook. *The Rehnquist Court: Justices, Rulings and Legacy* (ABC-CLIO Supreme Court Handbooks) Santa Barbara CA: ABC-CLIO Inc., 2006. Print.

Hill, Anita, and Emma Coleman Jordan, eds. *Race, Gender, and Power in America: The Legacy of the Hill-Thomas Hearings*. New York: Oxford University Press, 1995.

_____. *Speaking Truth to Power*. New York: Doubleday, 1997.

Hillstrom, Laurie Collier. *Roe v. Wade*. Rpt. Detroit. Omnigraphics, Inc., 2008. Print.

Hine, Darlene Clark, William C. Hine, & Stanley Harrold. *The African-American Odyssey*. Combined Vol. 2nd ed. Upper Saddle River, NJ: Pearson Education, 2005. Print.

Hirshman, Linda. *Sisters in Law: How Sandra Day O'Connor and Ruth Bader Ginsburg Went to the Supreme Court and Changed the World*. New York: HarperCollins, 2015. Print.

Hogan, Lisa Shawn. 2013. "Elizabeth Cady Stanton, 'The Solitude of Self' (January 18, 1892)." University of Maryland: *Voices of Democracy* 8, 23-41.

Holmstedt, Kirsten. Band of Sisters: American Women at War in Iraq. Mechanicsburg, PA: Stackpole Books, 2008. Print.

Holton, Sandra Stanley. *Feminism and Democracy: Women's Suffrage and Reform Politics in Britain,*

*1900-1918*. Cambridge: Cambridge University Press, 2003. Print.

Horowitz, Daniel. *Betty Friedan and the Making of the Feminine Mystique: the American Left, the Cold War, and Modern Feminism*. University of Massachusetts Press, 2000.

Huffman, Brian. "United States v. Virginia Case Summary." *UH Law Library*. Honolulu: William S. Richardson School of Law Law Library, 2017. Web. 7 August 2017.

Hull, Gloria T. "Alice Dunbar-Nelson (1875–1935)." Cengage Learning Web site. http://college.cengage.com/dunbarnelson_al.html.

Hull, N. E. H. & Peter Charles Hoffer. *Roe v. Wade: The Abortion Rights Controversy in American History*. 2nd ed. Lawrence, Kansas: University of Kansas Press, 2010. Print.

_____. *The Woman Who Dared to Vote: The Trial of Susan B. Anthony*. Lawrence KS: The University Press of Kansas, 2012. Print.

Hunt, Lynn. *Inventing Human Rights: A History*. New York: W. W. Norton, 2007.

_____. *The French Revolution and Human Rights: A Brief Documentary History*. New York: Bedford Books, 1996.

Irons, Peter. *A People's History of the Supreme Court*. New York: Penguin Books, 2000.

Isenberg, Nancy. *Sex and Citizenship in Antebellum America*. Chapel Hill: University of North Carolina Press, 1998.

Johnson, Karen A. *Uplifting the Women and the Race: The Lives, Educational Philosophies, and Social Activism of Anna Julia Cooper and Nannie Helen Burroughs*. New York: Garland, 2000.

Johnson, Wilma J. "Dunbar-Nelson, Alice Ruth Moore (1875–1935)." BlackPast.org Web site. http://blackpast.com/dunbar-nelson-alice-ruth-moore-1875-1935.

Jones, Beverley W. "Mary Church Terrell and the National Association of Colored Women: 1986–1901." *Journal of Negro History* 67 (1982): 20–33.

_____. *Quest for Equality: The Life and Writings of Mary Eliza Church Terrell, 1863–1954*. New York: Carlson Publishing, 1990.

_____. "Mary Eliza Church Terrell, 1863–1954." *Tennessee Encyclopedia of History and Culture* Web site. http://tennesseeencyclopedia.net.

Justia. "Stenberg v. Carhart: 530 U.S. 914 (2000)." *Justia*. Mountain View: Justia, 2017. Web. 24 October 2017.

Jütte, Robert. *Contraception: A History*. Translated by Vicky Russell, Polity Press, 2008.

Kantola, J. *Gender and the European Union*. New York: Palgrave Macmillan, 2010. Print.

Katin, Ernest. "*Griswold v. Connecticut*: The Justices and Connecticut's Uncommonly Silly Law." *Notre Dame LR* 42 (1967) 5.

Kauper, Paul G. "Penumbras, Peripheries, and Emanations, Things Fundamental and Things Forgotten." *Michigan LR* 46 (1965): 2.

Keetley, Dawn & John Pettegrew. *Public Women, Public Words: A Documentary History of American Feminism*. Vol. 2. Lanham, MD: Rowman & Littlefield, 2005. Print.

Kennedy, David M. *Birth Control in America: The Career of Margaret Sanger*. New Haven: Yale UP, 1970.

Kennedy, John F. "Remarks upon Signing the Equal Pay Act." White House, Washington, DC. 10 June 1963. *American Presidency Project*. Santa Barbara CA: University of California Santa Barbara: American Presidency Project, 2017. Web. 14 November 2017.

Kettler, Sara. "Malala Yousafzai." Biography.com, A&E Networks Television, 17 Aug. 2017, www.biography.com/people/malala-yousafzai-21362253.

Korey, William. *NGOs and the Universal Declaration of Human Rights: "A Curious Grapevine."* New York: St. Martin's Press, 1998.

Kraditor, Aileen S. *The Ideas of the Woman Suffrage Movement, 1890-1920*. New York: Anchor, 1971. Print.

Lasch, Christopher, ed. *The Social Thought of Jane Addams*. 2nd ed. New York: Irvington, 1997.

Legal Information Institute. "Webster v. Reproductive Health Services." *Legal Information Institute*. Ithaca NY: Cornell Law School, 2017. Web. 27 October 2017.

Legal Law Institute. "United States v. Virginia et al. (94-1941), 518 U.S. 515 (1996)." *Legal Law Institute*. Ithaca: Cornell University Law School, 2017. Web. 8 August 2017.

Lemert, Charles, and Esme Bhan, eds. *The Voice of Anna Julia Cooper*. Lanham, Md.: Rowman and Littlefield, 1998.

Lemmon, Gayle Tzemach. Ashley's War: The Untold Story of a Team of Women Soldiers on the Special Ops Battlefield. New York: HarperCollins Publishers, 2015. Print.

Lerner, Gerda. "Early Community Work of Black Club Women." *Journal of Negro History* 59, no. 2 (April 1974): 158–167.

Levin, Phyllis Lee. *Abigail Adams: a Biography*. St. Martin's Griffin, 2001.

Levine, Suzanne Braun and Mary Thom (editors). *Bella Abzug: How One Tough Broad from the Bronx Fought Jim Crow and Joe McCarthy, Pissed Off Jimmy Carter, Battled for the Rights of Women and Workers, Rallied against War and for the Planet and Shook Up Politics along the Way (An Oral History)*. New York: Farrar, Straus and Giroux, 2007.

Lewis, Jone Johnson. "President's Commission on the Status of Women." *About Education*. About.com, 2015. Web.

Linkugel, Wil A., Martha Watson, and Anna Howard Shaw. *Anna Howard Shaw: Suffrage Orator and Social Reformer*. Westport CT: Greenwood Press, 1991. Print.

Linton, Paul Benjamin. "Planned Parenthood v. Casey: The Flight from Reason in the Supreme Court." Louis U. Pub L. Rev. 13 (1993): 15.

Lunardini, Christine. *Alice Paul: Equality for Women*. Boulder: Westview Press, 2013.

———. *From Equal Suffrage to Equal Rights: Alice Paul and the National Woman's Party, 1910–1928*. New York: New York University Press, 1986.

Mabee, Carleton, and Susan Mabee Newhouse. *Sojourner Truth: Slave, Prophet, Legend*. New York: New York University Press, 1993.

Mani, Bonnie G. *Women, Power, and Political Change*. New York: Lexington Books, 2007.

Manning, Jennifer E., Ida A. Brucnick, and Colleen J. Shogan. "Women in Congress: Historical Overview, Tables, and Discussion." *Congressional Research Service*. Washington: Congressional Research Service, 2015. Web. 23 October 2017.

Marable, Manning, and Leith Mullings, eds. *Let Nobody Turn Us Around: An African American Anthology*. Lanham, Md: Rowman & Littlefield, 2009.

Marshall, Megan. 2013. *Margaret Fuller: A New American Life*. Houghton Mifflin Harcourt.

Marso, Lori Jo. 2007. "A Feminist Search for Love: Emma Goldman on the Politics of Marriage, Love, Sexuality, and the Feminine." In *Feminist Interpretations of Emma Goldman,* Penny A. Weiss and Loretta Kensinger (eds.), 71-89. Pennsylvania State University PRess.

Mason, Laura, and Tracey Rizzo. *The French Revolution: A Document Collection*. Boston: Houghton Mifflin, 1999.

Matteson, John. 2013. *The Lives of Margaret Fuller: A Biography*. Norton.

McBride, Alex. "Expanding Civil Rights: Landmark Cases: *Roe v. Wade* (1973)." *The Supreme Court*. PBS, 2006. Web.

McClain, Linda C. & Joanna L. Grossman, eds. *Gender Equality: Dimensions of Women's Equal Citizenship*. Cambridge: Cambridge University Press, 2009. Print.

McClosky, Robert. *The American Supreme Court*. 4th ed. Chicago: University of Chicago Press, 2005.

McGerr, Michael. *A Fierce Discontent: The Rise and Fall of the Progressive Movement in America, 1870-1920*. New York: Free Press, 2003.

McMillen, Sally. *Seneca Falls and the Origins of the Women's Rights Movement*. New York: Oxford University Press, 2008.

Medwick, Cathleen. *Teresa of Avila: The Progress of a Soul*. New York: Knopf, 1999.

Menand, Louis. 2005. "Stand By Your Man: The strange liaison of Sartre and Beauvoir". *The New Yorker*, September 26, 2005.

Miller, Claire Cain. "Women Actually Do Govern Differently." *The New York Times*, 10 Nov. 2016, https://www.nytimes.com/2016/11/10/upshot/women-actually-do-govern-differently.html.

Miller, Grant. "Women's Suffrage, Political Responsiveness, and Child Survival in American History." *The Quarterly Journal of Economics* 123. 3 (2008): 1287–1327.

Mills, Kay. *This Little Light of Mine: The Life of Fannie Lou Hamer*. Lexington, KY: U P Kentucky, 2007. Print.

Morrison, Toni, ed. *Race-ing Justice, En-gendering Power: Essays on Anita Hill, Clarence Thomas, and the Construction of Social Reality*. New York: Pantheon Books, 1992.

Morsink, Johannes. *The Universal Declaration of Human Rights: Origins, Drafting, and Intent*. Philadelphia: University of Pennsylvania Press, 1999.

Moye, J. Todd. *Ella Baker: Community Organizer of the Civil Rights Movement*. Lanham, MD: Rowman & Littlefield Publishers, 2015. Print.

Mungarro, Angelica, et al. "How Did Black Women in the NAACP Promote the Dyer Anti-Lynching Bill, 1918–1923?" Women and Social Movements in the United States, 1600–2000, Web site. http://womhist.alexanderstreet.com/lynch/intro.htm.

Murray, Pauli, and Mary O. Eastwood. *Jane Crow and the Law: Sex discrimination and Title VII*. Durham,

NC: Sallie Bingham Center for Women's History and Culture, 1965. Print.

Mutua, Makau. "The Ideology of Human Rights." *Virginia Journal of International Law* 36 (1996): 589–657.

Naparsteck, Martin. *The Trial of Susan B. Anthony: An Illegal Vote, a Courtroom Conviction and a Step Toward Women's Suffrage*. Jefferson, NC: McFarland & Co., 2014.

Nash, Margaret A. "'Patient Persistence': The Political and Educational Values of Anna Julia Cooper and Mary Church Terrell." *Educational Studies* 35 (April 2004): 122–136.

National Equal Pay Task Force. *Fifty Years after the Equal Pay Act: Assessing the Past, Taking Stock of the Future*. Washington: White House, 2013. Print and Web. 14 November 2017.

National First Ladies Museum. "First Lady Biography: Eleanor Roosevelt." *National First Ladies Library*. Canton OH: National First Ladies Museum, 2017. Web 24 October 2017.

*National Organization for Women Official Website*. National Organization for Women, 2015. Web.now.org.

National Park Service. "Equal Pact of 1963." *Civil Rights*. Washington: National Park Service, 2016. Web. 14 November 2017.

_____. "Notable Women's Rights Leaders." *Women's Rights National Historical Park*. Washington: National Park Service, 2017. Web. 25 October 2017.

National Public Radio Web site, 14 August 2015, http://www.npr.org/sections/itsallpolitics/2015/08/14/432080520/fact-check-was-planned-parenthood-started-to-control-the-black-population.

National Women's History Project Web site. http://www.nwhp.org/. Accessed on March 4, 2008.

National Women's Law Center. *Titleix.info*. National Women's Law Center, 2015. Web.

New York Times, The. "July 3, 1919: Dr. Anna H. Shaw, Suffragist, Dies.". *The New York Times: On This Day Learning Network*. New York: The New York Times Company, 2010. Web. 25 October 2017.

O'Brien, Michael. *John F. Kennedy: a Biography*. Macmillan, 2005.

O'Neill, William L. *Everyone Was Brave: A History of Feminism in America*. Chicago: Quadrangle Books, 1971.

Ohles, John.F. *Biographical Dictionary of American Educators* Vol 1. Greenwood Press, 1978.

Orr, Katie and Megan Kamerick. "Trump's Election Drives More Women to Consider Running for Office." *NPR*, 23 Feb. 2017, http://www.npr.org/2017/02/23/515438978/trumps-election-drives-more-women-to-consider-running-for-office.

Osnos, Evan. "The Biden Agenda." *The New Yorker*. Condé Nast, 28 Jul. 2014. Web.

Oyez. "United States v. Virginia." *Oyez*. Chicago: Cornell's Legal Information Institute, Justia, and Chicago-Kent College of Law, 2017. Web. 7 August 2017.

_____. *Body Politic: The Supreme Court and Abortion Law*. Chicago: Oyez and the Institute on the Supreme Court of the United States, 2017. Web. 22 October 2017.

Painter, Nell Irvin. *Sojourner Truth: A Life, A Symbol*. New York: W. W. Norton, 1996.

Pankhurst, E. Sylvia. *The Life of Emmeline Pankhurst: The Suffragette Struggle for Women's Citizenship*. Whitefish, MT: Kessinger Publishing, 2010.

Pankhurst, Emmeline. *Suffragette: The Autobiography of Emmeline Pankhurst*. New York: Hearsts's International Library Co., 2002. Print.

Payne, Charles. *I've Got the Light of Freedom: The Organizing Tradition and the Mississippi Freedom Struggle*. Oakland: University of California Press, 2007. Print.

Pernoud, Régine; Clin, Marie-Véronique. *Joan of Arc: Her Story*. Trans. Jeremy Duquesnay Adams. New York: St. Martin's Griffin, 1999. Print.

Phelps, Timothy M., and Helen Winternitz. *Capitol Games: Clarence Thomas, Anita Hill, and the Story of a Supreme Court Nomination*. New York: Hyperion, 1992.

*Planned Parenthood of Southeastern Pa. v. Casey*, 112 S.Ct. 2791 (1992). Justia: US Supreme Court https://supreme.justia.com/cases/federal/us/505/833/case.html [accessed October 31, 2017].

Pollis, Adamantia, and Peter Schwab, eds. *Human Rights: Cultural and Ideological Perspectives*. New York: Praeger, 1979.

Popkin, Jeremy. *A Short History of the French Revolution*, 5th ed. Englewood Cliffs, N.J.: Prentice Hall, 2009.

Proceedings of the Thirtieth Annual Convention of the National American Woman Suffrage Association. Philadelphia: Alfred J. Harris, 1898.

Purvis, June. *Emmeline Pankhurst: A Biography*. New York: Routledge, 1987. Print.

Ransby, Barbara. *Ella Baker and the Black Freedom Movement: A Radical Democratic Vision*. Chapel Hill: The University of North Carolina Press, 2005. Print.

Reed, Miriam. *Margaret Sanger: Her Life in Her Words*. Fort Lee, NJ: Barricade Books, 2003.

Roberts, J. M. *The French Revolution*, 2nd ed. Oxford, U.K.: Oxford University Press, 1997.

Robinson, Jo Ann. *The Montgomery Bus Boycott and the Women Who Started It: The Memoir of Jo Ann Gibson Robinson*. Knoxville, TN: UT Press, 1987. Print.

Roosevelt, Eleanor. "On the Adoption of the Universal Declaration of Human Rights." *American Rhetoric* Web site. http://www.americanrhetoric.com/speeches/eleanorrooseveltdeclarationhumanrights.htm.

_____. *The Autobiography of Eleanor Roosevelt*. (reprint edition of 1961 text) New York: Harper Perennial, 2014. Print.

Rothman, Sheila M. *Women's Proper Place: A History of Changing Ideals and Practices, 1870 to the Present*. Vol. 5053. Phoenix, AZ: Basic Books, 1980.

Rubinstein, David. *A Different World for Women: The Life of Millicent Garrett Fawcett*. Columbus, OH: Ohio State University Press, 1991. Print.

Rugoff, Milton. *The Beechers: An American family in the nineteenth century*. Harper & Row, 1981

Sahni, Urvashi. *Reaching for the Sky: Empowering Girls through Education*. Brookings Institution Press, 2017.

Sanger, Margaret. *My Fight for Birth Control*. New York: Farrar & Rinehart, 1931.

Schneider, Dorothy and Carl J. Schneider. *American Women in the Progressive Era, 1900-1920*. New York: Facts on File, 1993.

Schultz, Kristina, ed. 2017 *The Women's Liberation Movement: Impacts and Outcomes*. New York: Berghahn.

Scott, Joan Wallach. 1996. *Feminism and History*. New York: Oxford University Press.

Seigfried, Charlene Haddock. "The Social Self in Jane Addams' Prefaces and Introductions." *Transactions of the Charles S. Peirce Society: A Quarterly Journal in American Philosophy* 49.2 (2013): 127–156.

Shapiro, Ian, editor. *Abortion: The Supreme Court Decisions 1965-2000*. Indianapolis: Hackett Publishing Co., Inc., 2001.

Sherr, Lynn. *Failure is Impossible: Susan B. Anthony in Her Own Words*. New York: Three Rivers Press, 1996

Smith, Christopher E. *Critical Judicial Nominations and Political Change: The Impact of Clarence Thomas*. Westport, Conn.: Praeger, 1993.

Smith, Harold. *The British Women's Suffrage Campaign: 1866-1928*, 2nd Edition. London: Pearson, 2007. Print.

Spruill, Marjorie J. *Divided We Stand: The Battle over Women's Rights and Family Values that Polarized American Politics*. New York: Bloomsbury, 2017.

Stanton, Elizabeth Cady, and Ann D. Gordon. *The Selected Papers of Elizabeth Cady Stanton and Susan B. Anthony*. Edited by Susan Brownell Anthony, Rutgers University Press, 2006.

Stebner, Eleanor J. *The Women of Hull House: A Study in Spirituality, Vocation, and Friendship*. Albany: State University of New York Press, 1997.

Steinem, Gloria. *My Life on the Road*. New York: Random House, 2015. Print.

_____. *Outrageous Acts and Everyday Rebellions*. New York: Henry Holt & Co., 1987. Print.

Stephens, Carolyn King. *Downer Women, 1851-2001*. Sea King Publishing, 2003.

Sterling, Dorothy. *Black Foremothers: Three Lives*. 2nd ed. New York: Feminist Press, 1988.

Steven R. Morrison, "Personhood Amendments After Whole Woman's Health v. Hellerstedt," *Case Western Reserve Law Review*, 67 (2016): 447-499.

Streitmatter, Rodger. "Josephine St. Pierre Ruffin: A Nineteenth-Century Journalist of Boston's Black Elite Class." In *Women of the Commonwealth: Work, Family, and Social Change in Nineteenth-Century Massachusetts*, ed. Susan L. Porter. Amherst: University of Massachusetts Press, 1996.

_____. *Raising Her Voice: African-American Journalists Who Changed History*. Lexington: University Press of Kentucky, 2009

Strum, Philippa. *Women in the Barracks: The VMI Case and Equal Rights*. Lawrence: University of Kansas Press. 2002. Print.

Susan B. Anthony House. "Biography of Susan B. Anthony." *National Susan B. Anthony Museum & House*. Rochester NY: Susan B. Anthony House, 2013. Web. 25 October 2017.

Teresa of Ávila. *The Interior Castle*, trans. Kieran Kavanaugh and Otilio Rodriguez. New York: Paulist Press, 1979.

_____. *The Way of Perfection*. Christian Classics Ethereal Library Web site. http://www.ccel.org/ccel/teresa/way.html.

Terrell, Mary Church. *A Colored Woman in a White World*. New York: G. K. Hall, 1996.

The Equal Rights Amendment Web site. http://www.equalrightsamendment.org/. Accessed on January 15, 2008.

Theocharis, Jeanne. *The Rebellious Life of Mrs. Rosa Parks*. Boston: Beacon, 2014. Print.

Thomas, Tracy A. *Elizabeth Cady Stanton and the Feminist Foundations of Family Law*. New York University Press, 2016.

Thorpe, Helen. *Soldier Girls: The Battles of Three Women at Home and at War*. New York: Scribner, 2014. Print.

Thurman, Judith. 2009. "Introduction to Simone de Beauvoir's *The Second Sex*." Random House: Alfred A. Knopf.

Tilly, Louise A., and Patricia Gurin, eds. *Women, Politics, and Change*. New York: Russell Sage Foundation, 1990.

Todd, Janet. *Mary Wollstonecraft: A Revolutionary Life*. New York, Columbia University Press, 2000.

Tong, Rosemarie, and Tina Fernandes Botts. *Feminist Thought: a More Comprehensive Introduction*. Westview Press, 2018.

Truth, Sojourner, and Olive Gilbert. *Narrative of Sojourner Truth*. New York: Arno Press, 1968.

Underhill, Lois Beachy. *The Woman Who Ran for President: The Many Lives of Victoria Woodhull*. Bridgehampton, NY: Bridge Works Press, 1995.

United Nations. "Human Rights." http://www.un.org/en/rights.

VanBurkleo, Sandra F. *"Belonging to the World": Women's Rights and American Constitutional Culture*. New York: Oxford University Press, 2001.

Walters, Margaret. 2006. *Feminism: A Very Short Introduction*. New York: Oxford University Press.

Walton, Mary. *A Woman's Crusade: Alice Paul and the Battle for the Ballott*. New York: Palgrave MacMillan, 2010. Print.

Ward, Geoffrey and Ken Burns. *Not For Ourselves Alone: The Story of Elizabeth Cady Stanton and Susan B. Anthony*. New York: Knopf, 1999.

Wellman, Judith. *The Road to Seneca Falls: Elizabeth Cady Stanton and the First Woman's Rights Convention*. University of Illinois Press, 2004.

White, Barbara. *The Beecher Sisters*. Yale University Press, 2003

*Whole Woman's Health v. Hellerstedt, 136 S.Ct. 2292 (2016).* Justia: US Supreme Court https://supreme.justia.com/cases/federal/us/579/15-274/ [accessed October 31, 2017].

Williams, Rowan. *Teresa of Avila*. London: Geoffrey Chapman, 1991.

Winslow, Barbara. "The Impact of Title IX." *History Now*. The Gilder Lehrman Institute of American History, 2015. Web.

Withey, Lynne. *Dearest Friend: A Life of Abigail Adams* Paperback. Touchstone , 2002.

Woloch, Nancy. *Women and the American Experience*. New York: Alfred A. Knopf, 1984.

Wright, E. A. & Halloran, S. M. *From rhetoric to composition: The teaching of writing in American to 1900*. In J. J. Murphy (Eds.). A short history of writing instruction: From ancient Greece to modern America. Mahwah, NJ: Lawrence Erlbaum Associates, Inc., 2001.

Yarbrough, Tinsley E. David Hackett Souter: Traditional Republican on the Rehnquist Court. Oxford, UK: Oxford University Press, 2005.

Yousafzai, Malala, and Christina Lamb. I Am Malala: the Girl Who Stood up for Education and Was Shot by the Taliban. Weidenfeld & Nicolson, 2016.

Yuval-Davis, Nira. *Gender and Nation*. Thousand Oaks, CA: SAGE Publications. 1997

Zahniser, J. D.; Fry, Amelia R. *Alice Paul: Claiming Power*. Oxford University Press, 2014.

# Index